Women and the Military System

Women and the Military System

Edited by
Eva Isaksson

Proceedings of a symposium arranged by the International Peace Bureau and Peace Union of Finland

St. Martin's Press
New York

First published in the United States of America in 1988

Printed in Great Britain

ISBN 0–312–01976–9 (cloth)
0–312–01978–5 (paper)

Library of Congress Cataloging-in-Publication Data

Women and the military system / edited by Eva Isaksson.
p. cm.
'Proceedings of a symposium arranged by the International Peace Bureau and Peace Union of Finland.'
Bibliography: p.
Includes index.
ISBN 0–312–01976–9 : $35.00 (est.). ISBN 0–312–01978–5 (pbk.) : $15.00 (est.)
1. Women and the military—Congresses. I. Isaksson, Eva, 1953– . II. International Peace Bureau. III. Peace Union of Finland.
U21.75.W66 1988
355'.0088042—dc19 88–15803
CIP

Contents

Introduction

Eva Isaksson

The study of women and the military system is a growing, interdisciplinary branch of women's studies. Current research has long since exploded the myth that war and military are matters primarily reserved for men; we now know that both men and women have been socialized to support ideologies of national security and defence, and to serve the military system in their particular countries. Forms of this support vary from hidden militarization to open large-scale mobilization of women.

Military historians once believed that women's military participation (apart from some isolated cases of female soldiers) dated back to the First World War. However, this is not so. As historian Barton Hacker has described in his work, women have served mobile armies as camp followers for centuries, sometimes more than equalling in their numbers those of fighting men. When state machinery evolved, military efficiency—closely related to industrial efficiency—demanded a more rigorous military control of women. Military's own support systems replaced women, so that only a few women followed men to war by the turn of the century.

The First World War marked the establishment of the large-scale industrialization of the war effort and of society's support services. Women were recruited to replace mass conscripted male workers. However, this happened only 'for the duration', with the assumption that women's wartime work was expendable. War did not, in reality, increase the number of women in paid employment, but instead created a passing discontinuity in the growing percentage of women who had been working outside their homes long before the war began.

This pattern was repeated, even more pointedly, during the Second World War. Massive wartime mobilization of women in Britain and in other countries left little if any trace in patterns of women's postwar employment, except for new areas of women's work gained in low-skill, repetitive factory jobs. There was a marked tendency in wartime job training opportunities. Men were given training while women might be merely taught to repeat a series of movements necessary to master a particular task.

Women served in the two world wars, not only as a manpower reserve but as a support service to the armed forces as well, whatever their official capacity in relation to the military. The initial small-scale mobilization of women during the First World War was changed to mass recruitment of women during the Second World War. Ruth Roach Pierson describes in her study how military needs forced society to find ways to accept women in uniform by assuring that they did not challenge the approved gender roles in any way.

The variety in women's military roles during the Second World War was great. Russian women served in armed combat, while Canadian women, in their well-designed 'feminine' uniforms were placed far from the actual theatres of war. Yugoslavian women partisans were induced to fight both for a new socialist Yugoslavia and for a new, more equal society where women's rights would be respected; Finnish and Scandinavian women had been recruited in hundreds of thousands into women's sections of conservative right-wing Home Guard organizations and were made to fulfil the traditional, supportive ideal of womanhood. In all cases, whatever their wartime experiences, women were forced to make room for the men, returning from the front to take over their rightful places. No places existed for women returning from their wartime military duties.

Women's services were maintained in the armed forces of most countries after the war, although the number of women serving in them were greatly reduced. Militaries were unwilling to give up the structure of women's services entirely. Through the 1950s and 1960s, women continued to serve as soldiers, always in very subordinate positions. At one point, military planners were ready to believe that there would be no more need for women soldiers (or male conscripts for that matter) in the nuclear war scenarios. However, after the escalating yet increasingly exacting balance of nuclear armaments was established, interest in maintaining and developing conventional armies increased. Diverse national security scenarios designed by military planners have been gaining support by citizens who are given to understand that however frightening the prospects of possible global nuclear annihilation, national militaries are still doing their best to protect them. The role of the armed forces as an employer worthy of consideration has served it in its efforts to make defence more popular in many countries.

The US armed forces opened their ranks for mass enlistment of women after the end of the Vietnam War. Coinciding with the rise of new feminism, this development raised much debate about women's social status as connected to their possible military careers. Women comprise now 9.5 per cent of the personnel of the US armed forces; a disproportionate amount of these women are Black women, who have been unable to find other employment. Instead of a step towards full citizenship of women, their entrance into the US military has so far happened as a part of military plans very far out of their control as women and citizens.

Cynthia Enloe has convincingly argued in her book *Does Khaki Become You? The Militarization of Women's Lives* (1983) that women serve a wide variety of military needs, not only as soldiers but also as military wives, prostitutes, nurses and workers in armaments factories. Despite its reliance on women, the military remains as society's bastion of male identity, thus 'to allow women entrance into the essential core of the military would throw into confusion *all* men's certainty about their male identity and thus about their claim to privilege in the social order'. The military is, in the words of Judith H. Stiehm, a male-defining institution. Yet women do serve, but their roles are always controlled by male military decision-makers. A few token women in combat training in the armies of some NATO countries do not challenge this status quo; in reality, few women qualify for combat tasks specifically tailored for men, and most probably none would be sent to direct combat missions in case of war.

Women's less visible military roles are connected to civil defence, which is increasingly being used as an excuse for bringing new areas of civilian social structures under military influence and control. Civilian women, such as nurses, social workers and teachers, are being trained to be able to participate in increasing military security and military preparedness of their country. Some of this training is becoming obligatory, although women's participation in paramilitary and military activities still remains largely voluntary.

A notable exception to this is Israel, where Jewish women are conscripted to serve in the women's corps of the Israeli army. Nira Yuval-Davis has analysed the sexual division of labour in the Israeli army and the connected differences in class, ethnic background and religion. Israeli women are predominantly engaged in clerical occupations; a minority are engaged in technical, mechanical and operational duties. Of the latter, a significant number are engaged in welfare duties and teaching. None have served at the front since 1948, despite the popular image of liberated women soldiers with machine-guns in their hand. Instead, women are filling low-skilled secretarial and support duties in subordinate positions to men. The division of labour bears similarity to that in the civilian sector. It has to be noted that only Jewish women are recruited into the army: in 1976–7, 51.5 per cent of Jewish women, 0 per cent of non-Jewish women were recruited out of the eligible age group. Women are released from military service on various grounds; some are simply rejected, some have already started to fulfil their reproductive roles, while some are released for religious and conscientious reasons.

The strong symbolic identification between the people and the state in Israel is reflected in the role of the army as a major mediating mechanism for solidifying national consensus. The role of Israeli Jewish men as soldiers is their most important national role, while women's most important national role is as reproducers, to bring new small soldiers in the world.

Marie-Aimée Hélie-Lucas describes similar strong ties between sex roles and nationalism in the case of Algeria. Women participated in the liberation of Algeria in large numbers. However, they were not liberated as women through the process of global liberation of their country. Women's task was symbolic; the people had to build a national identity and women became the keepers of this threatened identity. Women were seen as bearers of tradition, while men had access to modernity. Wearing the veil became thus a symbol of national resistance; obedience, morality, and conformity were necessary conditions for becoming a participant in the revolution. Religion has been used increasingly by Muslim fundamentalists as a means of societal control of private life, as reflected in the reactionary Family Code of 1984.

Although it is evident that women as well as men have the capacity for violence, this does not necessarily mean that women's position in relation to the military system can be described in the same terms as that of men. Women play a subordinate role both in society and in the military; the terms of their military participation have been determined by men, as well as many other terms of women's participation. Women have been assigned system-maintenance roles as nurturers and bearers of the next generation of soldiers. As Elise Boulding points out in her contribution, every war has renewed pressure on women to maintain women's services in the household and in the community and in rebuilding them. As pointed out by Wendy Chapkis, dominating, aggressive behaviour in men is complemented by passive, nurturing behaviour in women. Thus femininity will not be the peaceful alternative, since it is a complement of aggressive masculinity instead of an alternative to it. According to Elise Boulding, men's capacities for gentleness and nurturing have been overlooked. Certainly they do exist.

In the case of Chile, as described by Ximena Bunster, women active in pro-Junta organizations have become patriotic mothers, subordinate to 'father of the nation', who promises to defend them and their traditional roles as mothers and home-makers. These women are not the originators nor the creators of a new social order but instead propagandists whose task is to project the goals and desires of the leader in a society in which order and authority have replaced participation. Yet women organized against Pinochet have used the same cultural model of womanhood for empowerment for a totally opposing political programme.

Scilla McLean stresses in her contribution that illegitimate use of power depends for its success on a lack of awareness on the part of the powerless. Women must assume their responsibility for changing the status quo; we are not to blame others but to ask them to recognize and accept their responsibility. For that purpose, we have to name what is going on. The information package compiled by Scilla McLean as a part of her work for the Oxford Research Group gives us important knowledge about nuclear decision-making processes in the modern military–industrial complex. Carol Cohn gives us in turn a glimpse into the abstract techno-strategic language of defence intellectuals. In learning it, 'one goes from being the passive, powerless victim to the competent, wily, powerful purveyor of nuclear threats and nuclear explosive power'. According to her, learning a language is a transformative process; however, those who created and mastered the language had already become members in a privileged élite group of nuclear strategists.

The requirements of the military system are shaping the world we live in. They distort the economy and the polity so that no goals of social justice can be achieved. As economist Marion Anderson has found out, military build-up leads to a significant net job loss for women. Military spending also affects society's resources in a multitude of ways, so that 'our children are deprived of basic goods so we can produce weapons that we cannot afford to build or to use'. Women bear the burden of militarism also when they are taking over support functions that are no longer being provided by the state.

The connections between the military system as a whole and women's role in a society subordinated to the needs of national security and defence are still known only sketchily. The international symposium 'Women and the Military System', arranged by the International Peace Bureau (Geneva) and Peace Union of Finland, served as a forum for both researchers and activists in this field. More than 100 women, among them some ten men, met at Siuntio Baths, Finland, from 22 to 25 January 1987, in an energizing atmosphere dedicated to an exchange of ideas and research strategies. Ilkka Taipale and Eva Isaksson organized and co-ordinated the symposium on behalf of the Peace Union of Finland. The symposium staff from the Peace Union of Finland as well as

the invited speakers and participants made the meeting a success with their energy, dedication and insight. Cynthia Enloe deserves special thanks for her networking skills and warm support during the process of organizing the symposium. Scilla McLean and Wendy Chapkis also helped us with contacts and suggestions. Special thanks also to Riitta Valkeila for making so much of her time and energy available.
We sincerely hope that this collection of papers serves as inspiration for further study on the important field of women and the military system.

PART 1

HISTORICAL PERSPECTIVES

1

From Military Revolution to Industrial Revolution: Armies, Women and Political Economy in Early Modern Europe

Barton C. Hacker
Visiting Professor of the History of Science
Oregon State University
Corvallis, Oregon, USA

Military institutions have always formed the core of states, ancient and modern, Western and non-Western, capitalist and socialist. Throughout history they have shaped, if not directed, social and technological change. They have, in particular, played key roles in making and keeping women subordinate. Military institutions arose from the fraternal interest groups of pre-state societies and persist in shaping the patriarchal form state societies invariably assume. Indeed, armies owe their very existence to women's structured social subordination. Although women have sometimes performed important military functions, the basic fact remains the same: subordination defines women's relationship to armies. Military institutions, in brief, explain much about past and present gender stratification. Maintaining the patriarchal basis upon which their survival hinges, in turn, explains much about the history of military institutions themselves.[1] Understanding that history—far more than the history of war which is chiefly its by-product—is vital to any peace movement.

Unfortunately, such useful kinds of military history scarcely exist. Military history retains much of the character its classic Greek practitioners first imposed: the war stories of Herodotos, the moral lessons of Thucydides, the memoirs of Xenophon. Professional study, first defined in the nineteenth century, chiefly furnished handy lessons for training young officers in the art of war. All these forms of military history stress battles, not armies. Peace studies tend to share the same preoccupation with war rather than military institutions. But this is not the place for a discourse on proper military history or peace research. Here my aim is more modest, though surely related. By choosing an unusual vantage point, I, like Eric Wolf in his recent study of the world since the sixteenth century, hope to explore new terrain.

An anthropologist with a historical bent, Wolf called his book *Europe and the People without History*.[2] Viewed from the bottom up and the outside in, modern history looks only vaguely like standard textbook accounts. I want to try something like that for military history, though limited time decrees a far smaller scale. This paper addresses only a limited time and place in the long history of women and military institutions: early modern Europe. Within such limits, however, I can at least suggest how looking more closely at changing modes of destruction and their social interactions may illuminate aspects of economic and political development otherwise left poorly explained or not explained at all.[3] As Max Weber insisted on his life-long debate with Marx's ghost, modes of production are not the only modes of human action that matter.[4]

Like Wolf, I shall begin by sketching things as they were at the beginning of early modern times. In the sixteenth century, women were still normal and vital parts of European armies. Usually dismissed as camp followers, they actually played indispensable support roles. That started changing with the military revolution of the sixteenth and seventeenth centuries. Among other far-reaching results, it began a process that sharply constrained women's military roles. It also set in train or promoted many of the economic and social changes leading to industrial revolution. Military women, I believe, significantly influenced those changes, both within the armed forces and in the larger society. My intent, perhaps needless to say, leans toward informed speculation rather than definitive analysis. Too much yet remains unknown and unstudied to allow more.

WOMEN IN EARLY MODERN EUROPEAN ARMIES

Contrary to common opinion, women were not merely victims of war. As we shall see, they worked for the system and benefited from their efforts, though never as much as men. Women in large numbers formed a normal part of armies at the beginning of the modern era. These armed forces appear quite foreign to modern eyes, and not only because of women's presence. Uniforms and drill remained in the future, while private enterprise governed large areas now subject to command. Military units might themselves be profit-making ventures, a company the business of its captain, raised and led in hope of gain, a regiment of its colonel, even an army of its general. In a very real sense, troops were skilled workmen who hired themselves out to the highest bidder. Mercenary forces, rather than national armies in the modern sense, were the norm.[5]

Civilian contractors outside the chain of command might provide and deploy the siege guns, or perform other functions now regarded as purely military. According to Robert Barret's 1598 treatise on *The Theorike and Practike of Moderne Warres*, 'horses, oxen, carts, waines, carters, wainemen, engineers, gunners, carpenters, smiths, founders, armorers, mariners, calkers, pioners, labourers, and other such service' were all 'conducteth under pay'.[6] At a time when Western Europe numbered scarcely a handful of cities of more than 50,000, such an army might indeed resemble the 'vast moving city with its own community life' that historians Geoffrey and Angela Parker describe, complete with 'shops, services and families, all defended by walls of iron—the weapons of its soldiers'.[7]

Distinctions between army and society, however, must not be too sharply drawn. Boundaries easily blurred when soldiers and peasants shared common class backgrounds and often lived cheek by jowl. Before 1600, as Myron Gutman notes, people in the countryside

> dreaded war because it enveloped their lives. They feared the presence of troops who, whether friend or enemy, literally camped in the villages,

fields, homes, and even the beds of the peasants, and, in short, entered into all aspects of everyday existence. The disruption caused by their presence could be overwhelming and the financial drain occasioned by the need to feed them was a heavy burden for peasants, no matter how prosperous.[8]

The horrors of war lurked, at least partly, in unavoidable friction between peasants and troops living off the same land.

Unofficially perhaps, but a fact none the less, armies comprised women as well as men in those years. Scenes of camp or train often included women. Though many were, in fact, soldiers' wives or widows, all female camp followers shared the label whore. In German armies a *Hurenweibel* commanded the baggage train: 'An old and experienced soldier is chosen and used', according to Fronsperger's *Kriegszbuch* of 1598, 'for in his power and under his command is the whole baggage train as well as whores and boys'.[9] Outlining the *Hurenweibel*'s duties, Fronsperger offered a glimpse of women's workaday army world:

He must see to it that they do not hinder the troops on the march, and that they do not come into camp before them, where they would take away everything usable from the combatants. Besides, he must see that whores and loose fellows keep clean the latrines, and further: That they wait upon their masters faithfully and that they are kept occupied when necessary with cooking, sweeping, washing and especially attendance on the sick; and that they never refuse either on the field or in garrison, running, pouring out, fetching food and drink, knowing how to behave mostly with regard to the needs of others and taking it in turns to do what is necessary according to orders.[10]

In both army camp and peasant village, much of women's work was hard physical labour, vital but seldom acknowledged. So at least the advice of seventeenth-century campaigner Sir James Turner suggests:

As woman was created to be a helper to man, so women are great helpers in Armies to their husbands, especially those of the lower condition. . .; they provide, buy and dress their husbands meat when their husbands are on duty, or newly come from it, they bring in fewel for fire, and wash their linnens, and in such manner of employments a Souldiers wife may be helpful to others, and gain money to her husband and herself; especially they are useful in Camps and Leaguers, being permitted (which should not be refused them) to go some miles from the Camp to buy Victuals and other Necessaries.

At one siege, Turner recalled, 'the married Souldiers fared better, look'd more vigorously, and were able to do more duty than the Batchellors; and all the spite was done the poor women, was to be called their husbands mules, by those who would be glad to have had such mules themselves'.[11]

Within the army as outside, women cooked, cleaned, laundered, nursed, and mothered, sometimes for pay, often not. Some women were sutlers, trading in meat, drink, and other needs or wants outside normal supply systems. No sharp line divided small-scale peddler from army wife eking out her husband's meagre and often tardy wages with needlework or laundry. Witness this passage from von Grimmelshausen's seventeenth-century picaresque novel, *The Adventurous Simplicissimus*:

In their misery, a few troopers took on wives (some of these formerly two-bit sluts) who could increase their income by such work as sewing, washing, spinning, or by selling second-hand clothing or other junk, or even by stealing. Among the women was a female ensign who drew her pay like a corporal! Another was a midwife and she was given many a good meal for herself and her husband. Another took in laundry and ironing; she washed shirts, socks, nightshirts, and other apparel for the bachelors among the officers and men, and she had quite a reputation. Others sold tobacco and furnished pipes for those who needed them. Still others sold brandy; it was generally thought that they were adulterating it with water distilled by their own bodies—but that didn't change the color of the liquor in the least! Another was a seamstresss who was able to earn money through hemstitching and embroidery. Still another could pick a living off the field: in the winter she dug up snails, in spring she picked salad herbs, in summer she took the young out of birds' nests, and in fall she could gather hundreds of other tidbits. Some sold kindling wood, which they carried to market like donkeys; others peddled still other merchandise.[12]

Like men in the ranks, women tended to come from the depths of the social order. For either camp follower or soldier, life might be short, for neither easy, though perhaps no shorter nor worse than the life of poor peasant or day worker. Pre-industrial Europe offered poor women few options. Describing their lot in a recent study of *Women, Work, and Family*, Louise Tilly and Joan Scott echo von Grimmelshausen:

They were women in precarious economic situations, since their husbands never earned enough money to cover household needs. These women had no skills, nor did they have capital for goods or a shop. . . So they became petty traders, and itinerant peddlers selling such things as bits of cloth or 'perishable articles of food from door to door' accompanied by their children. The street was their shop; their homes were their workplaces; and their work required no investment in tool or equipment. . . The women were lodging-house keepers and retailers or 'repairers of old clothes and hats, of rags and old ironware, buckles and hardware'. When they did not sell items they had scavenged or repaired, they sold their labor, carting goods, water, or sewage, doing laundry, and performing a host of other unskilled services which were always in demand in the city and usually outside the control of the guilds. Their work was an aspect of 'the economy of makeshift' which characterized their entire lives. . . 'A poor woman . . . goes three dayes a week to wash or scoure abroad, or one that is employed in Nurse keeping three or four Months in a Year, or a poor Market woman, who attends 3 or 4 mornings in a Week with her Basket[13]

Correspondence between women's lives in the army and outside declined in the waning seventeenth century, still more markedly in the eighteenth. Revolutionary changes in the art of war altered not only armies but states and societies as well. Army women, however, sooner than their civilian sisters, felt the weight of change. Regimentation affected women as well as soldiers. Although armies allowed fewer women, they also took better care of those who remained. The first stirrings of official concern for aged and disabled soldiers extended, albeit tentatively, to their widows and orphans as well.

THE MILITARY REVOLUTION

Michael Roberts coined the term 'military revolution' thirty years ago.[14] The idea won quick, widespread and lasting assent; it is now a commonplace, as corrected and revised by later historians.[15] In brief, European armies between the middle of the sixteenth century and the middle of the seventeenth, at last acquired the technical means to exploit gunpowder weapons on the battlefield. The problem had baffled Western minds since the fourteenth century, when such weapons began to transform siege and naval warfare. But neither guns nor small-arms, though ever more widely employed, could routinely achieve decisive results in the field.

That required tactical changes, which in turn demanded new kinds of units, new forms of training and discipline, a new division of military labour. All this had largely been achieved by the mid-seventeenth century.[16]

Technology limited choices, but weapons themselves are social products. Though new weapons demanded new tactics, they dictated nothing about the precise form of such tactics. Nothing compelled men to stress hierarchy and specialized division of labour in reorganized armies. Patriarchal culture, here as elsewhere, affected material organization. Strategy, in any event, revived as these changes took effect and armies regained their power to fight decisive battles. Decisiveness, now expected if not always attained, encouraged larger goals. Ambitious policies, in turn, demanded larger armed forces, forces more centrally controlled and efficiently administered. Larger armies became ever more clearly defined as agents of the state rather than hybrids of private and public enterprise.

Historians had known all this but overlooked its significance. Roberts stretched the chain of cause and effect from narrow tactical innovations to the reordering of polity and society. Expensive standing armies led everywhere to experiments in finance, taxing and economic policy of far-reaching import. Administrative machinery created to support enlarged armies could, and soon did, serve other state purposes. Schools founded to train technical officers pioneered all modern engineering and much professional education. As states altered to meet the needs of their armed forces, society altered to meet new state demands. Military discipline became the model for well-ordered civil society, and state control reached into areas of life once private. Although he ignored the cultural roots of innovation, Roberts traced to military institutions many traits of the modern nation-state, indeed modern society, that emerged in the seventeenth and eighteenth centuries.[17]

Professionalization and bureaucratization transformed women's military milieu during that period, as armies assumed greater control over their support services. Change proceeded neither smoothly nor systematically. By the end of the eighteenth century, though, hired military units—mercenaries—had become rare; civilian gunners and engineers had all but vanished. Military supply was slowest to come under direct army control. Sutlers did lose some freedom—they became, for instance, more likely to wear uniforms—but also gained state aid in filling beer kegs and brandy flasks.[18] This pattern of growing control partly offset by increased benefits marked women's military career throughout the eighteenth century.

Women who preferred the life found armies harder to follow. Marrying a soldier, once purely a private choice, became tangled in new rules. Officers feared that wife and child might distract the soldier from his duties. Restrictions on peacetime family life were, however, seldom strictly enforced and 'wife' could be loosely defined; garrison soldiers who ignored the rules might well escape penalty. Not so when war or overseas duty called units from normal stations. Commanders then often sought to limit numbers of wives who might follow husbands on campaign. Periodically, family life thus faced major crises. Army-controlled transport meant army-controlled movement; commanders could with little trouble bar 'excess' women at these crucial junctures, and they did. History is silent on likely efforts to resist such novel rules, but not on the outcome. By the eighteenth century, English custom decreed no more than six wives per company, or per hundred men, on active service. Other armies imposed similar limits.

Official efforts to control dependants highlight two sides of a changing relationship. The very rules that denied army places to all women sanctioned places for some. 'Wives on the strength', as the British army called them, could now draw rations in token of their legitimate military status, but must also accept duties defined in much greater detail. Regulations of the British 95th Rifle Corps in 1801 show the pattern. 'The marriage of soldiers being a matter of benefit to a regiment', begins the article on wives, it must be well ordered. 'The number of women allowed by Government to embark on service are six for every hundred men', including all sergeants' wives. This ample number 'should never be exceeded on any pretext whatsoever, because the doing so is humanity of the falsest kind'. The lucky few would find the Corps 'a home of comfort to those who are entitled to feel its benefits, [not] a source, as is too often the case, of multiplying misery and prostitution'.

The Corps must provide 'employment and comfortable livelihood to those women who remain', the article continues, but to none who 'are of immoral or drunken character, or who refuse work for the men'. Women would do the regimental needlework and washing. 'The Colonel requests that the officers will never give their linen to wash out of the regiment, and also that they will distribute it nearly equally among the sergeants' wives'. Soldiers' laundry was 'to be distributed in equal proportions among the other women of the companies. The number of shirts and socks which are washed for each soldier per week is two of each and at least two turnovers', for which each laundress received five pence from the pay sergeant: 'The Quartermaster will never give any needlework out of the regiment which can be done in it, and officers are requested to do the same; the women are also recommended to look for needlework in the neighbourhood of wherever the regiment may be, and the officers to give them any aid in their power to procure the same.'[19]

Although expressed as concern for women's well-being, these rules clearly worked both ways. Good housekeeping, in the largest sense, mattered as much to military communities as civil. Only in this century, for instance, has disease ceased to be the chief cause of army casualties. Paid or not, hard work still marked army life. Amenities were few, discipline harsh for women as well as men, in garrison scarcely less than on campaign. Yet women in large numbers clearly preferred army life to whatever options they may have had. Hardship might drive them as well as men into armies, but they were never impressed into service as men were; in that sense, women always volunteered. Their work, in any event, was crucial to the political economy of armies, though subject to scant thanks and much complaint. Never so easy to command as men even when formally carried on the regimental rolls—perhaps simply because children and other duties made them less single-minded about the job—women seemed to those in charge ever less suited to armies growing more rational, bureaucratic and hierarchical. Increasingly excluded from modernizing armies, women and civilian contractors gradually gave way to uniformed, paid, male support services under direct army orders.

TOWARD THE INDUSTRIAL REVOLUTION

Before the nineteenth century, the army alone among major social institutions might allow many women to escape the constraints of rural poverty or urban slum. John Childs may speak as much for women as men in noting the unlikely attractions of eighteenth-century army life:

> The lower levels of urban and rural existence were hard, with work often casual and seasonal. Life in the army . . . was . . . frequently a great deal better than their current lot. . . . Ninety percent of European soldiers hailed from the landless proletariat of urban and rural labourers or from the serfs and peasantry of the agricultural regions.[20]

Army life might also confer more positive gains. 'For many recruits the army must have opened up broader horizons', Childs also observes: 'Once an individual had been enlisted his experiences gave him a much wider outlook on life than if he had stayed in his village as a farm labourer.'[21]

Army women shared such experiences. A major who saw women in 'great number following the regiments' during the 1810–11 French campaign in Portugal thought, 'They preferred licentiousness and the affluence of marauding to purity and abstinence in the deserted countryside. . . They were quite free and were attracted by this new type of life.'[22] Major Pelet may have misread the novelty, but not the freedom, even within a patriarchal, gender-stratified system. Freedom attracted the women who chose army life by the thousands and tens of thousands, no less than the hardships of civil life repelled them. The novel scenes and expanded horizons of military life must have contrasted keenly with the tight little world of village or slum from which they mostly came. And surely the hundreds of thousands of women over the centuries who glimpsed a wider world in their military travels must have affected the civil communities to which sooner or later most of them returned. The men who returned certainly did, as André Corvisier reminds us: 'It is a mistake to underestimate the influence exerted by retired soldiers on those around them.'[23]

Still, women losing army places in the late eighteenth and early nineteenth centuries may no longer have wanted them very badly. Industrializing economies in the Western world opened new choices to the working-class women who might once have become camp followers. Conditions in the new factories of the Industrial Revolution, like those of army life, may seem harsher to our eyes than theirs; they knew what they fled, as we do not. Even amidst 'the record of excessive hours of labour, cramped housing, excessive child-bearing and terrifying rates of child mortality', observes E.P. Thompson, factories offered women a chance 'to achieve an independence unknown before'.[24]

Industrialization itself owed no small debt to military example. Entrepreneurs and captains of industry found much to admire, and to adopt, in the regimentation and redivision of labour imposed on modernizing armies. For one thing, John Nef observes, 'The rise of standing armies contributed to the divorce between gainful labour and family life which is a feature of the modern economic order'.[25] Military regimentation became a model for rationalized production. Sociologist Jacques van Doorn draws even tighter links between military and industrial revolution. He sees much in common between Maurice of Nassau, a key figure in the military revolution who restored drill to armies in the late sixteenth century, and Frederick Taylor, who devised scientific management in the late nineteenth:

> The similarity is not fortuitous. Both were confronted with the problem of how a mass of badly trained, moderately motivated individuals, who were also cut off from their old social milieu, could be welded into goal-attainment organization. Both had the proletariat as a recruiting pool, and in spite of all differences which can undoubtedly be pointed out, their mechanistic image of man was also a product of the circumstances in which they had to work. . . . The military as well as the industrial revolutions made their spectacular leap forward in the first place by a more efficient and concentrated organization of human effort.[26]

Military models, in fact, inspired Taylorism, something van Doorn neglects to mention. Actually, Lewis Mumford addressed this question more comprehensively fifty years ago in his masterly essay on *Technics and Civilization*:

> The general indoctrination of soldierly habits of thought in the seventeenth century was, it seems probable, a great psychological aid to the spread of machine industrialism. In terms of the barracks, the routine of the factory seemed tolerable and natural. . . . The regimentation and mass-production of soldiers, to the end of turning out a cheap, standardized, and replaceable product, was the great contribution to the military mind of the machine process.[27]

Military models also may have served in less direct ways. As the eighteenth century advanced, states began to accept responsibility for military families. Economic historian Fritz Redlich sees the roots of nineteenth-century *Sozialpolitik*, the policy of social security for industrial workers, in eighteenth-century armies. Conditions then prevailed among army families 'which became general for the workers' class in the nineteenth century: a risky occupation, entire dependency on income from wages, and no property to start with on which an old soldier or his family could fall back'. States in the eighteenth century at last agreed to provide, however meagrely, for the few authorized soldiers' wives and children, widows and orphans. This in turn provided a model for the benefits nineteenth-century states, fearing industrial strife, forced employers to concede workers and their families.[28]

The dialectics of women and military institutions in early modern Europe involve the inevitable contradictions that arise when women act independently within ultimately patriarchal institutions. Women were as much a part of early modern armies as men, and the lines between military and civil society could be quite blurred. Most women and men lived close to the margin outside the army as well as within, and women clearly received smaller rewards for greater work. Patterns like this are common to such agriculturally based peasant societies as early modern Europe. Still, women seem to have done better in the army than elsewhere, which may account for their apparent willingness to become camp followers despite harsh conditions and growing official opposition.

Even such modest success as women enjoyed stirred complaints. Official policy statements again and again reveal irritation with women's alleged disruptive influence and presumed diversion of male loyalty and obedience. Such pronouncements embodied an ideology defining army women's moral obligation to greater subservience than male soldiers, both to the institutions and to individual men. The military revolution of the sixteenth and seventeenth centuries first brought this conflict to a head. Technological change opened opportunities for social change in armies. Technology did not, however, dictate the direction of change. Increasing mechanization and greater regimentation, the exclusion of most women from armies with greater security for the few who remained, all were choices rooted in patriarchal culture. Military institutions thus helped shape the Industrial Revolution toward mass production and mass education, standardized parts and interchangeable men.

The nineteenth century saw the last vestiges of non-military support services pass under direct army control. Even as that occurred, armies were laying the groundwork for a vastly larger concept of support that has come to include the whole of society. When the arena shifted to industry in the nineteenth century, war became less a matter of armies than of production. Culminating in the First World War, that trend produced societies in certain ways almost indistinguishable from armies. The First World War also marks the starting point for most modern studies of women and the military system. My story ends, in other words, where most others begin.

The twentieth century—history since the First World War—lies outside the scope of this paper. Historians are seldom comfortable talking about their own centuries, still less trying to foresee the future; I am no exception. Yet I firmly believe that the past must guide the present, and I would like briefly to suggest how that might be done in this instance. Women have always participated in the military system, and in more ways than my relatively focused account suggests. Unlike men, women were never impressed into the armed forces, but the same social and economic forces moved women as well as men. That is still true. At present, however, we can take advantage of knowing what happened before. I will suggest three major approaches to thinking about women and the military.[29]

The first resembles classic liberalism in seeking equal rights for women within the armed forces. Economic and other benefits accrue to men who serve, ranging from the barest state-supported livelihood to such handsome rewards in the United States as advanced education, free medical care and cheap mortgage loans. Liberals argue that women deserve access to such returns.[30] They also have a deeper reason for seeking equal rights within the armed forces. Citizenship and arms have been linked in Western thought since Aristotle. Conscription and mass armies early in the nineteenth century meant political rights extended to classes of men formerly excluded. Women won such rights only a century later, after the First World War.[31]

Unexpectedly, the recent debate over the Equal Rights Amendment to the Constitution of the United States revived this issue. Equality for women, many came to believe, ultimately demanded women in combat: opportunity entails obligation, goes the argument, and if women expect to receive the benefits of military service, they must also accept the risks.[32] Attention to women's military past, as this paper suggests, might turn the debate into more fruitful channels. Unfortunately, that past remains largely unknown, and the debate proceeds on both sides as if the issue arose only yesterday. Late-twentieth-century liberalism, in any event, suffers a deeper flaw: attaining equal rights within the system leaves the system unchallenged, when the system itself may pose the greatest threat.

Socialist approaches largely ignore questions of women and the military in favour of women and revolution. Romantic images of women bearing a rifle in one hand, holding a child with the other, largely replace analysis. Historically, women have played active and visible roles in revolutionary armies, as they still do. But when the task shifts from war-fighting to state-building, women again revert to their proper places. Exhorting women to seize the means of destruction seems no more likely to produce results in the real world than urging them to seize the means of production.[33]

Radical feminism covers a wide spectrum. One prominent

strand relies on notions of women's unique nature or nurture, which somehow leaves them aloof from war and military institutions, or more strongly inclined than men toward peace. Given even the brief sketch I have offered in this paper, such views seem shaky. Other approaches—anarcha-feminism, for instance—see military institutions and states as inseparable from patriarchy. From that angle, the proper question becomes how women and other outsiders might focus their opposition to military institutions and strengthen efforts to build peace-oriented communities.[34] I have no answers, but that at least, I think, is the right question.

NOTES

1. This thesis is documented more fully in Barton C. Hacker and Sally L. Hacker, 'Military Institutions and the Labor Process: Noneconomic Sources of Technological Change, Women's Subordination, and the Organization of Work', *Technology and Culture* 28 (1987): 734–75. In the present essay I also draw heavily on Barton C. Hacker, 'Women and Military Institutions in Early Modern Europe: A Reconnaissance', *Signs* 6/4 (1981): 643–71.
2. Eric R. Wolf, *Europe and the People without History* (Berkeley: University of California Press, 1982).
3. I owe this usage to Jack Goody, *Technology, Tradition and the State in Africa* (1971; reprinted in New York: Cambridge University Press, 1980), Ch. 3, 'Polity and the Means of Destruction'. See also Max Weber, *Economy and Society: An Outline of Interpretive Sociology*, trans. Ephraim Fischoff and others, ed. Guenther Roth and Claus Wittich, 2 vols. (1968; reprinted Berkeley and Los Angeles: University of California Press, 1978), Vol. 2, pp. 1148–55.
4. For this phrase, see Irving M. Zeitlin, *Ideology and the Development of Sociological Theory* (Englewood Cliffs, NJ: Prentice-Hall, 1968), Part 3, 'The Debate with Marx's Ghost', Ch. 11, 'Max Weber', pp. 111–58, esp. at p. 121.
5. V.G. Kiernan, 'Foreign Mercenaries and Absolute Monarchy', *Past & Present* 11 (1957), reprinted in Trevor Astin (ed.), *Crisis in Europe, 1560–1660* (New York: Anchor Books, 1967), pp. 124–149; Fritz Redlich, *The German Military Enterpriser and His Work Force: A Study in European Economic and Social History*, 2 vols., Vierteljahrschrift für Sozial—und Wirtschaftsgeschichte nos. 47–8 (Wiesbaden, 1964–5); Geoffrey Parker, *The Army of Flanders and the Spanish Road, 1567–1659: The Logistics of Spanish Victory and Defeat in the Low Countries' Wars* (Cambridge: Cambridge University Press, 1972);

Michael E. Mallett and J.R. Hale, *The Military Organization of a Renaissance State: Venice c. 1400 to 1617* (Cambridge: Cambridge University Press, 1984); J.R. Hale, *War and Society in Renaissance Europe, 1450–1620* (New York: St Martin's Press, 1985); Simon Pepper and Nicholas Adams, *Firearms and Fortifications: Military Architecture and Siege Warfare in Sixteenth-Century Siena* (Chicago and London: University of Chicago Press, 1986).

6. Robert Barret, *The Theorike and Practike of Moderne Warres* (London: William Ponsonby, 1598; facsimile ed, Amsterdam: Theatrum Orbis Terrarum, and New York: Da Capo Press, 1969), p. 132.
7. Geoffrey Parker and Angela Parker, *European Soldiers, 1550–1650* (Cambridge: Cambridge University Pres, 1977), p. 34.
8. Myron P. Gutman, *War and Rural Life in the Early Modern Low Countries* (Princeton, NJ: Princeton University Press, 1980), p. 31.
9. Leonhard Fronsperger, *Kriegszbuch* (Frankfort, 1598), as quoted by the translators, Robert L. Hiller and John C. Osborne, in Hans Jacob Christoffel von Grimmelshausen, *The Runagate Courage* (Lincoln: University of Nebraska Press, 1965), p. 144n.
10. As quoted in Herman Heinrich Ploss, Max Bartels, and Paul Bartels, *Woman in the Sexual Relation: An Anthropological and Historical Survey*, revised and enlarged by Ferd. F. von Reitzenstein, trans. Eric Dingwall (1930; reprinted New York: Medical Press of New York, 1964), p. 99.
11. Sir James Turner, *Pallas Armata: Military Essayes of the Ancient Grecian, Roman, and Modern Art of War, Written in the Years 1670 and 1671* (London: Richard Chiswell, 1683; facsimile ed, New York: Greenwood Press, 1968), p. 277.
12. Hans Jacob Christoffel von Grimmelshausen, *Simplicius Simplicissimus*, trans. and ed. George Schulz-Behrend (Indianapolis and New York: Bobbs-Merrill, 1965), p. 221.
13. Louise A. Tilly and Joan W. Scott, *Women, Work, and Family* (New York: Holt, Rinehart & Winston, 1978), pp. 49–50.
14. Michael Roberts, *The Military Revolution, 1560–1660* (Belfast, 1956), revised and reprinted under the same title in Roberts, *Essays in Swedish History* (Minneapolis: University of Minnesota Press, 1967), pp. 195–225; the book also includes a related essay on 'Gustav Adolf and the Art of War', pp. 56–81.
15. Geoffrey Parker, 'The "Military Revolution", 1560–1660—A Myth?' *Journal of Modern History* 48 (1976): 195–214, reprinted in G. Parker, *Spain and the Netherlands, 1559–1659* (Short Hills, NJ: Enslow, 1979), pp. 86–103; Gunther E. Rothenberg, 'Maurice of Nassau, Gustavus Adolphus, Raimondo Montecuccoli, and the "Military Revolution" of the Seventeenth Century', in Peter Paret (ed.), *Makers of Modern Strategy: From Machiavelli to the Nuclear Age* (Princeton, NJ: Princeton University Press, 1986), pp. 32–63.
16. In addition to works by Roberts, Parker, and Rothenberg cited above, see William H. McNeill, *The Pursuit of Power: Technology, Armed Force, and Society since A.D. 1000* (Chicago and London: University

of Chicago Press, 1982), Ch. 4, 'Advances in Europe's Art of War, 1600–1750', pp. 117–43.

17. In addition to Roberts, see Charles Tilly (ed.), *The Formation of National States in Western Europe* (Princeton NJ: Princeton University Press, 1975), especially Samuel E. Finer, 'State- and Nation-Building in Europe: The Role of the Military', pp. 84–163, and Wolfram Fischer and Peter Lundgreen, 'The Recruitment and Training of Administrative and Technical Personnel', pp. 456–561; David D. Bien, 'The Army in the French Enlightenment: Reform, Reaction and Revolution', *Past & Present* 85 (1979): 68–98; Charles Tilly, *As Sociology Meets History* (New York: Academic Press, 1981), Ch. 5, 'War and Peasant Rebellion in Seventeenth-Century France', pp. 109–144, and Ch. 8, 'States, Taxes, and Proletarians', pp. 191–210; McNeill, (n. 16, above), Ch. 5, 'Strains on Europe's Bureaucratization of Violence, 1700–1789', pp. 144–84; Ronald W. Batchelder and Herman Freudenberger, 'On the Rational Origins of the Modern Centralized State', *Explorations in Economic History* 20 (1983): 1–13.
18. Andre Corvisier, *Armies and Societies in Europe, 1494–1789*, translated by Abigail T. Siddall (Bloomington and London: Indiana University Press, 1979), Part 2, 'The State and the Army', pp. 61–127; John Childs, *Armies and Warfare in Europe, 1648–1789* (New York: Holmes & Meier, 1982), Ch. 2, 'The Armies', pp. 28–100.
19. As excerpted in E.W. Sheppard (ed.), *Red Coat: An Anthology of the British Soldier during the Last Three Hundred Years* (London: Batchworth, 1952), pp. 48–9. Cf. Walter Hart Blumenthal, *Women Camp Followers of the American Revolution* (Philadelphia: George S. MacManus, 1952; reprinted New York: Arno Press, 1974); H. de Watteville, *The British Soldier: His Daily Life from Tudor to Modern Times*, 2nd ed (New York: G.P. Putnam's Sons, 1955), Ch. 11, 'The Soldier's Wife', 123–36; T.H. McGuffie (ed.), *Rank and File: The Common Soldier at Peace and War, 1642–1914* (New York: St Martin's Press, 1966), *passim*; Roy Palmer (ed.), *The Rambling Soldier: Life in the Lower Ranks, 1750–1900, through Soldiers' Songs and Writings* (Harmondsworth: Kestrel Books, 1977), *passim*; Myrna Trustram, *Women of the Regiment: Marriage and the Victorian Army* (Cambridge: Cambridge University Press, 1984).
20. Childs (n. 18, above), pp. 61–2.
21. *Ibid.*, p. 57.
22. *The French Campaign in Portugal, 1810–1811: An Account by Jean Jacques Pelet*, ed. and trans. Donald D. Horward (Minneapolis: University of Minnesota Press, 1973), p. 313.
23. Corvisier (n. 18, above), p. 193.
24. E.P. Thompson, *The Making of the English Working Class* (1963; reprinted New York: Vintage Books, n.d.), p. 414.
25. John U. Nef, *War and Human Progress: An Essay on the Rise of Industrial Civilization* (1950; reprinted New York: W.W. Norton, 1968), pp. 210–11.
26. Jacques van Doorn, *The Soldier and Social Change: Comparative*

Studies in the History and Sociology of the Military (Beverly Hills, Cal., and London: Sage, 1975), Ch. 1, 'The Genesis of Military and Industrial Organization', pp. 15, 17. See also Jacob de Gheyn, *Wapenhandelinghe van Roers Musquetten ende Spiessen* (The Hague, 1607), facsimile ed as *The Exercise of Armes* with commentary by J.B. Kist (New York: McGraw-Hill, 1971); Maury D. Feld, 'Middle-Class Society and the Rise of Military Professionalism: The Dutch Army, 1589–1609', *Armed Forces and Society* 1 (1975): 419–42, reprinted in M.D. Feld, *The Structure of Violence: Armed Forces as Social Systems* (Beverly Hills, Cal., and London: Sage, 1977), pp. 169–203; Gerhard Oestreich, *Geist and Gestalt des frühmodernen Staates* (Berlin: Duncker & Humblot, 1969), trans. David McLintock as *Neostoicism and the Early Modern State*, ed. Brigitta Oestreich and H.G. Koenigsberger (Cambridge: Cambridge University Press, 1982), esp. Ch. 5, 'The Military Renascence', pp. 76–89.

27. Lewis Mumford, *Technics and Civilization* (New York: Harcourt, Brace, 1934), pp. 84, 92. See also Gautam Sen, *The Military Origins of Industrialisation and International Trade Rivalry* (London: Frances Pinter, 1984).
28. Redlich, (n. 5, above), Vol. 2, p. 265.
29. I borrow the framework for the following remarks, in part, from Alison M. Jagger, *Feminist Politics and Human Nature* (Totowa, NJ: Rowman & Allenheld, 1983).
30. See Martin Binkin and Shirley J. Bach, *Women and the Military* (Washington: The Brookings Institution, 1977); Jeanne Holm, *Women in the Military: An Unfinished Revolution* (Novato, Cal.: Presidio Press, 1982); Mady Wechsler Segal and David R. Segal, 'Social Change and the Participation of Women in the American Military', *Research in Social Movements, Conflicts and Change* 5 (1983): 235–58; Lois B. DeFleur and Rebecca L. Warner, 'The Impact of Military Service on Women's Status: A Neglected Area of Inquiry', presented at American Sociological Society annual meeting, San Antonio, Texas, 1984.
31. Morris Janowitz, 'Military Institutions and Citizenship in Western Societies', in Gwyn Harries-Jenkins and Jacques van Doorn (eds), *The Military and the Problem of Legitimacy* (Beverly Hills, Cal., and London: Sage, 1976), pp. 77–92; Susan Moller Okin, *Women in Western Political Thought* (Princeton, NJ: Princeton University Press, 1979), pp. 48–50, 60–3; Jean Bethke Elshtain, *Public Man, Private Woman: Women in Social and Political Thought* (Princeton, NJ: Princeton University Press, 1981), pp. 92–9.
32. For a recent survey of this issue, see Nancy Loring Goldman (ed.), *Female Soldiers: Combatants or Noncombatants? Historical and Contemporary Perspectives* (Westport, Conn., and London: Greenwood Press, 1982).
33. See Janet Weitzner Salaff and Judith Merkle, 'Women in Revolution: Lessons of the Soviet Union and China', *Berkeley Journal of Sociology* 15 (1970): pp. 166–91; Jane S. Jaquette, 'Women in Revolutionary Movements in Latin America', *Journal of Marriage and the Family* 35

(1973): 344–54; Sheila Rowbotham, *Women, Resistance and Revolution: A History of Women and Revolution in the Modern World* (1972; reprinted New York: Vintage Books, 1974); Carol R. Berkin and Clara M. Lovett (eds), *Women, War, and Revolution* (New York and London: Holmes & Meier, 1980).

34. See Peggy Kornegger, 'Anarchism: The Feminist Connection', *The Second Wave* 4 (1975): 26–37; Pam McAllister (ed.), *Reweaving the Web of Life: Feminism and Nonviolence* (Philadelphia: New Society, 1982); Judith Stacey, *Patriarchy and Socialist Revolution in China* (Berkeley: University of California Press, 1983), esp. Ch. 4, 'People's War and the New Democratic Patriarchy', pp. 108–57; Cynthia Enloe, *Does Khaki Become You? The Militarisation of Women's Lives* (Boston: South End Press, 1983); Betty A. Reardon, *Sexism and the War System* (New York and London: Teachers College Press, 1985); Birgit Brock-Utne, *Educating for Peace: A Feminist Perspective* (New York: Pergamon Press, 1985).

2

'They're Still Women After All': Wartime Jitters over Femininity

Ruth Roach Pierson
The Ontario Institute for Studies in Education, Canada

In 1941 and 1942 official women's services were created within the Canadian armed forces, and for the first time in the history of Canada, women other than nursing sisters were recruited into the military. This paper examines the ideological accommodation made to this wartime development by the Department of National Defence and media supportive of Canada's war effort.[1]

'They're Still Women After All' was the title given, with an audible sigh of relief, by Canadian foreign correspondent Lionel Shapiro to a piece he did for a major Canadian magazine in September 1942. In a jocular vein, the article expressed one man's fears, aroused by the British wartime sight of so many women stepping into formerly male jobs, that women might cease to be women, that is 'feminine individuals', synonymous terms in Shapiro's vocabulary. Similar fears plagued many other Canadians, male and female, as they viewed women entering the munitions plants and, what in the eyes of some seemed even worse, joining the armed forces.[2]

As the primary purpose of the services is the provision of the armed might of the state, their male exclusivity had been in keeping with a deeply rooted division of labour by sex that relegated women to nurture, men to combat, women to the creation and preservation of life, men, when necessary, to its destruction. Closely connected to the sexual division between arms bearers and non-arms bearers was a gendered dichotomy of attributes that identified as masculine the military traits of hardness, toughness, action and brute force, and as feminine the non-military traits of softness, fragility, passivity and gentleness. Hence, the very entrance of women into the army, navy and air force sharply challenged conventions respecting women's nature and place in Canadian society.

Two specific sets of circumstances induced the Department of National Defence to admit women into the armed services during the Second World War: (1) manpower shortages and (2) a reserve of womanpower embodied in a Canadian-wide paramilitary movement of women volunteers eager to serve.[3] For the men in charge of Canada's military, efficient prosecution of the war was the reason for putting women in uniform and under service discipline. They had no desire to tamper with existing gender relations by altering the sexual division of labour or the male over female hierarchy of authority. Obviously the members of the women's volunteer corps eager to become part of Canada's official forces wanted to end the male exclusivity of the military. But even they gave no indication of a desire to erase the demarcation line between male and female spheres. There was thus a tension inherent in the admission of women to the armed services: the tension between the Canadian state's wartime need for female labour within those pre-eminently masculine institutions and Canadian society's longer-term commitment to a masculine–feminine division of traits as well as separation of tasks. This tension was also apparent, albeit to a lesser degree, in the entrance of women into non-traditional trades in war industry. In both cases, under the pressure of the war emergency, women appeared to be breaking sex barriers on an alarming scale.

Reactions to women's admission to the forces, similar to but more pronounced than those to women's mobilization for war industry, provide a good index of the social attitudes toward women prevailing in Canada at the time of the Second World War. And the records of the Department of National Defence provide a good source for those reactions. The Department had to be sensitive to values of the larger civilian society: its dependence on women volunteers, not conscripts, made it especially so. To inform itself of those attitudes it made use of opinion surveys and to influence public opinion it made use of the media. Also, as a part of the established order, the Department of National Defence itself incorporated and acted on widely held, unexamined notions of women's nature and capabilities. The dilemma facing the Department thus brought the current social attitudes towards women into high relief: by admitting women to the services it had violated the convention that the armed forces were no place for a woman; in seeking volunteers, it had to advertise its conformity with as many other received notions of proper womanhood as possible.

What were the reactions to women's entrance into the armed forces (as well as into non-traditional trades in war industry)? One was that the war was opening up for women a world of opportunity unrestricted by sexual inequalities. Army recruiters spoke of the war's having 'finally brought about complete emancipation of women'.[4] Evidence for this was to be found in the very admission of women to the forces and to an ever-increasing number of trades within the forces. With the punning title ' "Jill" Canuck Has Become CWAC of All Trades', a 1944 magazine article celebrated the expanding number of trades open to members of the Canadian Women's Army Corps and singled out in illustration the first 'qualified girl armourer in the CWAC' and the first CWAC to operate 'a Telecord recording machine'.[5]

This perception of the war's having fully emancipated women meshed with the view that women were participating in the war effort on an equal footing with men. 'Shoulder to Shoulder', which was an army motto adopted by the Canadian Women's Army Corps and made the title of their official marching song, epitomized that sense of the equality of women's and men's service.

Of a piece with the celebration of equality and emancipation was a kind of wartime advertisement which proclaimed the end of women's confinement to the domestic sphere. Many companies advertising in the Canadian press between 1939 and 1945, especially those trying to hold on to postwar markets, sought to give a patriotic cast to their messages. One such series of advertisements run by General Motors of Canada took as its theme women's movement into the wide open spaces of the public domain. Running for five pages the advertisement was set up so that a reader would encounter

'Woman's place . . .' on a right-hand page and then turn to find not 'is in the home' but 'is Everywhere . . .' followed on the fourth and fifth pages by the qualifier 'with Victory as Their Business' and a brief description of the many fields in which women were serving the nation at war.[6]

Canada's mobilization of women for the war effort necessitated violation of the social ideal of the woman dedicated to home and family. But even without challenging established patterns of work and behaviour considered appropriate to each sex, war cruelly disrupted and dislocated human lives. To contain the disruptive and destructive forces of war as far as would be compatible with its efficient prosecution seems to have been a goal tacitly agreed upon by those in charge of the war effort and by many in the media. Thus, with respect to women's participation in the armed forces, alongside the talk of emancipation, equality and the overcoming of tradition, recruitment propaganda and wartime advertising also sought to minimize the degree of change required and to hint at and occasionally even stress the expectation of a rapid return to normalcy once the war was over.

Westinghouse of Canada provided a graphic statement of the expectation that at war's end women would return to motherhood and childrearing as their principal life's work. A large two-page advertisement headed 'These Are Tomorrow's Yesterdays' showed the pride the future son of the female war worker would take in his mother's war service. Looking through a book on *Women at War* in the school library in 1955, the boy was surprised by a picture of his Mom, taken in a war plant in 1943. Overcome with emotion, the child has sat down to write his Mom to say how proud of her he is. The advertisement carried not only a tribute to Canadian women's role in Canada's struggle but also the projection that in ten or twelve years' time the women would all be back where they belonged, taking care of the home, rearing Canada's future generation, and buying Westinghouse appliances.[7]

Recruitment propaganda, promotional newspaper stories and patriotic advertising, then, reveal a deep ambivalence toward women's wartime mobilization. On the one hand was the celebration of the trail blazing and achievement of women in the services and, on the other, the assurance that joining the forces changed nothing in women's nature and place in Canadian society.

In 1943 the ambivalence intensified as more and more women were needed, but recruitment met resistance, and monthly enlistment figures dropped. Faced with this slowdown, the National Campaign Committee granted authorization to two opinion surveys in the first half of 1943:[8] (1) a general survey of public opinion[9] and (2) a study of CWAC opinion.[10]

Both surveys revealed that there was widespread disapproval of women joining the armed forces. In light of that sentiment, those in charge of women's recruitment for the three services sought to apply the lessons learnt from the results of the two opinion surveys and to play up any features that had elicited a positive response and to play down, deny, disguise or reinterpret the sources of disapproval.

One source of disapproval was the fear that the woman who joined the forces did so at the risk of her femininity. In the hopes of dispelling that notion, speeches of recruitment officers, recruitment literature, sponsored advertising and promotional news stories, were full of assurances that membership in the women's services was not incompatible with femininity. 'Our women in the Canadian Armed Forces are nothing if not thoroughly feminine in manner and appearance', recruiting officers instructed National Selective Service personnel being trained to help recruit servicewomen.[11] Clearly, while the armed forces could persuade a male potential recruit that military service would make a man of him, they felt they had to do the reverse with a female prospective volunteer, that is convince her that military life would not make her less of a woman.

From the start army authorities assumed women in the services would be concerned about their appearance. Opposition to wearing a uniform *per se* was not anticipated from the women in the volunteer service corps (as many such corps sported their own uniforms), only opposition to a poorly designed uniform. In general, the planners of the CWAC calculated they would have a better chance of attracting volunteers the more attractive the uniform. The 1942 CWAC brochure 'Women in Khaki' boasted: 'CWAC uniforms have been acknowledged by leading dress designers to be the smartest in the world'.[12] Certainly no one would have argued that pride in uniform was excusively or particularly feminine, for men also took pride in their uniforms. There was, however, an important difference. A long association linked male with military uniform and military uniform with the masculine traits of forcefulness, toughness and, in the case of an officer's uniform, commanding authority. When a man donned a uniform he stood to see his masculinity enhanced. Hence the popular notion that uniforms (on men implied) turned women's heads. Literary evidence exists that where the war effort was strongly supported and there were large concentrations of men in uniform, men of military age not in uniform felt threatened not only by the possible charge of cowardice but by the possible loss of girlfriends to the soldiers, sailors and airmen.[13]

Just the reverse was the fear in the case of servicewomen in uniform (or for that matter, of women war workers in overalls and bandanas). Here reassurance was needed that such garb did not diminish femininity. A magazine article appearing in 1943 entitled 'They're Still Feminine!' sought to convince readers that 'khaki, Air Force and Navy blue, or well-worn denim and slacks' had no lasting effect 'on the softer side of Womanhood'.

Clothes don't make the man
and uniforms and overalls
don't seem to be unmaking
the female of the species

was set out in bold print. Accompanying the article was a cartoon showing a group of women war workers and servicewomen, congratulating a member of the Women's Division of the RCAF, who blushingly holds out a diamond engagement ring for the others' admiration.[14]

One Combined Services recruitment advertisement developed in response to the opinion surveys of 1943 showed a mother before a framed photograph of her three uniformed daughters, one in each of the three women's services. The mother is confidently telling the public: 'My Girls are the real

Glamour Girls', and thus countering the association of women in uniform with loss of glamour.[15]

In the heyday of the 'pin-up girl', military officers in public relations never lost sight of the promotional value of female 'sex appeal'. To enhance the image of the woman in uniform, recruiting officers singled out the servicewoman with the beauty queen or movie star good looks of the day to advertise the women's services. Assuming that a function of good-looking women was to decorate, public relations officers also used 'glamour shots' to publicize events in support of the war effort. For example, to draw attention to an exhibit of armaments in Ottawa in May 1944, army photographers took a series of shots of war equipment with which they posed a pretty CWAC corporal. The caption to one photograph in the series read:

> The huge spot-light on display with a collection of modern war material in Ottawa, has a valuable use in searching out enemy night raiders, but Cpl. Wilma Williamson, CWAC of Dundas, Ont., has found another use for it . . . it provides an excellent reflection for straightening a crooked Service tie.[16]

A lot was conveyed by that photograph plus caption: the contrast between the serious operational function of the war equipment and the ornamental function of the CWAC; and the assumption of a narcissism on the part of the servicewoman so ingrained that she would even use a piece of war equipment as a mirror.[17]

Even though the intent of the military was not to alter conceptions of femininity, the campaigns to promote women's uniformed service did have an effect on fashion. The 'mannish' suit for civilian women, with its severe lines and padded shoulders, can be seen as inspired, at least in part, by servicewomen's uniforms. It was also during the Second World War that the popularization of pants for women began, a direct result of women's recruitment into armament, munitions and aircraft assemblage plants. Although eventually the overalls and bandana of the women war workers became symbols of service, in the early stages government officials were concerned that disapproving or ridiculing attitudes towards women wearing trousers would keep women from applying for essential jobs. The Department of Munitions and Supply for Canada considered it necessary to issue the message 'PLEASE DON'T STARE AT MY PANTS' in March 1942 and to illustrate it with the following picture. A middle-aged matron in hat, gloves and furs, has stopped to look disdainfully at the young woman in slacks, while a man in white collar and overcoat has a condescending smirk on his face. The fine print gives the supposed reply of the diffident object of all the attention: 'Would you like to know why I wear trousers like the men when I go about the streets? Because I'm doing a man's job for my country's sake.' [18] Just a year and a half later attitudes had changed enough that *National Home Monthly* could put on the cover of its September 1943 issue a humorous drawing that reversed the roles depicted in the earlier poster. Now it is the female worker, swinging her lunch pail and striding along confidently in her slacks, who wheels around to take a second rather scornful look at a passing kilt-clad member of a Highland regiment.

The extension of slacks as wearing apparel for female military personnel, however, remained slow and restricted. Only in 1944 did the navy's traditional bell bottoms begin to be issued for wear to members of the Women's Royal Canadian Naval Service, and then only to a select number of Wrens on coastal duty. To announce the new departure, a photograph was released to newspapers across Canada in June 1944, and when it appeared in the Toronto Telegram it carried the following caption: 'No wonder this husky sailor seems slightly puzzled. He has just spied a WREN wearing, of all things, bell-bottomed trousers!'[19]

Similarly, in the army, the wearing of trousers by women had to be justified by working conditions or by the task to be performed, but even then could still meet up with opposition. For instance, trousers were authorized early on as part of the winter (but not summer) uniform for CWAC drivers of trucks and jeeps, but not of staff cars.[20] Then in the summer of 1944 the Master-General of the Ordnance authorized 'Trousers . . . for summer wear by CWAC drivers' but 'of Trucks and Jeeps *only*', and went on to specify in no uncertain terms that CWAC drivers of staff cars would have to continue to wear skirts, both summer and winter.[21] The serious attention given to these regulations governing when servicewomen could or could not wear trousers, provides one example of the wartime politics of dress, indicating the symbolic power that could be invested in attire as a regulator of gender and class relations.

In the area of make-up, the army was prepared to make accommodation to current criteria of feminine attractiveness, as defined by officers' conceptions of gentility. The 1920s had seen the introduction of artificial cosmetics as commodities to be purchased on the market. Adoption by women of the middle and upper classes had established their use as fashionable if applied with restraint. Excessive use was associated with less-respectable women, especially prostitutes. The regulations for the Canadian Women's Army Corps permitted women in uniform to wear make-up, so long as it was applied lightly and in moderation. Similar restraint was to govern the use of nail varnish: clear or lightly tinted shades were all right but 'highly coloured' polish was not.[22] While finding it prudent to allow servicewomen the means to strive to meet the current standards of female beauty, military authorities felt constrained to regulate against possible 'vulgarity'. On the other hand, the personal decision of the first Officer Administrating the CWAC, Lieut.-Col. Joan B. Kennedy, to wear no make-up nor jewellery at all, was regarded as unnecessarily severe.[23] Concern lest the servicewoman acquire the image of a 'painted lady', was counterbalanced by concern lest she appear manly.

Both concerns lay behind the public-spirited decision of the National Council of the YWCA to offer 'beauty culture' classes at their Women's Active Service Club in Ottawa. 'Seated at long tables before individual mirrors', the servicewomen were 'taught the importance of good skin grooming'.[24] 'Rouge should be natural looking' was one piece of advice handed out by the 'well-known beauty consultant' who acted as 'volunteer instructress' of the classes.[25] Open to women of all three services, the classes were photographed by the army to use as further proof that genteel feminine beauty and membership in the CWAC were not incompatible.[26]

All three women's services enforced regulations governing the length at which women in uniform could wear their hair: it had to be off the collar. It was anticipated that this requirement might act as a deterrent to those women whose feminine self-image depended on long tresses and elaborate hair dos.[27] While recruits were warned that they would have to sacrifice their 'curls and glamour bobs', they were also assured that styles could still be beautiful and meet regulations.[28]

The 'attractiveness' so central to the prevailing notion of femininity ultimately meant attractiveness to men. Heterosexuality was certainly one of the norms of femininity subscribed to in official publicity about the women's services. While advertisements acclaimed the good wholesome fun women could have together in the services,[29] celebrations of female camaraderie stopped far short of any suggestion of lesbianism. Under military law, after all, homosexuality could be construed as grounds for discharge.[30]

The survey of CWAC other rank opinion had revealed that, after patriotism and the urge to travel, the third strongest motive for joining the service had been the desire 'to be near family, friends in the forces'. While 68 per cent had been influenced by having women friends in the forces, a larger proportion (77 per cent) had followed men friends into the military.[31] Recruitment propaganda, capitalizing on this information, came up with the poster: 'Are you the girl he left behind?' In army photo stories on life in the CWAC, public relations made a point of including material on dances and dates and boyfriends. The message of one army photo in a series on CWACs in Washington, DC, was that members of the Canadian Women's Army Corps stationed outside Canada could find dates in the armed forces of Canada's allies. It showed two CWAC privates stepping out with a soldier and a sailor of the United States Forces.[32]

Indeed, the concern whether life in the armed forces made a woman more or less attractive boiled down to a concern whether enlistment made a woman more or less marriageable. Thus, dispelling the fear that enlistment would scare away dates was not enough. Recruitment literature had to give the further assurance that membership in the women's services would not reduce one's marriageability.

The 1944 CWAC recruitment pamphlet assured the prospective volunteer that, yes, she could get married while she was in the service, provided she had her commanding officer's permission.[33] The army's Department of Public Relations encouraged news coverage of marriages between servicemen and servicewomen. Official army, navy and air force photographers took pictures of such weddings for release to the press.[34] Announcements of such military weddings became a regular feature of the women's activities columns of Canadian newspapers.[35]

One of the least examined and most unshakable notions of the time about women was that subordination and subservience to men were inherently female characteristics that dictated women's role and place in society. This assumption converged with the real position of servicewomen in relation to servicemen, for in jobs, pay and benefits and place in the command structure of the service, the servicewomen were in general subordinate. As reflected in mottoes and enlistment slogans, the very function of the women's services was to subserve the primary purpose of the armed forces: the provision of an armed and fighting force. Having been excluded/exempted from combat, the women of the Canadian Armed Forces could adopt as their motto: 'We Serve that Men May Fight'.[36] That general motto had been adapted from the airwomen's 'We Serve that Men May Fly'.[37] Even more expressive of the secondary status and supportive role assigned to army women was a slogan used on enlistment advertisements: 'The CWAC Girls—The Girls behind the Boys behind the Guns'.[38]

In preserving the male monopoly on armed service, the Department of National Defence was acting in harmony with social convention and conviction. The prevailing view was that men were by nature suited to dangerous, life-risking jobs while women were naturally adapted to monotony and behind-the-scenes support work as reflected in these remarks of one air force officer on the suitability of airwomen for the trade of parachute rigger.

> Take parachute packing. To a man it's a dull, routine job. He doesn't want to pack parachutes. He wants to be up there with one strapped to his back. But to a woman it's an exciting job. She can imagine that someday a flier's life will be saved because she packed that parachute well. Maybe it will be her own husband's life or her boy-friend's. That makes parachute packing pretty exciting for her and she does a much more efficient and speedy job than an unhappy airman would.[39]

Deeply entrenched as the assumption was that the female was the second sex, there still surfaced from time to time the fear that women who were serving with the army would lose their deference toward men and become 'bossy'. Mainly it was the prospect of female officers that seems to have aroused this fear. When Lionel Shapiro covered Major Alice Sorby's arrival in London to command the CWACs overseas, he approved of the fact that she was 'pretty' and had 'graciously submitted' to the press conference. But at the perception that she was also 'a woman full of the barbed-wire quality of a colonel in the Indian service', Shapiro confessed, 'my man's world was beginning to totter before my eyes'. But a question of his that 'penetrated her military façade and revealed her in all her feminine vulnerability' saved the day for Shapiro. 'Major Sorby', he asked, 'your husband is a lieutenant and you are a major. I assume he will have to salute you when you meet. Is that not so?' After a moment's thought, Major Sorby replied that, yes, she supposed that would be regulations, but as she had not seen her husband for more than a year, she doubted whether they'd 'bother about salutes'. Missing the irony of Major Sorby's retort, Shapiro was jubilant. 'Moment triumphant!' he exclaimed: 'My man's world returned in full flower. Major Sorby was really only Mrs Sorby with a King's crown on her epaulettes, and Mr Sorby, though a mere lieutenant, was still master of the Sorby household.'[40] The apprehension that women serving in the forces would lose their femininity included the fear that the male over female hierarchy of authority might be upset.

Just as importantly the public had to be assured that the work women in the forces were asked to perform was suitable for women. With an ambivalence typical of the promotion of the women's services, speeches or publications in one sentence applauded women's breakthrough into positions previously dominated by men and in the next denied that servicewomen were being asked to do anything inimical to their feminine nature. 'If a woman can drive the family car, she can drive a staff car', is an example of the recruitment line that sought to reassure the public that military jobs for female personnel, although performed in new settings and under different conditions, remained essentially 'women's work'.[41]

Thus the contradiction between the armed services' need for women in uniform and the ideology of woman's place being in the home (or in a paid job long sex-typed as female) was bridged through the redefinition of certain military jobs as womanly.[42]

In actual fact, the overwhelming majority of uniformed women employed by the army were assigned to jobs that had already become female niches in the civilian labour market or could be regarded as extensions of mothering or housework.[43] In propaganda and practice, a 'woman's place' was created within the wartime armed services. A similar ideological manipulation was performed in order to make acceptable women's employment in munitions factories. While the woman war worker shown in a photo that appeared in the Toronto *Telegram* appears to 'be preparing a batch of cookies . . . actually she is laying out ignition caps for smoke cartridges'.[44]

The very association of women with the military and with non-traditional trades had touched off fear of an impending breakdown of the sexual division of labour. Under the anxiety over the changed appearance of women lay a more profound but less often articulated fear that women were invading male territory and becoming too independent. Humour of various sorts provided an outlet for these fears. In a 1942 magazine article on 'Woman Power', for instance, a female journalist jokingly proposed a number of ludicrous possibilities. What if at war's end, she speculated, the thousands of war working women

> refuse to be stripped of the pants and deprived of the pay envelopes? What if they start looking round for some nice little chap who can cook and who'll meet them lovingly at the door with their slippers in hand? What if industry has to reorganize to give these women sabbatical years for having babies?[45]

These fears survived till the end of the war. In September 1945, despite the fact that approximately 80,000 women war workers had already been laid off by then, a popular Canadian magazine ran a cartoon that derived its humour from the preposterous yet feared possibility of a reversal of the sexual division of labour between male breadwinner and dependent female domestic. A husband wearing an apron and standing with a mop in his hand and a bucket at his feet frowns in annoyance at his overalls- and bandana-clad wife who, home from the factory, has headed straight for the refrigerator, tracking muddy footprints across his nice, clean floor.[46]

As Susan M. Hartmann has written in *The Home Front and Beyond: American Women in the 1940s*, 'Women's military service represented one of the greatest assaults on traditional practices and values'.[47] The great fear was that the war, by necessitating the mobilization of women on an unprecedented scale, might undermine the established male dominant sex/gender system. The outward expression of women's place in that system is summed up in the term 'femininity'. Through dress, deportment, mannerisms, speech, facial expression, cognitive style, and emotive range and mode, femininity 'both signifies and maintains'[48] women's difference from, deference towards and dependence on men. Thus the fear of the loss of femininity occasioned during the Second World War by the sight of women in uniform or slacks and bandanas, betokened a fear of structural changes in the sex/gender system—a fear of women's slamming the door on domestic dependence and assailing the segregation of jobs by sex. The preoccupation with preserving women's femininity was triggered by war's destabilization of gender relations, and the recruitment propaganda developed by the Department of National Defence to appease such fear simultaneously reflected and reinforced prevailing definitions of womanhood.

NOTES

1. This paper is a condensed version of Ch. 4, 'Wartime Jitters over Femininity', in Ruth Roach Pierson, *'They're Still Women After All': The Second World War and Canadian Womanhood* (Toronto: McClelland & Stewart, 1986), pp. 129–68, 271–6.
2. *Saturday Night*, 26 September 1942, p. 10.
3. According to the nationwide survey of CWAC other ranks, carried out in April–May 1943, 'about 20% of CWAC women belonged to a volunteer women's part-time service organization prior to enrolling in the CWAC. Most of these belonged to one of the unofficial uniformed women's corps or the Red Cross.' *Report of Enquiry—Canadian Women's Army Corps: Why Women Join and How They Like It*, April–May, 1943, p. 23. Copy at DND, DH, 168.009(D91).

4. Notes for the Assistance of Speakers at School for NSS Employment Office Personnel, February 1943, PAC, RG 24, Reel No. C–5303, file HQS 8984–2.
5. *Saturday Night*, 4 March 1944, p. 4.
6. *Mayfair*, May 1943, pp. 141–5.
7. *Women at War*, comp. and ed. J. Herbert Hodgins, David B. Crombie, Eric Crawford and R.B. Ruestis, with co-operation of the Department of Munitions and Supply and the National Film Board (Toronto: Maclean Publishing, 1943), pp. 70–1.
8. Minutes of the 89th Meeting of the National Campaign Committee, 22 February 1943. PAC, RG 24, Reel No. C–5303, file HQS 8984–2.
9. *Report: An Enquiry into the Attitude of the Canadian Civilian Public Towards the Women's Armed Forces* (Montreal/Toronto: Elliott-Haynes, 1943), p. 3, hereafter cited as Elliott-Haynes.
10. *Report of Enquiry—Canadian Women's Army Corps: Why Women Join and How They Like It*, April–May, 1943, p. 23. Copy at DND, DH, 168.009(D91).
11. Notes for the Assistance of Speakers for NSS Employment Personnel, February 1943. PAC, RG, 24, Reel No. C–5303, file HQS 8984–2; NSS Representatives Conference, London, Ontario, 15–17 February 1943, PAC, RG, 24, Reel No. C–5322, file HQS 9011–11–5.
12. CWAC, 'Women in Khaki', p. 20. Copy at DH, DND, 164.069 (D1).
13. Lionel Shapiro, *The Sixth of June* (Garden City, NY: Doubleday 1955); Geoffrey Cotterell, *Westward the Sun* (London: Eyre & Spottiswoode, 1952).
14. Lotta Dempsey, 'They're Still Feminine', *Maclean's Magazine*, 1 January 1943, p. 7.
15. PAC.
16. PAC, National Photography Collection, PA–141005.
17. Some Second World War servicewomen remember without fondness their having been used as sex objects. One wrote that 'as an RCAF (WD) I was involved in displaying my legs on a float in an advertising effort to recruit young men (so-called) still in high school. What a horrid memory'. Letter to author from Shirley Goundrey, dated 17 October 1977.
18. *Maclean's Magazine*, 1 March 1942, p. 3.
19. RCN photo by Photographer Sheraton, RCNVR, York University Archives, Toronto *Telegram* Collection.
20. PAC, Natoinal Photography Collection, Z–61–2, 'C.W.A.C. Winter Driving Uniform', 9 January 1942.
21. Emphasis in original. Master-General of the Ordnance Letter. No. 64/1944, 22 July 1944. PAC, RG 24, Vol. 2255, file HQ 54–27–111–33, vol. 3.
22. Section IX, para. 120(b), 'Regulations for the C.W.A.C., 1941', PAC, RG 24, vol. 2252, file HQ 54–27–111–2, vol. 1; Section IX, para. 40(b), 'Regulations for the C.W.A.C., 1942', HQ 54–27–111–44, DH, DND, 113–3C1 (D1).
23. W. Hugh Conrod, *Athene, Goddess of War: The Canadian Women's*

Army Corps, Their Story (Dartmouth, Nova Scotia: Writing and Editorial Services, 1983), p. 55.
24. Caption to army photo, PAC, National Photography Collection, Negative Z–2337–5, 3 December 1943.
25. Caption to army photo, PAC, National Photography Collection, Negative Z–2337–2, 3 December 1943.
26. See also PAC, National Photography Collection, 'C.W.A.C. Beauty Culture', Negative Z–2431–3, 8 January 1944.
27. 'Army hair-do regulations of no hair below collars caused a little trouble, but most C.W.A.C.'s were quick to the occasion, passed off glamorous tresses as a war luxury and now more and more appear with boyish and military hair cuts.' James C. Anderson, 'Police Women for the Army', *Saturday Night*, 24 April 1943, p. 26.
28. *Wings on Her Shoulder*, RCAF (WD) promotional film, 1944.
29. PAC, National Photography Collection, Z–2405–3, 27 December 1943.
30. Rosamond 'Fiddy' Greer's account of life in the Women's Royal Canadian Naval Service during the Second World War contains this personal recollection: 'When two sisters slept together in a lower bunk across from mine, the thought of lesbianism never crossed my mind. This is not at all surprising, as I had never even heard of it. The more worldly-wise than I (which was probably almost everyone) may have known about "it", but none spoke the unmentionable word and for some time I thought how nice it was that the girls could comfort one another when they felt homesick. However, one day I heard that they had been "found out": shortly afterwards they disappeared from *Stadacona*; and I surmised that "something funny" had been going on. I was learning; although not too swiftly . . . for a long time after the incident I thought lesbians were rather peculiar sisters'. Rosamond 'Fiddy' Greer, *The Girls of the King's Navy* (Victoria, BC: Sono Nis Press, 1983), pp. 83–4.
31. *C.W.A.C. Report*, pp. 18, 24.
32. PAC, National Photography Collection, army photo, Negative Z–1885–17, 11 August 1943.
33. *50 Questions and Answers About CWAC*, p. 11.
34. PAC, National Photography Collection, army photos 'C.W.A.C. Wedding', Negatives Z–2586–(1–9), 1 March 1944; 'C.W.A.C.—Navy Wedding at Kildare Barracks', Negatives Z–3796–(1–4), April 1945.
35. Private of C.W.A.C. Weds Army Corporal', *Globe and Mail*, 2 December 1942, p. 11.
36. NSS Representatives Conference re Recruitment of Women for Armed Services, London, Ontario, 15, 16, 17 February 1943. PAC, RG 24, Reel No. C–5303, file HQS 8984–2.
37. Mary Zeigler, *We Serve that Men May Fly: The Story of Women's Division, Royal Canadian Air Force* (Hamilton, Ontario: RCAF (WD) Association, 1973).
38. CWAC recruiting pamphlet used in M.D. No. 4 in January–March 1943 campaign, DH, DND, 164.069(D1).

39. Ziegler, pp. 66–7.
40. L.S.B. Shapiro, 'They're Still Women After All', *Saturday Night*, 26 September 1942, p. 10.
41. 'Suggested Notes for the Guidance of Speakers at the National Selective Service Schools', 9 February 1943, sent out from the Office of Director of Army Recruiting. PAC RG 24, Reel No. C–5303, file HQS 8984–2.
42. See Ruth Milkman, 'Redefining "Women's Work": The Sexual Division of Labor in the Auto Industry During World War II', *Feminist Studies* 8, 2 (Summer 1982): 336–72, for a discussion of the flexibility of what she calls 'the idiom of sex typing' as a component of 'the resilience of the structure of job segregation by sex'. Milkman shows how shifting composition and application of 'the idiom of sex typing' in the US auto industry both legitimated and curtailed the 'redefinition of the boundaries between "women's work" and "men's work" ' during the war and helped facilitate the return to prewar patterns of occupational segregation by sex during postwar reconversion. '[T]he reproduction of job segregation by sex', Milkman argues, is 'a process that is always occurring'. And this '*job segregation*', she further argues, 'coincides with a *gender hierarchy* within the labor market'.
43. See Ruth Roach Pierson, Ch. 3, 'CWAC of All Trades', in Pierson (n. 1 above).
44. York University Archives, Toronto *Telegram* Photograph Collection.
45. Thelma Lecocq, 'Woman Power', *Maclean's Magazine*, 15 June 1942, pp. 10–11, 40.
46. Drawn for *Maclean's* by Vic Herman, *Maclean's Magazine*, 15 September 1945, p. 32.
47. Boston, Twayne Publishers, 1982, p. 212.
48. Geraldine Finn, 'Questions of Appearance', review of *Femininity*, by Susan Brownmiller (Linden Press/Simon & Schuster, 1984), in *Canadian Forum* LXIV, 741 (August/September 1984): 45.

3

Women Soldiers in Yugoslavia's National Liberation Struggle, 1941–1945*

Barbara Jancar
State University of New York, Brockport, USA

The military role of women in Yugoslavia's National Liberation Struggle (NOB) is only one way of studying the participation of Yugoslav women in those decisive years which determined that country's postwar political shape. The official figure for women's total participation in the partisan cause is 2 million, or about 12 per cent of the prewar population. Of these, 100,000 were soldiers in the partisan guerrilla forces, of whom 25,000 died and 40,000 were wounded. Some 2,000 women achieved officer's rank. Some 282,000 of the women participants on the side of the partisans are estimated to have died or been killed in the concentration camps. A dedicated but indeterminate number were engaged in terrorist and guerrilla activities in the territories occupied by the enemy. The balance of the women were employed in logistic and supply operations in the rear in what were termed the liberated areas.[1]

Given the more massive participation of women in other aspects of Yugoslavia's revolution, why should we single out the women soldier? Above all else, the *partizanka* was the dual symbol of women's fighting contribution to the revolution and of her stake in the emerging socialist Yugoslavia which promised women an equal place with men. The Second World War in Yugoslavia was not one war but three. It was a war against the invader. It was a war between the country's feuding nationalities to achieve equal status in her political

* From *Women and Revolution in Yugoslavia,* 1941–45, forthcoming from Arden Press, Boulder, Colorado.

system. And it was a political war between the Communist-led partisans desiring to overturn the old order and create a socialist Yugoslavia along Soviet lines, and those who wanted varying degrees of a restoration of the *status quo ante*.[2] Women were caught up in all of these wars.

The typical woman of prewar Yugoslavia was a mother in a peasant household, illiterate, and whether Christian or Moslem, subordinate to the patriarchal rule of her husband. In the mountainous regions of Macedonia, Montenegro and Bosnia, peasant women had long held a reputation as fierce fighters for their homes and families against the invading Turk. This tradition came to life again in the Second World War, symbolized by the *partizanka*. In the industrializing cities, women were at the bottom of the labour ladder, the worst paid, the last hired, and the first to go when a crisis came.[3] It was not surprising therefore that they should have been active in the strikes and wage protests which characterized the interwar labour movement in Yugoslavia. The urban woman's most urgent demand was the right to vote, and the civil rights movement attracted the largest number of adherents. As constitutional government was washed away in the rising tide of dictatorship, the movement appeared to grow in strength. Its culmination was a massive demonstration for the right to vote in all of Yugoslavia's major cities in 1939. To no avail. The realities of fascism, German occupation and civil war cut short the dreams. The *partizanka* came to stand for women fighting not only for national liberation from the invader but for their own rights and freedom.

Who were the women who joined the partisan army? Official wisdom and analysis of available data indicate that the huge majority of them were under 25 and probably as much as 70 per cent under 20.[4] The partisans admitted women volunteers between the ages of 18 and 45, and accepted 17 year olds if they requested.[5] In Croatia, these young fighters were known as *djeca borci* (child warriors). Because of their youth, many women soldiers were still in school or holding first factory jobs. According to Danisa Milosavljevič, commander of the 1st Battalion of the 2nd Proletarian Brigade during the final operation in Serbia, the majority of the young women who served under her had never seen military service before. In the older age groups, the partisan women came from a variety of occupations. Some were Serbian Orthodox nuns.[6] Others were workers and teachers from the cities, but again the large majority were peasants. Most needed by the partisans were doctors and nurses. Because nurses in the interwar period had come from the nuns, young recruits had to be trained in medical work. For this reason, the partisan army treated women doctors with respect, and the few who joined, like Saša Božovič, developed legendary reputations.

The women came from all over Yugoslavia. Probably, the greatest number were Serbian, although there are no data to support this assertion. Very few Moslem women joined the partisans. But one would not want to insist on the preponderance of any one nationality. Young girls came from all nationalities and regions where the war was fought. The majority of these young women came from villages under occupation, or that had been a target of war. The chair of the Yugoslav women's organization, Săsa Javorina, drew a distinction between these women who joined 'by instinct'[7] and the more ideologically oriented women who volunteered in the first partisan units. Those mainly came from the large cities and towns, where they had come in contact with progressive ideas through literary circles and school clubs.

Motives for joining the partisan forces were diverse. In the forefront, doubtless, were personal reasons. A parent, brother, or fiancé had been massacred or sent to a concentration camp. In the hill country, where most of the battles were fought, the war entered women's lives directly, and personal tragedy forced them from the sidelines into action. Often whole families joined the partisans together.

Personal experience was not the only reason for joining. For many, the partisan life in the woods seemed infinitely preferable and safer than remaining in the exposed villages or cities, where enemy reprisals were sudden and unpredictable. Another factor was the camaraderie of the partisan experience. The single most precious memory for the former women partisans interviewed by the author in December–January 1985 was the common experience and danger of the war. They shared hunger and cold, and the exhilarating realization that one was tough and could bear infinite hardships. Such experiences forged permanent bonds between soldiers in the same unit. Women also joined because of the adventure and excitement the partisans offered. In some of the more remote villages, young women danced to radios for the first time in their lives. When the partisans were in town, the evenings were filled with music, dance and impromptu and professional theatre. The war brought not only danger but a new life-style to the village. Young girls wanted to be a part of that.

Because of their simple origins, many young women recruits had only the most confused idea of Tito or the Communist Party. One young courier thought the Party was a lovely woman from the Soviet Union who was stronger and more intelligent than the woman commissar of her unit.[8] In some villages, women were discouraged from joining the partisans. They were told that the Communists recruited young women for immoral purposes and that the women soldiers led dissolute lives or were raped for the partisans' pleasure.

Probably only a minority of the young women joined the partisans for consciously held political or ideological reasons. Most of these had either been active in the prewar anti-fascist or women's movements, or their childhood experience had led them to become convinced nationalists. The most politically aware were the first recruits from the cities. For the majority, political education began in the partisan forces. While most ended the war with respect for the Party and a special loyalty to Tito, most entered it because of personal tragedy, the need to survive and the overriding desire to defend home and family.

Initially, the Party leadership was not sure it wanted women soldiers. But the evident eagerness of women to serve changed its mind. Women were the first to volunteer when partisan detachments were organized. Thirty girls from the Bosnian village of Dvar were among the first to sign up in 1941, and the first woman national hero was from Dvar. Women actively participated in the abortive Montenegrin uprising of July 1941. Women were in the original partisan detachments of Macedonia, Slovenia and Serbia, and were also among the first to lose their lives.[9]

When a woman joined the partisans, she assumed definite

obligations. At induction she swore the partisan oath, pledging to destroy old habits of thought, commit herself to the 'working masses' and be full of love for her comrades-in-arms.[10] Once inducted, the woman soldier was assigned generally to a unit in the territorial forces, which operated close to her home village. If she had more experience, she might be assigned to a unit in the proletarian divisions which were authorized to fight all over Yugoslavia and were subject to the orders of the partisan command.[11] In both kinds of groups, there was strict discipline and a sense of commitment to an ideal which was larger than self. Many women embraced this new life eagerly. The 100,000 Yugoslav women who became soldiers[12] rank numerically among the largest contingents of women ever to go into battle under military command at any time in history.[13]

DISTRIBUTION AND FUNCTIONS

As noted above, women were exceptionally eager to sign up. Vladimir Dedijer, one of Tito's closest associates during the war, recalls that women wanted to join so badly that they were shaking lest they be rejected. When the first women's battalion was formed in Lika, a village of Serbian peasant immigrants in southern Croatia, 700 women volunteered. Only 110 could be taken.[14] A major disappointment was to be assigned a job that was not 'soldiering'. National Hero Albina Hočevar-Mali from Slovenia burst into tears when she was assigned her first duty as nurse. The doctor turned to her and said coldly, 'How can you cry? You, a SKOJka [a member of the Communist Youth League]'. Communists must do as they are told cheerfully and willingly.

The first all women's partisan *četa* (band or unit) was formed in Lika on 25 August 1942. In September of that year a second women's unit was formed in Turjanski, and a third and fourth a month later. These uniquely female units were later phased out by absorption into other *čete*. As a rule, a *četa* of 300 would have five or six women.[15] The *partizanke* were distributed in these mixed units throughout the territorial and operational commands.[16]

An analysis of the relative strength of women to men in the units of the I Corps of the National Liberation Army (NLA) in Croatia provides some idea of their functions. The largest percentage of women appear to be at staff headquarters in this corps, and the next largest percentage in the artillery. The smallest percentage of women are not in the specialized units but in the regular territorial units. In none of the units does the proportion of women reach even 10 per cent. Data on the distribution of women in Dalmatian units analysed earlier by the author,[17] show without exception a concentration of women in the medical assistance jobs, although the largest number of women served as soldiers (42 per cent). Specialized soldiers and service personnel were far fewer as were political officers.

While women did not form a very large part of the overall fatalities in the I Corps, the share of women who lost their lives relative to the total number of women in the corps was almost 20 per cent. The share of men who died compared to the total was 24 per cent. The corps would appear to be representative, perhaps even a little low in female fatalities, since the total number of women partisans who died as compared to the total number enlisted was 25,000, or 25 per cent.[18] In the VI Corps of the NLA Croatia, where 183 women had lost their lives as of 1944, we find that the common perception that nurses and staff personnel shared danger equally is illusory. The data suggest that it was far riskier to be a partisan soldier than a medic. The inexperienced peasant woman under 25 did not survive much beyond her baptism of fire.[19]

Even though the number of nurses who lost their lives was proportionately less than that of the soldiers, nursing had its dangers. The typical field hospital was little more than a tent or a peasant's hut. Medicines and medical supplies were very short. There was little or no anaesthesia. The enemy was all around, and one never knew when he would attack. Nurses and doctors came constantly under fire. The rear hospitals were better protected, but enemy offensives demanded strict security. At Hospital Franja in the mountains of western Slovenia, the wounded were brought in blindfolded so that they would not know how they came to hospital, and were blindfolded again when they left. The nurses also had their eyes covered when they went out, so that no one knew the hospital's exact location except a few trusted individuals. Even the wash could not be hung outside to dry; lest the white sheets attract the German's attention.[20]

Saša Božović, one of the foremost women physicians during the war, recalls that a doctor had very little rest. There was a chronic lack of medical personnel and the partisan doctor was always in demand whenever the troops came to a village. A village might be going through a typhus epidemic or have just been the victim of an attack. Doctors and nurses had to set to work immediately to tend the burnt and the dying. Many that were hurt and survived were children whose parents had been killed in the attack. The first day in a village could bring the medical staff close to exhaustion.

Although a medic's life was one of the most demanding in the partisan forces, the nurse did not have the status of the fighter. In traditional Yugoslavia, women had always tended the sick and taken care of the wounded in wartime. Thus, although a nurse's job was indispensable to the partisan effort, it never really was given the credit and the place of honour it deserved. Doctors, on the other hand, were recognized for their dedication to medicine. Božović rose to the rank of major, the highest rank ever reached by a woman in the National Liberation Army during the war. Given nursing's undervaluation in traditional society, there is little doubt that for a young girl not yet 20, the excitement and the challenge was on the battlefield not in a field hospital. Danisa Milosavljevič had to petition Tito directly to become a fighter. The Party decision to let her become a soldier marked one of the greatest days in her life. As the numbers of wounded increased, the soldier began to understand the task of the nurse better, but the nurse never acquired the same status as the fighter in the field.

While nursing was by far the most common role for women partisans outside that of the plain soldier, it should be remembered that in none of the military occupations were women ever in the majority. In the units of the 13th Croatian Division, for example, there were twenty-four women assigned to the hospital and 197 men. The difference comes in the ratio of male and female nurses to the total number of men and women in the division. In that division, male nurses constituted 4 per cent of the total number of men in the division, and women nurses, 24 per cent of the total number of women. By contrast, men constituted almost 90 per cent of the soldiers and women, 70 per cent. Again, the forty-six individuals enrolled in the officers' training course were all men. Interestingly enough, in this division, the band was all male as well.[21] It would not be correct to infer discrimination. Clearly, men provided the main fighting force. Women were used where their skills were considered the most useful. Nursing had primacy of place.

Women performed many others kinds of jobs, although they were not as routinely assigned to these. They were intelligence gatherers, couriers, telegraph operators, cooks and typists.[22] But these tasks did not require the person to be in the partisan army. Inspection of the 854 women's biographies in *Women of Croatia of NOB* indicates a large number of women who served as couriers, cooks and informants outside the partisan units. Women also did not perform the same task all through their military career. Hočevar-Mali may have started partisan life as a nurse, but she ended her army career working in the political section. Danisa Milosavljevič ended hers as a commanding officer.

The bravery of the woman soldier was legendary. National Hero Milka Kufrin became a symbol of partisan resistance for her courage in sabotaging the Zagreb–Karlovеć railroad line and 'cleaning' the area of enemy units. Javorina proudly asserted that women never deserted the units and were among the most heroic. Milovan Djilas, who later broke with Tito over postwar policy, insisted that women were braver than men.[23] Danisa Milosavljevič, one of the few women partisan officers, stressed women's stamina in the war and estimates that the soldiers in her command had walked over 4,000 miles of roadless terrain by 1945.

Such courage is even better appreciated when it is placed within the context of the difficult conditions in which the soldiers lived. As stated earlier, most of the first women partisans came from the cities, where they had been workers, students or teachers.[24] The peasant women were recruited later as the war developed in the mountains of Montenegro, Bosnia and Serbia. The professional women, in particular, were not used to physical work nor the rough primitive surroundings. Exposure to the harsh wartime conditions made it impossible for many of them to bear children after the war.[25] According to Saša Božović, numerous women, even the younger ones, ceased to menstruate or had difficulties with their periods, a condition which was not uncommon elsewhere in wartime Europe, where proper food was scarce and living conditions deteriorated.

Women partisans lived the same life as the men, slept in the same quarters, ate the same food, and wore the same clothes. A partisan strict moral code governed daily living. Sexual relations were severely discouraged among the common soldiers. Love, said, Javorina, showed itself in carrying a rifle for one's beloved or in giving an apple. Božović, however, recalled that youth would have its way, and that young people frequently succeeded in avoiding the strict eyes of the partisan command, even though they knew that swift punishment would follow if discovered. Women found the time to be women. The posed photographs in the published documents are full of handsome young women with smiling faces dressed in partisan uniform with surprisingly chic hairstyles under a partisan cap perhaps set a tiny bit askew to give a jaunty effect. Although the partisan code frowned on such frivolities, it seems only human nature that after the battle or before the camera, the girls would want to pretty themselves up, especially if there were evening activities scheduled.[26] But no young *partizanka* could openly admit she was interested in such things.

MILITARY RANK ATTAINED BY WOMEN

Some 2,000 women attained officer's rank in the partisan forces. Before ranks were introduced into the army in 1943, command structure was indicated by the kind of partisan group the commander led. The groups ranked from the lowest to the highest as follows: *desitina, vod, četa*, battalion, *odred*, brigade. Throughout the war there were two chains of command: party and military. From 1941 to 1943, the Party chain paralleled that of the military. When ranks were introduced, the commander distinctions were replaced by the military titles of ensign, lieutenant, captain, major. But the dual chain of command remained, with the Party commissars equalling in rank the parallel military officer.[27]

A comparison of the ratio of male and female staff officers to total numbers of men and women in six Croatian units, indicates that overall the percentage of male officers to male soldiers, and female officers to female soldiers, might not appear that significant. But the small difference in the figures means that in these units there were about 30 per cent more male officers among male partisans, than female officers among female partisans. In other words, there was a tendency to pick male officers over female officers. Second, the size of the officer ranks varied widely between units. The highest percentage of male commissioned officers in the six units was 8.37 per cent as compared with 2.86 per cent for women, while the lowest percentage of male commissioned officers was 0.42 per cent as compared with 0.72 per cent for women.[28] Such data suggest that men had greater opportunities for promotion or that women might have been deliberately discriminated against.

The case for discrimination also may be argued from the distribution of women's promotions. These appear to have been based primarily on their medical expertise or on their status in political work. The first women officers in 1943 were almost all medical people.[29] Of the ninety-two women national heroes, thirteen attained rank in the partisan forces as indicated in their official biographies. Of these thirteen, only three had military rank, the highest of which was that of second lieutenant earned by Danisa Milosavljevič. The other ten were party functionaries who held corresponding military ranks of lieutenant and captain.[30]

If women were not commanding troops in the field, they were in larger proportion responsible for the daily military and political morale of the partisan soldiers. The commanding staff of each *četa* was composed of four people: the commander, the political commissar, the supply officer and the deputy political commissar. At the beginning, only the first two existed. The others were added as the forces grew. The political commissar was a Party member, but not necessarily leader of the unit's Party group. The documents indicate that women were frequently leaders of the *desetina* Party group or head of SKOJ groups at various army group levels.

According to Javorina, no decisions could be made by the commander without the agreement of all four individuals. All documents were received and reviewed by both the commander and the commissar. The task of the commissar was to explain the main line of NOB to the troops, and, when required, to the villagers living in the area where the troops were bivouacked. The deputy political commissar was immediately responsible for Party work in the unit. He or she had to see that the partisan code was enforced, that difficult moments were overcome, that troop morale remained high. The deputy commissar also was the one responsible for organizing reading courses and troop entertainment, always of course with the consent of his/her superiors.

Given the Party control of partisan movements and strategy, the position of commissar was obviously a critical one, and the post tended to be filled either by experienced women in the Party before the war, like Liljana Maneva and Javorina, or by trusted younger people. Statistical analysis of data on women participants in NOB in Croatia derived from Croatian documents, indicate that the proportion of women Communist Party members tended to be lower in the partisan forces (26.8 per cent) than among the documentary sample population as a whole (30.6 per cent). This finding is significant because the population in the Croatian documents is skewed towards women active in NOB with known sympathies to the Communist cause. By contrast, the percentage of women teachers in NOV (the National Liberation Army) (19.4 per cent) was substantially higher than in the sample population as a whole (4.2 per cent). Teachers were the stuff from which political commissars were made. However, since the Party was organized hierarchically, the woman who became political commissar had first to work her way up through the ranks of ordinary Party membership to reach the more trusted and responsible positions. The documents suggest that very few women went much beyond the level of *odred* commissar.

If the bulk of the women recruits came from peasant backgrounds, so did the bulk of the male recruits, yet more male partisans were promoted. If a higher percentage of women teachers did indeed join the partisans than might be expected, these young women certainly must have formed an appropriate officer recruitment pool and not only for the rank of political commissar. Research has also found that a significantly higher percentage of women with some education joined NOV than was the case in the other partisan organizations in which women participated and for which we have data. Most of these were doctors, while the others all had political/bureaucratic functions. The nucleus of the partisan military command came from the male volunteers for the Spanish Civil War. What were the sixteen women volunteers doing at the beginning of the Second World War? While these data do not add up to proof of deliberate discrimination, they strongly point to a 'woman's place' in the partisan army.

Available evidence thus forces a modification of our picture of the Yugoslav *partizanka*. We cannot conjure up an image of equality where heroic women command major troop movements alongside men. Rather, we must limit our vision to young women shouldering their guns bravely to carry out the commands of their male superiors at the front, in hospital or in the political section—or spontaneously initiating some action in the field as the moment demanded. In this sense, courageous, determined and resourceful as they were, the woman partisan belonged more to the passive agents of battle rather than to the military planners.[31]

As regards the ability of women to hold higher military commands, there are those in Belgrade and Zagreb who believe that certain of the women officers were indeed of superior quality. But their husbands also held officer's rank and unfortunately were somewhat less able. The general staff in their view disregarded the promotion of the able women so as not to appear to discredit the husbands. Since the documents in no way suggest such a view, it is offered only as an opinion without confirmation. But the fact that this viewpoint is held at all indicates that all was not equal between male and female partisans, and that some women did not perceive the situation as equal either. Women did hold men's jobs: they were soldiers. But they did not rise through the ranks in any significant numbers to hold commanding military positions.

The conclusion is inescapable that in the partisan forces, women played the supporting roles, not those which created policy and drove the military machine. As in the Vietnamese revolution, only the exceptional few rose even to middle levels of responsibility.

TRAINING OF WOMEN RECRUITS

The documents and interviews provide no evidence of special military training for women. The standard formula was a one month's 'short course' for all soldiers before being sent to the front. Frequent references are made to one-month 'political military courses' where both men and women received training.[32] The partisans also offered courses in encoding and decoding, and artillery courses, but none of them was specifically directed towards women. The basic training courses were rudimentary at best, and in view of the urgency of the situation, could not last as long as they should have. The high mortality rate of young women suggests that women might have benefited from additional training.

Training and organization in the medical sphere were another matter. The partisans' development of medical facilities and medical training programmes is one of their most notable achievements of the war. By 1945, every theatre of the war had its medical installations, staffed primarily by women who had gone through the partisan nursing courses. At the beginning, medical care was haphazard and spotty. During the last years of peace, the Party started to provide courses in nursing. Danisa Milosavljevič recalls an illegal sanitary course held for her youth group. Her first assignment was in a partisan *odred* near Užice, where she received ten additional days of training as a nurse, based on the course she had taken earlier. At the time, the partisans needed nurses so desperately, there was no time to provide them with proper training.

Hočevar-Mali's first contact with nursing was to put three bottles of rakija, the Balkan brandy, and three bottles of spirit in an army bag and take them to the partisan field hospital. Upon completion of her assignment, she was told she had just gone through her first lesson in nursing. She was then sent for what she was told was real training, learning how to tie bandages. When her first patient came, she was told to take down the man's trousers. She was so embarrassed, she broke into tears. But the doctor's words about the obligations of a SKOJka rang in her ears and she set to work to be a nurse.

As the war progressed, the nursing courses became better organized until there was a network of courses of varying levels of difficulty and skill. At the same time, hospitals were set up in each military theatre attached to a division or battalion. The nursing courses were apparently small with the average class size around thirty. Among the factors determining the type of course available at any one moment and location, were the region where they were offered, the availability of trained teaching personnel and the immediate needs of the local units.[33] The successful administration and operation of the wartime military and public health-care facilities are testimony to the quality of the wartime medical training courses and to the dedication of the women who took them.

MEN AND WOMEN PARTISANS: MUTUAL ATTITUDES AND PERCEPTIONS

It was to be expected that all the women partisans interviewed had the highest praise for Tito and the High Command. The published documents also portray what they would like to have one believe was a virtually universal admiration for Tito. Tito appears in them like a mythic hero, a legend in his own time. Young girls are said to have died for Tito in battle, or to have attributed their feats of bravery to his influence.

It is virtually impossible to separate the reality from the legend in these materials. Tito was and remains the single most important person in the founding of the new Yugoslavia. For Javorina, Tito was 'the prince on the white horse'. Danisa

Milosavljevič particularly respected Tito for his insistence on the role of women in the war. In a more reflective mood, Mitra Mitrovic, wartime editor of the women's publication, *Zena danas* (Women Today) and former wife of Milovan Djilas, recalled that all the military leaders respected Tito for his excellent organization and political talents. In her view, there were many capable individuals in the top command. Some were more, some less capable than Tito. But during the war there was mutual respect and co-operation between them. This bond held the whole partisan effort together. Where there was criticism was in the High Command's appearance of having a light code of conduct for their personal lives and a strict one for the troops. In Mitrović words, such behaviour 'went with power'.

Male attitudes towards the women partisans appear to have been highly equivocal. First of all, there was the sexual double standard of the leadership.[34] Djilas writes on one page of his memoirs that the decision to join the partisans was more of a turning-point for women than for men, and for this reason, women tended to fight more bravely than men. On the next, he finds his dedicated partisan wife, Mitra Mitrović, hard, overassured, and 'overflowing with a sarcastic spirit'. And on the third, he deplores the fact that all the Party leaders seem to have pretty little secretaries. He takes particular satisfaction in citing those in the Party leadership, including Tito, who failed to follow the strict Communist moral code.[35] Dedijer stands apart in his enthusiasm for the participation of women in battle. In his sober assessment of the impact of the war upon women, he notes that the majority of the army was peasant and came from the most underdeveloped and hence most conservative regions of the country. These were the regions where before the war women were 'treated like slaves'. In his view, the women who joined the partisans from these areas made the greatest advances forward.[36] Editorials in the wartime Party journals support the contention of general male resistance to equal opportunity for women in the army.[37]

Perhaps one of the strongest factors operating in both male and female perception of women's role as armed fighter in the war was what George Zaninovich has called the partisan myth of equality. This myth focused on the equal share of all groups, nationalities and women, in the experience of national liberation.[38] Party educational courses in the army placed this myth within the historical context of the class struggle. On the one side were the forces of progress. On the other, the 'reactionaries' and 'quislings', the servants of fascism. Within this framework, both the Četniks, the non-Communist Serbian partisan resistance, and the Croatian Fascist Ustaše were (and still are) depicted as counter-revolutionary forces which humiliated and brutalized women. Party-sponsored journals did not need much encouragement to publicize every act of terrorism, rape or murder accomplished by the other side in the civil war. The result of such propaganda was that the partisan male knew he could not openly oppose the position of the woman fighter. The absence of public confrontation could only strengthen the positive perception of equality, already developed from the moments of camaraderie experienced by many *partizanke*, among both men and women in the partisan army.

Clearly, Tito could not have mobilized the numbers he did without massive confidence in his leadership. Nor would women have volunteered as enthusiastically to fight for the partisans if they had not attributed to Tito the qualities necessary to win the war and believed in his promises of postwar change. Yet while one may appreciate genius and leadership, the instrumental use of women in the army which came out in our analysis of the published data appears directly attributable to the persistence of patriarchal attitudes demonstrated by the personal behaviour of the High Command. Women were fighters because fighters were needed for the war, and the war needed to be won. But it was a man's war throughout, with men determining when, where and how women would fight. And while men may have commented over and over again on the *partizanka*'s remarkable courage and self-sacrifice, this recognition of the qualities of the woman fighter did not translate into giving even the most trusted of them a role in the wartime decisions nor in the final disposition of the victory.

Women thus participated in battle while remaining totally within the androcentric frame of reference. For some, participation alone meant equality. In Milka Kufrin's words, 'Equality was only in the *četa*'. In the military unit, men and women were summoned to equal courage, equal energy and equal determination. Outside the *četa* and above the *četa* in the military command, the patriarchal world continued as before. It is not surprising therefore that those women who did lead troops, or had a distinctly military role during the war, should feel that the war brought them liberation and provided the basic necessary conditions for liberating the rest of Yugoslav women. But the sense of togetherness achieved in participation in a common cause is not the same as equality. The proof is in postwar developments. Women's place in the modern Yugoslav army is as volunteers in the medical and logistic units.

CONCLUSION

How can we fairly assess the role of women as fighters and the impact of this role upon the consciousness-raising process? The data and interviews indicate women sought the role of fighter as indicative of higher status, commitment and adventure. When they were admitted into the partisan units, they proved excellent, dedicated fighters. For the women active in the prewar Communist underground, admission was nine-tenths of the battle. The prewar programme both of the non-Communist Women's Movement and the Communist Party demanded that women be permitted to acquire male roles. The male role *par excellence* was that of the warrior. Thus the old generation of urban-born women Communists accepted woman's fighting role as proof of the programme achieved.

For the younger generation of peasant women, the wartime warrior role represented both a continuation of a valued patriarchal tradition and an uprooting from this tradition in the Communist leadership's insistence on the equality myth translated into specific norms of conduct. This insistence expanded their sense of personal worth, giving them a *perception* of equality never before experienced. For both generations, the role of soldier was a personal breakthrough in which they successfully played a man's part in a man's world. For the Party leadership, on the other hand, the woman warrior represented the unique moment of women's emancipation in Yugoslavia. Beyond the admission of women to the most exclusive male role, its androcentric vision could see no further.

The above analysis is in no way intended to minimize the role of the woman soldier in the Yugoslav National Liberation Struggle. On the contrary, it suggests that perhaps the hierarchical organization of the military and the total demands of obedience on the battlefield may be an ideal arena for women to achieve a sense of self as *competitors* for male roles, but an inappropriate theatre for women to achieve a sense of self *as women*. Through their participation in the partisan forces, Yugoslav women proved to the world that women could fight as soldiers in a modern war as well or better than men. However, the very fact of doing something as well as men militates against women thinking and acting in a woman-centred world, where self-realization is not predicated on identification with male roles. It also tends to the glorification of war and violence. It is significant that the legend of the woman partisan bound up as it is with Yugoslavia's fight for freedom during the Second World War, has been able to dominate the definition of women's liberation in Yugoslavia for over forty years. Only now is a new generation of women beginning to look critically at that legend from a woman-centred perspective to set it in its proper context.

NOTES

This paper is a revised version of Ch. 3 of my book *Women and Revolution in Yugoslavia 1941–1945* (Boulder, Colo.: Arden Press, 1987). The book is the product of research into Yugoslav documents and interviews in Yugoslavia with women who participated in the National Liberation Struggle. The interviews were conducted between December 1984 and January 1985. Further information about the book may be obtained from the publisher.

1. The figures are from *Leksikon Narodnooslobodilački rat i revolucija u Jugoslaviji 1941–1945* (Dictionary of the National Liberation War and Revolution in Yugoslavia 1941–1945) (Belgrade: Narodna Knjiga, 1980), Vol. 2, p. 1251.

2. Denison Rusinow makes a similar point in *The Yugoslav Experiment, 1949–1974* (Berkeley and Los Angeles: University of California Press, 1978), pp. 3–7.
3. For a Yugoslav discussion of the status of working women in the interwar period, see Jovanka Keĉman, *Žene Jugoslavije u radničkom pokretu i zenskim organizacijama 1918–1941* (Women of Yugoslavia in the Workers' movement and Women's Organizations 1918–1941), (Belgrade: Navodna Knjiga and Institut za savremenu istoriju [Institute of Contemporary History], 1978).
4. The raw data are found in Marija Soljan (ed.), *Žene Hrvatske u Narodnooslovodilačkoj borbi* (Croatian Women in NOB) (Zagreb: Izdanje Glavnog odbora saveza ženskih društava Hrvatske, 1955), Vol. 2, pp. 446–504. See my analysis of the data in B. Jancar, *Women and Revolution in Yugoslavia* (Boulder, Colo.: Arden Press, 1987), Chs. 2, 3 and 4.
5. Author interviews with members of the Slovenian veteran and women's organizations, January 1985.
6. Bosa Cvetić, *Zena Srbije u NOB* (Serbian Women in NOB) (Belgrade: Nolit, 1975), p. 711.
7. Author interview with Saša Javorina, Chair of the Yugoslav Women's Organization, January 1985.
8. Author interview with Saša Javorina, January 1985.
9. Dušanka Kovačević *et al.*, *Borbeni put žena Yugoslavije* (Yugoslav Women's Militant Road) (Belgrade: Leksikografski zavod 'Svazjanje', 1972), pp. 52, 127, 161 and 232.
10. For the full text of the partisan oath, see *Leksikon*, Vol. 2, p. 829.
11. Author interview with Vojislav Subotić of the Institute of Military History, Belgrade, January 1985.
12. This number did not join immediately. In 1941 there were only twelve women in the Croatian detachments of the partisan army: in 1942, 479; in 1943, 1,211; and in 1944, 6,610. Kovačević, *et al.* (eds.), *Borbeni put*, p. 127.
13. The number of women in the Red Army during the Second World War who served at the front in combat or support roles was much higher. However, we are speaking of a larger population pool.
14. Vladimir Dedijer, *With Tito Through the War* (London: Alexander Hamilton, 1951), p. 121; and *Zene Like, Bore se rade govore* (The Women of Lika: They Fight, Work, Walk) (Zagreb: Izdanje Glavnog odbora AFŽ Hrvatske, 1953), pp. 5–6.
15. Author interview with Vojislav Subotić of the Institute of Military History, Belgrade, January 1985. As quoted in Kovačević *et al.*, *Borbeni put*, p. 195.
16. For further data on the recruitment of women into the partisan army, see Kovačević *et al.*, *Borbeni put*, pp. 89–90; Stana Gerk, Ivka Križnar and Stefanija Ravikar-Podbevsek (eds.), *Slovenke v Narodnoosvobodilnem boju: Zbornik dokumentov, člankov in spominov* (Slovenian Women in NOB; Collection of Documents, Articles and Remembrances) (Ljubljana: Zavod 'Borec', 1980), pp. 121–8; and Vera

Vesković-Vangeli, *Ženata vo revolucijata na Makedonija 1941–1945* (Women in the Macedonian Revolution 1941–1945) (Skopje: Institut za nacionalna istorija, Zavod za unapreduvanje na stopanstvoto na SRM (Institute for National History, Department for The Advancement of Society in SRM] 1982), pp. 281–91. According to Veskov-Vangeli, in 1943, about 30 per cent of the fighting force in Macedonia were women.

17. Barbara Jancar, 'Yugoslavia, War of Resistance', in Nancy Goldman (ed), *Female Soldiers: Combatants or Noncombatants*? (Westport, Conn.: Greenwood Press, 1982), p. 97.
18. Analysis made from Soljan (ed.), *Žene Hrvatske*, Vol. 5, pp. 179.
19. Summary data compiled from *Ibid*., pp. 301–312.
20. According to Irina Lah, once Italy capitulated and Tito was recognized by the western Allies, Slovenia benefited from shipments of medications from the Allied lines. The Franja Hospital, already one of the better equipped hospitals of the partisan forces, became the best stocked with medical supplies.
21. Soljan (ed.), *Zene Hrvatske*, (1955), Vol. II, p. 241.
22. Fitzroy Maclean, *Eastern Approaches* (London: Cape, 1957), p. 132.
23. For Djilas' views, see Milovan Djilas, *Wartime* (New York: Harcourt Brace Janonovitch, 1977), p. 210. It is simply impossible to count the number of published reports of the bravery of the women partisans and their sisters in the rear during the war. In my talks with Yugoslavs in January 1985, not only was there never any doubt raised about women's bravery, women's courage was the first thought that came to virtually every one interviewed.
24. The predominantly urban composition of the first women partisans is striking in the list of the first Slovenian women partisans referenced in Footnote 7.
25. Author interview with Danisa Milosavljević.
26. In his diary, Dedijer recalls with obvious pleasure the theatrical and musical performances given for the partisans by professional entertainers. Dedijer (1951), p. 121. Bailey also emphasizes the contribution of the professional performers. Bailey, pp. 132–135.
27. *Leksikon*, Vol. I, p. 197.
28. Figures as developed from data presented in Jancar, 'Yugoslavia: War of Resistance', *Female Soldiers—Combatants or Noncombatants*? p. 100.
29. *Žena danas* [Woman today], November 1943, p. 16.
30. Data derived from Peter Kacavenda and Dušan Zirković (eds.), *Narodni heroji Jugoslavije*, Institut za Savremenu istoriju Beograd (Belgrade: Partizanka knjiga, Narodna knjiga, 1981), Vols. 1 and 2, *passim*.
31. Freeman Dyson, *Weapons and Hope* (New York: Harper & Row, 1984), pp. 3–10.
32. Kovačević *et al*., pp. 63–4.
33. In February, March and April 1942, for example, first-aid courses were started in Croatia to train medics at the *četa* level. In May 1942, a

fifteen-day more advanced course was organized under the direction of a medical doctor for medics at the battalion level (*ibid.*, pp. 128–9). Saša Bošović gave basic nursing courses in her field hospital.

34. A similar double standard existed among the Chinese Communists during the Chinese Civil War. The dislike and reservations with which Mao's divorce and remarriage to a common actress were viewed by the other members of the CPC leadership is dramatically presented in Françoise d'Eaubonne, *L'Impératrice rouge, moi Jiang quing, veuve Mao* (The Red Empress, Me Jiang quing, the Widow of Mao) (Paris: Encre, 1981), pp. 57–106.
35. For Djilas description of his wife, see Djilas, *Wartime*, pp. 109–110. His observations on Party leaders are found throughout his memoirs.
36. Dedijer, *With Tito through the War*, p. 241 and *passim*.
37. An editorial in the March/April 1941 edition of *Proletar* strongly criticizes 'some outdated and unworthy views that women cannot bear arms in the struggle, that they should not perform various functions in the army headquarters. . . . These are the views of the fifth column'. Cited in Kovačević *et al.*, pp. 128–9.
38. George Zaninovich, 'The Yugoslav Variation on Marx', *Borbeni put*, Wayne S. Vucinich (ed.), *Contemporary Yugoslavia: Twenty Years of Socialist Experiment* (Berkeley and Los Angeles: University of California Press, 1969), p. 287.

PART 2

WOMEN, MEN AND THE MILITARY

4

Beyond 'Rambo': Women and the Varieties of Militarized Masculinity

Cynthia H. Enloe
Clark University,
Worcester, Mass., USA.

Several months after the revolution which toppled Ferdinand Marcos and brought to power Corazon Aquino, a British friend showed me a newly published report of the events precipitating those changes. 'Wait till you see what NPA guerrillas are watching on their Betamaxes up in the Luzon mountains—*Rambo*!' 'No, you must be joking', I replied. 'It's true', my friend insisted with obvious relish, and she promised to send me a copy of the book. When it arrived soon after, I put aside other books to immediately begin reading this lively and surprising account. And, sure enough, there was the description of young Filipino men in their mountain redoubt telling of their reactions to watching *Rambo* on VCR. How perfect.

Why did I take such perverse pleasure in this account? I think this is worth some collective exploration. For it may raise serious questions about how women, feminists in particular, build an international analysis to inform an international strategy to resist galloping militarization.

Rambo has caught the imaginations of millions of people. For a time it was the top film in both the United States and Britain. It has gone on to inspire fashions, dolls and television series. 'Rambo' has slipped quickly into the global lingo of adults as well as children, of militarism's critics as well as its enthusiasts. For many of us who are working as feminists to resist the spread of militaristic values and policies, *Rambo* has become, I think, a handy shorthand for a complex package of ideas and processes that we believe are dangerous to all women and many men. So when I read James Fenton's journalistic report that even Filipino men apparently committed to fighting a repressive state's army were eagerly watching Sylvester Stallone's portrayal of the post 'post-Vietnam' era hero's exploits, I felt confirmed. It *did* seem as though men everywhere, even those in progressive movements who take up arms, yearn to prove their manhood through military adventure.

But now I'm not so sure. Maybe it's not quite so simple. Maybe charting the 'Rambo-ization' of the world's male population isn't the most useful enterprise for anti-militarist feminists.

One of the most important contributions that feminist writers and activists have made to their respective countries' peace movements is describing how notions about masculinity and femininity have helped promote and sustain the military. While other critical analysts have given economic, racist and bureaucratic patterns their prime attention, feminists have concentrated on the social constructions of gender. As we have accumulated more and more evidence from more and more societies, we have become increasingly confident in this assertion that to omit gender from any explanation of how militarization occurs, is not only to risk a flawed political analysis; it is to risk, too, a perpetually unsuccessful campaign to roll back that militarization.

Precisely at this juncture in the historical development of feminism, *Rambo* has appeared. Its alarming popular appeal—an appeal fuelled by immense infusions of corporate capital—has seemed to confirm our assertion. The social construction of masculinity—not just élites' interests or bureaucracies' cosmologies—is what is serving to entrench and extend the grip of militarism. Furthermore, as my own response to the Philippines report revealed, many of us are coming to believe, as well, that militarism's reliance on particular forms of masculinity holds for societies with otherwise different cultures and at different levels of industrialization.

I still believe both of these theories are valid bases for political action. But I'm beginning to wonder whether that is enough. Specifically, I think we may need to add two new questions in our continuing exploration:

(1) Even if masculinity does have to be militarized in any society, for militarism to survive, are there important differences in *how* militarism and masculinity are made to 'mesh' in societies with different cultures and economic systems? If there *are*, what does this mean for feminists' organizing internationally?
(2) Do military systems of the 1980s (and soon 1990s) require *more* than just a single form of masculinity to make them work? If they do, what does *this* mean for feminists?

The problem with fixing on the international 'Rambo' phenomenon, I'm coming to believe, is that it lures us into imagining that the process of militarizing masculinity is identical in all societies and communal cultures. Moreover, while charting 'Ramboization' is a politically significant task for feminists, doing only that tempts us into a preoccupation with only one sort of militarized masculinity, that of the low-ranking combat soldier; whereas, in reality, today's military systems need at least three or four *other* constructions of masculinity to sustain themselves. These other forms may not be quite so amenable to box office hits, but they will need watching—and feminist critiquing—too.

LOCAL MEMORIES, FOREIGN DRILL SERGEANTS AND MASCULINITY

We don't know enough about the constructions of masculinity in different militarized societies. What we do know is that in virtually all of the societies today in which militarization is rampant—the United States, Chile, Afghanistan, Taiwan, South Korea, North Korea, Honduras, South Africa, Ethiopia, the Soviet Union, Britain, Israel, Iraq—men are assigned roles to enhance that militarizing process that are strikingly different from those assigned to women. But we have less information about exactly how masculinity is being reshaped in order to ensure that that process continues. This in turn means that we are less clear than we need to be about the precise nature of women's experiences of militarization. What are the daily lives women live with Chilean, Iraqi, British, American men whose sense of their own 'manhood' is being manipulated so as to sustain the authority and public legitimacy of the military? But the research has begun, and we need to listen to feminists from diverse countries carefully—not just to have our own theories confirmed, but to learn of the differences between women.

Let me offer a few examples, starting with 'Rambo'. This recent creation is not a simple mainstream American military hero. He is not 'GI Joe'. He defies his superiors. He tries to continue a war his commanders have declared over. He is a rebel. He is solitary. He is a peculiarly 'post-Vietnam' type of militarized male. Rambo's message for American men is about how to cope with national humiliation: resort to individualistic military adventurism that defies hierarchies but restores a nation's pride in its military.

But do men in other societies have the same responses to national humiliation? 'Humiliation' is both a gendered and an enculturated emotion. So we might expect it to be militarized in quite different ways in different countries, with the consequence that 'Rambo' will be absorbed (or rejected, perhaps) in quite dissimilar ways. For instance, military comic books based on American military escapades are being translated into Italian and marketed for young and not-so-young men in Italy today. But the Second World War, the Korean War and the Vietnam War do not have the same meanings for Italian men—or women—as they do for their American counterparts. So what are the effects on Italian boys and men who are reading these American-generated military comics in the 1980s? The comics might make Italian men more contemptuous of their own country's far less adventurous army. They might make some men endure their own compulsory army conscription with less resentment than they otherwise would. They might make US domination of NATO, or US endangering of Italian lives with its bombing of nearby Libya more palatable, even vicariously enjoyable, to some Italian men who might otherwise protest such threatening policies.

Let's take another example—and, once again, this is not idle speculation in 1987. How does humiliation resonate among women and men in contemporary Japan? Despite US government pressure on the Japanese to remilitarize and despite Prime Minister Nakasone's apparent desire to play down Japan's Second World War errors and revive the nation's military strength, Japanese popular notions of masculinity so far do not seem easily remilitarized. Norwegian, Egyptian, Filipino, French, German (East and West) and South African Afrikaner women and men also each have collective memories of defeat that some think of in terms of 'humiliation'. But do each of their societies' men sift that alleged national humiliation through a militarized sieve in ways that make them respond to 'Rambo' in precisely the same individualistically defiant way that American men seem to? I doubt it. Feminists in every country where 'Rambo' seems to have become a cultural hero might take a closer look to see exactly *what* it is in the character and the narrative that seems most attractive to men. What do those tendencies, in turn, tell us about how men in their countries might be drawn to support militarism. And where has 'Rambo' been a cultural flop? We need to know where this peculiar form of militarized masculine response to national humiliation appears to have no resonance and what that implies for the ongoing reconstructions of 'manhood'.

There is a second territory for our investigation of possible varieties of militarized masculinity: cross-national military training programmes. *Is* 'a drill sergeant a drill sergeant a drill sergeant'?

The British government is an old hand at militarization. One of its successful empire-building strategies was to build armies out of local colonialized labour. To do that, British officials had to find ways to persuade local male rulers that their personal authority and status would be enhanced if they would allow the British to build them 'proper' armies filled with 'proper' soldiers. Then they had to persuade thousands of male peasants and nomadic herdsmen that *their* manhood would be enhanced within their own communities if they would enlist in the newly created British-controlled armies. There was nothing automatic about either of these processes. Both required that men persuade men of something new—with an occasional dose of coercion thrown into that 'persuasion'.

But was this complex historical process no more than a

matter of British (English? Scottish?) notions of militarized manhood being 'exported' to different ethnic communities in India, Nigeria and Malaysia? Reading old training manuals and eavesdropping on British colonial officials' reminiscences suggest that considerable adaptation had to go on to make this imperial strategy work. That is, masculinity could *not* be militarized in Scotland in exactly the same ways that it could be militarized in India or Nigeria.

These colonizing experiences are relevant for women in 1987. For the British government, despite a shrunken empire, still energetically exports its military training expertise. In November 1986 the British government signed an agreement to start training Mozambiquan (male?) soldiers. Reports suggested that it was the Zimbabwean regime of Robert Mugabe, a supporter of the besieged Mozambiquan FRELIMO-led government, which smoothed the way (the Western press called it 'acting as the midwife') for this military training agreement. Evidently, Zimbabwean officials have been pleased with the British military programme's impact among its own military, a force that has been quite systematically remasculinized since the end of the Zimbabwean revolutionary war. Does this mean that contemporary British military strategies for turning 1980s British middle-class men into officers and working- (often in fact unemployed) class urban men into useful soldiers, can be applied to rural Zimbabwean men of different ethnic groups with no adjustment?

Many observers are concerned about the escalating trade in arms between countries, with Brazil, South Korea and Israel now joining the arms sales competition along with the larger international players. But maybe there is another international militarized commerce going on too that deserves to be monitored and resisted: the export in strategies for turning civilianized masculinity into a kind of masculinity deemed especially useful to military commanders and their pro-military civilian superiors.

To monitor *this* trade, feminists in the 'exporting'—that is the training—countries will have to pay attention to what their governments claim are the advantages of their particular ways of turning civilian men into military men. We also will need to keep track of just *who* in our country's military is selected by élites to do that training of men from other countries. For instance, which branch of the armed forces is used for overseas training? Each branch is likely to have a slightly different ideology of militarized masculinity. For instance, in the United States, the army prohibits its men from carrying umbrellas, declaring the practice unfitting, while the air force scorns such nervousness and permits its men to carry umbrellas.

Also, we need to watch which ethnic group's men within our own militaries are deemed most appropriate to do this training. This may be a reflection of the racial ideology that overlays the gender ideology, or it may reflect a presumption about the culture of the foreign men to be trained.

Feminists in the United States especially will have their work cut out for them. The US government currently is passing along its peculiar notions of militarized masculinity to men in Honduras, El Salvador, Jamaica, Barbados, Mexico, the Philippines, Indonesia, Saudi Arabia and most of the countries in NATO. What is this doing to the ongoing social constructions of masculinity in each of these societies? Few women are consulted; they just have to make the adjustments to live with the results. Military planners depend on women being able and willing to adjust their notions of feminine behaviour to complement the newly revised ideas about manhood.

The flow of consequences from military training and trade probably won't be one-way. It is likely that the men who act as 'foreign advisors' will come home from their training assignments with long-lasting notions about what masculine traits in their own societies make them 'naturally' better—braver, more inventive, more loyal, more disciplined—soldiers than the men from other cultures they have been sent to train. Usually there's a strong element of ethnocentrism or outright racism mixed into these militarized, masculinized memories; they could have far-reaching effects on future foreign policy.

In the January 1987 issue of an American magazine called *Vietnam Combat*, devoted to recalling the brave deeds of rank-and-file American men who served in Vietnam, there is a full-page photo showing a tall white American soldier wading through a Vietnamese rice paddy carrying a toy-like M–16 rifle. Next to him walks a shorter Vietnamese man in battle fatigues; he's carrying a much more potent piece of weaponry. The American advisors referred to their Vietnamese advisees as 'indigs'. What ideas did this American militarized Big Brother bring back to the United States about his militarized Little Brother's bravery, loyalty, intelligence, sexuality? Whatever those masculinized, militarized memories are, they almost certainly are shaping US military advisors' training strategies among Honduran and Salvadoran men today.

Feminists in the 'importing' countries—whose governments are on the receiving end of this trade in militarized gender ideologies—might start keeping track of just what it is their government officials hope to gain by subjecting their military men to foreign training. Does it imply an official disappointment with their society's current construction of masculinity? Perhaps the acceptance of British or US—or French or Cuban or East German or Israeli—training suggests that the country's élite men are imagining their own male citizens to be too 'undisciplined'. That is, perhaps they believe the 'traditional' construction of masculinity in their own societies (or at least in the ethnic communities from whom they've decided to draw most of their soldiers) to be too 'wild', or 'disorderly', to serve the current regime's goals of national unification, national order and national security. Alternatively—or perhaps simultaneously—maybe the present élite imagines the conventions of manhood among their male population to be too dismissive of the sorts of modern weapons technology that requires literacy and patience. Thus they have concluded that American or British or East German men's approaches to militarizing masculinity will produce the sorts of soldiers they think they need.

Elites who invite foreign soldiers to train their men may go so far as to imagine that their own men, subjected to such manipulation, will return to civilian society after their military service being more productive male farmers or more disciplined government supporters or more responsible fathers. What do they assume, then, about women's reactions to their fathers', husbands' and brothers' new attitudes?

Feminists can trace this export in forms of militarized masculinity by monitoring the gendered repercussions of specific military policies, even mundane decisions. Feminists might watch for any changes in the cut of military uniforms. What do design changes suggest about the new masculine images for soldiers? We might also watch for changes in the presumptions informing rules or penalties concerning VD. What do any rule changes presume about militarized men's sexual needs? Though it probably will go unstated, any revised VD regulations will rely on reformulations of élite presumptions about women's sexuality. We already know from monitoring boot camps in the United States that verbal threats take on a gendered colouring as they're used to frighten or humiliate men into obedience and aggressiveness. Does the language used by foreign drill sergeants match a local misogynous convention? Or do foreign trainers bring in harangues based on *their own* society's men's fear of being seen as 'feminine' or 'queer'?

If these foreign military trainers and their local male trainees each have to make *no* adjustments in their ideological formulas for militarizing the standards of manhood, then perhaps the notion of the 'universal Rambo' *is* valid. That is, *if* an American male sergeant of Anglo ethnic background can employ precisely the same recipe of symbols, rewards and threats to turn a Honduran young man into what both US and Honduran senior officials deem a 'good soldier' that he deploys when training a group of black, Hispanic and white men in the United States—and *if* the Honduran young man and his counterparts respond in the same way as the American young men (towards the sergeant, towards women as 'sweethearts' and women as 'whores', towards 'the enemy')—only then can we assume that there is a process of militarizing masculinity that is so fundamentally similar that it is politically wasteful for feminists to spend scarce resources paying attention to variations in the workings of class, ethnicity and national culture.

My own suspicion is that, while there are some striking similarities that have resulted from common state manipulations and cultural imaginings, there are also significant differences. And these differences have generated confusions, compromises, resentments, even open conflicts between military men that they would rather we didn't know about.

'JOINT MANOEUVRES'

There is a third arena in which feminists can investigate how masculinity is militarized in various cultures and economic systems: joint military manoeuvres.

As the major powers grow more determined to create separate and competing networks of military alliances around the world, more women and men are being pressed to co-ordinate their resources, skills and fears so as to guarantee centralized strategic military actions. Most critics of these sprawling global alliances focus on the problems of co-ordinating legal and industrial conditions. For instance, in recent years there have been rumbles of discontent throughout the European members of NATO: their American partner's call for 'standardization' of NATO tanks, rifles or computers seems one more attempt by Washington to compel everyone else to 'Buy American', to the disadvantage of their own needy defence contractors. Within the Warsaw Pact, similarly, there are simmering discontents over the Moscow-imposed divisions of labour rationalized by references to military alliance cohesiveness.

What is much less talked about inside these alliances is how incompatible forms of militarized femininity and masculinity are reconciled. Most obvious are alliance members' differing policies toward allowing women to serve in uniformed services; for example, in 1986 the US military comprised 9 per cent women, while its Italian and Spanish allies still prohibit women from serving. Within NATO there also are differing policies towards women in combat: the Dutch now allow women to serve in jobs defined as 'combat', while the British take a firm stand against combat assignments and the Americans are on the brink of another public legislative debate over both the definition of 'combat' and the military rationale for excluding women from such jobs. In fact, as each male élite tries to negotiate its way between gender conventions and military 'manpower' needs, each is developing a different definition of what exactly is 'combat'.

There are also growing differences among NATO's militaries concerning the alleged relationship between homosexuality and 'national security'. The Canadian Parliament in 1986 was pressed by feminists to drop the exclusion of lesbians and gay men from the Canadian armed forces; the US government is now facing multiple court cases brought by women's and civil liberties groups challenging the legality—and logic—of discharging women and men accused of homosexuality. The various policies—and their rationales—for protecting the military from AIDS suggests another dimension of difference in sexual politics among alliance members.

In virtually every NATO military the constructions of masculinity and femininity—and the relation of each to military preparedness and national security—are in flux. But they are not being resolved in precisely the same ways. The strength of each country's women's movement and lesbian and gay movements differ. The historic ties between civilian manhood and the state's military, the current regime's sense of national insecurity, the availability of young men from the classes and ethnic groups the military commanders trust—each and all of these factors together vary, even within the 15 societies whose governments have brought them into the NATO alliances.

What would the Warsaw Pact's internal politics look like through similar lenses? As ethnic Russian men at the top of the Soviet military command structure worry more about their seeming dependence on Asian Soviet men for rank-and-file soldiery—worrying that has been intensified by what has happened during their war in Afghanistan—will they move towards using more women, especially 'European' Soviet women, in uniformed military jobs? And if they do (there is evidence that this is already happening), and if they find they can control the dynamics of masculinity and femininity sufficiently not to damage their military performance, will they then encourage other Warsaw Pact regimes to recruit more women as a complement to, not a substitute for continued pressure on women from trusted ethnic groups to produce more future soldiers? Already, Rumania and Yugoslavia make more use of women in their national security formulas—especially in local militias and in the name of 'home defence', thus not fundamentally challenging existing ideological ties between manhood and militarism. But both of these regimes are outside the core of the Warsaw Pact, making their gendered military innovations less likely to affect intra-alliance dynamics.

Nor should we watch just the major East–West military constellations. Bilateral joint manoeuvres are proliferating today. The Honduran army is holding repeated joint manoeuvres with its American patron. The Japanese Defence Force is engaging in joint exercises along the Pacific Rim with the US navy. The Egyptian military has co-operated in joint manoeuvres with the US military. The armies and militarized units of the Jamaican, Barbadian and now Grenadian soldiers and militarized policemen participated in not only trial-run scenarios but actual invasion operations with the US military.

In November 1986, 5,000 British troops held 'war games' together with Omani soldiers in what was called 'Operation Swift Sword'. Military attachés from other countries were invited to observe these joint manoeuvres, partly to share lessons, partly to be persuaded of the superiority of British-made weaponry. According to the *New York Times*' long-time military affairs reporter, also among the invited guests, lessons generated by this Omani–British joint manoeuvre concerned not only strategy and hardware but also masculinity. British officers concluded that Omani men were perhaps better material for warfare in the harsh desert conditions of the Persian Gulf than any other men: 'They are willing to learn from their British teachers, they are adaptable and by tradition they are accustomed to the use of firearms.'

Some of the British officers were even willing to trade potential arms sales for the right kind of masculinity: 'One argument against the introduction of armoured personnel carriers, a British officer said, is that their use might lead the Omanis to forget their natural skills as mountain fighters and (instead) "ride everywhere" ' (*New York Times*, 14 December 1986).

Joint manoeuvres are feats of logistical and political management. They are also tests of militarized gender management. For the success or failure of any joint manoeuvre hangs on whether soldiers and officers of different cultures can learn to trust each other. And trust depends on some shared understandings of 'bravery', 'loyalty', 'reasonableness', 'reliability' and 'skill'. Each of these concepts is gendered; each is infused with presumptions about proper behaviour for 'real men' and proper behaviour for 'real women', as well as how men and women should relate to one another. But are they each gendered in precisely the same way in each society whose soldiers are thrown together on a supposedly hostile battlefield? If they aren't, how do sergeants, majors and generals each try to reconcile those differences so the joint manoeuvre will 'work'?

It may be that different militarized masculinities are not fully reconciled; they are only band-aided over with misogyny. How often do Honduran and American men on 'Big Pine' joint manoeuvres camouflage their basic distrust of one another by trading jokes about the Honduran women working as prostitutes around their camps?

Joint manoeuvres are one of the most potent tools for cementing different societies together with a glue of militarism. Thus any of us concerned about how militaristic presumptions are being spread might pay attention to these bilateral and multilateral performances. West German and British peace activists have been perhaps the most energetic in charting and protesting this tool of international integration. But we should not imagine that joint manoeuvres are easy to manage. In fact, they are fraught with problems. Once again, there are fault lines running through contemporary inter-military relationships that their designers and boosters would rather we didn't notice. And one of those fault lines may be the fundamental differences between allies' formulas for militarizing masculinity.

BEYOND PLURALIST PARALYSIS

Looking at possible differences between militarized masculinities as an antidote to seeing Rambo as a global archtype does *not* mean surrendering to debilitating pluralism. Quite the opposite.

'Factor juggling' can leave researchers and their audiences paralysed by endless 'it all depends'. Most of us are much more likely to act when we see powerful commonalities. This is the political appeal of the 'Ramboization'. If it is true that men in societies as different as Britain, the Philippines, Honduras and the United States, respond to the masculine traits celebrated by Sylvester Stallone, then there must exist a common platform on which feminists in widely disparate countries can mobilize to criticize and resist militarization of relations between women and men, women and women, and men and men.

Still, recognizing that there may be varying relationships between masculinity and militarism need not stop us in our tracks.

It is the spread of militarization from country to country that is particularly alarming in the 1980s. Yet this spreading is not an inevitable or unstoppable process. It requires subtle manipulation and no small measure of ideological camouflage precisely because men and women do not have identical notions of 'manhood' and because state militaries have not played identical historical functions in sustaining the myths of manhood. Moreover, governments need the co-operation of women when they seek to retrain men, to build new bases, to cement alliances or to conduct joint manoeuvres. And we know from new feminist histories that nowhere has that requisite women's compliance come automatically: it has taken at least a cultural sleight-of-hand, frequently political coercion.

By exploring differences within and between societies, feminists may expose conflicts and confusions that militarizing élites would rather hide. Can the 'Rambo' myth inspire leftist Filipino men to challenge a formidable state army while at the same time assist American military recruiters in getting the American men they need in their state forces? Is the current rift within NATO more than just a matter of military-industrial rivalry? Can Honduran, Afghan and Zimbabwean women undercut the militarizing policies of their governments by exposing the alienness of the foreign drill sergeants' boot-camp misogyny?

What is operating in the world today is not merely diffuse pluralism. There are formal institutions. These institutions are designed to disguise some cultural and ideological differences for the sake of military alliance maintenance, while dichotomizing other differences for the sake of constructing objects of fear. None of these institutions—multilateral alliances, bilateral alliances, foreign military assistance programmes—can achieve their militarizing objectives without *controlling women for the sake of militarizing men*. And that, in turn, necessitates attempting to sustain and reconstruct beliefs about masculinity and about femininity. Neither of these militarizing enterprises can be undertaken without élites trying to alter the daily lives of women. That is the common reality that allows us to build international networks of women working to roll back militarization.

RAMBO AND THE STAR WARRIOR

Contemporary militaries in the most advanced industrialized societies need more than foot-soldiers and generals. They need underground missile silo technicians; they need cartographers; they need factory managers; they need highly trained engineers and physicists. The further away any of these military functionaries are from whatever is defined as 'combat' or considered state authority, the more possible it seems to use women to fill such posts. But, for the most part, these jobs are being filled by men. Yet are the standards for masculinity the same in each of them? While the frontline infantryman—or even an action-seeking lieutenant-colonel sitting in the White House basement—may respond to the Rambo-esque mix of masculinity and militarization, will the scientist sitting at his laboratory computer designing a satellite laser weapon?

Most of our descriptions of civilian workers, business managers, scientists and intellectuals who have been co-opted into military contract work, describe American men. For instance, William Broad has reported on the emerging subculture at the Lawrence Livermore Laboratories in California, the site of President Reagan's Strategic Defense Initiative's ('Star Wars') most esoteric research. His book, *Star Warriors*, is not feminist—he is only slightly curious about the women whose less dramatic labours or emotional validation sustain SDI research and political lobbying. Yet he does provide considerable information about how these male scientists talk, dream and joke. Few of them are married or have girlfriends. Most of them seem to live at their computer terminals, except when they take breaks to drink coke or consume great quantities of ice cream. They don't appear particularly violent; they don't wear army surplus fatigues; they don't have rifles mounted on the backs of their pick-up trucks. They do have a penchant for boyish pranks. They do seem to thrive on competition and to see both the scientific world and the larger world as places where rivalry is the norm.

The latter is the ideological trait that seems to make them likely candidates for militarization. In fact, the men who recruited these young scientists made a point of playing upon their competitiveness to attract them to SDI weapons research. Still, they appear unlikely candidates for a military's basic training. They are too contemptuous of collective discipline. Their notions of action seem more cerebral than physical. And yet they clearly find deep reassurances about their own manhood in the militarized science they do. And the US élites who see militarization as the bedrock of American security, *need* these men to feel those reassurances. That, as much as grant money, is what makes these male scientists militarizable. Admirers of Sylvester Stallone might hold these Livermore men in contempt, branding them 'nerds', but they are no less critical to the 1980s militarizing of American society than M–16 wielding 'grunts'.

The men who lure scientists into militarized laboratory communities appear to have notions of their recruits' sexual needs not shared by their army or navy counterparts. For instance, institutionalized homophobia doesn't seem to send off warning sirens when a young male engineer eschews girls. Nor do the men responsible for the morale of the Livermore scientists seem to think they require brothels just outside the laboratory's gates. Has anyone suggested that these 'Star Warriors' be sent to VD classes? Why not?

It may be that militarized masculinity takes one form when men are socialized into the world of *nuclear* warfare planning, while it takes quite a different form when men are socialized into the world of what is euphemistically called *conventional* warfare.

Carol Cohn is a feminist who has had the unusual opportunity to spend time inside a civilian think tank at the Massachusetts Institute of Technology (MIT) devoted to strategic theorizing. She describes still another breed of militarized American masculinity—the 'defence intellectual'. These men seem more likely to have social relations with women. More are married. Many of them seem able to turn on 'the charm'. Though all of their professional peers are men, they interact more regularly with women who work for them as secretaries. As yet, though, we don't know much about what sorts of femininity their wives, lovers and secretaries are pressed to adopt in order to maintain smooth relationships with men who get satisfaction out of being defence intellectuals.

What Carol Cohn reveals, however, is the elaborate and often surprising linguistic and ideological formulas that these men construct to enable them to discuss death and destruction day after day. Some of the language is embarrasingly (at least to the feminist ear) phallic. They talk constantly about 'penetrations', 'thrusts'. But Cohn finds that many of the terms these American men have created to discuss efficient death and destruction are unexpectedly domestic: they pat a missile not as if it were a sexual object but as if it were a baby or a puppy. As Carol Cohn observes, 'The creatures one pats are small, cute, harmless—not terrifyingly destructive. Pat it, and its lethality disappears'. These men's subculture isn't quite as isolated as that of the men at the Livermore Laboratories, but they have created a language and cosmology that seems to permit them to reduce their emotional investment in the actual outcomes of their abstract 'scenarios'.

This sort of militarized man, the defence intellectual, has come to play an increasingly influential role in those political systems which have—or wish to have—a regional or even global military role and which have technologically and industrially complex infrastructures to back up that role. In societies with this brand of militarization, military planning has become too complex, presumably, for generals, politicians and weapons producers.

Still to be written are feminist descriptions of how masculinity—and thus femininity—are constructed within companies and factories reliant on defence contracts. From Hilary Wainwright, we do have a sense that at least some British women working today in the usually feminized electrical units of defence factories do not seem to get the ideological or monetary rewards that their male counterparts do from working on weapons. However, they may be encouraged to see themselves as supporting 'our boys' as sort of surrogate militarized mothers. But what of white-collar middle managers and senior executives, the largely masculinized strata of aerospace, armaments and electronics companies, who have made conscious decisions to pursue local and foreign defence contracts? Perhaps they get some boost to their sense of manhood from being involved with such products, being in regular contact with military officers.

Women as wives and lovers have to make adjustments in order to support or validate these choices. Marriages are affected when men become more and more involved in secret work, when their business days are shaped by state security concepts or when their professional colleagues are military professionals. When a corporate contractor's wife refuses to make these adjustments in her marriage, she may send small tremors through her country's military-industrial complex.

I think it would be a mistake to imagine that, because each one of these cogs in the increasingly complex military machine appears to rely on notions of masculinity, all the parts automatically work together in smooth precision. 'Grunts', 'nerds', 'defence intellectuals', 'captains of industry', 'the brass'—all may be masculinized, but those masculinizations may not create bonds of trust or respect. William Broad's SDI scientists and Carol Cohn's defence intellectuals both talk of the military officers and the civilian politicians they deal with quite contemptuously. Conversely, uniformed military men of various ranks may dismiss scientists and intellectuals as too removed from reality (as they see it). It would not be surprising if some of this mutual derision were translated into comments about the others' tenuous manliness and the others' failed relations with women.

So, once again, sorting out possible varieties of masculinity—here within a single militarized society—need not induce factor juggling paralysis. It could equip feminists with more accurate portraits of the ideological requirements any technologically sophisticated and spatially interventionist militarizing government has to try to meet. It may shed light on tensions and contradictions within those military systems, exposing them as less impermeable, more fragile.

Still, we should avoid Americanizing our analysis. It doesn't follow that every militarizing society is constructing the same divisions of labour or the same varieties of masculinity to sustain its military system. The Soviet Union, France, Britain, Israel and South Africa may come closest to replicating the current American masculinized, militarized division of labour. Each of these states has been trying to build its own scientific and industrial-military infrastructure. Each prides itself on its capacity to absorb information and make plans. But are Soviet engineers afraid of other men calling them the Russian equivalent of 'nerds' if they carry calculators clipped to their belts?

Are Israeli defence intellectuals as prone as their American counterparts to looking down upon uniformed military men? They—as well as Israeli men working as engineers in the country's large weapons industry—are said to be able to sympathize with their male counterparts in uniform because they too serve in the military as reservists until the age of 55. Not many societies, however, have a conscription system that helps to ensure this empathy between men socialized into different forms of militarized masculinity. In each country there may be slightly different sorts of tension between militarized masculinities. Consequently, roles that different groups of women are pressured to play in order to reduce or mask those tensions in the name of a smoothly running military machine might be somewhat different. Feminist organizing to exploit contradictions among the several militarized masculinities and to overcome the man-made divisions separating women will have to grow out of the specific conditions in each country. The time is ripe for feminist analyses of military-bureaucratic-academic-industrial complexes.

Morocco, Norway, Finland, Italy, Canada, Mexico, East and West Germany, Japan—each of these societies' governments presently seems willing to forgo having a self-sufficient military system and/or militarily expansionist ambitions. They are more resigned to relying on someone else's advanced weapons research; they are more willing to purchase certain weapons abroad; they feel less need to generate abstract strategic doctrine to cover a myriad of military contingencies; or they define 'national security' in a way that assigns top priority to civilian manufacture and thus channels most scientists and engineers into civilian research. Any of these tendencies will affect the status and ideological role of those Norwegian, Italian or other men who *do* become militarized. Will they have less capacity to serve as a standard for manhood in that society? We should watch closely to see *which* countries' male scientists and industrial managers are most able to reject US offers of SDI research money.

It could be that the alliance structure each of these countries has entered will influence how this question is answered. Perhaps men in Italy or Mexico will disparage their own military men for being so dependent on outsiders for their weaponry and their doctrine and thus begin to look longingly to the notions of manhood in the more dominant militarized countries. What *do* young Italian men think about while immersed in imported American military comics?

CONCLUSION

There is common terrain on which women from different cultures and societies can organize to resist militarizing tendencies. This is terrain that has been mapped by feminists from Chile, Japan, Italy, Canada and other countries. Despite their cultural and historical differences, these women have noted that:

1. Militaries depend on the maintenance of a popular presumption that the most rewarded, highest status military activities can go only to the masculinized members

of society. When women are used in the military, it is only 'for the duration' and only in roles defined as 'auxiliary'.

2. Militaries need to keep alive the notion that, for men, having intimate relationships with the military is the best proof that they are 'real men'.
3. Both of these military-serving ideological pillars will topple if they aren't constantly supported by certain myths about what it takes to be a 'real woman'.
4. This necessity, in turn, leads militarizing élites (in and out of the uniformed military) to try to control women—their hopes, their fears, their labour, their sexuality.
5. Any woman who succumbs to this control finds her life becoming militarized—willingly or unwillingly.
6. When a woman exposes or resists those ideas or structures, she throws a wrench into the works by which not only women but men, too, are militarized.

My own response to 'Rambo's' globalized career was, I think, inspired by this new understanding of how widespread, seemingly universal, the gendered dynamics of militarization are. I was both appalled and energized by what seemed this latest evidence of the common threat women in all countries have to confront.

My 'second thoughts', that I've tried to sketch out here, aren't a retreat from this pursuit of a common ground. Rather, I think they suggest that we may have to add to that sense of basic commonalities a fresh understanding of how various are the ways that those common dynamics actually work themselves out in our different countries.

Usually, when we look at how internationalized the forces of militarization have become, we feel pretty disheartened: it was hard enough to expose and reverse the tides of militarization before international alliances, arms sales, basing networks, training programmes and war-glorifying videos became so tightly woven. Now even those women peace activists who are the most internationally active—for instance, the network of women's peace camps—feel like Alice, always running just to stay in one place. If the gendered politics of militarization are becoming daily more international, isn't this cause for more despair?

Maybe not. For *if* masculinity and femininity have to be militarized for militarization to occur, and *if* those ideological constructs are embedded in the specific histories and memories of particular societies, *then* any one of these apparently potent alliances may be surprisingly vulnerable to feminist critique. As awesome as the spiralling arms sales may be, some national security officials might prefer that we focus on them rather than shine our feminist torches on the murky waters of masculinity. It could be that proponents of international militarization have a very great stake in 'Rambo's' global saleability.

Similarly, many of us living in the highly industrial nations find it dismaying to realize how many different parts of our complex societies now seem to be drawn into military service: universities, advertising agencies, research laboratories, electronics companies, garment factories, aerospace firms, energy ministries, secondary schools. We rightly wonder whether all men are being seduced by the 'Rambo' myth.

My own tentative hunch is that we are correct in noting how many sorts of institutions are prone to militarization; but this may not be producing an ever-stronger military grip on our societies. For the appeals to the men who try to fulfil their 'manly' ambitions through each of these institutions may be subtly different. Underneath the military-science-industrial complex in any of our countries may run a gendered fault line.

The most resilient organizing among women will be organizing that looks differences straight in the eye. But in the process we may uncover conflicts among militarizing men that reveal their internationalizing and expanding enterprises to be more fragile than they would like us to know.

REFERENCES

Conversation with Italian economist and feminist Elisabetta Addis, Cambridge, MA, November, 1986.

Conversation with Philippa Brewster, feminist publisher, London, October, 1986.

Conversations with Japanese feminist Yumi Iwai, Clark University, Worcester, MA, 1985–6.

William J. Broad, *Star Warriors* (New York: Simon & Schuster, 1985; London: Faber & Faber, 1987).

Bunster, Ximena, 'Surviving Beyond Fear: Women and Torture in Latin America', in June Nash and Helen Safa (eds.), *Women and Change in Latin America* (South Hadley, MA: Bergin and Garvey, 1986).

Cohn, Carol, 'Sex and Death in the Rational World of Defense Intellectuals', in Jean Beth Elshtain and Sheila Tobias (eds.), *Thinking about Women, Militarism and War: Essays in History, Politics and Social Criticism* (New York: Rowman & Allenfield, 1987).

Edwards, Paul, 'The Army and the Microworld: Computers and the Militarized Politics of Gender Identity', special issue on women and computers, *Signs*, forthcoming.

Enloe, Cynthia H., *Ethnic Soldiers: State Security in Divided Societies* (London: Penguin, 1980; Athens, GA: University of Georgia Press, 1980).

Does Khaki Become You? The Militarization of Women's Lives (London: Pluto Press, 1983; Boston: South End Press, 1983; Helsinki: Peace Union of Finland, 1986.

'Bananas, Bases and Patriarchy', *Radical America* 19(4); reprinted in *Trouble and Strife* (Britain) 9, 1986, and in Jean Beth Elshtain and Sheila Tobias (eds.), *Thinking about Women, Militarism and War: Essays in History, Politics and Social Criticism* (New York: Rowman & Allenfield, 1987).

Fenton, James, 'The Snap Revolution', in *Granta* (London and New York), 1986.

Mikiyo, Kano, 'Remolding Terroism for Modern Japan', in a special issue on 'The Challenge Facing Japanese Women', *AMPO* (Tokyo) 18 (2–3).

Pastor, Roxanna, 'How the US Militarized Honduras', in *Sojourner* (Cambridge, MA), November, 1986.

Wainwright, Hilary, 'Women Who Wire', in Dorothy Thompson (ed.), *Over Our Dead Bodies: Women Against The Bomb* (London: Virago, 1982).

5

The Effect of Myths about Military Women on the Waging of War

Judith Hicks Stiehm
Provost and
Professor of Political Science
Florida International University

My first scholarly work involved a study of the theory of non-violent action. In the 1960s in the United States non-violence was an approved, even honoured, form of social action. In the mid-1960s, though, Martin Luther King Jr, declared his opposition to the Vietnam War and began to organize support for low-income workers such as the Memphis, Tennessee, garbage collectors. Almost immediately King's public support began to erode; so did interest in and enthusiasm for non-violence.

I then began to study violence, in particular, legitimate violence, that is violence which is both legal and approved. Usually legitimate violence is not called 'violence'. It is called 'law enforcement' or 'national defence'. Neither ends nor means are often questioned. What is fascinating, though, is the fact that legitimate violence has until recently been for men only. That is, it has been reserved for men. Women were excluded; they could not be patrol officers or combat soldiers.

I have been trying to understand why women have mostly been barred from legitimate violence. My recent work has focused on the military. Earlier I studied male officer élites at the military academies. Currently I am writing a book on enlisted women in the four services (army, navy, air force, marines.) What I have found is that there are firmly held beliefs about military women which are not necessarily verifiable. These I call myths and they are the primary object of my study. What I am interested in is their tenacity and by implication their utility. Why, I have asked, are these beliefs so strongly held, and what is their effect on a nation's or an organization's ability to wage war?

In this paper I shall discuss the meaning of three persistent beliefs about military women. These myths appear to lend support to the military's ability to conduct warfare. They are (1) that women are participants in war, (2) that military women are whores or lesbians and (3) that even military women require the protection of men.

MYTH I: WOMEN PARTICIPATE IN WAR

At one point I began a collection of pictures of men in skirts and women with guns. Among the former were Scots in kilts, Indians in dhotis and Fiji police officers. Among the latter were US women in basic training, Vietnamese women at war and Israeli home guards. Then I began to notice that the second kind of picture was not at all scarce. It was not difficult at all to find pictures such as those of (1) Arab women in khakis—with black veils over their faces—(2) Iraqi women at a firing range as depicted on a governmental calendar and (3) armed Libyan women (who were shown on front pages of US papers all over the country shortly after the US bombed Libya.)

Supporters of wars of liberation from Frantz Fanon on have enthusiastically described women participants in those wars and many observers have, like Fanon, suggested that women who had served their nation in war became so liberated that they would never accept their prewar status. What we know now, however is that many a revolution failed to rewrite its family law when it rewrote the nation's governmental law, and that this failure has led directly to women's return to their prewar status. Indeed, in many countries family law is a category of religious law. Seeking change, thus, puts women at odds with God—an opponent far more formidable than the colonialists challenged in the interest of national sovereignty.

It was a Nicaraguan poster, though, that finally led me to understand the myth of women's military participation. That poster portrayed a woman dressed in military fatigues and wearing a broad smile and a rifle. In addition, the woman was carrying a well-nourished baby and her full breasts suggested she was a nursing mother. The woman was obviously not going to war. Then it dawned on me. The other women in my picture collection were not going to war either. In fact, few women (as compared to men) ever go to war.

The historical record tells us that women rarely participate as combatants even though they are often the victims of combat. Again, some women have always been a part of partisan forces and many Russian women have fought to defend their motherland. But the pictures of women with guns and particularly the Nicaraguan picture described above and a now famous picture of Iranian women with ammunition belts, guns and chadors which so encumber the women that they could not use the weapons even if they were ordered to, do have a most important purpose. That purpose is made clear by the timing. The pictures of women with guns appear when a country is under siege. Their purpose is to mobilize civilians. Their purpose is to demonstrate unified commitment. It is to tell an enemy that it will have to occupy the country and pacify every citizen before it can claim victory. But, perhaps most importantly, it is a way of mobilizing young men.

It is young men the military most wants to mobilize. Militaries are run by old men who send young men—or boys caught up by the desire to prove they are men—to risk and sometimes give their lives. Pictures of women training to shoot are guaranteed to bring men to the enlistment halls. The implicit message of such pictures is 'even women . . .'. Given a basically male military, few men are able to resist the call to service when women are serving. For men the shame of refusing to serve would be intense. Women's mere presence, in effect, blackmails men into service.

It is not clear that this blackmail is intended. Women do rally to their nation's defence in times of peril, and the press publishes pictures of women with guns because they are unusual. The problem, though, is that as long as the military is primarily male, as long as women's relationship to the military is significantly different from that of men, women who join it are not just acting on grounds of conviction; they are also pressuring men to join. To the degree that women's enlistment is permitted, not permitted or manipulated by men decision-makers, women are being used by men to manipulate other men.

Many young men do not want to serve in combat or even to join the military. To get them to do so, governments conscript men. They punish men who will not serve. They also use young men's insecurity about their sexual identity to get men to enlist and also as a means of controlling them. When women accept exclusion from service or from combat, then, they assist policy-makers' exploitation of young men by making it possible for policy-makers to describe some behaviour as 'manly' and other behaviour as 'unmanly'.

MYTH II: MILITARY WOMEN ARE WHORES OR LESBIANS

After the Second World War, Colonel Mattie Treadwell prepared a voluminous official history of women's participation in the US army during that period. (The air force was not then a separate service and navy women have not been the subject of a separate volume; thus, this comprehensive study is far and away the best single source of information about American military women of the period.)

Chapter 11 of Treadwell's book is titled 'The Slander Campaign'. It presents a detailed account of attacks on the morals of military women which had the effect of lowering the morale of women in service and of discouraging the recruitment of others. (Since all military women in the United States have been volunteers, 'discouragement' means low enlistments. Men, of course, are drafted no matter how discouraged or reluctant they may be.) Such a campaign (the slander campaign) was not unanticipated. Therefore Women's Army Auxiliary Corps (WAAC) officials had been careful to ensure that military women were of high quality by requiring private doctor's health certificates, personal references and high test scores. These standards were higher than those to which men were held, and WAAC officials displayed statistics showing that uniformed women were much above the average of uniformed men and of civilian women. Such statistics included venereal disease rates and unwed pregnancy rates. Still, in spite of the data, rumours swept both military camps and the public alleging, for instance, that virgins were not accepted in the military, and that Waacs were required to carry prophylactics whenever they left the barracks, and that large numbers of pregnant Waacs were being returned from overseas.

The slander campaign's effects were so disruptive that Eleanor Roosevelt stated in a press conference that the rumours were Nazi propaganda, and a full-scale military intelligence investigation was launched. What was found was that the strongest opposition to service women came from service men overseas; no trace of Axis propaganda was uncovered.

The conclusion must be that moral accusations have been, are and will be used to keep women out of certain public arenas. This will occur regardless of the facts and regardless of the plans of official policy-makers. In part such slander campaigns are effective because women are susceptible to them. Some women accept a double standard which makes the same gossip about sexual assignations mortifying to a woman but gratifying to a man. Or, even if a woman does not accept such a standard, she may be concerned about her standing with men who do accept such a standard—or with men who do not, but who expect her to be 'easy', to be available for casual sex.

Treadwell's book does not index 'lesbian' and there is only one reference to 'homosexuality'. Nevertheless, the frequency and casualness of references to the presence of many lesbians among military women is not innocent. First, many women who are not lesbians do not like to be thought lesbians. They are harassed by such labelling. Second, women who are lesbians and even those who are wholly comfortable with being lesbians, are threatened by such labelling. This is because the military is the one institution in the United States which specifically prohibits homosexuality, and which can (almost) instantly discharge personnel who are found to be homosexuals. This can occur, for instance, with nineteen years of service and only one year to go to retirement. Third, because pregnant women were discharged, and married women discouraged prior to the all-volunteer military, most young women in the services have been single and subject to being pressured to 'prove' that they aren't lesbians. Finally, women's military uniforms have mostly been designed to look like men's uniforms, and military culture is so steeped in maleness that it is almost impossible to separate 'male' from 'military' elements in military values and customs. (See my *Bring Me Men and Women: Mandated Change at the US Air Force Academy**.) This means that women in the services appear to look and act like men more than civilian women. This causes some to conclude that they look and act like lesbians. This causes some military women to conclude that they are on the defensive—that they bear a certain burden of proof.

What, though, is the effect of myths about military women's whoredom and lesbianism on the nation's ability to conduct war? On the strategic level it is debilitating because it makes it hard to recruit women. Some anti-war women might therefore conclude that such rumours are to be endured. These rumours, however, appear to be spontaneous, heartfelt, and widespread—especially among men away from home—and they are harmful to the women about whom they are created. What may be happening is something like this. Where young men greatly outnumber potential marriage partners, proximate women become both highly visible and also unattainable for most men. A not unnatural response is to suggest that the unattainable is undesirable. When the unattainable is obviously similar in background and competency (if not superior), vague accusations about the unattainable's sexuality can bolster the ego of men peers. If a woman is sexually active, then, she can be described as a whore; if she is not, or if she is simply very private, she can be assigned the label 'lesbian'.

But what is the effect on a nation's 'war effort' of this myth, a myth whose origin seems so easily explainable? As noted above, it makes it harder to integrate women in an effective way. It is debilitating for women's service. But if women are not 'needed', if a war is winnable with men only (e.g. see the

* Stiehm, 1981.

United States v. Grenada), the myth may support the waging of war. It may do so in two ways. The first is simply by enhancing men's solidarity by making them perceive their military units as 'exclusive' of a full half of the population. Second, the fact that there are actually some women around need only slightly diminish 'exclusivity', if the women are few in number and can be classified as deviant and as not worthy of or interested in being mates. The second way the myth can support the war, then, is that because near women are not dear, their presence need not be disruptive. Men will not be tempted to offer them chivalrous protection. Deviant women, then, have to take their chances. They are expendable.

Military policy-makers make similar arguments, but they use slightly different language with slightly different meanings. First, they would be likely to argue on behalf of 'cohesiveness'—on the need for the kind of bonding which cannot tolerate homosexuals, and which also finds it hard to tolerate women—of any kind.

However, because military policy-makers are likely to acknowledge military men's need for access to women, they are also likely to decide it is as well to monitor and regulate the professional services of local 'working women' (prostitutes). This does not make these policy-makers tolerant of the free sexuality of women in uniform. Indeed it is much easier if military men use women who are not in uniform to fulfil their sexual needs. The military has no long-term responsibility for prostitutes, no mandate, for instance, to evacuate them in a period of conflict. Thus, in 'forward' areas where wives are not allowed, whores are still present, and it is in just such areas that military women's presence is most debated, because the military is not sure whether the best analogy for military women is the civilian dependant or the prostitute. The fact is military women are fundamentally different from both, but they are not the same as military men.

The problem is that in the United States women may not serve in combat. Military policy-makers, however, know that even if one does not shoot to kill, one can easily be killed if combat comes. Yet policy-makers are distinctly uncomfortable about evacuating women military personnel along with women and children. Thus keeping them in place may be easier, if they can be discounted in some way.

In sum, at the macro level this second myth is counter-productive. But it is not a macro-level myth. It is a grass-roots myth. At that level it may be productive. In the small unit, and especially aboard and in combat zones, the myth may be productive for men. For women, surely, accusations, labelling, name-calling, stereotyping and isolation are always counter-productive. They have the effect of diminishing women's capacity for self-definition. For men, though, the myth can be absolving. It can remove or reduce responsibility they may feel but which they cannot effectively meet. It may also make the unavailable seem unattractive.

MYTH III: EVEN MILITARY WOMEN NEED PROTECTION

I take non-violent theory seriously. I have found, though, that I am unable to make a full commitment to non-violence. Ironically, this inability is rooted in my motherhood. My commitment flounders precisely on the hypothetical case of my being able to offer protection to innocent others, especially children, especially my own children. Knowing this about myself makes it easier for me to take seriously men's assertions about their responsibility to protect. It makes it easier for me to understand the energy with which men cling to their role of defender. It makes it easier for me to accept men's apparent ability to do deeds which sometimes seem too awful to be human.

What seems clear is that human beings will do more terrible things and will endure more terrible things on behalf of others than they will do or endure for themselves alone. This argument is developed in Reinhold Niebuhr's *Moral Man and Immoral Society*. Its point is that the bigger, the better, the truer, the more abiding generate 'beyond human' behaviour. Only men, though, are asked to use violence in a 'beyond human' fashion.

When a culture defines the bulk of its population as in need of protection, when it declares women, the old, and the young as ineligible to defend themselves, it imposes a grave burden on those defined as protectors (solely) because of their age and sex. Again, a certain portion of a country's population is usually assigned the duty of protecting the whole population, and that assignment is usually given on the basis of the most core elements of a person's identity: age and sex. This is experienced as very compelling. Further, when a culture is successful in establishing such a definition, it makes it more likely to succeed at war. This is so because its protectors (government officials and uniformed personnel) develop a capacity for both ruthlessness and sacrifice.

US officialdom has been quite successful at defining the bulk of its population as in need of defence. In fact, it has even succeeded in defining some of its military personnel as needing defence! Those personnel are, of course, military women.

One might think that all uniformed personnel would be expected to share the demands of the 'profession of arms'. This is not the case. US military women are barred from participation in combat, and the debates over the definition of combat make it clear that what is at stake is not a matching of skills, not a testing of competency, but a far more profound division of labour by sex, a division which serves to entrap men because their sex is, like the law of gravity, virtually unalterable.

The myth that military women require protection and, therefore, should not serve in combat, is established by law, policy and, for many, belief. There is a paucity of evidence, however, and more debate occurs over whether or not something is or is not combat than over whether women can or cannot do it.

The air force, for example, engages in periodic debate about which of its activities is 'combat'. At one time missile duty (in silos, for instance, in South Dakota) was considered combat. Later it was decided it was not combat, perhaps because the silos were as safe as anywhere in the country, or perhaps because missiles are not aimed by 'line of sight' (a distinction the army believes relevant to a definition of combat.) The navy bases its definition not on activity but locality. Women are prohibited from most at-sea billets. Clearly it is assumed that jeopardy rather than work assignments should control in the navy's definition. The army uses both locality and activity and adds as a further exclusion physical strength. The latter is particularly interesting because when the army recently developed its definition of required strength for infantry service, the requirements it set excluded virtually all women. A problem quickly developed. That was that by setting standards which eliminated all women, the army had also excluded a substantial number (between 10 and 20 per cent) of men! Later the army reset its strength cut-offs in such a way that virtually all men were eligible for combat. This meant that the fraction of women who met the stength qualifications would have to be eliminated on grounds of sex. They were. This was apparently perceived as a better solution than the previous proposal which would have excluded so many men (on the grounds of strength) from a sex role their gender required of them.

Perhaps the transparency of assertions about women's need for protection and their incapacity for defence becomes most apparent when one considers America's relationship with its military allies. The US military has never suggested that it could not train Vietnamese or Jordanian men even though their size and strength is substantially less than that of the average US male. Nor has the military doubted the efficacy of its training and the cohesiveness of troops who have a minimal command of the language of their trainers. Clearly correct gender confers possibility; incorrect gender precludes it.

CONCLUSION

I used to believe a scholar's job ceased with demythologizing—that a demonstration, a compiling of evidence was sufficient. Now I believe that it is important to explore the meaning and context of widely shared and deeply rooted beliefs, especially those which are not supported by evidence or which are not logically consistent.

In this essay I have discussed three beliefs about women in the military and their likely effect on that institution's capacity to wage war. The first myth—that women do participate

—has been shown to have as an important function the mobilization of young men. This is important to understand because in many ways military service is a patriarchal initiation rite more than it is a contribution to national defence. Western women have no comparable rite, and I, at least, find it hard to grasp why men are so eager to accept membership in an organization which brutalizes them as the price of entry.

The second myth, which derogates women who do join the military, was shown to be dysfunctional as far as overall rational planning was concerned, but, perhaps, to be functional at the unit level where a grave disproportionality in numbers between men and women may exist, and where the possibility of being asked to make a chivalrous sacrifice also exists.

The third myth, which extends patriarchal protection to some uniformed personnel, is in some ways the most intriguing. It appears to be the most certain proof of the necessity of maintaining the all-male nature of warfare if warfare is to be conducted. This myth became necessary only recently when the United States committed itself to the maintenance of a large, peacetime, volunteer army. This army has approximately 10 per cent women personnel; they serve in every job category which does not involve 'combat'. That is where the line is drawn, and that, of course, is the defining activity of an institution which appears to function as a male-defining institution.

All this means, I suspect, that women's entrance into the military in equal numbers and as full equals *would* change that institution. It would not suddenly be infused with either womanly or feminist values, but it would cease being an all-male institution, and in doing so it would lose some coercive power which such institutions hold over men. Women's inclusion would also give women a stake in the formulation of national security they do not now have. That stake, analogous to the stake a working woman has in the economic system as opposed to the stake of a dependent wife, has the possibility of creating more informed and more intense involvement by women in matters of security, defence, war and peace. In my estimate US women who focus on peace and on nuclear disarmament are not sufficiently serious. Their interest too often stops when they are no longer threatened, and US women feel threatened only by nuclear war. A serious and consistent critic should analyse the wars fought by surrogates, the consequences of profiting from arms sales, the effect of 'winning' miniature wars (e.g. Grenada).

Direct 'Great Power' conflict has been avoided for almost forty years. Can progress toward the elimination of military stockpiling and spending, towards the elimination of wars between smaller nations (e.g. Iran and Iraq), and towards the elimination of the domination of domestic governments by national militaries (e.g. Central America) be made without understanding how deeply gendered the institution which monopolizes legitimate violence is? I think not. Further, I do not believe that the egalitarian perspective offered here necessarily leads to an increased militarization of women or a country, as is feared by many peace activists. I am confident that even equal legal status will not lead to either equal participation or interchangeability of women and men in the military. I am equally confident that no country, however peace-loving or however militarized, is prepared to permit such a radical experiment. Moreover, I believe that militarization develops from (1) conscription (legal coercion) and from (2) high rewards for military volunteers (economic conscription). Thus my own plan for demilitarization would encompass three points: (1) equal and identical responsibilities for national security for men and women, (2) a volunteer military and (3) a guaranteed civilian job for every citizen at the same level of pay as is offered by the military.

REFERENCES

Niebuhr, Reinhold (1932) *Moral Man and Immoral Society*, New York: Scribner.

Stiehm, Judith Hicks (1981) *Bring Me Men and Women: Mandated Change at the US Air Force Academy*, Berkeley: University of California Press.

6

Sexuality and Militarism

Wendy Chapkis
University of California at Santa Cruz, USA

In the 'New Feminism of Yin and Yang', author Alice Echols notes that some contemporary feminists seem to have adopted a position on gender in which masculine and feminine characteristics are inseparable from essential maleness and femaleness. This aspect of the movement, which Echols labels 'cultural feminism', tends to espouse the position that women are more concerned with such issues as ecology (preserving Mother Earth) and peace, and less with sexuality than men.[1] For these women, aggressiveness is seen as inherently, indeed biologically, male. In an article on 'Feminism and Non-violent Revolution', Marion Bromley cites with approval an argument made by Evelyn Reed that

> the male animal suffers from a biological liability. This stems from the violent characteristics of male sexuality in nature, propelling males to strive for 'dominance'. . . . Females, on the other hand, far from being handicapped by their maternal functions, acquired from them the very traits conducive to advancing from animality to human life and cooperative labour. Insofar as the sexes were unequally endowed by nature, the biological advantages for humanizing the species were on the side of the females not the males.[2]

This idea of women as 'Moral Mothers' has been criticized by other feminists such as Micaela di Leonardo:

> The powerful image of selfless maternality and the symbolic associations of women-children-earth versus men-bombs-annihilation limit our theory and activism in relation to militarism. . . . The Moral Mother argument is a poor organizing tool: it does not challenge us to think in complex ways about the sources of military threat, nor about women's own consciousness and social activity.[3]

It is my contention that the essentialist arguments about masculinity and men, femininity and women are not only limited as a basis for organizing opposition to militarism but are in fact dangerously counter-productive and personally self-defeating. One indication of the danger of essentialist arguments is the very strange bedfellows we would share by espousing such a position. In her book *Three Guineas*, Virginia Woolf notes that 'Herr Hitler and Signor Mussolini have both often in very similar words expressed the opinion that "There are two worlds in the life of a nation, the world of men and the world of women" ';[4] 'Both [dictators] repeatedly insist that it is the nature of man and indeed the essence of manhood to fight. . . . Both repeatedly insist that it is the nature of womanhood to heal the wounds of the fighter'.[5]

One attempt to salvage the essentialist position has been to argue that there is a crucial difference between socially constructed femininity under patriarchy and true female nature. Femininity is then equated with passive and submissive behaviour while female nature is defined as 'nurturing, loving, open and egalitarian'.[6] But even this distinction does not really get us very far. The idea of females as inherently nurturing and loving, for example, fits distressingly well into military ideology about the role and purpose of women in the military. Nira Yuval-Davis has made the point that the role of women in the Israeli women's corps is explicitly to function to 'raise the morale of the male soldiers and make the army "a home away from home". . . . In the words of the Zahal [Israeli army] spokesman: "Chen [the women's corps] adds to Zahal the grace and charm which makes it also a medium for humanitarian and social activities" '.[7] This view of the role of women in the military is clearly not limited to the Israeli example. In the United States, two women veterans of the Vietnam War recently commissioned a bronze statue of a female veteran to be unveiled at the site of the Vietnam Memorial in Washington, DC. They decided to make the woman a nurse since 75 per cent of the women who served in Vietnam were nurses. The women have explained that the statue is meant as a 'composite of the ideal for which all women performed their duty . . . to aid, to heal, to insure the survival of others'. Among women's unique contributions to service in Vietnam were, they said, their 'nurturing qualities'.[8] Or again, in the words of Virginia Woolf, 'it is the nature of womanhood to heal the wounds of the fighter'.

As long as women continue to insist on this narrowly gendered image of womanhood, we will not only fail to effectively challenge the ideology on which current military practice is based, but we will leave ourselves open to direct use by the military to pick up the bloody pieces in time of war. As Donna Warnock says, 'If the peace movement is to be successful in putting an end to war, it must work to eliminate the sex-role system which is killing us all by rewarding dominating aggressive behaviour in men'.[9] And, I would add, by rewarding passive and nurturing behaviour in women. For while this kind of female gendered behaviour may seem to be the antithesis of militarism, it is in fact a central component within it.

Masculine dominance and feminine submissiveness as exclusive categories are necessarily complementary, each enabling the other to exist. In an article by two men on masculine sexuality and violence appropriately entitled 'More Power than We Want', authors Bruce Kokopeli and George Lakey argue that

> The sexual politics of domination/submission is so reinforced by militarism that one cannot be eliminated without the other. . . . If the masculine character ideal supports militarism, what can support peace? Femininity? No, for that character ideal also has been shaped by patriarchy and includes . . . a kind of dependency which breeds the passive–aggressive syndrome of curdled violence.[10]

The implication of what I am saying is that women's personal, social and indeed sexual repertoire must be expanded to include the possibility of dominance and control just as that of men must come to include the possibility of surrender.

As odd as that may sound, this may well be the most effective avenue to unmasking the hidden tensions that give militarism its power and enduring appeal. It is my belief that militarism is fuelled by deeply held but generally unspoken fantasies of domination and submission found in both men and women. In fact, I would go as far as to say that the military myth (which is quite distinct from the reality of life within the military system) is essentially a highly gendered erotic fantasy.

Within contemporary Western society, power has a deeply erotic component. The reason for this relationship between power and sex is very much the subject of continuing debate. Some argue that early childhood experiences of power and powerlessness between mother and child create an enduring connection between eroticism and power play centring on self–other boundaries. Others stress the role of power inequalities in adult life and argue that power is eroticized in a creative move to derive pleasure from otherwise objectively oppressive conditions. Whatever the reason, and for better and worse, power has an undeniable erotic charge. And the military myth has become one of the most significant cultural symbols for the re-enactment of these submission–dominance rituals.

Again, I want to emphasize that I am talking here about the popular fantasy of the military experience, not the actual reality of militarized life. No one is really empowered—sexually or personally—by real military discipline and domination. Indeed, men as well as women are often destroyed emotionally and physically by the reality of the military. But the popular fantasy of the military experience tells us important information about the contemporary construction of desire.

The American film industry has recently provided us with an alarming number of movies in which the military myth is given expression in all its glory and allure. I think it worthwhile to turn briefly to a consideration of what the fantasy is that is being played out in uniform in such films as the 1986 'blockbuster', *Top Gun*. Young American 'heart-throb' Tom Cruise plays the hero, Lieutenant Pete 'Maverick' Mitchell, a top US navy pilot sent to the 'Fighter Weapons School'—nicknamed 'Top Gun'—for a course in Air Combat Manoeuvring. Only the top 1 per cent of all navy pilots are selected for this course and Maverick is one of the best among the best.

The film is unquestionably about eroticism: the boys' bodies are oiled and displayed at every opportunity, often in slow motion. Shown equally lovingly are aerial shots of the fighter planes in action. The air combat manoeuvring is explicitly meant to be sexually stirring: 'This gives me a hard-on', says a pilot while viewing training films of F–14s in action. During the final air-battle scene, another pilot responds to the glories of war by remarking, '[the enemy aircraft] must be close, I'm getting a hard-on'. Competition and conflict between the boys is the motor for this erotic charge. Despite a heterosexual love angle, the tension between the hero and the woman is strikingly unconvincing compared to the electricity between the military men. *Top Gun* can only be said to be typical in this regard for the military is a sexual fantasy built around images of masculinity.

Only other men can pose a sufficient threat and a sufficient challenge to serve as worthy objects of desire. Masculinity is the ultimate and forbidden conquest in the eroticized battle between the boys. The true moment of sexual contact and completion in this film is the long-awaited clenched fist embrace between Maverick and his Top Gun rival, the Iceman.

What I am arguing here is not simply that the military has strong homo-erotic overtones, though of course it does. But more importantly, the military fantasy effectively exploits the eroticism of power. The sexuality in these films is a celebration of distance, danger, expertise, control and violation of individual boundaries through physical exhaustion, self-sacrifice and even death. The power play is not merely domination *or* submission, it is the constant interplay between the two. The best opponent, like the most attractive object of desire, must be able to offer sufficient resistance before succumbing.

For related reasons, the other key features of most military fantasy films is the symbolic breaking and building of men in basic training. Basic training is the symbol of submissiveness, the necessary counterpoint to high-profile dominance rituals of war. The military fantasy thus offers satisfaction of both desires for control and forced surrender. The existence of an 'enemy' provides the justification for otherwise forbidden male bonding, submission to the power of a commander and the relinquishment of individual identity and agency in the unquestioning obedience to orders—in short, an enemy offers a justifiable pretext to be forced to be femme. Men are thus offered a fantasy of crossing gender boundaries and coming out not only intact but even more of a man.

Women are offered a rather less direct and certainly more ambiguous fantasy in the military myth. None the less, it holds undeniable appeal for many women either as an avenue to personally transgress gender boundaries or as a means to project the eroticism of power on to male objects of desire. For women interested in directly engaging with power, the military is eager to exploit the illusion that they are a path. Recruitment material for women tends to emphasize that the military is 'The Challenge You Need'. 'No longer is a woman restricted to a traditional role', claims the recruitment leaflet, 'now you can do the totally new. You can be a missile repairer, carpenter/mason, a construction equipment operator or missile crew member.' Or at least so they promise.

The military myth is no more a reflection of reality for women than it is for men. Most women in all national militaries are overwhelmingly segregated in traditional female jobs such as nursing, secretarial and administrative work. In fact, women who believe the military myth and expect to defy civilian gender boundaries are likely to discover that the military is tremendously uneasy with unfeminine females. The very existence of the military system is founded on rigid distinctions of gender. As we have seen, the ghettoizing of women in traditionally feminine occupations in the military reinforces—even right in the midst of the machine itself—the image of women as Other: nurturing, supportive and affectationally essential but practically dependent and therefore defenceless. Women then remain in need of male protectors which the military has been designed to create.

This may explain why the same army that promises women the freedom of the unconventional and new, is so eager to reassure us—or perhaps more to the point, itself—that the same old you can do the job: 'you can make it in the army and still be a woman'. Perhaps this is also an important reason why in an already homophobic institution, lesbians—the gender outlaws—are singled out for even more obsessive search and destroy missions than gay men. In her book *Does Khaki Become You*, Cynthia Enloe reports that according to a 1981 study, women were discharged from the US navy and air force on the grounds of homosexual conduct at a rate two and a half times higher than men. And in the US army, women were six times more likely than men to be discharged on grounds of homosexuality.[11]

Even women who fail to respond to the military myth of personally gaining access to masculine power by joining up, may find themselves enjoying the fantasy of at least consorting with those who do. In her book, *Sleeping with Soldiers*, Rosemary Daniell initially explains her passion for macho men in terms of the reassurance they offer to her own gender identity: 'The more macho the man, the more traditionally feminine, passive and virtuous I felt.'[12] But gradually she becomes aware that it is not only the otherness of her soldier lovers but indeed her deep identification with them that attracts her to them:

> in my most confident moments, the man with whom I most identified was the maverick who apparently had escaped the dictates of conformity—who against great odds controlled his own life, embodied the activity and assertion that I, as a Southern woman, had been brought up to deny in myself. Freely and fearlessly, it seemed, he took the risks, acted out the aggressive impulses I had learned early to repress, or else judge myself crazy. . . . He was my embedded twin, the part of me that—rather than staying put or doing what I'm told—flies: simply the man I would have been.[13]

I would accept, like Daniell, the idea that each of us, male and female, embodies the desire for both control and surrender, daring and dependency, authority and compliance, heroism and passivity, and a desire for freedom from the gender roles that make it necessary to choose between these qualities. If we start with this simple awareness, we can begin to separate out our desires from the military fantasy in which they are now enfolded. This would allow us to self-consciously fight the exploitation by the contemporary military system of our richly conflicting passions.

NOTES

1. Alice Echols, 'New Feminism of Yin and Yang', in Ann Snitow *et al.* (eds.), *Powers of Desire* (New York: Monthly Review Press, 1983), p. 440.
2. Marion Bromley, 'Feminism and Non-violent Revolution', in Pam McAllister (ed.), *Reweaving the Web of Life* (Philadelphia: New Society Publishers, 1982), pp. 149–50.
3. Micaela di Leonardo, 'Morals, Mothers, Militarism', *Feminist Studies* 11(3): 611.
4. Virginia Woolf, *Three Guineas* (London: Hogarth Press), p. 180.
5. *Ibid.*, p. 186.
6. Echols, p. 443.
7. N. Yuval-Davis, 'Front and Rear: The Sexual Division of Labor in the Israeli Army', *Feminist Studies* 2(3): 663.
8. Kate Rix, 'Metal of Honor', Santa Cruz, CA: *City on a Hill Press*, 8 January 1987.
9. Donna Warnock, 'Patriarchy is a Killer', in McAllister, p. 28.
10. In McAllister, p. 231.
11. Cynthia Enloe, *Does Khaki Become You*? (London: Pluto Press, 1983), p. 143.
12. Rosemary Daniell, *Sleeping with Soldiers* (New York: Holt, Reinhart and Winston, 1985; London: Grafton, 1986), p. 17.
13. *Ibid.*, p. 64.

7

Women and War: Victims and Collaborators

Astrid Albrecht-Heide
Technische Universität Berlin, FRG

While in many countries of the world women have access to the military, in the Federal Republic of Germany a group of women have begun to fight for the right of entry into this institution of 'specialists on violence' (Lasswell, 1941) by going to the Federal Court. 'Frauen zum Bund' (Women into the Federal Military) is the name they have given themselves (Auth, 1986).

The hesitancy in the Federal Republic is, among other things, due to the fact that during National Socialism the voluntary and involuntary involution of women into warfare on all levels was extreme: from military motherhood, via labour in the war industries, serving alongside the military within anti-aircraft defence or medical and clerical jobs, down to wardresses in concentration and extermination camps. There is no doubt that during this time women were victims of as well as collaborators with, a destructive and imperialistic system. It may well be that this hesitancy, which became part of the West German constitution, at the present stage is more adequate than women fighting their way into the military with equal-rights' initiatives.

I shall develop my arguments along three lines:

1. I shall try to give a paradigmatic analysis of the situation of women in patriarchal societies. This will be done under the metaphorical keyword of 'colonization' (Albrecht-Heide, 1986), which I owe to a certain extent to my colleague Claudia von Werlhof. This shall not be a global or general one, but one which gives the chance to understand and distinguish between active and passive

involvement of women, that is victimization and collaboration.
2. The next step will be an attempt to illustrate the colonized situation of women with respect to war and military.
3. Finally, I shall try to show that, under present circumstances, women empower the military to such an extent that the world of civilians has become endangered.

COLONIZATION OF WOMEN

A Paradigmatic Analysis of the Situation of Women in Patriarchal Societies

I don't want female soldiers, because I am against the military and soldiers generally. On the other hand, I think, if women are that blockheaded and want to become soldiers, it's their own business and nobody should hold them back. But I feel the armies of the world shouldn't get extra support by the way that women support them. It's enough if those machos are stupid enough for it. I am for anarchy, although nowadays it's quite unrealistic, because of the monstrous size of the world population.

Anyway, I'm also contradicting myself, as on the one hand I'm a pacifist and violence makes me vomit, and on the other hand I feel: why don't they shoot each other, there are too many of them anyway. Additionally I believe that you can change conditions only with money or by using violence. If women ultimately want to fight in an army, they should rather go to a 'women's force' for emancipation, anarchy and so on. They should fight for their own rights and if it looks likely to succeed, use violence at the right place. Rather fight at the women's front than in the Federal Military!

Oh yawn, what an ideological letter, but you wanted to know what I think. I'm looking towards the future rather pessimistically but I'm trying to make the best of it. To join the military would be the very last thing that I would demand of myself or other women. Also this whole bullshit of hierarchy and so on. Oh, Woman! That's been of course invented by all those machos; who else could have had such a rotten idea?

This is part of the answer of a 17-year-old girl to my question: female soldiers, yes or no? Remarkable with respect to the paradigm of 'colonization' is that the normally amalgamated unity of male heroism and female tears (Huston, 1983) is no longer guaranteed, although the counter-arguments are wild and bewildering, and not yet productive in any anti-militaristic sense.

An appreciation of the interior, or physical, occupation of women in our culture is an essential element in developing an understanding of the fact that girls and women actively and passively develop and/or internalize patterns and values which may be called, metaphorically, 'colonial elements of patriarchy'.

In his book on the effects of French colonization on Algier (*Les Damnés de Terre*), Frantz Fanon described the imperialistic occupation of the souls of the colonized people. It seems to me that a comparative approach was followed by those Afro-Americans who used the metaphor 'Uncle Tom' to describe the psychological conditions of their brothers and sisters. A few years ago at an international workshop of the two universities of Groningen (Holland) and Oldenburg (West Germany) critical psychologists tried to get more insight into the aspects of colonial assimilatory pressure under the topic of 'inside and outside colonization' (Jos Gerwin *et al.* 1982 and 1983).

The effort to understand the interior structure of occupied souls—under any rule whatsoever—as a process of contradictory adoption of norms and values of the colonists, will serve as new elements in developing an understanding of the situation of women within patriarchy.

1. Colonization is a violent act. Foreign territory is being expropriated and exploited according to the interests of the colonists.
2. The colonists are dependent on the acceptance, at least, of their norms and values by the occupied.
3. Colonists feel themselves endangered by deviating norms and values; they are perceived as uncategorized, disorganized, chaotic and threatening.
4. In the minds of colonists, territories which are not (yet) organized according to their own structures, or are not related to these, have the quality of blank spaces on a map.
5. Colonists are dependent on patterns of explanation which legitimize the relations between themselves and the colonized. They also need confusion, disorientation and collaboration. However fictive it may prove, they need an apartheid of the world of occupants and occupied organized by division of labour.

6. The colonists need to wipe out the history of the colonized. In doing so, deviating norms and values can be reinterpreted as innate, basically primitive, and in need of suppression.

But:

7. In colonies, insurrections, riots, mutinies and rebellions (sometimes even liberation) are unavoidable. These mutinies may be performed secretly or openly; they may be suppressed and forbidden or extensively gone through; they may be directed against their own person/group or against the colonist; they may be irritated and bewildered, collaborative, rebellious or liberating.
8. (Self) liberation of the colonized includes liberation of the colonists even if these first grasp only their territorial loss.

Illustrations of the Paradigm of Colonized Women

To a certain extent the paradigm of colonization of women in patriarchy is self-evident. But this, I have learnt during my academic career, is not sufficient. So I shall also offer evidence in the form of stories, scenes and pictures.

Male War-Activities and Female Tears

As I have mentioned, Nancy Huston described (in her essay on 'Tales of War and Tears of Women') the amalgamation of male war-activities and female tears. Together they lend a somewhat metaphysical sense to a destructive context of action. Huston describes a necrophilic and obsessive pattern, from the *Iliad*, via the Nibelungenlieder, up to modern war correspondence:

> the *New York Times* could not publish, on the front page, a photo of Iraqi or Iranian prisoners of war, kneeling in the age-old posture of male humiliation, hands on their heads, eyes filled with fear and hatred—without publishing on an inside page along with the continuation of the article, a photo of Iraqi or Iranian women, kneeling in the age-old posture of female bereavement, rocking back and forth, arms crossed over their breasts, eyes closed and cheeks streaming with tears. The second photograph is there in order to give the first one its full meaning. (Huston, 1983: 179).

Collaboration or Slavery?

I remember my first Marine Corps Ball in the gym of Knoxville's Reserve unit: we ate peanut butter and jelly sandwiches, danced to records, but we listened attentively to the 21st commandant, Gen. Randolph McC Pate's message, and stood at attention for the Marines' Hymn. Tears of pride streamed down my face as I began to realize what it meant for the first time to be a Marine Corps spouse.

We have also been fortunate to attend many Marine Corps Balls in every clime, be it far off northern lands of Korea or the sunny tropic scene of the Philippines. Each time the Marines' Hymn is played, troops march or stand at attention, I get bumps, blurry eyes, and a knot in my stomach. Our military men—our Marines—are the best anywhere in the world; everyone knows from pride in appearance, erect lean stature, and behaviour that once a Marine, always a Marine. . . .

When your fiancé proposed, I presume he made it clear to you that duty always comes first—before you, family, home ties, or anything else. For Marines, the guiding principles are 'duty, honor, country . . . and the Corps'. I am not too sure that in some instances this order is not reversed. Remember this, regardless of a Marine's crusty, hard-boiled exterior, his salty language at work, his ferocious fighting prowess on the battlefield or in the air, he has one weakness—and that is you, his spouse. Marines have a certain gallantry, pride, and love when speaking of their wives. Marine wives are on pedestals; and we sincerely believe that while the Corps always comes first, 'the flag is a jealous mistress'. In his heart, your Marine fights for you and his loved ones first, last, and always. By giving him the freedom to grow as a Marine and by learning more about his commitment, friends and traditions of the Corps, you will feel more loved and understood. . . .

If you play your part as a helpmate, although not recognized officially, one half of every promotion, one-half of every success, and one-half of every medal belongs to and depends on you. (Quoted in Bowers, 1984).

These are parts from a speech given by a Marine Corps wife for her colleagues on Military Spouse Day, 23 May 1984, at Marine Barracks, Subic Bay, Philippines.

This collaborative attitude towards the female status of the defeated in a male-occupied area undoubtedly is not limited to the military. We can find it in nearly all sectors of our lives. The speech of this Marine Corps Spouse gives a hint to the ambiguity of female tears. Female tears of pride and those of suffering related to male activities or even 'only' values obviously are the decisive element in giving (metaphysical) sense to male action. The sentimental adoration of the macho dismantles the function of male (military) life as a surrogate. The interior architecture of occupied souls is dependent on an artificial composition and exaggeration of the colonists (pride in appearance, erect lean stature). The élitist status is being supported by pin-up qualities. It is not difficult to recognize the pride of girls and women in civil life in their tough guy.

Important, it seems to me, is the privatized interpretation of the relation between the incarnation of patriarchal institutions of specialists on violence and the dependent spouses. They are standing on pedestals; they are the real reason for combat, and the flag is a jealous mistress. . . . For you, for you, for you—that is the *cantus firmus* throughout the history of violence of patriarchy; and in cases of defeat it will be reinterpreted as 'because of you'!

But there is something else in this speech. The enthusiasm of the speaker appears exhausted, if not overexhausted. It is obviously difficult to explain one's own status of being colonized. This is also true in a case—as the above illustrated—where there is absolutely no consciousness of having become 'foreign territory'. This enormous stress could be a possible reason for the breakdown of the status as a collaborator and/or slave.

Masterful Man and Cultivable Woman

There exists a colonial woman's problem not only in the metaphorical sense used so far but in the literal sense of an occupation of foreign territory. In the colonization process women have been camp followers, and workers in society's communication zone, products of and producers of colonial power and violence.

Temptingly, Magdalene Prince wrote the following to future colonial spouses:

> The man founds the house, the woman keeps it! This sentence is more true than ever for our colonies. Could you, young women and girls be won for our young Germany overseas. Any loss of comfort, amusement, social activity, and inspiring activities of any kind, will be more than paid back for by those activities and duties which you have to fulfil side by side with a beloved husband. Truly, it is a wonderful lot to be allowed to take one's proper place within the victorious march of German culture. (Prince, 1902).

Colonists need legitimation and irritation by division of labour. Male hordes colonize, female camp-followers 'culturize'. Legitimation and irritation have been initiated by colonial racism. Colonial racism does not differ from anti-feminism which also knows female protagonists. The interior caging of women in this case is actively being adopted by the exterior caging of the competitors of other races. Colonization of foreign territory remains dependent on occupation by high birth rates. The specific female ability to give birth is not only alienated but actively been given away with a colonialistic mentality.

Fostering: Placebo Against Patriarchy

Cultivating patriarchy: this is being arranged and handled between the 'masterful man' and the 'cultivable woman'. Female social character, projected on and into women in our culture from early childhood finds its metaphysical climax in Red Cross service, with Florence Nightingale as a symbolic figure.

Independent of the question of whether patriarchy just functions better or really becomes more humane by this service, is that fact that fostering is not a remedy but a placebo, and a placebo is not without impact. But the impact is of a character in which reality and illusion are being combined; they are combined in such a way as to make illusory and real elements hard to disentangle.

Wilma Ruediger (German Red Cross), reports in her autobiography (1962) on an event in a military hospital during the First World War:

> At the end of the ward non-commissioned officer Urban had his bed. His lower leg had been badly injured; his leg was now partially in a plaster-of-Paris dressing, and he already felt a little better. He had proudly shown me photographs of his wife and children and told me joyfully that he was expecting the visit of his wife within the next days. But when I entered the ward next day his bed was empty. What had happened? Urban had had a heavy secondary bleeding and despite of all efforts (blood transfusions did not yet exist) he had died in the morning. I was bewildered and went to our nice sergeant at the door in order to talk to him. In this very moment the door opened, and a woman came in. She looked young and at her arm she carried a bag with a bottle of wine.[1] One of the warders went over to her,

and the woman asked him something. And then I could hear the answer, 'Yes, he died this morning; I carried him out myself'. I had a feeling, who this woman was and hurried over, but the sergeant had already told her, 'It is true, he just died; who are you?' The woman started to scream. She screamed like an injured animal, with a suffering, piercing tone. She screamed and screamed. . . . The doors of the ward went open; injured, warders, nurses and doctors came in; the woman screamed. I had pressed her tightly into my arms, and by this I tried to mitigate the tone, but it did not help much. It took a very long time until this terrifying screaming finally stopped (Ruediger, 1962: 22).

Screaming is the problem; this has to be fostered away. The placebo has its impact; but what a wild mixture it is! Irritation is being initiated at nearly all levels . . . and this changes reality.

Insurrection, riot, mutiny, rebellion, liberation

History proves that in all colonies insurrections, riots, mutinies, rebellions and sometimes even liberation may happen. The patriarchal system of apartheid has not yet left the level of innate, biologistical interpretation, but it has been differentiated. By differentiation this system of apartheid became more unintelligible.

In all colonies parts of the native population have tried to improve their lot by collaborative participation of power up or down to the level of mercenary.[2] Others put their hope in a balance of interest; and this can only be achieved by at least some readiness to be rebellious. Liberation from the patriarchal system of apartheid requires that the status of colonization vanishes. As the colonized status is supported by a system of psychological occupation (cultural imperialism) not only the colonists but also many of the colonized value rebellion and insurrection as 'indecent'. (It would be enlightening and tempting at the same time to look into the whole history of women's movement under this metaphorical aspect.)

Nevertheless, I am tempted to develop some recommendations for 'indecent' decolonization activities. They all have in common that they oppose the interests of the colonists (as described above):

1. The territory will be regained; in an emergency case it shall be left first.

2. Norms and values of the colonists will no longer be accepted.
3. Norms and values of the 'natives' shall be put under the suspicion of life and not of chaos.
4. Decolonization includes the discovery of one's own multitude. The territory is multi-cultural and multi-coloured, not white.
5. The division of labour within the patriarchal system of apartheid will no longer be accepted.
6. One's own history will be discovered; wishes and desires are related to this history and not to nature.
7. Rebellion is liberative and not an egotistic revolt.
8. In the long run decolonization will urge also the colonist to a non-colonial existence.

WOMEN AND WAR: A SPECIAL ANALYSIS OF THE COLONIZED SITUATION OF WOMEN WITH RESPECT TO WAR AND MILITARY

In this section I shall not go into a detailed history of women and war. Some of it has been developed in other papers already been discussed here.[3] I am trying to do something smaller. I shall go through the indicators of colonization in order to find out elements of them in the specific relation between women and war (military).

1. *Colonization is a violent act. Foreign territory is being expropriated and exploited according to the interests of the colonists.*

We can find a certain amount of evidence for the truth of this general observation. Expropriation and exploitation of the female labour force is more than obvious. Never in modern history women could decide whether they wanted to be part of the war business or not. They were one of the 'reserve-armies of army labor' (Enloe, 1979). It has always been a colonized illusion of women that any of their emancipatory efforts had a decisive impact on (male) military agencies to recruit them for war-labour.

2. *The colonists are dependent on the acceptance, at least, of their norms and values by the occupied.*

Throughout modern history and in nearly all parts of the world governments have repeatedly had to counteract legislative deficits in their defence politics; central values of governmental policy were questioned; and it was necessary to widen the basis of approval by giving occupied parts of the population the illusion of being part of the whole. This can either be along sexual (female soldiers) or racial (Ethnic Soldiers: Enloe) or age lines (boys or elderly men during the Second World War, Ireland, Iran/Iraq, etc.) or whatever discriminatory layers the specific society knows of.

3. *Colonists feel themselves endangered by deviating norms and values; they are perceived as uncategorized, disorganized, chaotic and threatening.*

Repeatedly, governments and military leaders are confronted with the fact that the troops do not function according to their expectations; for example lack of morale in troops as well as disciplinary problems and opposition within the military quest for measures. As long as things work smoothly, female attitudes are of no interest; but they can become vitally important. As long as they seem to be disorganized and therefore chaotic with respect to military aims, they need to be re-/overshaped. Thus they function as a sort of plastercast holding together the shaking basis of military policy, and this may give them quite a feeling of strength.

4. *In the minds of colonists, territories which are not (yet) organized according to their own structures, or are not related to these, have the quality of blank spaces on the map.*

To go into detail of this sub-aspect of military colonization of women, could fill volumes—because it would require a description of the process of militarization of women between the extremes of victims and collaborators as a whole. By militarization of women I mean precisely that process which progressively integrates all aspects of female lives into the logic of a war system

—Their ability to give birth to life is militarily integrated under the aspect of birth rates for future military manpower.

—Their existence as a 'civil' part of the population still serves as one of the central (illusionary) defence motivations of militaries all over the world.

—Their reproductive woman-power serves military man-power at home and in clerical and medical jobs within the military;

—Their productive woman-power in the military or militarily relevant industry and as female soldiers are a sort of a mercenary to the (male) war system.

It is against this background that the role-distinction of women within the war system, derives its specific importance.

5. *Colonists are dependent on patterns of explanation which legitimize the relations between themselves and the colonized. They also need confusion, disorientation and collaboration. However fictive it may prove they need an apartheid of the world of occupants and the occupied by a division of labour.*

Throughout modern history it was a male domain to occupy foreign territory or property by violence. Nevertheless, this does not mean that women were the peaceful sex. We generally speak about sex-specific division of labour, but we may also speak about sex-specific division of violence (Albrecht-Heide, 1979).

—There are female actors of violence. While public life dominently knows male actors of violence, private life knows female actors of violence too.

—Besides this, according to the interpretive framework of colonization, we more often have female supporters and applauders of violence, the latter especially by identifying with the aggressor.

6. *The colonist needs to wipe out the history of the colonized. In doing so, deviating norms and values can be reinterpreted as innate, basically primitive and in need of suppression.*

We know that besides history through mankind there exists a 'herstory'. Many aspects of this herstory have been wiped out so that it is quite difficult to reconstruct its basic elements. All speculations with respect to peaceful and/or warful attitudes are due to this 'wiping-out-effect'. Whether it is true or not, whether it is real or projective: the interpretation as a sort of natural peace-resource on the side of women includes this as a 'primitive' and necessarily 'naïve and 'inadequate' answer to the challenges of history.

7. *In colonies, insurrections, riots, mutinies and rebellions (sometimes even liberation) are unavoidable. These mutinies may be performed secretly or openly; they may be suppressed and forbidden or extensively gone through; they may be directed against their own person/group or against the colonist; they may be irritated and bewildered, collaborative, rebellious or liberating.*

In my opinion, it is still much easier to illustrate this thesis on the level of geographical colonization than with respect to women and war/military. A general anti-militaristic attitude remains so far metaphorical. At the present stage of herstory it probably is vital to be multi-cultural, multi-coloured, pluralistic, pacifist, feminist, herstorist, anti-militarist. . . .

WOMAN EMPOWER(S) MILITARY: THE/A PRESENT STATE OF AFFAIRS

The title of this chapter implies the hypothesis that women had an active collaborative part in the process of their own military colonization. In the second section I went into this on a superficial level. In this section I shall try to indicate the more subtle impact on women and the society as a whole (cf. Albrecht-Heide, 1984). I shall do this with respect to highly industrialized societies and militaries against the background of present arms technology. Here I shall not be dealing with women and war for all times and in all countries but with the very specific, present situation with its huge overkill capacity.

We live in a prewar situation, equipped with mass-killing instruments—which are, I pray, something different from weapons. In my opinion, such a fundamental qualitative change has not really been realized up to now. The relationship between general policy and military violence is still dominantly understood (explicitly or implicitly) in the way it was in the nineteenth century, that is military as an instrument of politics. Our consciousness is pre-atomic (Anders, 1980) and inadequately developed to meet the essential conditions of the atomic age.

Women are offered a number of roles with respect to the war-business, and often they fulfil them actively. As mothers, wives and partners of soldiers they actively collaborate with destruction. By identifying with the defence of their country they are able to ignore its full destructive potential. In this way they establish a psychologically stable basis for substituting the female dimension of fostering for aggression. Women do not only collaborate with the modern military in a nurturing way, but also aggressively, although they may not (and indeed are not allowed to) notice it. Thus they function as instruments of a mystification of military violence and war.

In those countries where marriages between male and female soldiers increase a profound process of militarization on a new qualitative level is taking place. Women here seem to act on the one side privately and on the other publicly, although in both cases it is of public importance. Often it is only barely understood that there is a breakdown in the traditional military–civilian relation between man and woman ('society of defenders', Judith H. Stiehm, 1983). At the same time, and this seems to me the more important development, defence starts to lose its basis as an act of civilian society. In its place we are confronted with a sex-independent, though nevertheless patriarchal, destructive tendency. We again become victims of a process of mystification—which colonists love—if we stop with an analysis at the point of 'society of defenders'. The confusing power of mystifications like this is strong; it helps us to forget that the civilian basis of defence has already collapsed, or imploded, because of the predominant strategic concepts.

Mystification also may take place with respect to those women who work as civilians within the military. These women have, superficially, at least two reasons for turning their backs on their own relevance for the military: the civilian clothes they wear and the type of jobs available to them outside the military. On another level, women working within arms production or a militarily relevant industry add to mystification. Given their female socialization, these workers may understand and define their production of destruction as fostering activities. Their key-dimension in this process is their own role in defence. A profound inversion of the dimension 'protection of life' towards (potential) destruction is taking place. In conventional arms this invertive connection between protection and destruction has already been established. In modern systems of mass destruction the element of protection converges towards nothing: protection and destruction become identical.

Another development of disorientation is taking place, where workers cannot distinguish between civil or military use of what they are producing (and which are not their products). They are released from relating their activities to anything; indifference and unconcern are the psychological effects. While female labour within high-tech and militarily relevant production is silently and rapidly increasing, the destructive impact of this fact is wholly underestimated by those involved.

Female soldiers who are most visibly related to the business of war, are involved directly in mystifying tendencies through their reinterpretation as 'defenders'. This tendency is enforced by a number of socio-psychological effects of the interior structure of the military and the change of military combat. The military is characterized, even more after women became soldiers (Albrecht-Heide *et al.*, 1982), by a fundamental atmosphere of maleness and machismo. The male role of military violence obviously needs a distance from social and emotional needs of interpersonal relations. This leads to a brutalization in the relationship to women (pin-up culture, sexual harassment). In addition, modern military instruments—to avoid such misleading words as 'arms' or 'weapons'—lead to combat situations where male-against-male activities are exceptions. Button-pushing killing predominates—superficially aseptic killing by distance. And this seems to be sex-neutral. But this is only superficially the case, because male readiness to kill and take risk in combat has been incorporated into modern killing instruments.[4] If a woman allows herself to analyse the fact that men maintain that, on this basis, women can do combat jobs too because it does not need much physical strength, if woman dares to approach this fact with categories of psychoanalysis, this macho-produced sex-neutrality may be dismantled as an obscene highlight of patriarchy.

NOTES

1. Notice the naive fairy-tale like aesthetics à la Little Red Riding-Hood.
2. I owe this qualified impudence to Utemaria Bujewski and love to make use of it.
3. Together with Utemaria Bujewski I have elaborated some historical aspects in a book (Albrecht-Heide and Bujewski, 1982).
4. Masculine ways of acting and thinking have not only been incorporated into military science and technology but also into civil science and technology. In her foreword to the German edition of Brian Easlea's *Fathering the Unthinkable: Masculinity, Scientists and the Nuclear Arms Race* (Weinheim u. Basel: Beltz, 1986) Doris Janshen speaks of 'intellectus erectus'.

REFERENCES

Albrecht-Heide, Astrid (1979) 'Das Verhältnis von Mädchen und Frauen zur Gewalt: Fragen zu einem vernachlässigten Bereich' (Relation of Girls and Women to Violence: Questions Concerning Neglected Problems), in Christiane Rajewsky (ed.), *Rüstung und Krieg* (Arms and War) Frankfurt: Haag and Herchen, 1983.

Albrecht-Heide, Astrid (1981) 'The Peaceful Sex', in Wendy Chapkis (ed.), *Loaded Questions: Women in the Military*, Amsterdam/Washington: Transnational Institute.

Albrecht-Heide, Astrid (1984) 'Frau Macht (macht?) Militär' (Women (Em?)power Military) in Barbara Schaeffer-Hegel (ed.), *Frauen und Macht. Der alltägliche Beitrag der Frauen zur Politik des Patriarchats* (Women and Power: Everyday Contribution of Women to the Policy of Patriarchy), Berlin: Publica.

Albrecht-Heide, Astrid (1986) 'Männliche Helden—Weibliche Tränen. Über die innere Kolonisierung von Mädchen im Patriarchat' (Male Heroes—Female Tears: Psychic Colonization of Girls inside Patriarchy), in Christian Büttner *et al.* (eds), *Die Rebellion der Mädchen* (Rebellion of Girls) *Jahrbuch der Kindheit* Bd. 3 (Yearbook of Childhood, Vol. 3), Weinheim u. Basel: Beltz.

Albrecht-Heide, Astrid, and Bujewski, Utemaria (1982) *Militärdienst für Frauen*? (Military Service for Women?) Frankfurt/New York: Campus.

Anders, Günther (1980) *Die Antiquiertheit des Menschen* (Humankinds' State of Obsolescence), 5th edn, Munich: Becks.

Auth, Edgar (1986) 'Verfassungsklage soll Frauen den Weg zum Bund ebnen' (Going to the Federal Court Will Pave Women's Way into the Federal Military), *Frankfurter Rundschau*, 26 November.

Bowers, Paula (1984) 'The Marine Corps Marriage', in *Marine Corps Gazette*, November.

Enloe, Cynthia (1979) 'Women: The Reserve Army of Army Labor', Worcester, Mass., August (manuscript).

Enloe, Cynthia (1980) *Ethnic Soldiers: State Security in a Divided Society*, Harmondsworth: Penguin.

Gerwin, Jos and Mergner, Gottfried (eds.) (1982), *Innere und äussere Kolonisation* (Interior and Exterior Colonization), Oldenburg: Bibliotheks und Informationssystem der Universität Oldenburg.

Gerwin, Jos and Mergner, Gottfried (eds.) (1983), *Alltäglichkeit und Kolonisierung* (Every Day's Life and Colonization), Oldenburg: Bibliotheks und Informationssystem der Universität Oldenburg.

Huston, Nancy (1983), 'Tales of War and Tears of Women', in Judith H. Stiehm (ed.), *Women and Men's Wars*, Oxford: Pergamon Press.

Lasswell, Harold D. (1941), 'The Garrison State and the Specialists on Violence', in *American Journal of Sociology*, January, pp. 455–68.

Lasswell, Harold D. (1962), 'The Garrison State Hypothesis Today', in S.P. Huntington (ed.), *Changing Patterns of Military Politics*, New York.

Prince, Magdalene (1909), *Südwestafrikanische Eindrücke* (Southwestafrican Impressions), Berlin.

Ruediger, Wilma (1962), *Frauen im Dienste der Menschlichkeit* (Women as Servants of Humanity), Munich: J.F. Lehmanns.

Stiehm, Judith H. (1983), 'The Protected, the Protector, the Defender', in Judith H. Stiehm (ed.), *Women and Men's Wars*, Oxford: Pergamon Press.

PART 3

MILITARY ECONOMY

8

The Impact of the Military Budget on Employment for Women

Marion Anderson
Employment Research Associates, Lansing, MI, USA.

This paper is based upon research done by Employment Research Associates on the impact of military spending upon the economy of the United States.

Since 1950 the military has been the largest purchaser of goods and services and the largest employer in the federal government. The military's share of the GNP has ranged from 5 per cent to 10 per cent depending upon whether or not we were at war. But at no time has it fallen to the minuscule level which it was before the Second World War. Nor has the size of the armed forces fallen below 3 million people during this period.

The question we are addressing here is: what is the impact of military spending upon employment for women? Does it create or destroy more job opportunities for them?

Our most recent study, *The Empty Pork Barrel: The Employment Cost of the Military Build-up 1981–1985*, shows what happened to jobs in our major industries in each of the fifty states during the Reagan military build-up. Our point of departure was the 1981 Pentagon budget. We said, give the Pentagon increases for inflation, and then measure the amount over and above this sum that was spent on the military between 1981 and 1985. During this period, 190 billion was spent in excess of the amount needed to cover inflation. This was the cost of the military build-up.

We then analysed how many jobs were created in the economy with this expenditure and found that there were 7,224,000 jobs. This included direct, indirect and induced jobs, including the jobs added to the armed forces.[1]

We then determined the number of jobs which would have been generated if this same 190 billion had been spent on normal civilian economic activities. This includes personal consumption expenditures; investments in factories, public works, and housing; and state, local and civilian federal government. If this sum had gone for expenditures on normal civilian economic activities it would have generated 8,370,000 jobs. *This is 1,146,000 more jobs than those generated by the military spending*.

So, military spending when compared to civilian spending caused a net loss of jobs in the nation. Thirty-five of the fifty states showed a net loss of jobs. Seventy per cent of the American public live in states which suffered a net loss of jobs.

This was the overall jobs impact. But what about women? How did women fare under this build-up? Worse. Over 80 per cent of the jobs forgone were jobs which would have gone for women.

The reason is straightforward. Neither the industries which are major employers of women nor the occupations in which women are engaged have a significant military component. There are relatively few women in the armed forces, only 9.5 per cent of the total, and virtually no women who are high executives in major military firms. The workforce in the military firms is also disproportionately male.[2] The Rockwells, General Dynamics and Lockheeds of the world are the preserves of white males.

Additionally, while there are relatively few women employed in military production,[3] there are many more employed in the production of consumer durable goods. Jobs in this high-wage industrial sector are among the first to be eliminated when consumer incomes are reduced by military-induced taxation. A hard-pressed consumer will focus first on necessities and will forgo larger purchases like a new car or refrigerator.

Even non-durable goods like textiles and food processing show a decrease in jobs when military and civilian spending are compared. There were, for instance, 10,700 fewer jobs for women in textile factories, and 95,000 fewer womens' jobs as food service workers during the 1981–5 period due to the military build-up.

Other occupations historically held by women were also hard hit. There were 288,000 fewer jobs for women secretaries and clerical workers, 125,000 fewer jobs for sales workers, 156,000 fewer jobs for teachers, and 55,000 fewer jobs for nurses. However, for the women who were aero-astronautic engineers there were 2,160 more jobs (Tables 8.1 and 8.2).

Table 8.1. Employment impact of the military build-up on industrial and government sectors 1981–5 (compared to spending the same sum on normal civilian economic activity 1981–5)

Industry	Net job gain or loss	% women	Net job gain or loss for women
Durable manufacture	1,562,135	0.2602	406,410
Non-durable manufacture	−196,940	0.4114	−81,030
Mining	−25,172	0.1233	−3,104
Construction	−133,583	0.0985	−13,155
Transport & public utility	−91,888	0.2658	−24,427
Finance, insurance, real estate	−141,554	0.5996	−84,875
Retail trade	−798,732	0.5074	−405,301
Wholesale trade	−88,480	0.2748	−24,311
Services	−610,644	0.5981	−365,237
State & local government	−837,119	0.5113	−427,986
Federal government, civilian	−84,245	0.3393	−28,588
Federal government, military			
Uniformed	114,100	0.0950	10,840
Non-uniformed	186,100	0.3393	63,151
Total number of women's jobs forgone			−977,613

Table 8.2. Employment impact of the military build-up on occupations, 1981–5 (compared to spending the same sum on normal civilian economic activity 1981–5)

Industry	Net job gain or loss	% women	Net job gain or loss for women
1 Aeronaut engineers	31,309	0.069	2,160
2 Chemical engineers	1,027	0.061	63
3 Civil engineers	−2,829	0.04	−113
4 Electrical engineers	31,945	0.061	1,949

Table 8.2. (contd.)

Industry	Net job gain or loss	% women	Net job gain or loss for women
5 Industrial engineers	15,314	0.11	1,685
6 Mechanical engineers	17,199	0.028	482
7 Metal & materials engineers	1,806	0.058	105
8 Mining-petro engineers	−578	0.058	−34
9 Sales & other engineers	6,511	0.058	378
10 Computer programmers	5,154	0.325	1,675
11 Computer analysts	3,643	0.313	1,140
12 Computer specialists & not elsewhere counted	1,220	0.296	361
13 Health technologists	−23,725	0.843	−20,000
14 Nurses, therapists	−59,259	0.928	-54,992
15 Physicians, dentists	−36,151	0.133	−4,808
16 Agri. bio. technicians	−1,196	0.291	−348
17 Chemical technicians	512	0.296	152
18 Draftspeople	16,462	0.175	2,881
19 Electrical technicians	20,163	0.125	2,520
20 Industrial engnr technicians	3,035	0.184	558
21 Mechanical engineering technicians	2,076	0.184	382
22 Math. technicians	−24	0.184	−4
23 Not elsewhere counted technicians	7,945	0.353	2,805
24 Pre K, K–6 teachers	−93,544	0.86	−80,447
25 7–12 teachers	−115,077	0.518	−59,610
26 Editors & reporters	−2,402	0.484	−1,163
27 Public relations	−2,202	0.501	−1,103
28 Not elsewhere counted writers & artists	−2,199	0.427	−939
29 Religious workers	−10,408	0.509	−5,298
30 Social scientists	−3,811	0.468	−1,784
31 Soc. & rec. workers	−30,776	0.431	−13,264
32 Post-secondary teachers	−42,677	0.363	−15,492
33 Accountants	-589	0.387	−228
34 Airline technicians	−340	0.021	−7
35 Architects	2,022	0.127	257
36 Farm & environment	−3,089	0.16	−494
37 Lawyers & judges	−5,726	0.158	−905
38 Librarians	−1,021	0.873	−891
39 Bio-phys. scientists	−1,260	0.205	−258
40 Math. specialists	−65	0.313	−20
41 Systems analysts	9,540	0.313	2,986

Table 8.2. (contd.)

Industry	Net job gain or loss	% women	Net job gain or loss for women
42 Labour relations workers	−5,415	0.523	−2,832
43 Not elsewhere counted research workers	−125	0.291	−36
44 Not elsewhere counted technicians & engineers	−6,842	0.184	−1,259
45 Vocational educational counsellors	−2,173	0.531	−1,154
46 Financial managers	−16,614	0.386	−6,413
47 Farm produce managers	−544	0.121	−66
48 Wholesale & retail buyers	−7,426	0.472	−3,505
49 Health administrators	−9,586	0.57	−5,464
50 Inspectors	−16,482	0.231	−3,807
51 Not elsewhere counted public administrators	−44,246	0.385	−17,035
52 Railroad conductors	−234	0.02	−5
53 Restaurant managers	−22,133	0.635	−14,054
54 Sales managers	−17,210	0.284	−4,888
55 College administrators	−98	0.414	−41
56 1–12 school admins	−479	0.414	−198
57 Not elsewhere counted administrators	−102,703	0.409	−42,005
58 Sales & advert agents	−520	0.372	−193
59 Insurance agents	−23,344	0.251	−5,859
60 Real estate agents	4,292	0.484	2,077
61 Stock & bond brokers	−5,415	0.236	−1,278
62 Not elsewhere counted sales workers	−179,253	0.697	−124,939
63 Insurance adjusters	−7,181	0.65	−4,668
64 Info. processing workers	−2,233	0.889	−1,985
65 Secretaries	−46,292	0.982	−45,458
66 Not elsewhere counted clerical	−284,895	0.852	−242,731
67 Electrical lineworkers	−1,852	0.056	−104
68 Electricians	13,144	0.015	197
69 Telephone installers	−4,879	0.099	−483
70 Not elsewhere counted construction	−11,304	0.018	−203
71 Forge & hammer workers	1,770	0.035	62
72 Furniture finishers	−840	0.167	−140
73 Locomotive engineers	−145	0.023	−3
74 Machinists	42,356	0.041	1,737
75 Repair & mechanics	−35,419	0.03	−1,063

Table 8.2. (contd.)

Industry	Net job gain or loss	% women	Net job gain or loss for women
76 Printing trades	−5,698	0.256	−1,459
77 Sheet-metal workers	14,590	0.045	657
78 Tool and die makers	17,035	0.012	204
79 Not elsewhere counted craftspeople	55,716	0.081	4,513
80 Machine operatives	34,400	0.421	14,482
81 Textile operators	−13,052	0.821	−18,716
82 Not elsewhere counted operatives	307,597	0.328	100,892
83 Mass transit workers	−8,713	0.078	−680
84 Railroad brake workers	−47	0.023	−1
85 Truck drivers	−36,880	0.032	−1,180
86 Not elsewhere counted transit operatives	−19,951	0.048	−958
87 Construction labourers	−17,611	0.021	−370
88 Other labourers	−84,322	0.194	−16,358
89 Cleaning workers	−33,899	0.386	−13,153
90 Food service workers	−150,022	0.633	−94,964
91 Health assistants	−102,367	0.892	−91,312
92 Personal service	−86,834	0.792	−68,772
93 Private household workers	−81,882	0.961	−78,689
94 Protective service	−177,831	0.128	−22,762
Federal gov. military			
Uniformed	114,100	0.095	10,840
Non-uniformed	186,102	0.437	81,326
Total number of women's jobs forgone			−955,923

The drastic shift in federal budget priorities, which has occurred over the last six years, clearly diminishes women's opportunities in the paid workforce. But at the same time the militarization of federal government activities constitutes an attack on women beyond the workplace.

High levels of military spending means less tax money going to the critical services which state and local governments provide. Less funds are available for schools, hospitals, libraries, social work, nursing homes, parks and recreation.

These are services to the entire community which decline as taxes are siphoned off year in and year out into the voracious maw of the Pentagon (see Appendix B at the end of this chapter, p. 141).

The decline of these services is especially hard on women. It robs them of job opportunities and it also diminishes services on which they rely. In recent years the United States has had an explosive growth in the number of families headed by single women. These people are especially dependent upon services generated by the state as they cannot afford to pay for private schools, expensive health care or costly recreation.

Cuts in social programmes not only affect women but also children and indeed the whole family structure, especially in the lower-income sectors of society. Because poverty in the United States affects women disproportionately, cuts in these programmes hit women the hardest. Increased military expenditures have come at a cost of reduced social programmes.

Since 1981 there have been real cuts in AFDC, food and nutrition programmes, medicare and medicaid, and in education and educational assistance. Since 1979 the number of poverty-stricken children has risen by 33 per cent.[4] America's infants die in greater numbers than those in twelve other industrialized countries. Our children are deprived of basic goods so we can produce weapons that we cannot afford either to build or to use (see Appendix A, p. 140).

Cuts in education to fuel the military build-up similarly harm women and children as we trade books for bombs. Even with the recent educational gains, women still have less education and job training than men.[5] Cutbacks in education will only maintain or exacerbate this inequality.

So as the cutback in critical public services causes a decline in the quality of life for all, it means a special deterioration in the quality of life for women.

There is evidence that the Soviet Union faces similar problems and corresponding social costs. As the global arms race intensifies, the Soviet government also drains resources from their people-oriented sectors into their military sector. *Their* society, *their* women, *their* children suffer needlessly as a result. When looking at the social costs of military spending, we must realize that this is not simply an issue for certain nations: it is a global problem. Any country that diverts resources to its military is doing so at a high cost to its civilian sector.

The implications of just this one particular example of a military build-up (not even military spending in general) are disturbing. Our work at Employment Research Associates clearly demonstrates that women bear a disproportionately large share of the economic burden of sustained high military spending.

APPENDIX A: EXAMPLES OF CUTS IN SOCIAL PROGRAMMES

Between 1986 and 1990, the Reagan administration has proposed $37.6 billion in cuts to federal support for families. These families are usually single-parent and often headed by women (*A Children's Defense Budget*, p. 29).

In 1983, Medicaid (a low-income health insurance plan) served only 70.7 children for every 100 in poverty. The President, none the less, has proposed a $1.1 billion cut in Medicaid. Other programmes for low-income families have been similarly cut and even eliminated in order to free up funds for the military budget (*ibid.*, p. 31).

Five billion dollars has been cut from child nutrition programmes in the past four years, and more cuts are proposed. Several million children have already lost school lunches as a result, and more cuts will simply mean more hungry, malnourished children (*ibid.*, p. 35).

The programme known as Revenue Sharing has been completely eliminated. This programme returned over $4 billion of federally collected tax dollars to state and local governments in 1986; it will return none in 1987. This money helped provide many services, including fire and police protection, education and health-care facilities. Thousands of jobs, primarily women's jobs, will be lost as a result.

APPENDIX B: FACTS ABOUT UNITED STATES SOCIAL PROGRAMMES AND WOMEN

Under present proposals, by 1990 each American will be spending $91 less in taxes on the needs of low-income families and $656.50 more on the military (*ibid.*, p. 29).

During the period from 1979 to 1984 the number of female-headed households below the poverty line increased by 2.9 million, a 21 per cent increase in only five years (*Statistical Abstract of the United States*, 1986, p. 458).

AFDC payments have not kept up with the cost of living. The maximum AFDC benefit for a family of three in January 1985 was less than 75 per cent of the poverty level in all but four of the fifty states. The President has proposed an additional $325 million cut to the AFDC programme (*A Children's Defense Budget*, pp. 33–4).

The number of poor and homeless families is rising, but funds for public housing were reduced by more than 15 per cent from 1985 to 1986 and the remainder will be halved in 1987 under administration proposals. Some 170,000 poor New York City families face a wait of between fifteen and eighteen years for housing. The wait is ten years for Washington, DC, six years for Pittsburgh, and similarly long in other US cities. Many of these poor families are headed by women (*ibid.*, p. 35.).

NOTES

1. Induced jobs are the jobs generated when people hired to make the armaments go out and buy clothing, cars and so on.
2. See Thomas Karier, Eastern Washington University, 'Wages in Defense Industries'.
3. Ibid.
4. Children's Defense Fund, *A Children's Defense Budget: An Analysis of the President's FY 1986 Budget and Children*, 1985.
5. *Statistical Abstract of the United States*, 1986, p. 134.

9

The Effect of Military Spending on Women in Italy

Elisabetta Addis
University of Abbruzzi, Italy

INTRODUCTION

Women and men may argue against militarism on many different rational or moral grounds because peace is, especially in our times, rational and moral. Women, though, are in a special position with respect to the military system.

The military system is a system which organizes people for a violent solution of a conflict between nations. Women's historical work was to create life and to nurture children, therefore 'feminine' and 'maternal' came to be associated with meekness, caring and mediation at times of conflict, rather than with aggressiveness, fighting and death. Hence women's exclusion from armies and their special ability to contribute to a culture of peace.

Feminism, moreover, has taught women new ways to deal with the problems of conflict and dispute—ways that can be applied to the problems of peace and war. Feminist women learnt to oppose male violence. Violence is a way of solving conflict by destroying the enemy. Feminist women chose to endure conflict with the men in their lives—fathers, husbands, sons—who are enemies to be loved and not to be destroyed. They have practised nonviolent conflict-solving in their daily lives and they have been the backbone of the anti-nuclear pacifism in the recent past.

Women's opposition to the military system is deeply grounded in their culture, as is the opposition of military people to feminine attitudes and values: the worst insult for a soldier is to be called feminine.

But there is more to it than that. As I am an economist by training, the natural question for me to ask was: what happens from the point of view of economics?

Cynthia Enloe has shown that women have been used by armies through the centuries: as nurses, camp-followers, prostitutes, secretaries, wives of officers and so on. In these roles, they received only a pittance from a considerable distribution of resources.

From the economic point of view, military spending, like all public spending reallocates resources exactly as taxation and public spending may reallocate resources between different areas of a country or between different classes of citizens. Military spending redistributes resources among genders when, as is the case in most countries, the employees of the army are only or mostly men.

In this chapter I document the extent of such redistribution in Italy. I try to measure, as well as I can, given the fact that economic accounting is not done by gender, how the employment, job opportunities, wages and economic status of women are affected by military spending.

Usually, pacifism's economic argument runs along the line: 'we oppose military spending because it uses resources to build guns instead of butter'. This is certainly true. Military spending wastes resources on nuclear weapons instead of giving women what they need, be it nurseries, health care, or in some countries, food.

But there is more—military spending is like a State subsidy which helps perpetuate the economic power of the male in society. It is an expenditure in favour of a special sector of society where women are either excluded or underrepresented; it creates job opportunities, education, and a network of economic influence for men; and it gives only to men, control over a large chunk of public consumption and army supplies. In this way it creates power for men in the civilian society as well. Women have an immediate economic reason to ask for the reduction of military spending because it perpetuates male economic power and female economic inferiority in civilian society.

The conclusion of such an analysis is not, and cannot be, that women must enter armies as they are and be soldiers exactly as men, and thus give up all their culture and values. But women must not be indifferent to military matters, especially today when new laws are about to be enacted which would enable women to enter the army in subordinate positions.[1]

Women and feminists must take a political initiative in two directions: first, to ask for a change of armies, weapons and defence systems as they are conceived today for there are alternative, nonviolent and non-nuclear models of defence. Secondly, and this is where my work may be useful, to measure the advantages that the military system creates for men, and to ask that the same amount of resources be spent on women and that the same opportunities should be given to them.

This chapter is organized in sections. In each section, I examine one of the channels of the economic impact of military spending. The channels along which military spending affects civilian redistribution of resources are:

a) employment
b) wages and income
c) economic power
d) education and training

I will deal with them in order and will introduce a digression on equity in the redistribution of economic resources, which is needed to make the discussion clearer. The amount of economic research, other than small sectoral studies, measuring the different impact of public spending on men and women is still very small. I also hope that this research may contribute to the development of gender-oriented economic research.

EMPLOYMENT

What is the impact of military expenditure on the employment of men and women? We consider employment in the all-male army equivalent to a massive programme of public employment, and we want to know its impact on male unemployment and what would be the impact of a programme of the same size on female unemployment.

In Italy, the Defence Ministry permanently employs 243,534 people. 190,028 of them are officers (therefore all male) and 53,364 are civilian. Moreover, at any given time, there are 272,057 serving one year of compulsory service which is mandatory for all men aged 18, and may be postponed until 26 by students.

There are, moreover, 11,000 young men who are conscientious objectors and choose the 20-month civilian service instead of enlistment. This raises the total to 525,449 people. They are all men, other than 3499 women among the civilian employees (0.6 per cent). Therefore we may say that there are 550,000 males employed by the Italian army.

Let us compare this with the data on the labour force, employed and unemployed.[2] First, those who are permanently employed by the Defence Ministry are included in the economic data as employed, whilst young draftees are counted as 'out of the labour force' like housewives and retired people.

This fact forces me to undertake a somewhat long and boring calculation to readjust the data to include them. Table 9.1 presents the results of my calculations.

In Table 9.1, heading A, I briefly present the situation today. Notwithstanding the fact that only 8 million women are in the labour force, and 15 million men, the unemployment rate for women is 17.10 per cent and for men is 6.7 per cent. In the age bracket of the draftees, the unemployment rate for women is 41.02 per cent and for men 27.4 per cent (including the draftees as out of the labour force).

If, instead, as I show under B, we consider the draftees employed, the unemployment rate for men decreases to 24.5 per cent at the draft age and 6.6 per cent for men of all ages. These are the numbers I will use in the following calculations.

We could have a decrease in youth unemployment and overall unemployment if a law such as that proposed by the women elected to the Lazio Regional council were enacted. This law introduced a civilian service of one year for women, similar to the law for conscientious objectors—to help in works of public utility, like environmental preservation, assistance to old and handicapped people, and so on. Such a service would be either mandatory or voluntary, and let us

Table 9.1. Four different scenarios of the effects of a civilian service on women employment (absolute values in thousands)

	Females		Males		Total	
	abs.val.	rate	abs.val.	rate	abs.val.	rate
A TODAY						
Labour force	8052		14986		23038	
Employed	6675	82.90%	13972	93.23%	20647	89.62%
Unemployed	1377	17.10%	1013	6.76%	2390	10.37%
AGE 14–24						
Labour force	1972		2316		4288	
Employed	1163	58.98%	1681	72.58%	2844	66.32%
Unemployed	809	41.02%	635	27.42%	1444	33.68%
B MALE LABOUR FORCE						
CORRECTED FOR DRAFT			15258		23310	
Employed			14204	93.09%	20879	89.57%
Unemployed			1013	6.64%	2390	10.25%
AGE 14–24			2588		4560	
Emp. 14–24			1953	75.46%	3116	68.33%
Unemp. 14–24			635	24.54%	1444	31.67%
SCENARIOS						
C						
Labour force	8052		15258		23310	
Employed	6946	86.26%	14204	93.09%	21150	90.73%
Unemployed	1105	13.72%	1013	6.64%	2118	9.09%
AGE 14–24	1972		2588		4560	
Empl. 14–2	1463	72.82%	1953	75.46%	3389	74.32%
Unemp. 14–24	537	27.23%	635	24.54%	1172	25.70%
D						
Pop. 14–70	21217		20477		41694	
Lab. F. Corrected	8221		15258		23479	
Employed	6947	84.50%	14204	93.09%	21151	90.08%
Unempl.	1274	15.50%	1013	6.64%	2287	9.74%
Pop. 14–24	4769		4818		9587	
LF 14–24	2141		2588		4729	
Emp. 14–24	1435	67.02%	1953	75.46%	3388	71.64%
Unemp. 144	706	32.98%	635	24.54%	1341	28.36%
E						
Employed	7187	87.42%	14204	93.09%	21391	91.11%
Unempl.	1034	12.58%	1013	6.64%	2047	8.72%
Empl. 14–24	1436	67.02%	1953	75.46%	3388	71.64%
Unempl. 14–24	537	27.23%	635	24.54%	1172	24.78%

Table 9.1. *(contd.)*

	Females		Males		Total	
	abs.val.	rate	abs.val.	rate	abs.val.	rate
F						
Employed	7038	85.61%	14204	93.09%	21242	90.47%
Unemployed	1183	14.39%	1013	6.64%	2196	9.35%
Empl. 14–24	1435	67.02%	1953	75.46%	3388	71.64%
Unempl. 14–24	706	32.98%	635	24.54%	1341	28.36%

assume it would be of the same size as the military service, that is 272,000 young women might be employed in it. Moreover, women of all ages might be permanently employed, either in the army or in civilian service, as men are permanently employed as army officers.

We might therefore envisage four scenarios, which are described under headings C, D, E, and F. In scenario C we assume that civilian service for women is voluntary. Therefore only those girls who today declare that they are either employed or looking for a job would enter it. Those who study or choose to work inside the family do not.

Therefore the female labour force participation rate would not change. Under such a hypothesis, the rate of unemployment of young women would fall from 41.02 per cent to 27.2 per cent, that is, would already be reduced almost to the male unemployment rate in the same age group.

In scenario D civilian service for women is mandatory. Therefore a number of girls who would not otherwise enter the labour force are included. The participation rate of young women in that age group is 44 per cent of the population. Therefore those 272,000 jobs will be shared, giving 44 per cent of them to those in the labour force and the other 56 per cent to those who are called in. This number (56 per cent of 272,000) must be counted in the labour force and in the number of employed. The results are shown in the table: the unemployment rate in the age group would decrease to 32 per cent. It is worth noting that the overall unemployment rate for women would also decrease.

In scenario E I assume that there is permanent employment of adult women in the same proportion as for adult men, under the hypothesis that women who are already in the labour force will be employed. This is, of course, the most favourable scenario. In it, the overall unemployment rate of women falls to from 17.1 per cent to 12.5 per cent, an improvement which cuts total female unemployment by 40 per cent.

In the last scenario again I take into account the fact that women have a lower participation rate in the labour force, and I assume, therefore, that women are permanently employed by the army only in the same proportion as they participate in the labour force, instead of in the same number. Even such a solution would, as it is shown in F, greatly improve the present situation.

We have been talking only of the direct effect of military employment. There is also an indirect effect of military spending on employment—that men and women are employed in providing military supplies. There is no reason to believe that the proportion of women in this kind of industry is greater than the average, and certainly it is not enough to counterbalance the bias created by male employment in the army.

THE QUESTION OF TAXES

The objection that I mentioned at the end of the above chapter brings forward the question: how much of public resources are women entitled to?

There are different concepts of fiscal justice. Some economists claim that each taxpayer should receive from the State as much service as he or she pays in taxes. Alternatively, fiscal policy should be progressive, taking more from the rich and giving more to the poor. How progressive?—of course, not so progressive as to make the rich poor. In fact, the progressiveness of the fiscal system is usually only apparent at the moment of contribution (rich people pay a more than proportional share) but less so at the moment of expenditure (rich communities and people get better public services than poor communities and people). Roughly speaking, in order to keep a fiscal regime acceptable to the taxpayers, public spending will redistribute resources according to criteria which take account of the political (electoral) power of the recipients and the amount of tax paid. What will count will be their number, their degree of political organization, and the contribution to the economy.

Women, we know, are little more than half the population. Their degree of autonomous political organization is still small, but it is improving. What about their contribution to the economy?

There is no doubt that since fewer women than men work for a wage, they do not contribute as much to public finances and therefore it might be argued that they deserve less transfer of public expenditure than men. But, as we all know, all women's work in the home, even if it had a value in the market, does not have any economic value when it is given in the household. All economic accounting related to the contribution of women will be distorted by the fact that the housewife's work does not enter national accounting.[3]

The Finance Ministry, which collect taxes, does not give data on the sex of the taxpayer, therefore we do not know exactly how much each gender contributes, even among participants in the market. Even if provided, the information would be very distorted because, due to the peculiarity of Italian tax law, joint filing with a non-working wife is a way to descend the tax bracket, and a number of women report earnings which are not theirs so that the family pays less. However, if we count as taxpayers only women who earn their income working for wages or have an independent income from property and assets, probably women contribute less because their wages are lower. The discrimination against women in wages would therefore be accounted against them.

For this reason, as well as because of the unaccounted housework, I believe that in the case of women less attention should be paid to the amount of their contribution (which is still such that they are entitled to some of the benefits denied them because of military spending) as to their number; however, it will of course be of paramount importance that women organize politically to benefit in the fiscal compromise.

WAGES, INCOME AND INCOME DISTRIBUTION

Distribution of income is a key feature of a society. What commodities are produced depends on who has the money to buy them. Income distribution affects the very shape of our daily life.

The distribution of income and income differential between men and women are affected by the fact that as large an employer as the army discriminates in favour of male employment. There is a direct and an indirect effect of army employment on the distribution of income. The direct effect is due to the fact that only men are employed and only men are allowed to earn an income through the army. This income accrues only to the male sector of society.

Moreover, the salaries of the officers who are permanent army staff is in the same scale as for other civil servants, even though the standard of education of the army is lower than that of other government employees. The seniority of officers at a given age, therefore, tends to be higher, and the salary accordingly; moreover, unlike civil servants, officers did not pay for their education. The government, in other words, discriminates in favour of officers and against other civilian government employees, which includes women. These are two direct effects of military spending on income distribution among genders.

INDIRECT EFFECTS ON INCOME

Employment and wages show direct effects of military spending; in addition, there are indirect effects.

The first one occurs because employment in the army reduces the supply of men in the civilian labour market and therefore (allowing for imperfect substitution of women for men) increases the wages of men. In plain English, there are fewer men to be hired, and therefore, if you really want a man and you do not want to hire a woman instead, you have to pay more. This kind of effect is very difficult to measure because it is difficult to evaluate the elasticity of substitution between male and female labour.

I have tried to measure this indirect effect but it proved impossible. In a country like Italy where enlistment affects men of between 19 and 24 years, such an effect might have been deduced from the fact that the earnings of young women (of the age at which enlistment drains the male labour supply) are proportionately lower than the earnings of young men than the earnings of older women compared to those of older men (when the effect of army employment on labour supply is smaller).

Although some estimates exist of the overall wage differential among the sexes (women earn 82 per cent of what men earn for comparable work, but 60 per cent if we take account of the fact that women are in lower tiers of hierarchy, seniority and qualification) I could not find in the official data of the ISTAT (the National Institute of Statistics) a disaggregation of earnings by sex *and* age (either one but not both).

Although the high unemployment rate may reduce the difference between earnings of young people of different sex, it is probably true that young women enter adulthood with a feeling of incompetence, because nobody wants their skills and a greater sense of insecurity because they are not able to earn a living. This feeling of inadequacy would certainly change if 300,000 young women were called into some useful activity at the same age at which men are called into the army.

EDUCATION, TRAINING AND OTHER ACCUMULATION OF HUMAN CAPITAL

Training—job training—is given to men when they are recruited by the army. This geographical, mechanical, and also political knowledge acquired in military training is denied to women. This knowledge is valuable *per se*, and also it is marketable. It therefore increases the wages of the young men who enter the civilian labour market after having been in the army. The net benefit of this job training is spread over a lifetime.

The army widely advertises this kind of benefit. I was not able to find an indication of the number of young men who find a civilian job based on the skills they earned in military service. This applies mostly to young men who are called up as soon as they are 18, and who did not have the opportunity for better education. It does not apply to the increasing number who postpone enlistment until they have left college. However small and decreasing this number might be, it is still true that some young men do benefit from job training in the army, and that no woman does.

This increase in skills that men acquire in the army adds to the difference in skills among men and women which already exists. The difference becomes one of the channels through which unequal earnings accrue to men and women, and thus affect income distribution.

THE NET OF ECONOMIC POWER

It is important to point out that the army's high-level officers decide on contracts for materials, from food to clothes to weapons. Because of this power high-ranking officers can be compared to managers of large industries and the existence of contractors depends on their decisions. They build a network of economic relationships and even of economic control which provides them with respect, influence, opportunities and often financial reward.

This is an important source of social power and economic decision-making from which women are excluded. The exact measure of this kind of power is not easy to define but the flow of expenditure can be traced back to those who made the decisions and therefore one can at least describe and map such a power.

THE QUESTION OF MANDATORY MILITARY SERVICE

Employment in the army as a permantly employed officer is

certainly a benefit. Enlistment, however, is considered by most young men as a nuisance that they would be willing to forgo if they only could.

However this is mostly due to the unnecessary hardships of the barrack environment. The requirement of discipline often results in a need to obey orders which defy intelligence and the requirements of physical fitness may mean working men to exhaustion. The all-male environment induces permanent competition to establish internal hierarchies, to prove manhood at the expenses of 'wimps' and older soldiers traditionally may submit newcomers to cruel practical jokes that stand for initiation rites.

I would not hold, nor would anybody, that enlisted men are the main beneficiaries of employment in the army—the main beneficiaries from employment in the army are the professional officers and men in general as part of society.

CIVILIAN SERVICE

In Italy those who are willing to pay the cost of doing civilian instead of military service are allowed to do so.

Military service lasts one year, civilian service lasts two years. The pay is the same for civilian and military and is very low, about 120 US$ per month. The military draftees get free room and board, and those who choose civilian service get an equivalent of 135 US$ which, even accounting for the difference in purchashing power, is still only about one-fourth of minimum wages, and not enough to provide room and board.

These conscientious objectors become firefighters, work in communities for handicapped, in charities, in reforestation programmes, in museums and the restoration of art, in civilian service with organizations which distribute government subsidies in third world countries, in trade unions and in other non-profit making organizations and institutions.

Notwithstanding the 'penalty' of serving double-time, the preference for civilian service has increased sharply—from 624 in 1976 to 11, 359 in 1983—and is still increasing. This rapid growth is probably due to the 'nominative call' regulation. In the first years of the civilian service programme, very few institutions used conscientious objectors, and the government decided to allow personal approaches for work. Since then, when applying for civilian service, young men can lobby an institution so that when their request is approved they can be allocated to the same institution. This gives institutions and organizations a cheap supply of work for two years, and offers young men a period of paid apprenticeship. Often, young men who start work in reforestation, museums or trade unions are then hired permanently by the same, or related, jobs.

Serving double-time is clearly meant to punish young men who are pacifists or consider military training a waste of time. Conscientious objectors' associations complain with good reason, that the law assumes that work for the community is not as valuable as that for the army.

Nonetheless, working for two years as a conscientious objector in a community or a project will give a young man training experience, and often the possibility of finding a permanent job in related areas. This is an opportunity for personal advancement that is denied to young women.

Of all the 'privileges' of the military condition, this is the one I believe women must begin to claim. The civilian service should be reduced to one year, paid at a minimum-wage level so as to allow independent subsistence and be open to men and women.[4]

CONCLUSION

Military spending is part of a public spending which belongs to both men and women. Women contributed to public finance as workers in paid employment and as workers in the household. Military spending redistributes this in favour of men and creates employment opportunities, income opportunities and economic power in favour of male citizens only.

Women should therefore ask for a reform of the army, to allow the inclusion of women, and the changing of the present model of defence in favour of a model which is non-nuclear and purely defensive.

They should, moreover, claim from the State resources comparable in size to military spending which is to be used to organize civilian service for young women in public utilities (defence of the environment, cultural and artistic monuments, assistance to the old and the handicapped and so on). Older women could also be employed. Such a programme would improve the statistics of female unemployment and give women new opportunities for income and career.

This would be a step towards the civilization of armies and the demilitarization of society, which is the best guarantee for a long-lasting peace.

NOTES

1. The Italian government approved a law proposal presented by the Defence Minister, Mr Spadolini. The main points of this proposal, which of course may change during the parliamentary process, are:
(1) Military service for women only on a voluntary basis and only at the career level, that is at the level of petty officers, starting from corporal on. Women would, in other words, enter as if they were men who, after the two years of draft, ask to be permanently employed by the army.
(2) The economic status would be the same as that of men of the same level.
(3) The proposal states that women cannot be employed in combat units and direct fighting.
(4) The military academies are open also to women. Women would have special uniforms. Maternity leaves and benefits would be the same as in the other governmental jobs (rather good, five months maternity and other benefits). I, and the group of pacifist women to which I belong, are rather critical about this law.
2. Let me remind non-economists that the labour force is by definition made up of two parts: employed, who declared to the census officers that they held a job and unemployed, who declared that they do not hold a job and that they are looking for one. Those who are not looking for a job, either because they are housewives, retired, under military obligation, or independently wealthy are not counted in the labour force. The unemployment rate is the percentage of unemployed over the labour force.
3. This is a problem which will reappear often when discussing gender-oriented economic topics, and which needs to be addressed urgently.
4. Recently, a very authoritative figure has supported this view, which we have been promoting for some time, the Archbishop of Milan, Cardinal Pappalardo. Even though I am not religious, I would welcome the support of the Catholics for the request of voluntary civilian service for women, as an alternative possibility, or else as a complement, to the proposal to Parliament.

10

The Impact of Industrial Development: Military Build-up and Its Effect on Women

Tsehai Berhane-Selassie
Institute of African Alternatives, UK

This paper is divided into two parts: the first part, intended to demonstrate the magnitude and basic character of the arms industry, deals generally with the Third World, with emphasis on Africa. It concerns itself with the contemporary arms industry and trade. The second part intends to demonstrate the long-term impact of the arms trade on women and societies in the Third World. A part of Ethiopian history is used to demonstrate the point, tracing the historical process whereby state and international politics affected the position of women in Ethiopian society, marginalizing them and forcing the rulers of the country to adopt a Eurocentric view about women. It will be noted that the process was very gradual, producing almost an unconscious result which made the history of women almost intractable.

The first part of the paper is based on research made by British peace campaigners such as Campaigns Against the Arms Trade (CAAT) and Third World First. The second part is based on my own research on Ethiopian military and political systems. A useful reading on Ethiopian women is my report for the *Change* series, entitled 'In Search of Ethiopian Women'.

Both sections are from the perspective of the Third World, so that the concerns of Western peace campaigners, such as sexuality and the military, do not feature in the discussion. More pressing issues of life and death through war and threatened livelihoods—such as through the economic pressures which affected food production, and therefore access to land—are the main topics.

Before we go into the subject there are two generalizations that must be made in order to remind ourselves of the background to industrial development and the place of women in it. The first is that industrial development, which began in the eighteenth century and culminated in intensive commercial competition among people in the northern hemisphere, left women in the margin. In addition, the newly developing European nations which competed among themselves for the control of raw materials for the manufacturing plants, conquered and then made the rest of the world dependent on them. Competition for the control of resources was and has remained the mainstay of politics and diplomacy among states in the northern hemisphere, leaving no room for fair and equal interplay with those in the south. The quest for raw materials was thus at the core of nineteenth-century colonialism, and control of it is now at the core of neo-colonialism. This domination has severe consequences for women in the so-called Third World which we will mention later.

Related to this is the emphasis on technological science which has run away with itself. Advancement in technology has led to indiscriminate manufacture of goods which are dangerous to health and the environment. In areas such as nuclear power, electronics and even seemingly innocent electricity, women have been kept out of decision-making positions. Yet some of them, especially from the Third World, are found in the industry as line workers; even when they are not involved in it, they have to bear the brunt of its consequences. In a thinly disguised activity, industrialized countries use their technology ruthlessly not only for expanding and protecting their commercial interests but also for their dangerous and uncontrolled experiments. Especially the nuclear industry is the most powerful because it enjoys open support of governments. It has therefore been instrumental in escalating conflict using dangerous weapons.

The experiments, too, have been directly hitting women in the Third World as local populations there have neither the knowledge nor the power to stop them. The follow up to this is the massive migration, famine and severe environmental and health problems affecting women.

The second generalization we have to remind ourselves of is the impact of industrialization on the order of society. The Industrial Revolution in Europe intensified urbanization as opposed to rural life and dependency on agriculture. In the process women became established in the service sector, for the industries and the style of life required for sustaining them. Men developed the skill that put them in the fore of employment, innovation and self-advancement. They continue to dominate society so much so that Western societies are the most intensely patriarchal. A whole way of life, the expectation of individuals, and so on, have become standardized according to Western men's position in the industrialized world. Regarding women as subordinate and inferior has gained currency because of the industrialized society's domination. The more the industrialized world gains control of the rest of the world, the more these ideals have travelled to the detriment of women elsewhere. A century of the women's movement has not yet managed to alter this state of affairs despite the challenges it has been posing to patriarchy.

Even though male domination is more or less universal, the boost industrialization has given it must not be underestimated. We must remember that the concept of the 'lady', the feminine woman is a particularly European mode of mannerism and behaviour. Those who follow the Marxist line of analysis will recognize that the idea of the feminine lady began when class distinctions became acute with the emergence of the working classes servicing the industries. Jobs that men and women can do became redefined with whatever women can take being designated as 'women's work'. Often these gendered jobs are lowly paid and are seen against the background of the work done. With these two broad generalizations in mind, I will narrow the discussion to a particular sector of industry, the arms industry, as it is most directly relevant to the question of military build-up and the direct impact it has on women. In particular I will deal with the impact it has on women in the Third World.

Commercializing the arms industry has two strands both of which still pertain to competition among states in the northern hemisphere. Competition extends also to the extraction of raw materials and to the selling of skills and services. The arms-manufacturing world perpetuates the conditions of war in ways that are intractable. Nevertheless, I will try to demonstrate the potential that exists for selling any category of arms in Africa before I go on to demonstrate how the ideals of the 'feminine' and the 'lady' were transmitted to our societies, how that is done through war, the arms trade and the need to keep the buying options open. The impact of creating the atmosphere or the conditions for sustaining the market for the industry is more long-lasting and substantial than the immediately visible impact of poverty and the loss of life.

If we study the map of the world, we will note that there are endless trouble spots around the globe, most of them in parts of the Third World which do not have the capacity to manufacture the arms required for them. In this context, and especially with regard to African countries, we should understand warfare as any conflict generated and sustained by deliberately organized armed groups incurring the loss of life and damage to property. In the case of Africa this will include the so-called arms gangs raiding and pillaging villages, for instance in north western Uganda before Savimbi came to power in 1986. Whether their impetus is 'tribal' or nationalistic, we should carefully examine it before we dismiss the conflict they generate as non-militaristic.[1] From that point of view very few African countries are free from conflict which entails the buying and selling of arms.

It is essential to enumerate the war spots in Africa in order to show the correlation between the horrific and short-term economic problems of famine which has affected women and children the most.

One of the major area of famine has been Southern Africa, including countries such as Mozambique, Angola, Tanzania, Zimbabwe and Zambia. These countries have suffered famine and general economic downfall while at the same time conducting warfare against organized groups supported by the so-called Republic of South Africa. That country has a nuclear plant which produces bomb-grade plutonium which it built with the help of Israel. The racist regime is supported by Israel, because there is profit to be made out of producing bomb-grade plutonium and indeed bombs.[2] Israel and South Africa also conduct joint experiments, tests and other programmes in collaboration, thus strengthening the apartheid South Africa's political status and economic power just when Africans are fighting for their independence. Its economic position in the whole region of Southern Africa has dire consequences for women. In particular, the structure of migrant labour from neighbouring countries to the mines and industries of South Africa has helped create such a dependency that the manufacturing industries of South Africa are sustained by male migrant labourers, who because of the laws of apartheid, have to remain separated from their rural-based wives, children and extended families, often for good. Women are left behind with neither sustained help in agricultural work from their men nor with the wage earned by them. South Africa gains from the cheap labour it thus recruits, and maintains its political power by its alliance with Israel and other arms suppliers. Moreover, inside South Africa itself it operated a system of pushing Africans out of the fertile lands into the arid regions where formerly self-sufficient farmers are dying of starvation.[3] The same situation exists in Namibia, which South Africa is occupying illegally.

Further to the north, in Uganda, Sudan, Ethiopia and Chad, there is conflict which again is being fuelled by arms dealers such as Adnan Khashoggi, who have not a speck of political or moral justification—only the desire for profit. In Ethiopia and Chad there is direct involvement by foreign government: in Chad, Libya and France; in Ethiopia, the Soviet Union and the United States, alongside a host of individuals and other elements.

It is interesting to note that in these countries the conflicts have local reasons, at least in their immediate background, which, had everything been equal, could have been resolved politically and peacefully. It is too long and complicated to go into these reasons, which partly and directly link to the availability of weapons escalating the simple conflict into full-fledged wars. One of the direct results is the creation of refugees, the majority of whom are women. According to the United Nations High Commission for Refugees (UNHCR), there are at least half a million Ethiopian refugees fleeing to surrounding countries. The number is difficult to pinpoint as it fluctuates according to the political relationships between

Ethiopia and her neighbours, some of whom, such as Djibuti, manage to return the refugees some of the time while others, such as Sudan, sometimes manage to attract more of them out. Such intervention in the lives of refugees depends on whether it is exigetical to the politics of the leaders in power. In the last days of the deposed Sudanese president Numeiri, about 7,000 people were going into Sudan each day due to his alliance with Israel, which was then stealing out the Falasha, the Jews of Ethiopia. Similarly, the conflict between northern Sudan and southern Sudan, which is for the most part local in origin, is generating refugees into Ethiopia.

As stated above, the majority of the refugees in Sudan and the other neighbouring states around Ethiopia are women. Some, notably the 'Eritreans', seek domestic employment in the Middle East, while most remain in the most horrendous situations in the refugee camps in Sudan. The sad thing is that none of these countries inside Africa are economically better off than the others so that refugees fare far worse than in their own homes. In addition, the women are open to sexual exploitation both within the refugee camps, by their own men, and by the men of the host societies. Most young women who pass into exile through the neighbouring countries are subjected to humiliations of all sorts.

In all of these countries there are internal refugees who run away from areas of conflict and the subsequent poverty. Sometimes this has been aggravated by many seasons of drought. Refugees from Tigre have been deliberately brought out to Sudan by the party at conflict with the Ethiopian government for justifying its war in the eyes of the world. Some of them are in camps 'under the control of the guerillas'. Whatever the reason for the existence of refugees, women form the majority among the refugees. Both locally and abroad, they are also lumbered with the care of their children. Very often the men are away either looking for economic opportunities, or in some instances fighting on one side or the other of the conflict. Although it was traditional for women to participate in Ethiopian battlefields (as discussed below), nowadays it is only men who decide and lead the battles which generate all the conflicts and refugees. However, some people sing the praises of the advances made in the Tigre refugee camps in terms of self-realization, and laud that the women can also join and fight on the battlefield. This distorts the historical background of the region in general and that of women in particular. What is interesting is that not only are guns supplied and conflicts fuelled, but political myths are also created and sustained in the process, often by foreigners.

Similarly destructive, confusing and, for women, detrimental conflicts exist in Chad and in Morocco. These and other Third World wars are important to note in order to understand the wider ramifications of the arms industry. In Latin America there is war in Nicaragua, Colombia, El Salvador, Peru, Guatemala, Chile and so on. In South-East Asia there is war in the Philippines, in Thailand and Sri Lanka. Some of the wars are international: Iran–Iraq, Palestine/Israel/Lebanon/Syria complex, and all the latent territorial and neighbourhood conflicts in Africa. Although all of these have local reasons and the responsibility may lie with the local governments, the condition is effectively a result of the commercialization of the arms industry. (This is not saying that it is a result of a conspiracy, but that it is undeniably a situation which is being successfully exploited by arms-dealer governments and individuals.)

This is best demonstrated by the latest item of arms trade: that of nuclear power, which is being exported from the northern hemisphere to the 'Third World' countries. Currently in the Third World there are no less than forty-one nuclear reactors, allegedly introduced for producing power for civilian use but actually producing bomb-grade plutonium. A close study made by Asa Moberg in *Links: 'Critical Mass'*,[4] show that the International Atomic Energy Agency of the United Nations has estimated that only between ten and twenty countries have the power grids and infrastructure to make nuclear development possible. Where nuclear plants have been installed they have been left unsafe (being only single reactors instead of the normal two). Among others, these are installed in Colombia, Zaire, Morocco and Egypt. In other parts of Africa there are three in South Africa and two in Algeria. Not only is the need for them dubious, but they are also extremely expensive to maintain.

The link with women's position is that the local governments subject their population to austerity programmes and repressions, the brunt of which fall on women. In some ghastly instances such as the Morong plant in the Philippines, the reactor was forced on the state by the World Bank when a loan was being contracted from it. It would not give the loan without agreement on the installation of a nuclear plant! Only a few 'Third World' countries such as South Africa, China and Israel have developed their own reactors without external pressure of this sort. The bomb-grade plutonium produced is often exported back to the northern hemisphere. Using the arms industry through nuclear plants are of course additional to the extraction of uranium from places like Niger, Namibia and India. At least in Namibia and Niger the population around the mines have very little protection from the plutonium.

The production and testing of bombs have had severe consequences for the health of women, and at least in Africa there is a total blackout of information both from the French, who carry out their tests in the Sahara, and the South Africans and the Israelis, who test theirs in the Kalahari. The impact of the nuclear industry on Africa is not fully researched, but I would submit that the atmosphere changes and the severe famine period that occurred over the last decade in the Sahel and in Southern Africa are interconnected.[5]

From the perspective of women's history, the introduction of any weapon into the 'Third World' is sometimes less direct than the case of the Morong plant in the Philippines and the World Bank or the sale of arms by Adnan Khashoggi. As a result of the ethos of competition by the arms industry, which needs to find *and control* markets and resources for its trade, there have developed intricate, thoroughly intertwined, political and economic systems of influence. Some of the channels of influence do not even relate directly to gun-running, as it were. What I am trying to say is better demonstrated by an example. I will cite how Ethiopian women lost their access to land and their means of asserting their right to it. The reader will note that the historical reference required to demonstrate the point is neither a romantic nor a nostalgic flashback to a historical period that is no more. Rather it is a necessary *recognition of women's past, Africa's historical heritage and a simple demonstration of a process of change in a traditional society.*

Historically, in Ethiopia land was owned theoretically by the 'king of kings', wrongly translated as 'emperor' or 'queen of kings', also wrongly rendered as 'empress'. In reality, it was owned communally, although it was often controlled by the most powerful warrior, which could be either a man or a woman, though very often the former. The system is too complex to deal with here,[6] but, roughly, it worked as follows. Warriorhood was a means of asserting control over a large tract of communal land, access to which would be granted to the retainers. Men and women who failed to ensure their rights of access to property by proving their warriorhood qualities were not allowed to even inherit their parents' communal land rights; nor were they able to acquire land elsewhere as land was not commercialized. This system brought women to the battlefield (admittedly sometimes by proxy) and to positions of political power, which I have talked about elsewhere.[7] Even during the first colonial encounter of 1886, when Italian invaders were beaten back, women's participation was quite substantial. Women's participation on the battlefield changed as a result of further, anachronistic, colonial pressure by Fascist Italy in the 1930s.

It is these pressures which partly demonstrate how the industrial system of Europe collectively worked against women in Ethiopia. In Italy, a combination of building up the nation, the economic crisis of the 1930s causing massive unemployment, and the defeat in 1896, was used by the Fascist dictator Mussolini to seek a diversion, preferably a colonial base in Africa for strenghtening his power. Ethiopia was his target. His political bureau, staffed by racist ethnographers and ambitious politicians, successfully campaigned and convinced the world that an arms embargo should be imposed against Ethiopia. An image of Ethiopia as a savage, barbaric and undemocratic society and government was promoted with all possible means. At the same time, the Ethiopian rulers, including 'Emperors' Yohannes IV (d.1879), Menelik II (d.1913), 'Empress' Zawditu (d.1930), had been cultivating friendships with both sides of the conflict in the First World War, and later with everybody who could extend friendship. The younger courtiers, including the late 'Emperor' Haile-Selassie, were brought under the influence of European values to the point of accepting certain precepts of European culture.[8] One of these was the idea that women were 'ladies' and 'feminine' in the European sense of the word. Thus, with the decrease in the volume of the arms trade as a result of the embargo, Haile-Selassie decreed that 'no woman should carry the gun'. There was a lot of objection to the decree, especially in the rural areas, and administrators found it difficult to implement it. The decree stayed in force until the Italian invasion in October 1935.

However, as soon as the mobilization drum was beaten throughout the country in response to Italian aggression, women simply took their guns and went to the front. After the battles at the front of invasion were over by May 1936 (October 1936 in the southern front), most resorted to the guerrilla warfare which was sustained throughout the five-year period of Italian occupation.[9] When it was over in 1940/1, and Haile Selassie was brought back to Ethiopia by the British forces in alliance with the guerillas after Italy declared war on Britain, the women were effectively told that they had no place in the army. Indeed, the army was 'modernized' with the help of the British, who set up a standing army and recruited only men accordingly.

In 1971 I was interviewing one of these women veterans when something extraordinary happened which kept me puzzled for a long time afterwards. During the interview her daughter and grand-daughter were with her, and I was quizzing her why and how she mustered troops and fought during the occupation period. My question arose of course out of my own experience as a postwar generation with very little knowledge of the history of Ethiopian women. She suddenly became on her guard and said, 'You want me to get killed!' Then she asked the other two to leave us alone. After they did, she brought out a five *birr* (Ethiopian currency) note and pressing it into my hands said that I should keep up my good work and write that she fought because 'she did not want to lose her father's property to anybody else'. She also intimated that when she started her guerilla activity, in defiance of the government decree, she had to dig out her father's gun, which was hidden in 1930. It was clear she was not bribing me, although she was not giving me the money in front of witnesses; she was rewarding me for something: for asking the right questions. Before then she had simply been telling me, like all the resistance fighters used to do, that she fought against the Italians to protect her country, her religion and her 'king of kings'. When I later came to realize the history of the past, this particular gesture encapsulated for me the simmering resentment women like her had towards the 'modern' system, which had deprived them of access to the main means of production, land.

The trade embargo on Ethiopia had a dramatic effect on the military tradition of the country and the economic position of women. Indeed, its consequences were far-reaching. In the decades following 1941, the emperor continued to give land grants for services rendered, especially for military service. Because women were not allowed into it, they were left out of the new redistribution of land by his government. Moreover, land eventually became commercialized, and with women having no economic power to purchase it, they continued to lose out. Also the idea of the man as 'head of the household' became so entrenched that when the socialist revolution of 1974 occurred, and total redistribution of land took place, quite a large proportion of rural women were left in the lurch. They either had to migrate or struggle for recognition as 'heads of households'. Ethiopia being an agricultural-based country, it is not difficult to see the dire consequences this has for women whose livelihood, too, derives from the land.

Relating this to the current arms trade reveals yet another historical process: that of myth-building by various groups interested in turning the society into a heavily militarized system. The guerilla fighters of Eritrea and Tigre are now celebrating the 'new' progress made in the equality between men and women to the point where they can now fight on the battlefield. The liberalism in terms of the equality for women that go into that celebration is a political point with which support and firearms are raised on behalf of the guerilla war which has been going on for more than two decades. It ignores the history of women's participation in the past, and facilitates the militarisation process, meanwhile creating a new myth.

CONCLUSION

As the example of the arms industry, with its inherent character of competition for the control of markets and resources for the arms trade show, those who own the industry are still in control of what the Third World societies can or cannot buy. Thus even if Third World societies put themselves in a position which requires them to buy arms, the lives of women become determined by the diplomatic relations between arms dealers and producers in the northern hemisphere. Italy got away with having a trade embargo against Ethiopia. Whereas Ethiopian women were formerly within a structure which enabled them to compete with men for positions of political power, the arms embargo facilitated a change whereby they were totally marginalized in the political and economic power structure. In the short term, the effect of Italian military build-up, at the expense of the Ethiopian, was traumatic for women. It essentially undermined their political and economic *power base* in the society. The impact of the industry is more subtle and the sources of its influence intractable. In Africa where societies are constantly in danger of fragmenting into linguistic groups and fighting among themselves, the long-term effects of similar decisions can be eventually destructive. Moreover, the growing volume and magnitude of the weapons in the market, including nuclear plants, are absolutely beyond the control of even the dealers involved in the trade.

NOTES

1. There is a false assumption that weapons used only by regular troops are harmful. However, transactions by weapons are required equally by those who systematically use weapons. These range from marauding bands of either liberation movements or any opposition groups to straightforward bandits. All of these invoke government reaction if

nothing else and ultimately involve regular troops in armed conflict. Indeed, superpowers use such bands to destabilize Third World governments they dislike. The conflicts they generate should not be underestimated by those who concern themselves with militarization.

2. Jane Hunter, *Undercutting Sanctions: Israel, the U.S. and South Africa*, (Washington: Middle East Associates, 1986), pp. 8–9, 12–17; Jenny Hammond 'The Real Costs of Nuclearisation', *Links: Critical Mass* 26 (1986): 2, 6.
3. Hunter, pp. 41–2; Lesley Lawson, *Working Women in South Africa* (London: Pluto Press, 1986), pp. 94–7; 20 South African Photographers, *South Africa: The Cordoned Heart* (Cape Town: The Gallery Press, 1986), pp. 9, 10, et passim.
4. Asa Moberg, 'Nuclear Power in Crisis', *Links: Critical Mass* 26 (1986): 30–1.
5. Hammond, pp. 6–7.
6. R. Pankhurst, *Economic History of Ethiopia* (Addis Ababa, 1968), pp. 135–81, 545–608.
7. Tsehai Berhane-Selassi, 'Women Guerilla Fighters', *North-East African Studies*, Vol. I, no. 3 (Michigan 1979/80), pp. 73–83; idem, 'In Search of Ethiopian Women', *Change, International Reports: Women and Society*, No. 11. (London [1984]), pp. 4–6.
8. Haile-Selassie was brought up under the influence of French tutors. See for example his autobiography.
9. See Berhane-Selassie, 'Women Guerilla Fighters', pp. 73–83.

PART 4

LIBERATION STRUGGLES AND THE LIBERATION OF WOMEN

11

The Role of Women during the Algerian Liberation Struggle and after; Nationalism as a Concept and as a Practice towards both the Power of the Army and the Militarization of the People

Marie-Aimée Hélie-Lucas
Women Living under Muslim Laws
International Solidarity Network, Algeria and France

This paper is about the role of women during the Algerian liberation struggle and after; about nationalism as a concept and as a practice towards both the power of the army and the militarization of the people. This paper is about our ignorance and fundamental distrust of peace movements; how this has been built into our consciousness; about how we have been locked into nationalism. This paper is about how long and difficult a process it is to become a dissident without betraying one's loyalties, without losing one's own identity.

1. *The role of women during the Algerian liberation struggle—in the military struggle, in the political struggle and in the cultural struggle (women as keepers of tradition and national identity); the nature of underground struggle and the concept of 'people at war'; their effect on obedience, morality and conformity of the citizen; nationalism and the military as a long-term ideology shaping people's consciousness; women as the carriers of the warriors.*

The image that the outside world formed of women in the Algerian liberation struggle is shaped by Frantz Fanon's books, a very widely distributed film called 'The Battle of Algiers', and the true story of a few national heroines. From these sources, the Algerian woman appears as a freedom fighter who carried arms against French colonialism and its army, a 'terrorist' who put bombs in the city during the 'battle of Algiers', an equal to men in the struggle, a person in her full right who shared decision-making both at the political level and at the military level.

These myths hardly match with personal experience; they are now also contradicted by the only scientific study done on this subject since independence, by Djamila Amrane, who herself was a freedom fighter from 1957 to 1962. She has been registered as a veteran in the archives of the Ministry of Veterans, and this allowed her access to these archives when she started the first and only study of women in the struggle ever attempted in twenty-five years, since independence.[1] As Djamila Amrane's work is based on the statistics of the Ministry of Veterans, I think it is useful to make a few remarks before presenting and commenting her statistical data.

Who was registered as a veteran by the Ministry? The request for registration had to be backed by a documented file, requiring lots of testimonies, requiring stamps in various offices, a whole bureaucratic procedure which made it difficult for any peasant or working-class man or illiterate people to register, and it was certainly very difficult for women, as Amrane pointed at in her introduction, because *they* were illiterate, from a peasant background, veiled and often partly secluded. Furthermore, this registration procured some advantages mainly for workers: specific jobs, promotion, retirement payments, and so on. It did not benefit women, since only 2.1 per cent were employed. This explains the fact that few women bothered to get registered and that they represent in official statistics of veterans only 3.25 per cent of the male population of veterans.

On the official side, there was no desire that women register as veterans, and a strong move to push women back in 'their place' began immediately after independence. Therefore statistical data drawn from the archives of the Ministry of Veterans is not representative of the number of women who could have been registered as veterans.

The second remark is about the concept of fighter (or veteran) itself. Numerically speaking, most of the struggle took place in the countryside, and little in the cities. Numerous tasks performed by the population in the countryside allowed the armed freedom fighters to survive: guiding, hiding, feeding, carrying messages, buying arms, watching the French army moves and taking the arms of those who had died. If it is easier to draw a line between people engaged in the struggle in the cities, it seems hardly possible to do so in the countryside, and the definition of 'fighter' cannot exclude all those, men and women, who performed all these intricate tasks.

But if a man, at the risk of this life, carried food to the armed fighters over long distances in the mountains, it is acknowledged that he was a fighter—while if a woman did so, she was only 'helping' the man in her traditional and natural way of nurturing; if a man, at the risk of his life, hid armed fighters or 'wanted' political leaders, he was certainly called a fighter—while if a woman did so, she was simply performing her normal woman's nurturing task. Although she could have died in the process, as well as her fellow men, she was not seen as a fighter; when she collected fuel for the fighters, nor when she collected food for the fighters, nor when she carried guns for the fighters, nor when she guided the fighters through the mountains. . . . She was 'helping' men. Only the French army acknowledged her action by jailing her, putting her into concentration camps, torturing her, killing her, as well as men.

This explains why even fewer women are registered as veterans, in the countryside. The official data is therefore even more biased and not representative of the reality. Reality is that in these types of guerilla liberation struggles, the whole population is involved, if not by will, by force, and we can consider rightly that nearly all women were actively involved in the struggle in the countryside.

Keeping in mind all these comments on the representativeness of the data, it is far from being uninteresting, and it still says a lot about Algerian women in the liberation struggle.

Out of 10,949 registered women, 9,194 are considered to be 'civilians' and 1,755 to be 'military', which means that 81 per cent work for the Civil Organization of the National Liberation Front (OCFLN), supporting the guerilla and urban terrorism, while 19 per cent are part of the army and work in the bush. Some 78 per cent of them worked in the countryside, and 20 per cent in the cities, which corresponds to the national population distribution. 1 out of 5 of them were jailed, tortured or killed. They were from all age groups from under 20 to over 50 years old, but it is interesting to note that 41.7 per cent were between 31 and 50 years old: they were all married and mothers; if we consider only the civilian branch (OCFLN) 47.3 per cent were between 31 and 50 years old.

These few figures show the overall participation of women, the heavy repression which fell on them, and the involvement of mature women and mothers.

The forms of activities both of civilians and military women were labelled as follows:

(i) In charge of hiding places and food collection: 63 per cent in the civilian branch; 2.9 per cent in the military. This means that only six performed such tasks in the military; Amrane's comment on this figure is that several women worked together in these tasks and only one of them (the leader) was allowed to register as veteran. It also supports my earlier comment: numerous women performed such tasks but were only considered as performing their feminine role and therefore were not considered as fighters. It also says very clearly that women in the struggle were employed in feminine tasks in their quasi totality.

(ii) Liaisons and guides: 22.1 per cent in the civilian branch, none in the military out of a total of 677 women.

(iii) Collection of funds, medicines, ammunitions; 286 women (9.3 per cent) in the civilian, none in the military. Nurses: 56 women in the civilian (1.8 per cent), 101 women in the military (49.3 per cent).

(iv) Cooks and clothes washers: none in the civilian, 44.4 per cent in the military, i.e. 91 women.

(v) Terrorists: 65 in the civilian (2.1 per cent).

(vi) Clothes makers and repairers: 19 women in the civilian (0.6 per cent) and 1 in the military.

(vii) Secretaries: 5 in the civilian (0.7 per cent), and 3 in the military (0.4 per cent).

(viii) Political commissaries: none in the civilian, 2 in the military (1 per cent).
(ix) Armed fighters: none in the civilian, 1 in the military (0.5 per cent).

Athough we know for sure that many more women were involved in the struggle, these biased figures still give a fair idea of the fact that even in the hardest times of the struggle, women were kept in their place and confined to a kind of task which would not disturb social order in future. Although the fulfilment of these tasks was absolutely necessary, they should not have absorbed the totality of female energy. Nurturing and maintenance were the tasks of women Algerian freedom fighters, plus an occasional medical service. We had no women in arms, we had no women in a position to make decisions neither in political matters, nor in military ones.

To sum up, there was only one woman in arms in the military. There were 65 women dealing with bombs in urban sectors (carrying spare parts or sometimes the whole pack as far as I know . . .) There were only two women political commissaries!

This gives a blow to Fanon's mythology (and followers) of the liberated Algerian woman—liberated through the process of global liberation of the country. We now know for sure where the liberated women were: in the kitchen, sewing clothes (or flags?), carrying parcels, typing. Nevertheless, since 'there is no humble task in revolution', we did not dispute the roles we had. It would have seemed so mean to question the priority of the liberation of the country and raise issues which would not be issues any more after the liberation: all the remnants of women's oppression were going to disappear with independence.

What makes me more angry, in retrospect, is not the mere fact of confining women to their place, but the brain-washing which did not allow us, young women, to even think in terms of questioning the women's place. And what makes me even more angry is to witness the replication of this situation in various places in the world where national liberation struggles are still taking place—to witness women engaged in liberation fronts covering the misbehavings of their fellow men, hiding, in the name of national solidarity and identity, crimes which will be perpetuated after the official liberation.

This is the real harm which comes with liberation struggles: people mobilize against such a strong, powerful, and destructive enemy that there is no room for the practical action of mobilizing women at the same time; but worse, it erases from our mind the very idea of doing so, which is seen as anti-revolutionary, anti-nation; this vision remains after independence and alienates generations of young women.

The overall task of women during the liberation struggle is symbolic: faced with colonization, the people had to build a national identity, based on values of one's own, traditions, religion, language, culture. Women bore the heavy role of being the keepers of this threatened identity; and they paid the heaviest price for accepting (but were there choices?) to play this role.

Probably most of the women present at this Symposium take for granted that they belong to a country, a nation, which does not have to prove its existence; it allows for transcending the concept of nation, and to criticize it. It has not been so for us; it has not been so for many people in ex-colonized countries; and it is not so for many people in still-colonized countries, or countries facing imperialism at war. Therefore it has been, or is much more, difficult to come to criticize the nation, and even the state which claims to represent the *nation*.

One of the early slogans of nationalism in Algeria was promoted by the Ulemas, the Doctors of the Faith—the religious leaders. It said, 'Arabic is our language, Islam is our religion, Algeria is our country'. Women, especially, were in charge of raising their sons within the religious faith, reviving traditions, keeping up moral standards, teaching the language of the forefathers.[2]

Women had to behave according to 'tradition', while men could have some access to 'modernity'. These, of course, are the concepts which were in use—not mine. It is now a well-known fact that what is kept as truly traditional among traditions, is only that which suits the purposes of those who are in power and those who rule for their own benefit. Tradition is seen as something a-historical, fixed, of the past, immutable, while modernity, in Algeria as well as in many other parts of the world, inevitably draws from the wealthy West—whatever it is thought to mean.

I'll give two examples of traditions as symbol of national identity during the struggle.

The veil

Although there is no doubt that veiling women—and women only—is part of the control and the oppression of women, the veil became a symbol of national resistance during the years of struggle for national independence. The French officials insisted that Algerian women should be freed from the oppression of the veil; with the help of the French army, they even went to the point of bringing women from villages in army trucks and forcing them to publicly unveil themselves, thereby renouncing their backward traditions. Of course, Algerian males—and women too—resented it as a symbolic public rape, (unfortunately mass rapes also took place in reality throughout the war for liberation). At the same time Fanon praised the revolutionary virtue of the veil, which allowed urban women freedom fighters to escape from control from the French army; they could hide guns under their veil and travel incognito for underground purposes.

In this context, how was one to take up the issue of the veil as oppressive to women? How could we do it without betraying both the *Nation* and the *Revolution*. Not surprisingly, many young women, even those brought up in families where they were not forced to wear the veil, chose to wear it, as a visible symbol of their belonging to the oppressed Algerian people, oppressed twice: in their lives, but also in their symbolic existence.

Needless to say, the FLN encouraged such attitudes together with the modesty which suits Algerian women—as well as all other women. All this was wrapped into the most appealing packaging: fighting for the Cause.

Closer to us in history is the example of Iranian women in their 'revolution'.

Tobacco and Alcohol

It is important to see this anti-women programme as part of a wider one which denied the people any private choice in private matters: around the time that the battle of Algiers took place, the FLN engaged in a campaign against tobacco and alcohol; their consumption became the sign of anti-national and anti-revolutionary feelings which lead to the death sentence and execution of the culprit.

The use of these drugs has been forbidden by religion, and whoever was not a believer was an ally of colonialism. The FLN actually killed people who were smoking in public, or cut their noses out in mild cases. Similarly, the practice of Ramadan-fast became compulsory, as an identification with the struggling nation; even non-religious people started fasting in solidarity. To be Algerian became synonymous with being a Muslim. Slowly but surely, the entwining of concepts as heterogeneous as nation, religion and ethnicity shaped the future of independent Algeria.

Again, I feel the need to remind us all that we women, we non-religious beings, we internationalists, did not raise our voices (it would have been difficult and risky), but moreover we did not 'raise our minds', did not see all the implications of this ideological confusion. We too believed that somehow this would be a betrayal of the people, of the revolution and of the nation. At no point did we see that a power structure was built on our mental confusion, which used control of private life and control of women as means to get access to power and maintain itself in this position.

Obedience, morality and conformity were necessary conditions to be part of the revolution. These were promoted under the cover of underground necessities. In a form of struggle where secrecy is the basis for action, one cannot question the decisions of the comrades in charge of organizing the struggle; it therefore leads to blind obedience. In a form of struggle in which one has to be as anonymous as possible, militants are asked to behave in the most conformist way, wear traditional clothes (including a veil, eventually), behave themselves. There soon appears a control of morality exerted on militants, and not surprisingly it is directed more especially on their sexual behaviour; needless to say that women are first concerned. But how could we speak about what (even to our blind minds) sometimes appeared excessive? To whom could we speak about what may have been needed by the nature of the struggle: clandestinity. How could we resist the fear of becoming marginalized?

It is in this context that I would like to set the forms of activities to which women were confined within the liberation movement. During this crucial period, women were assigned a place in society which could not be challenged without questioning both the past (traditions and history, the basis of an independent nation) and the future (revolution, which was reincarnated in the Algerian struggle for national independence). The roots for a tightly controlled society were set; nationalism will be the leading thread of interpretation of any side of our reality.

2. *After independence (1962): twenty-five years of oppression for women; steps in losing the mythical advantages women 'gained' during the liberation struggle; steps in the general political evolution; what the Algerian 'socialism' did to women (nationalism, religion, identity and women); women and the state; the policy of birth control in two decades, 1962–72 and 1972–82; the Islamic policy.*

Immediately after independence, the Algerian leaders started evolving a discourse about Algeria which grew more and more distant from the living experiences of Algerian people. Nevertheless, the mental rigidity acquired during the historical events of struggle for independence, the habit of not questioning, the fear of losing one's roots and identity, all these elements led to actual political schizophrenia: we used to elaborate on the discourse, and the discourse on the discourse became our reality. For instance, we endlessly talked of the Algerian socialism, where there was no socialism,[3] not even an attempted one; we were in state capitalism as a transition to plain capitalism, for the simple reason that there was no private national capital available to be invested at the time of independence.[4] We also endlessly talked about the self-management-Algerian-model, when self-management in industry was converted into state-owned industries less than one year after independence, and self-managed farms into state-owned farms soon after. We also discussed democratic institutions, when the police state was getting stronger and stronger and the power of the army grew by the day.

We denied the political use of religion and the growth of Islamic groups, later to become powerful Fundamentalists, since proclaimed socialism prevented us from such evils. And of course we congratulated ourselves for the freedom that women gained during the liberation. We were in the myth, talking about the myth.

In fact, what started during the liberation war was developing. Indeed, by law, women were equal to men in the Constitution, but as long as it was in conformity with Islamic religion. Later developments made us learn what it meant. Indeed, by law, the age of marriage for girls was fixed at 18. But it was not enforced. By law, girls should go to school, but there were not enough schools, so boys were sent there first. By law, women could and should have work, but there were no jobs, so men had to have them, as heads of families. Women could walk freely in the streets, but men harassed them and the police sided with the men: 'what is an honest woman doing outside her home?' Even when men started beating women in the streets when they dared say a word of protest, other men gathered and watched without helping women. Even liberal men did not intervene for fear of questioning by the police: 'you sided with her; did you know her? what were you doing there?' and so on.

The very summer of independence, the FLN army (ALN) patrolled the streets of the capital, arresting young people where males and females were walking together in groups: 'who is married to whom here. This one, is she someone's sister, wife?' One had better produce a good marriage certificate.

People retreated inside their homes, fearing the authorities and afraid of being denounced by their neighbours. More women wore a veil: we were now free so we could really be ourselves; beware of foreign ideologies. More people submitted to the Ramadan-fast: police locked up those who did not. Hypocrisy grew; one hid from neighbours, colleagues, 'friends', and even family ('my mother must not know that I am not fasting').

More people officially did not drink alcohol, or smoke in the presence of their father; a law was passed which forbids Algerian citizens to buy alcohol. It is applied or not, depending on the political seasons. But one never knows when it will be enforced again. Forced marriages took place and numerous suicides of young girls occurred, numerous women were ill-treated by their male relatives, beaten and secluded. There was no organization to report to.[5]

Those who denounced the state of affairs were persecuted as traitors—to the authorities, to the *state*, therefore to the *nation*, therefore to the *revolution*. One developed a split personality. What was seen did not exist: reality was the nationalist interpretation of it.

In this context of increasing lack of political liberties, of morality, of emphasis on religion, where women were losing openly what in fact they never gained, it is important to stress the role of what was officially labelled 'specific socialism' in Algeria. Why specific? To differentiate itself from 'scientific socialism', which stands for atheism; our socialism was supposed to combine with Islamic religion. Looking back, it was just another trick from the people in power to quieten those who have given so much for national independence.

As I have tried to describe, we were already silenced by all the fears of being accused of betrayal, and by the nationalist myth; but the best way to silence us has been the socialist label. Because it was a socialist state, one could not oppose the politics of the state without opposing socialism; because *the people* was in power, one could not criticize the regime without being anti-people. This rhetoric, as stupid as it appears when one has stepped out of it, has proved to work successfully in silencing the left in most of the East European communist countries.

It takes years to dare become a dissident and to speak out, knowing that our unveiling the truth will not only serve our purposes, but, also, be used by rightist elements, both inside and outside the country, to denigrate and destroy the aspirations to justice and equality which we believe should be the basis for socialism. As long as we do not link, inside and abroad, with people from the left at large, with other dissident socialists, the guilt feeling is immense, and the accusation of betrayal a painful wound.

I will now give two concrete examples of the policy of the state against women, and how nationalism, socialism and religion were entwined and successfully worked against women. The first example is the birth policy of Algeria. At independence, Algeria was still under the old natalist French law of 1920 which forbids not only the use of but also the knowledge of contraception. This law, like many others, could not be replaced all of a sudden, so it was temporarily prolongated ('tacite prorogation').

Obviously, we women hoped that after independence we would have access to some means of contraception. But many men died during the liberation struggle and the policy of the state was clearly to replace them. As well as during the liberation struggle, having children was encouraged as a main accomplishment for women and a duty to the nation. Women were the bearers of warriors. Nevertheless, it would have been difficult to have us accept, without a protest, such a blunt policy.

But—fortunately, if I may say so—the United States were, at that very time, trying to enforce a brutal policy of birth control in the Third World, which culminated with their attempt to put pressure on governments to make them adopt their world plan, called 'fertility target', at the World Conference on Population in Bucharest. As the champion of the liberation of Africa, as the champion of socialism, Algeria was not to allow such a policy to step in. As we all know, population policies are not *the* way to development.

Could we, women, disapprove of that? Could we, as socialists, not support the international policy of our government? We indeed supported its views, and as a result, did not protest when the natalist law was not changed. Although we managed to get statements from the highest Islamic authorities stating that contraception practices were not forbidden by religion, nothing was to change for a whole decade. This is a good proof that people in power use religion only when it suits them. At that time, they needed both that women produce children and to strengthen their control on the people by controlling also their private life in all possible respects.

The anti-imperialist stand that they took on birth policy perfectly suited also the needs of their internal policies: women had to pay a high price for it. In about ten years, the average number of children per woman was 7.9; pregnancies ranged from 14 to natural fecundity; we do not know about illegal abortions, nor about maternal death. The annual population growth reached 3.5 per cent, one of the highest, at that time, in the world.

To make a long story short, ten years were enough to turn a socialist bureaucracy into a more conventional bourgeoisie, owning means of production. The Algerian ruling class felt threatened by the growth of lumpen masses, and suddenly reversed its policies: birth control was legalized, contraception clinics were opened and their number increased rapidly, therapeutic abortion was legalized. Population growth came down to 3.2 per cent within a few years. In January 1981 the law of finances suddenly penalized large families: the more children, the more taxes. In both cases women had no say. They are the producers of goods whose control is in the hands of the state.

The second example concerns the use of religion. Although the Constitution guarantees equality to all citizens, it was stated shortly after independence that we should have a Family Code more in accordance with Islamic values. Three projects were drafted, one under Ben Bella, the first president of Algeria, two under Boumediene, the second president. All were circulated amongst small groups: all legalized the inferiority of women, submitting them to the authority of a man who was her legal tutor (father, brother, husband or . . . elder son . . .). None was passed because of the opposition of well-known personalities. But since 1963 women have been under the threat of such a law.

In 1981, under the present President Chadli, a new project was drafted, but kept totally secret. Ministers and deputees were allowed to read it in the course of a special session: they were given a copy of the project when they entered the room and it was taken back from them when they left at the end of the session. We do not know that any of them protested. No information came from them about the content of the project.

Women succeeded in stealing a copy and demonstrated in the streets, for the first time since independence. By doing so they succeeded in postponing a law which was highly unfavourable to women: women had no right to marry, they had to be given in marriage; no right to divorce; no right to work without permission of the male tutor; restricted rights to inheritance, and so on. All this was said to be Koranic, therefore no argument should be made against it.

In May 1984 a Family Code was finally passed, without warning and discussion, which reproduces the fourth project that women had challenged in 1981, except for the clause on permission to work. Is it because this paragraph appeared to be too far from the officially proclaimed socialism, or because they did not dare state that the Prophet also mentioned wage earning?

It is now a legal fact that women have lost many rights which were guaranteed by the Constitution, on the grounds that these rights were anti-Islamic. All supporters of religion will always tell you that religion stands for equality between all human beings; Muslims also have this language, and see no contradiction with the inequalities that Muslim laws enforce on women. With little sense of humour, they also claim that Islam asks from each believer to be fair to his women (polygamy and repudiation are now legal in socialist Algeria); if each man were a true believer, women would be well treated and would not need to seek formal equality. This evolution goes with the taking over of the male population by rightist Muslims, known in Algeria as Muslim Brothers, and in other countries as Fundamentalists. The rise of religious elements challenging the state in Algeria and channellizing the discontent of the population is not an isolated phenomenon; it occurs in most Muslim countries at present. One of the most striking elements of their philosophy is nationalism, entangled with a 'going back to traditions', a search for roots and identity, a rejection of all the evils of Western imperialism. One of the commonalities of these Fundamentalist tendencies in Muslim countries is the growing oppression of women.

In many countries or communities, new enforcement of Muslim laws have toughened the situation for women; not only in Algeria but in Egypt, in Pakistan, in India, in Sudan, and so on—not to speak of the unspeakable situation of Iranian women.

In Algeria the number of mosques have increased in such a way that each block has a huge room for prayer, each school or university has at least one. . . . These improvised mosques gather huge numbers of young men and teenagers, who rule their female folks according to the prescriptions of their leaders. We have recently discovered that Fundamentalists train young leaders in several countries and that huge amounts of money are involved in such training. For instance, Pakistani young men might be trained in Iran, with Saudi Arabian money, Sudanese might be trained in Pakistan with Egyptian money, and so on. We hope to encourage research on such matters.

We also found out that both in the Arab world and in South Asia, Ministers of Justice meet and attempt to unify Family Codes in a way which is even more restrictive to women. There is no doubt about the international dimension of this attempt to use religion as a unification device in the present world situation.

3. *Women in liberation struggles: national struggles as fronts; how women indulge in alienation for the common goal; the private and the public (how the ideology of national liberation affects women in their private life); what would be the conditions for gaining rights for women within the liberation struggles.*

We are made to feel that protesting in the name of women's interests and rights is not to be done *now*: it is never, has never been the right moment; not during the liberation struggle against colonialism, because all forces had to be mobilized against the principal enemy; not after independence, because all forces had to be mobilized to build up the devastated country; not now that racist, imperialist Western governments are attacking Islam and the Third World, and so on. Defending women's rights 'now'—this now being *any* historical moment—is always a betrayal of the people, of the nation, of the revolution, of Islam, of national identity, of cultural roots, and so on, according to the terminology in use, *hic et nunc*.

This narrow approach of nationalism is very effective: the

women's movement in my country is still weak—numerically, ideologically, theoretically—too weak to challenge an interpretation which suits so well the dominant males, including those on the left, who are the first ones to accuse us of betrayal, of 'imported ideologies', of 'Westernism', using the same terminology which our governments use against the Left at large. Women are caught in between two legitimacies: belonging to their people and/or identifying with oppressed women.

It is very hard to persist in total isolation in denouncing the stepping back of so many once 'revolutionary' countries, on the women's question, and to go on organizing the struggle. My deepest admiration and regard goes to those of us who stubbornly trace their way into this ideological jungle, to promote the cause of women.

Not only are we prevented from speaking for women but also to think, and even to dream, about a different fate. We are deprived of our dreams, because we are made to believe that leading the life we lead is the only way to be a good Algerian, a good Pakistani or a good Sudanese—and a good Muslim. We are not even aware of the differences which exist from one Muslim country to another, of situations which may be more favourable to women than others, of the intrication of culture, traditions and religion. Let women from Muslim countries step out of their national ghettos; let them see that female circumcision practised in Africa is unthinkable in Asia, that the veil worn in Arab countries is not there in Africa, that none of these practices rely on religious principles, but that religion everywhere backs such practices whenever they allow more control on women.

Moreover, let us dream of secular states, let us dream of the separation of religion and the state, of ending with nationalism justifying all the crimes against oppressed groups—including women. One of the most ugly crimes is the brainwashing we undergo. Although, in so many cases, we cannot organize inside our own countries—and not even speak without facing heavy repression—we are made to feel that we should not either speak outside, that we should hide, in the name of national loyalty, the crimes committed against women and against other oppressed fractions of the people.

We are thus made to identify with 'the nation', 'the people', conceptualized as an atomized and undifferentiated mass, without conflicting interests, without classes and without history; in fact, we are made to identify with the state and the ruling class as legitimate representatives of 'the people'.

Unfortunately, one can find many recent examples of such attitudes in women's groups, in our countries. I recently heard in Pakistan comments upon exiled Iranian women: their detractors said that they should not describe, in the West, details of the crimes committed against Iranian women, for this will be used against Islam and Muslim countries by racist and rightist Westerners—and against the Iranian people. This leaves the whole question open: are the Iranian people in power, or oppressed? Were the Germans who denounced Hitler during the Second World War anti-Germans or anti-Nazis? Whom did silence benefit? What legitimacy should one have chosen to side with?

In Algeria, many of us, including myself, kept silent for a whole decade after independence, in order not to give ground to the enemies of the glorious Algerian revolution; by so doing, we only have given time to those in power to strengthen and organize, allowing them, amongst many other things, to prepare and enforce discriminatory laws on women. Even now in Algeria, feminists try to analyse their oppression from within the Algerian context only, refusing to see the international side of it, for fear of being accused of betrayal.

Right now in India, in the name of the riots and massacres led by Hindu Fundamentalists against the Muslim community, Muslim Fundamentalists have succeeded in persuading Muslim women activists to stop their campaigns against Muslim Personal Law—campaigns which may be used 'against the community'; women should therefore suffer discrimination both from the dominant Hindus, and from their 'Muslim community'.

It is certainly true that some rightist forces will exploit our protests especially if they remain isolated, but it is as true to say that other rightist forces exploit our silence. I believe the question is not there.

We have everything to gain in being truly internationalist—

in exchanging all useful information, solidarity and support. We can create such a solidarity that it will become more and more difficult to exploit our protests in a way which does not suit our purposes.

We have recently set up a network of Women Living under Muslim Laws. Women and women's groups from seventeen countries or communities now communicate with each other through the network, ask for documentation, compare so-called Muslim laws in different countries, send appeals for solidarity, inform others about their strategies in very practical terms, such as writing marriage contracts which give maximum space to women, and so on. Through the network we have been informed of projects of unification of Family Codes, both in Arab countries, and in South Asia, as I earlier mentioned. We have also been informed about how young Fundamentalists are trained; we hope to find out where the training takes place and who is funding it. We have been informed about progressive interpretations of Islam, from the times of the Prophet till now, and about what happened to the courageous pioneers, men and women, who spoke in favour of an equalitarian interpretation of religion.

We have realized in concrete terms that most of our regimes leave no room for agnosticism or atheism, that religion is forced down our throats because of the constant ideological confusion between religion, culture and nationality—and that we should work towards a clear-cut identification of these concepts.

Now that we start supporting each other 'from within' it becomes more and more difficult to limit our action to a mere imitation of the West. Speaking against discriminatory situations in Algeria or crimes against women in Iran can less and less be used by reactionary forces both inside and outside our countries, because support comes from both inside and outside. We leave less and less ground to nationalist justification for silence. It is our very interest that internationalism should prevail upon nationalism, and that we should link such struggles from one country to the other, for reasons of ethics, as well as from the point of view of efficiency, and in the hope that more of such struggles will start and be backed, nationally and internationally.

We are indebted to the early Western internationalist feminists who twenty years ago started inviting women from the 'Third World' to international feminist gatherings, granting some of us the privilege to not only be in contact with the feminist movement at large but also meet other 'Third World' women. It is through international feminist gatherings that we came to know each other and later found associations at regional, continental and international level.

NOTES

1. Djamila Amrane, *La Femme Algérienne et la guerre de libération nationale (1954–62)* (Actes du Colloque d'Oran, 1980).
2. We will not discuss here the legitimacy of Arab language in a country where the dominant communities are Berber and speak Berber languages.
3. Tahar Berahouryia, *Economie de L'Algérie* (Paris: Maspéro, 1980).
4. Damien Hélie, 'L'autogestion Industrielle', thesis, Paris, 1964; 'Le socialisme était simplement une bonne recette pour l'accumulation primitive du capital'.
5. Fadila Mrabet, 'Les Algériennes', in *La Femme algérienne* (Paris: Maspéro, 1965 and 1967); Mahfoud Boucebci, *Psychiatrie et Société* (Alger: SNED, 1980).

12

Women and War: The Case of Nicaragua

Hermione Harris, UK

The symbol of the Nicaraguan Women's Association (AMNLAE) includes a profile of a woman's head crossed by a gun. Women were crucial in the war against Anastasio Somoza, who was both a hated dictator and a symbol of North American domination, and since the victory of the Sandinista National Liberation Front (FSLN) in July 1979, they have been involved in defending Nicaragua against continued US attack.[1] Defence of the revolution is also conceived of in political and economic terms. AMNLAE's logo incorporates a coffee branch and is encircled by a cog-wheel in the FSLN colours of red and black.[2]

The integration of women's organizations with the revolutionary party and its programmes is familiar from other socialist societies, and until now the experience of women in similar situations has not always been positive.[3] When revolutionary governments come to power committed to gender equality, women become recognized in political and economic life. But countries as diverse as People's Democratic Republic of Yemen, China and Mozambique have shown that these same states fight shy of tackling patriarchy, the institutionalized inequalities and ideologies of male superiority built round reproduction rather than production. In Castro's Cuba, in spite of women's progress and the much-vaunted Family Code, women's greater involvement in the public sphere has both exacerbated their dual role and added a third: political responsibilities. Until recently, the Cuban Women's Federation had prioritized the needs of state and party rather than women's specific demands.

But Cuba has had to survive US military and economic aggression, necessitating military mobilization. The negative effects of this for women have been explored for countries such as the USSR and Mozambique, besides Cuba, and some feminist analysts, suspicious of militarization in any form, because of what it usually means for women, argue that even in a revolutionary state women will be manipulated by a male-dominated military in the name of defence.[4]

Certainly, pressure from the counterrevolutionaries, the *contras*, have exacerbated the conflicts in Nicaragua's political project as a whole; the two tasks the Sandinistas face, transformation of society and defence against aggression, lie uneasily together. Popular democracy entails the voicing of sectional interests, allowing space for diverse demands and political inexperience. National security requires a strong state and centralized control, and brings the temptation to utilize grass-roots organizations to put across the party line. To some extent the tension between these principles has been reflected in the FSLN's policies on women, and in its relationship to AMNLAE.

But what makes the Nicaraguan experience unique is the extent to which, through pressure from women themselves, both the women's association and the FSLN have moved from a position of subsuming women's specific interests to what were seen as military and economic priorities, to the incorporation of women's demands as an intrinsic part of the revolution itself. To understand both the nature of these demands, and the process whereby they have been asserted, it is essential to look first at the experience of women in the pre-revolutionary period, and their role in the war against Somoza.

WOMEN AND THE STRUGGLE AGAINST SOMOZA

In the final offensive against Somoza, 30 per cent of the FSLN's fighting force were women. This was a higher proportion than in any previous Latin American liberation struggle, including the Cuban revolution twenty years before. And it was largely women, of all classes, who set up the structures of civilian support without which the guerillas could not survive. These 'collaborators' hid Sandinistas in their houses, set up first-aid posts, carried messages, gathered information, provided food, sewed uniforms by candlelight and transported arms.

Much of this activity came to be coordinated by the Women's Association. Founded in 1977, the Association of Nicaraguan Women Confronting the Nation's Problems (AMPRONAC) brought together women from different backgrounds to publicize the atrocities committed by the National Guard and cámpaign for the release of political prisoners. As links with the FSLN strengthened, AMPRONAC served to integrate women into organized resistance to Somoza. This rendered them vulnerable to the full force of the regime's repression: physical harassment, violence, imprisonment, rape, torture and death.

Why were women prepared to take such risks? Why were they so prominent at all levels, from clandestine *barrio* supporters to commanders in the guerilla ranks? To some extent they responded as members of their class. The middle classes, apart from Somoza's small and corrupt clique, felt stifled by his stranglehold on the country's social, political and economic life, and were outraged by his disregard for basic human rights and by the brutality of his National Guard. They saw in the armed FSLN the only means of confronting the Guard, and a progressive minority of the bourgeoisie shared the alternative vision of society which the Sandinistas offered. But for the majority of Nicaragua's 3 million population—the *campesinos* (peasant farmers), urban and rural wage workers and semi-proletariat—the motive was self-preservation in the face of both National Guard harassment and deepening poverty. Lacking basic education, housing and medical facilities, 70 per cent of the population suffered some degree of malnutrition, and infant mortality stood at some 200 per 1,000.

But women also mobilised for reasons specific to their gender, not only to their class. The level of female participation in the anti-Somoza struggle reflects the fact that it was women who suffered the full consequences of these conditions, since they bore the brunt of family responsibilities.

Nearly half of household heads in Nicaragua were women, and in the capital, Managua, this rose to two-thirds. Men came and went, driven not only by *macho* whim whereby women are available for mate selection, but also through the search for work. *Campesinos* had been expropriated by large producers of export crops, leaving few with farms large enough to support a family. The majority joined the flood of seasonal workers picking coffee, cotton and tobacco and cutting sugar cane, but outside harvest time regular work was scarce and wages insufficient to support a family.

In spite of this male mobility, traditional Catholicism still maintained that a man is master in the home. There his woman should dutifully remain, caring for the children. The high level of domestic violence showed a desperate attempt to uphold this male authority, emasculated by instability and unemployment, and frustrated by political impotence. But the real meaning of being a mother in these conditions was independent activity, and work outside the house to support the children. Some 85 per cent of single mothers worked, either on the land or as street vendors or domestic servants. Women also went with their children to work in the plantations at harvest time. Children contributed to the family income from an early age, working alongside their mothers in field or market, or selling in the streets. In the absence of state provision, a mother depended on them, not on their father, in her old age.

The ties between mothers and their children were therefore often strong, both in a material and emotional sense, and further explain the participation of many women in the war. Nearly three-quarters of the people who took to the streets in the popular insurrection were under 25, and supporting them in their clandestine activity, coming to their defence when threatened and tortured by the National Guard, seemed a natural extension of motherhood. The qualities needed to take part in their children's fight—stamina, toughness ingenuity and experience outside the home—were already part of a woman's armoury in her daily life. As the ferocity of the threatened dictatorship increased, the role of mother assumed a political dimension.

AMPRONAC actively recruited women around this aspect

of their lives 'We women experience this political crisis as citizens, mothers, wives and housewives', declared its programme: 'As mothers and women we feel the effects of this social crisis'.[5] By contrast, guerilla life, at least in theory, submerged gender differences and the traditional division of labour in dedication to a common cause. As many women have said of their life in the mountains, 'There were no men, no women, only fighters'. But AMPRONAC appealed to women in their traditional roles, which they tried to extend, rather than attempting to transform women's identity. The opportunity to take part in politics through development of their normal roles was a significant factor in the extent of women's involvement in the war.

AMPRONAC activists, therefore, were not vocal on the particular problems of women in a male dominated society, for although AMPRONAC included gender equality in its demands, this was seen as inseparable from the replacement of the dictatorship by a popular progressive government and the association's overriding aim was to integrate women into the anti-Somoza movement. AMPRONAC recognized that its campaign:

> would not please the big international feminist movements, for in content it rather laid emphasis on the general struggle of our people for a free country. But this corresponds to the real need of Nicaraguan women, who lay the foundations of the equality of their sex on equal participation in the construction of a new Nicaragua.[6]

This did not mean, however, that women's participation in the war had no positive effects in terms of their own liberation. Apart from the fact that women could indeed have no hope of emancipation under the old regime, the nature and level of their contribution to the war won them a new respect. This is echoed in a 1980 speech by Commander Tomás Borge, a founder of the FSLN and leading Sandinista:

> Women were in the front line of battle, whether they threw home-made bombs or were in the trenches. They were in the leadership of military units, on the firing line during the war, and therefore have every right in the world to be in the front line during the period of reconstruction. In the future, when structural changes are being made, we must cease thinking of a government of men and begin thinking of a government of men and women.[7]

Respect for war veterans is a common feature of liberation struggles. The danger is that it may die with their generation. How far this respect would be built into new structures as Borge optimistically predicted depended on the persistence of women themselves, not on the benevolence of male leaders. Perhaps the most important result of women's involvement, apart from their contribution to the overthrow of Somoza, is the confidence they gained, the independence they asserted and the capabilities they discovered in themselves. This is continually confirmed by fighters and collaborators alike, and is apparent in their lives. As one young woman soldier told me, after describing her horrific rape and torture:

> When I came out of jail, I said to myself, 'How do you feel now? Are you getting out, or hanging on a little longer?' Well, there was no question about it. I felt more of a woman; my experiences had shaped me; I was more sure of myself. And now, with the new situation that we're living in, at each stage I'm reaffirmed. And I think that this is what nearly all women feel.

This confidence in a general change in women's consciousness is an exaggeration: perhaps only a minority of women feel themselves so transformed. But their dedication, energy and public presence has made their influence greater than their numbers, and their contribution has been crucial to the FSLN's recognition of women's rights and their role in the new society.

WOMEN, WAR AND REVOLUTION

Nicaraguans refer to 1979 as the 'Triumph'; the 'Revolution' is what followed: the attempt to reconstruct the country along popular democratic lines to benefit the majority rather than a privileged élite. The Sandinistas have developed their own brand of socialism in which a strong public sector is incorporated in a mixed economy and an amount of political pluralism exists within a Sandinista state.

The initial context for the FSLN programme was a war-wrecked and bankrupt country. With the benefits of central planning, agrarian reform and foreign aid from East and

West, both economic recovery and social development began to take shape. But the mounting of the counter-revolutionary war by the United States rapidly made defence the top priority. Since 1982 Nicaragua has become increasingly militarized: imports of heavy weaponry have escalated, the number under arms grown considerably, and the civilians in vulnerable areas have been given guns. The war effort dominates FSLN policies and pervades public and private life. President Reagan portrays this militarism as the menacing stance of totalitarian communism against Nicaragua's 'democratic' neighbours, but the Sandinistas argue that mounting incursions from the Honduran and Costa Rican camps, the increased Contra presence inside the country, and CIA-directed sabotage—mining of harbours, bombing of strategic targets—have necessitated self-defence. While the US Congress imposed a total trade embargo in 1985 and voted for a multi-million aid package for the Contras in 1986, war damage amounted to 60 per cent of Nicaragua's export earnings, and defence took up half the national budget.

At a human level the cost is devastating: over 1 per cent of the population has been killed, wounded or kidnapped, and whole communities have had to be resettled in safer areas. Every family mourns a member, neighbour or a friend. There was therefore no opportunity to demobilize in face of continued aggression by the United States. Nevertheless, the FSLN reiterated its commitment to opening a space for women's emancipation. 'Women will be given a more dignified place in society', the FSLN programme promised, 'and all their rights in society will be enforced so that they are not subject to discrimination'. In 1979 AMPRONAC was appropriately renamed the Luisa Amanda Espinoza Women's Association (AMNLAE) after the first young woman guerilla to be killed by the National Guard, and took on the main responsibility for implementing these aims. AMNLAE's policies were outlined at their first National Assembly at the end of 1981 when Contra aggression was escalating. AMNLAE pledged to fight inequality and discrimination and to help create the conditions for participation in public life. This included a re-evaluation of domestic labour. The emphasis however was on the defence of the revolution as the political guarantee of women's emancipation, and the promotion of the education and politicization of women to enable them to play a full part.

This is reflected in the structure of AMNLAE, which does not claim to be a mass organization, seeking membership of all women. Rather, it calls itself a 'movement', promoting the public presence of women and encouraging them to join other organizations such as the Agricultural Workers' Union (ATC), Labour Union (CST), neighbourhood committees (CDS) and Sandinista Youth. It aims not only to alert women to the benefits of government programmes but to involve them in planning and implementation. Through such participation, it is argued, women will achieve their emancipation.

Initially, therefore, despite internal debates, the association continued AMPRONAC's integrationist approach, aiming to incorporate women both physically and ideologically in the revolution, rather than to focus on women's specific demands. This coincided with FSLN's view that *feminismo* was the mirror image of *machismo*, and that exacerbation of conflict between the sexes was divisive of the national unity essential in time of war. This does not mean that there was no genuine commitment to women's rights, but that this was set within the context of reconstruction and defence. Despite its limitations, this integrationist approach, and even the Contra war itself, did stimulate aspects of women's progress, and consolidated, rather than reversed gains made in the liberation struggle. This is especially true of the first three or four years of the revolution, before the war had wreaked as much economic ruin as it now has.

Firstly, for political as well as humanitarian reasons, women became the particular targets for government programmes. For women constitute over half the population, and so of the FSLN's potential political support. If they were to identify with the revolution, women had to see that it was serving their best interests.

The array of social projects improving women's lives have been described elsewhere—producer co-operatives, children's canteens and day-care centres. Many of the programmes which affect the whole community particularly benefit women through their family responsibilities: housing, health and educational campaigns. Attempts have been made to reach women in their localities, which may be isolated, rather than expect them to travel to the towns. For example, briefly trained health workers complement new hospitals and clinics, and go out into the communities to vaccinate, teach basic hygiene and carry out first aid. Maternal and child health is a priority in the new health service; polio was eradicated and infant mortality has dropped to 70 per 1,000 by the mid-eighties.

Social campaigns are often presented in the familiar military idiom, widening the concept of national defence: the battle against illiteracy, crusades against poverty, brigades, columns and squadrons of volunteers. The paradigm of this model was the 1980 Literacy Crusade when 60,000 young *brigadistas* set out from schools and colleges to teach *campesinos* to read and write. They found that 90 per cent of rural women were illiterate, compared with 50 per cent of the population as a whole. During the six months of the Crusade, illiteracy dropped to 12 per cent.

On the other hand, especially over the last four years, while the war had increased the necessity for social programmes, it is now destroying them. Illiteracy has risen once again, especially in the countryside. Adult education classes have been disrupted by the war, by national service, lack of resources shifting populations and Contra action. Schools, along with health centres and co-ops, have been reduced to rubble and the people working in them assassinated. Polio has reappeared. The war is also having a disastrous effect on the economy. Inflation, scarcity of staples and shortages of essential consumer goods have made it harder for women to maintain their families. There is a danger that the goodwill they have created will be dissipated by this hardship, just as the Contra intend.

ACTIVISM, EXPERIENCE AND EMANCIPATION

But secondly, women's participation in these programmes have made women agents of their own emancipation, not just objects of reform: one of the most significant effects of women's involvement is what has happened to themselves. Some 60 per cent of the Literacy *brigadistas* was female, and the time in the countryside proved a crucial formative experience, especially for girls from urban, middle-class homes. The FSLN opened a space for women. Those who have entered into it bear witness to the changes in their lives.

In one sense AMNLAE is right to insist that integration into the revolution is the road to their own emancipation. Just as participation in the struggle against Somoza earned self-confidence and the respect of others, so activity in mass organizations, civil defence, voluntary harvesting brigades, health campaigns, self-help housing construction teams or adult education classes has had the same effect. To be part of a group helps overcome domestic isolation and confirms efficacy in the public sphere. Opportunities for training and travel push back traditional boundaries and break taboos encircling feminine behaviour. Confidence and the sense of worth gained in these situations are reflected in domestic lives: as women take responsibility instead of orders, so they face up to husbands who seek to limit their activities. There is no doubt that for those who take part in public life the consciousness of their oppression and the confidence gained to confront this are grounded in their collective involvement in the wider struggle, rather than in campaigning around 'women's issues'.

Factors of individual ideology cannot be quantified and are difficult to assess. Some accounts written in solidarity with the Sandinistas tend to overemphasize the transformation in consciousness achieved. The interviews with activists on which they base their judgement bear eloquent witness to women's self-discovery, but give the false impression that most women are so inspired. In reality, many women have never been actively involved and remain indifferent or hostile to change. On the other hand, some feminist analyses of the position of women in or after liberation struggles focus almost entirely on state policies and the army's aims. They therefore lose sight of factors of consciousness, such as changes in women's self-confidence and capacity for independent action, and do not explore the implications of these developments for analysis. In the Nicaraguan case, they have been crucial in pushing forward the boundaries of FSLN policies on women.

THE FSLN AND THE SPECIFIC DEMANDS OF WOMEN

In preparation for its second National Assembly to be held in September 1985, and for its submission to Nicaragua's new Constitution, AMNLAE organized some 600 local assemblies throughout the country to discuss women's problems. Different preoccupations surfaced according to locality and class, but certain themes recurred repeatedly, raised with particular vehemence by women in or nearby the towns: sexual harassment, domestic violence, rape, contraception, abortion, *machismo* and women's double day. Both AMNLAE and the FSLN itself were taken to task for failing to tackle these issues.

When these concerns were reiterated in the September Assembly, FSLN Commander Bayardo Arce revealed the official reluctance to take them seriously, and questioned the need for a separate women's organization in a revolutionary society. Flor Ramirez, a *campesina* heading the Tobacco section of the ATC, describes how women like herself put him right:

> Women never used to have a say like they do now. I never spoke up: I went dumb. I got so nervous whenever I had to talk to people, and now I talk more than a parrot. I'm no intellectual and talk a bit plain, but I'm afraid of no one. At this year's Women's National Assembly I even told our Commander Bayardo Arce that I thought he was up the spout on women. That would never have happened in Somoza's day, you'd never have been some common upstart shouting her mouth off, the Guard would have beaten the living daylights out of me.
>
> Whereas as the Women's National Assembly we talked straight: 'Look Commander, what we're proposing is this, and you. . . .' Intellectuals and ordinary women alike all let ourselves be heard.[8]

And the FSLN had to listen. At AMNLAE's third Assembly in March 1987 Arce committed the party to fighting discrimination against women on the ideological as well as the social and economic fronts. Basing his speech on an FSLN commission on *machismo* during the intervening eighteen months, he analysed the ideology of male superiority which excluded women from rights, privileges and activities defined as 'male' and which sanctioned the abuse of women. He also stressed that women needed 'their own specific mechanisms' to mobilize around their particular concerns. AMNLAE was thus legitimated, but women's oppression analysed as a problem for the whole society, and thus for the revolution.

The means of conducting this campaign are still developing. After the Second Assembly, sexual education, contraception, and the hitherto taboo topic of abortion were featured in the media. The issues were debated within AMNLAE's own publications and assemblies, in unions and the meetings of mass organizations. The radical wing of the Church continues its work raising women's consciousness of their own position. The army initiates debates within its ranks, and militia training is taken as an opportunity to discuss personal relationships. In the police force, courses are run on the sensitive handling of special groups such as prostitutes, and AMNLAE's Women's Legal Office runs groups for state employees who deal with women in their work. This office was set up in 1983 to advise women on their legal rights, particularly regarding child maintenance, divorce and physical abuse, and has recently expanded into educational projects and launched a campaign against domestic violence.

No one in Nicaragua argues that campaigns and constitutional commitments in themselves bring rapid transformation. *Machismo* in all its manifestations remains a deep-rooted facet of Nicaraguan culture, reinforced by the conservative Church hierarchy and political parties which are still potent forces in pluralist Nicaragua. Abortion, for example, is still illegal, and bungled backstreet operations are still the main cause of maternal death.

There is also the question of how far Tomás Borge's pledge has been fulfilled, and to what extent women's influence has been translated into political power. Given the ground women must cover since their previous obscurity in public life, it is understandable that today there are only two female ministers and a handful of women in top government positions, although a third of second-level executive posts are filled by women, and they comprise 40 per cent of the National Assembly delegates. In the FSLN, the major political force, only 25 per cent of the members are women. There are several women in senior positions in the party, but as yet none in the nine-man National Directorate.

But what is significant is that women's issues are now on the agenda, both of AMNLAE and the FSLN, and that they have been put there not by party dictate but from women's pressure from below. They have been asserted, too, during a time of war, when defence and national unity are priorities both for the Sandinistas and for the men and women who support them.

WOMEN WORKERS AND THE WAR

The marked shift in FSLN policy can be seen as a response both to women's own demands, and the weight these carry given women's role in the war economy. As men are mobilized, women have moved into production, 'women now feed the nation', it is said.

Both to increase food production and to consolidate political support, the FSLN have prioritized the countryside during the war. This has affected the lives of rural women who now form 40 per cent of the rural workforce, double the proportion of the early 1980s. Agrarian reform has handed land to individual producers and provided access to inputs through service co-operatives. The 1981 Agricultural Cooperatives Law established a woman's right to hold land in her own name and, at least in theory, to participate in co-ops on equal terms. Especially in the war zones, women now run peasant farms. Formerly they tended to work on family land, with men taking both the decisions and the proceeds. In the waged sector, women by law should receive equal pay. As men are called up for military service, the number of women in full-time employment has increased, rather than being confined to the pool of seasonal labour. For those that harvest, their pay now goes into their pockets, instead of to the man in the family unit as before.

The move into 'male' employment during wartime is nothing new, and does not necessarily secure permanent gains for women. Whether they maintain their new positions when the men return, or go back to the *status quo ante*, often the home, depends on the extent to which they will be able to consolidate their new roles. Training is one important factor: for the first time women are encouraged to study agriculture and engineering. Well over half the technical and professional students are now women, as are nearly all medical students.

Another crucial factor is organization, and the extent to which women both join their unions and are accepted as permanent additions. In some unions, such as the *campesino* Farmers and Ranchers Association (UNAG), female membership is low and there is no systematic attempt to increase their participation in the co-operatives. But in the rural wage-earners union, the ATC, women formed 40 per cent of the membership in 1986 and 15 per cent of the elected leadership. There they see their role not just as recruiting more female members but also to ensure that the ATC represents women's interests. They challenge the traditional definitions of 'male' and 'female' labour, and argue for equal opportunities in employment. They agitate for increased child-care facilities for working mothers. Refusing to confine their activities to a woman's committee, they insist that the union as a whole takes up their demands.

MILITARIZATION AND MOTHERHOOD

Women have also come to prominence in wartime around national defence. Although their energies are now being depleted by the struggle to survive in war conditions, they have been active at the community level, such as in neighbourhood committees, the CDS. There they deal with a range of *barrio* affairs, including civil defence, and the local guards patrolling the streets at night have been almost entirely female. Women have a strong presence in the police force too, which is headed by a woman, and in the voluntary militia they learn how to handle arms. In the countryside women fight alongside male militia to defend their co-operatives against Contra attack.

But despite their military role during the struggle against Somoza, they now form only a fraction of the regular army. Women in army fatigues—or olive-green maternity smocks—are still a common sight on the streets. Nicaragua has followed a familiar post-liberation pattern by deploying women out of combat roles. Army officers argue that women soldiers are often better educated and more politicized than their male counterparts and are needed to fill administrative and logistical positions. The Ministry of the Interior now employs many women recruited from the army, including some at senior levels. There has been some opposition to this trend: AMNLAE fought successfully against the exclusion of women from military service, although accepting that for them this should be voluntary.

The problems associated with the demobilization of women have become apparent in comparable situations. How far does military action command higher status than civilian work? How far does the militarization of society, combined with female demobilization, reinforce *macho* values of violence and male power, and promote the image of dependent womanhood? These questions have yet to be researched in the Nicaraguan context.

The demobilization of women also raises the issue of motherhood, a further rationale for removing women from the front. Some in AMNLAE accept the argument that military life is incompatible with the maternal role. As Gladys Baez, a long-serving guerilla and FSLN militant, put it, 'women have proved themselves to be heroic, combative, courageous and able. But we *are* less tough, we march slower, and above all we have children. You can't have a regular army poised for instant mobilization based on a floating population.'[10]

Following AMPRONAC, AMNLAE too tries to recruit or retain women for the revolution in their role as mothers. The Patriotic Front of Mothers and Relatives organizes support for the young people doing military service; the Mothers of Heroes and Martyrs bring together the women whose children have been killed in action. Military service is unpopular with parents, and the loss of children traumatic, in both the psychological and economic sense. Through these groups personal comfort in anxiety and grief is offered, as well as a positive political meaning to individual tragedy.

Younger Nicaraguan women are now criticizing AMNLAE for its overemphasis on mothers, but it is in the eyes of some western feminists that the promotion of motherhood has the most disturbing connotations derived, for example, from Nazi Germany. These still resonate with writers who are wary of the issue even when analysing societies with a commitment to women's rights. To these writers the glorification of bearing and caring for children smacks of manipulation of the maternal role in order to renew a war-depleted population or breed a new generation of soldiers. It sidesteps the question of transforming gender roles and challenging the traditional division of labour.

This caution is understandable: there are real dangers here from which Nicaragua is not exempt. But the problem must be set in the context of Nicaraguan culture and FSLN policy, rather than viewed from a Eurocentric perspective which incorporates very different values. In Britain, for example, a woman's problem is rather that motherhood is downgraded and children socially marginalized, while state provisions for them are whittled away. At the risk of making crude contrasts, I would argue that children are central to Nicaraguan culture. Now women have more opportunity to plan their families, but children are still much desired and enjoyed. Through economic necessity, the threat of infant mortality and inadequate contraceptive facilities, mothers bear, on average, six or more children. AMNLAE's aim is not to destroy the status they confer on a mother, but to rescue it from the sentimental mystification of the traditional Catholic Church, and to emphasize its extra-domestic aspects. The FSLN also supports the maternal role materially through social programmes and has given greater recognition to the reality of motherhood, as opposed to its romanticized image, not only through health and welfare programmes but also by rewriting Somoza's Family Code.

Under the old regime this image of the nuclear family and the dutiful housewife promoted by the Church were in fact contradicted both by daily life and by the statute book. Elevated and revered from the pulpit, they were trampled on by the state. Legally men had no responsibility as fathers, yet had the right to remove their children from the mother's home. But in 1981 the Law of Maintenance enabled a woman to claim a financial contribution from the absent father of her child, and the Law of Family Relations gave her equal rights over the children. In practice, custody is now most often given to the mother, but AMNLAE, consistent with its aim of combating a purely domestic view of woman's role, rejected the proposal that she should have automatic rights in this respect. The aim was not to exclude men, but promote paternal responsibility within the context of the family.

The emphasis on the family in law reform might also at first sight seem anomalous to Western women who have identified this institution as the locus of women's oppression. But in the absence of a welfare state, the extended family is an essential system of support. AMNLAE revealed an awareness of the inequalities entrenched within the family in its 1982 draft of a Provision Law, enjoining all members to contribute to the family unit. This included sharing the housework, recognized as 'one of the pillars on which the family rests'. Although yet to be ratified, the law engendered much public discussion on the social and economic importance of domestic labour.

The new National Constitution, published in January 1987, confirmed these principles, restating the need for responsible paternity and promising legislation on the sharing of domestic duties. The Constitution also promises that women will have equal rights to sue for divorce, as yet mainly a male prerogative. It also states that there must be job security during pregnancy and during paid maternity leave, for the emphasis on motherhood is not coupled with a campaign to send women back into the home.

CONCLUSION

'Without the participation of women, there is no revolution', shout Nicaraguan women, not only at AMNLAE meetings but at the wide variety of gatherings they now attend. The slogan has a dual meaning. Just as women's contribution to the anti-Somoza struggle was indispensable, so now they are essential to the revolution's defence. But the slogan is not just a summons to further involvement, it is also confirmation of the claim that unless radical change in women's role is built into the revolution, there can be no true social transformation.

Inevitably, reality does not match up to aspirations. A recently published report by the government Women's Office concludes that despite the changes engendered by the war, the traditional division of labour and the ideologies that sustain it remain deeply entrenched in Nicaraguan society. Some women see little change in their situation from Somoza's time, except rising prices, fewer goods, greater distribution problems and further problems from an economy in trouble. But others see their lives transformed. They contrast their position as silent drudges under Somoza to their present activism in running a revolution. They talk of the 'space' that the Sandinistas have created for women, the 'doors' and 'windows' opened on the world.

The war has sharpened both perceptions, for it has had contradictory consequences for women. On the one hand, militarization of the country has directed resources to feed, clothe and arm those in uniform at the expense of the civilian population. It puts intolerable strain on the economy, which particularly affects female household heads. It increases family instability, and takes away a woman's children, sometimes for ever. It promotes images of masculinity which combine more readily with the traditional figure of the Virgin Mary than with the 'new woman' of the revolution. On the other hand, war has retained women at the centre of the national stage. It has precipitated their involvement in political and productive life, and forced action around factors that stand in the way of their participation. Through this, women have had opportunities to expand previous horizons and gain a new sense of self through their experience.

In Nicaragua the potential transformation of women's consciousness through a high level of involvement provides the thread of continuity between the war of liberation and the present military conflict. Comparative analysis might show that it is the combination of women's own determination with the democratic commitment of the FSLN that distinguishes

Nicaragua from the aftermath of other liberation struggles with regard to women's rights. For those women who enter into the new space opened to them, it is this confidence which helps them deal with *machismo* in their domestic lives, voice women's demands in the public arena and push forward the boundaries of official policy. Even given the overriding priority of war, what we can call 'feminist' demands around reproduction are now on the agenda.

But at present, even though the FSLN has the will to prioritize women's demands, they do not have the resources, or the political space. The key question for women themselves is whether their exhaustion at combining their additional responsibilities with trying to maintain themselves and their families under present conditions will erode their enthusiasm. For despite the Central American Peace proposals signed by the Central American presidents in August 1987, and President Reagan's failure to obtain further official funding for the Contra in February 1988, the economic effects of the war are crushing the country. For Nicaragua is now fighting for its survival, and women's hopes stand to be crushed by President Reagan's determination to wreck the Sandinista revolution.

NOTES

1. The peoples of Nicaragua's Atlantic Coast—Latino, indigenous Indian and Creole—form distinct cultural and politico-economic groups, and were geographically isolated from the anti-Somoza struggle. They are deeply affected by the Contra war, but the context of coastal women's lives requires a separate analysis which cannot be undertaken in this paper.
2. For background on women in Nicaragua see: Elizabeth Maier, *Nicaragua, La Mujer en la Revolución* (Mexico City: Ediciones de Cultura Popular, 1980); Margaret Randall, *Sandino's Daughters* (London: Zed Press, 1981); Jane Deighton *et al., Sweet Ramparts: Women in Revolutionary Nicaragua* (London: War on Want and Nicaragua Solidarity Campaign, 1983); Hermione Harris, 'Women in Struggle: Nicaragua', *Third World Quarterly* 5 (4); Hermione Harris, 'War and Reconstruction: Women in Nicaragua', in Olivia Harris (ed.), *Latin American Women* (London: Minority Rights Group, 1983); Maxine Molyneux, 'Mobilization without Emancipation? Women's Interests, the State, and Revolution in Nicaragua', *Feminist Studies* 11 (2). Maxine

Molyneux, 'Women's Role in the Revolutionary Process', in T. Walker (ed.), *Nicaragua: The First Five Years* (New York: Praeger, New York, 1985); Adriana Angel and Fiona Macintosh, *The Tiger's Milk: Women of Nicaragua* (London: Virago, London 1987).

3. See Maxine Molyneux, 'Socialism Old and New: Progress towards Women's Emancipation?' *Monthly Review* 34(3).
4. See Wendy Chapkis (ed.), *Loaded Questions: Women and the Military* (Amsterdam: Transnational Institute, 1981); Cynthia Enloe, *Does Khaki Become You? The Militarisation of Women's Lives* (London: Pluto Press, 1983).
5. *Programa de AMPRONAC*. Reprinted in Maier, p. 150.
6. *Documento de AMPRONAC*, Nicaragua, 1978, p. 6.
7. Speech concluding Women's Week, March 1980. Translated and published by WIRE, *Nicaraguan Women and the Revolution*, New York, 1982, p. 8.
8. Angel and Macintosh, p. 128.
9. Enloe, Ch. 6.
10. Quoted in Molyneux, 'Women's Role in the Revolutionary Process'.

13

The Mobilization and Demobilization of Women in Militarized Chile

Ximena Bunster
Instituto de Estudios Democraticos de la Mujer, Chile

The last thirteen years of Chilean history have witnessed and recorded the social evils brought about by one of the most brutal militarized governments in the world today. Under Pinochet's military state—ruled by a junta made up of representatives of the army, navy, air force and police—citizens have been living within the boundaries of what Chilean women have labelled 'the culture of death: kidnappings, torture, extra-legal executions, 'missing' relatives and friends and the irrational punishment of exiles that has torn so many families asunder. Integral to this culture of death has been the junta's misconceived economic policies: they have made the wealthy wealthier and the poor, poorer. The long democratic tradition of Chile has been thwarted by the junta's closing of Congress and the banning of political parties. Education at all levels—university, secondary and primary—has been interrupted by the military government: student leaders have been assassinated and jailed.

The ideological rationale for this culture of death has been the military élite's 'doctrine of national security'. This doctrine has allowed Pinochet to claim that the junta is waging both an international war against foreign communism and a domestic, internal war against local subversion.

Repression, flowing from and to this doctrine, has been handled by the armed forces, the police and civilians hired by the military. Increasingly, while unified behind the junta's survival, the army, navy, air force and police have engaged in rivalry with each other. For instance, one woman and her daughter and children recently had the army's intelligence agents at their door searching their house at one hour, only to be followed by *each of the other* three agencies' officers in succession throughout the night. In other words, shared masculinized militarism does not preclude rivalries between militaristic men; and these rivalries can only intensify the repression experienced by women.

Fear immobilized most of the Chilean population from 1973 on, when the military overthrew the Allende government. Fear froze any attempts at social mobilization to show massive rejection of the regime.

It was women who, in 1979, unbalanced the silent anti-dictatorship *status quo* by stepping out of the family, leaving the allegedly protected environments of their homes to invade the streets with their presence and demand a return to participatory democracy. They did so many years before men dared manifest themselves publicly against the regime. Chile's highly politicized male population seemed paralysed by the junta's continuing ban on political parties, for parties had always been the arenas in which Chilean men traditionally proved the adult manhood. By contrast, Chilean women broke the political silence by using the 'social construction' of femininity, by making legitimate their cultural female resources—'mother power'—in the political arena. They have consciously used their nurturing role as a powerful political instrument aimed at destabilizing the military junta (Bunster, 1986).

This large and diverse group of women is made up of women of the working class, by professional women and some women from the upper classes. They have come to realize that they share in common a rejection of the regime: shanty-town women have organized in the last few years around soup kitchens to give a collective solution to the problem of hunger brought about by joblessness or disappearance of the male breadwinners; women who have been the direct victims of the regime's torture and incarceration have networked around human rights organizations, organizations which hitherto had no feminist analysis or political base; mothers have flocked to the Vicariate of Solidarity under the aegis of the Catholic Church asking for the whereabouts of their missing family members. Both professional and non-professional women have put pressure on arms of the government, (and many of them *head* these organizations) through activism in the Chilean Association of Relatives of Disappeared Persons, in the Association of Relatives of Political Prisoners, and in different human rights groups—the Human Rights Commission, the National Commission Against Torture and in the group for the Protection of Helpless Children under States of Emergency. Chilean women lawyers put their lives in danger defending victims of the dictatorial regime, and woman psychiatrists, psychologists and social workers form part of medical psychiatric teams treating victims of torture and using their therapeutic resources on suffering relatives of the missing and the tortured.

An important new step in Chilean women's anti-militarism organizing and analysis was the formation of the collective Mujeres por la Vida (Women for Life). Its founders saw it as an umbrella organization bringing all of these politically and socially diverse groups of women together, including The Movement of Shanty-Town Women (Movimiento de Mujeres Pobladoras), The Women's Union Co-ordinating Committee (La Coordinadora Sindical Femenina) and the Feminist Movement, not to mention the MEMCH (Movimiento de Emancipación de la Mujer Chilena) and the MUDECHI (Mujeres de Chile), which co-ordinate all the women's groups in the country.

Mujeres por la Vida have strategized the mobilization of thousands of women in Santiago, the capital city and all along Chile. The organizers belong to male-led political parties of the centre, left and independent groups as well as feminist organizations. They have fashioned the slogan, 'Democracy in the country and at home'; they want radical changes in power relations in the nation and in interpersonal relations in the home, as well as changing the actual separation between the private and the public domain. Thus they have come to direct their demands not only at the current military regime but also at the anti-military men in their own parties. Mujeres por la Vida has become the political frame of reference for all women opposing Pinochet's government and has given this segment of Chilean women a new identity as political actors in the political arena. The political importance of Mujeres por la

Vida was recognized in 1986 by the Common Citizen's Assembly (la Asamblea de la Civilidad), a national umbrella association made up of over 200 organizations—mostly male led—articulated in twenty-three institutions for drafting Chile's Demand for a Return to Democracy (La Demanda de Chile). Mujeres por la Vida was represented by Antonieta Saa, a socialist and a feminist who was jailed for two months and later released due to international feminist protest.

The Common Citizen's Assembly managed to bring about a national strike against the regime during 2 and 3 July 1986. The military junta responded by escalating its brutal militarized repression and heinous crimes, including the burning alive of two young students and by the incarceration, torture and murder of many leaders. Even Mujeres por la Vida, who had defied violence and fear to take over the streets, have been pushed back by this new wave of regime violence.

Many Chilean and foreign feminists have devoted their attention to these smart and brave anti-militaristic women. In part their focus has been prompted by the American and European media's ignoring of Chilean women's political influence. But, at the same time, as Mujeres por la Vida was mobilizing women, the military was also busy mobilizing thousands of *other* Chilean women in order to turn them into a base of support for Pinochet. This is something that feminists must analyse and understand at the same time as we listen to and celebrate anti-militaristic women. But only by exploring this development can we as feminists expose the deeply *patriarchal* politics without which militaristic regimes cannot survive. The exploration which follows, therefore, does *not* mean to 'blame the victim'; rather, it is intended to reveal that even hyper-masculinized militarism remains dependent on rigid constructions of femininity.

Since 1973, Pinochet's military government deliberately has tried to exert its power and control over thousands of women all over Chile through community organizations which by 1987 branch out from the established military government bureaucracy further permeating civilian life with military values. The two most important organizations, because of their sophisticated structure and management and their massively articulated impact on women from all social classes are Cema-Chile (Chilean Mothers' Centres) and the Secretaría Nacional de la Mujer (Women's National Secretariat), or SNM.

The influence wielded by these two all-women pro-Pinochet government-controlled organizations is especially potent because political parties have been banned and because anti-junta women's organizing has been assaulted.

By 1983 Cema-Chile had 6,000 volunteers responsible for organizing and indoctrinating 230,000 members in more than 10,000 mothers' centres: the SNM boasted of having 10,000 volunteers in 321 branch offices; and it is estimated that during the ten-year period, 1973 to 1983, its activities had involved more than 2 million women (Lechner and Levy, 1984).

Both political institutions are perceived by the military regime and its élite civilian male allies as part of their structure of defence. Opposition women's groups have called them the 'junta's civil trench'. Cema-Chile is a private institution emphasizing and delivering economic assistance to its members; the SNM is a government agency specifically designed, equipped and articulated to serve as the ideological channel through which the military regime indoctrinates women on a daily basis. The SNM is a 'standing army' of women volunteers whose primordial task is to serve as agents of ideological propaganda of the military project superimposed on the Chilean population and to act as a network supporting activities of economic aid to the poor, where most women and youth find themselves within the socio-economic structure. Pinochet had acknowledged publicly that he relies heavily on the support of women, young people and government-appointed union leaders for the prolongation of his regime.

Though allegedly a private organization, the Cema's national president is Pinochet's wife, Lucía Hiriart de Pinochet. The executive director is appointed by Pinochet's wife. There are regional vice-presidents, provincial and communal ones along Chilean territory. Most of the women doing volunteer work are wives of officers of the armed forces and police. There is one volunteer for every ten mothers' centres; each volunteer acts as the representative of the 'First Lady of the Nation' and national president of Cema. Thus the militarization of 'wifely duty' has been crucial to the junta's cooptation of these women.

The SNM is a state institution whose aim is to implement state policy. Unlike Cema, it is not organized into base communities. Rather, SNM women see themselves as ideological-political advisors and teachers spreading Pinochet's political gospel. Therefore the task of the volunteers from the SNM is strictly political. Yet, like Cema, but even more so, the SNM is a women's organization at the service of a militarized patriarchal order.

The SNM focuses its political energies and brain-washing methods on the preservation of the conservative-historical-cultural model of the 'female condition'—*la condición femenina*—addressing Chilean women as mothers and 'bearers' of the values of the Fatherland. These two feminine priorities are not new to Chile. One can even see past democratic and socialist Chilean male politicians stressing these notions of Chilean femininity. What *is* new is harnessing these constructions of femininity to a militarized doctrine of national security.

The image of the Chilean woman manipulated by the SNM is that of a patriotic, self-sacrificing mother whose 'apolitical-feminine-private' social behaviour develops solely within the territorial boundaries of her home (Lechner and Levy, 1984; Munizaga and Letelier, 1987). However, 'home' is stretched so as to allow certain affluent women (especially from the newly upwardly mobile military class), to leave their own physical houses to do 'homely' volunteer work in poor neighbourhoods. This volunteer work has had an effect on the way upper middle- and upper-class women see shanty-town women—they *don't*. SNM's women have literally moved poor women's fragile houses out of Santiago's affluent neighbourhoods.

Pinochet himself, in one of his speeches to the women volunteers of the SNM, synthesized his appraisal of the ideal woman's role during his government by stating:

> When a woman becomes a mother she does not expect anything more on a material plane; she searches and finds in her own son the purpose of her life, her only treasure and the finishing line where her dreams come true.

The military regime perceives its women supporters as identifying themselves with the fatherland through their families, through their private experience as mothers. In another speech addressed to women of the SNM, Pinochet summed up this process thus:

> Fatherland and patriotism are concepts derived from the Latin pater, which means father. Therefore they indicate a filial relationship with the fatherland equivalent to the relationship between the concepts filiation and familiar paternity.

The 'patriotic mother' drummed up by the Pinochet regime is therefore strictly subordinated to the *pater familias* and particularly to the *pater patrias* (father of the nation); the 'patriotic mother' has a derived secondary identity stemming from her unconditional admiration for the 'father of the homeland', Pinochet himself. The thousands of volunteers from the SNM are guided by the image of this strong charismatic leader who promises to defend them, their families and the nation from the evils of international communism and offers them the attainment of a perfect social order built on a rejection of 'politics' and anything 'political'. In Pinochet's eyes, 'politics' is the equivalent of violence and chaos. Whenever the leaders of the outlawed political parties and the women of the opposition demand the participation of political parties and a return to a democratic government, Pinochet threateningly warns through the national television network, 'It's either me or chaos'. The crucial corollary of this warning is: women must be in the 'civil trench' to hold back that chaos; women are the preservers of Chile's moral order. Many Chilean women in the 1980s have been lured into accepting that identity and thus militarized in the process.

With the help of the SNM, women volunteers and their followers become the needed supporters of a government that intends to perpetuate itself indefinitely as a 'protected democracy'.

Women volunteers are portrayed as being at the lofty service of the fatherland, and this is what *defines* their voluntary work. They give of themselves generously out of a feminine love for sacrifice to a superior cause. When the social-political order contravenes the social-natural order, the survival of the nation is at risk. Therefore the universal mother acts on behalf of the Fatherland *with* and *under* the authority of the universal father. He is the epitome and the reincarnation of the values of the military in the sense that he can generate the necessary energy to keep the nation safe and alive and apply technical and scientific know-how on its behalf with no vested political interests (Munizaga and Letelier, 1987: 49–50).

The woman volunteer becomes a public mother. Yet she cannot do or say anything herself because she is not supposed to display any initiative of her own; her speech and her activities have to project the goals and desires of the leader in a position of authority. It follows then that the woman volunteer needs to be indoctrinated so she can spread the truth, she has to 'receive the word' in order to transmit it faithfully. She is no more than a delivery channel (Munizaga and Letelier, 1987: 50).

The president of the SNM is the 'first lady', Lucía Hiriart de Pinochet, appointed to the presidency for an indefinite period of time by Pinochet himself. Women volunteers get no salary, as their motivation is to promote and channel the support of women to the Pinochet regime. This in turn guarantees that they will serve the poor *but not be from the poor*. There are four categories of volunteers: (1) leaders with a strong ideological commitment to the government, basically from an upper-middle or upper economic status; (2) professional women who collaborate with the SNM through their areas of expertise—law, social work, education, nutrition, obstetrics and research; (3) monitors in charge of literacy campaigns, consumer education, civic orientation and national current events, and (4) community volunteers who have been trained to tackle specific problems.

The activities generated by the members of the SNM are varied. Among the most important are the following: (1) training and indoctrination in government policies (the core lectures are given to the women by men who are working closely with Pinochet cabinet ministers, secretaries of state, and other outstanding official power figures; (2) regular seminars to train volunteers in government ideology, who will, in turn, train other women; (3) a variety of talks and speeches targeted to different audiences—government-controlled or sympathetic to the government.

Targeted audiences are diverse in composition. Among these groups are found: (1) wives of cabinet ministers, secretaries of state and wives of officers and generals of the armed forces (courses are organized in conjunction with the Superior Academy of National Security); (2) women leaders (seminars co-ordinated with the Inter-American Committee of Women under the auspices of OEA—the Organization of American States); (3) volunteers of the National Foundation in Aid to the Community; (4) wives of officers of the War Academy and of the air force; (5) Corporation of Ladies involved in National Defence; (6) female personnel of the Polytechnic Military Academy; (7) Corporation in Aid to the Aged; (8) Secretaries' Association; (9) female personnel of the state operated railroad system; (10) junta-elected women union leaders in the area of public health, railway system and telephone operators; (11) PTA (parent–teacher associations in schools across the Chilean nation); (12) neighbourhood associations and other community associations; (13) women workers in the Chilean public administration system and in private companies; (14) mothers' centres (Cema); (15) fathers' centres; (16) shanty-town mothers who are in the process of being '*erradicados*' (these are women whose families are living in unsanitary crowded conditions to whom the Pinochet government has offered subsidized housing).

The SNM publishes a monthly women's magazine called *Amiga* (friend), which is a printed vehicle of state indoctrination. It also publishes the *Rural Teacher's Handbook* and booklets on civic topics, cultural themes, cooking and health tips.

Volunteers of the SNM are women from the upper middle and upper classes who have a private income. Typically, the volunteer is a middle-aged woman whose children are already married and who finds that she has too much free time and nothing to fill it with. There are also single women and widows who feel that life is made up of stages, that life has a purpose and that they should pursue some goal in life to fulfil themselves. According to Lechner and Levy, what characterizes these women is that they have clear ideas and that they love their president; these women are *committed* to the authoritarian government and they are the *civil militants of the regime*. These volunteers make up something like the dictator's party; the SNM is an organization whose existence depends on the total identification of its members with the president (Lechner and Levy, 1984).

Women volunteers of Pinochet's party also wear uniforms. The media refers to them as 'the ladies in pallet colours'. Ladies in Red (Damas de Rojo), are hospital volunteers, Ladies in Yellow (Damas de Amarillo) raise money to buy clothes for the indigent in hospitals, Ladies in Baby Blue (Damas de Celeste) look after the Chilean aged, Ladies in Calypso (Damas de Calypso) do volunteer work in children's hospitals and the Ladies in Lilac (Damas de Lila) do volunteer work in CONIM (Corporation of Child Nutrition).

We have seen how the vast network of pro-Pinochet women has been spread all over the country and how they have been made to represent to the public eye a 'living affirmation', a tacit approval of the oppressive junta regime. These militarized women stand in stark contrast to the resistance to the dictatorship strategized by Mujeres por la Vida, who do not affirm but loudly negate and refuse to accept the prolongation of the militarized Chilean government and the concepts of femininity on which it depends (Valdeś, 1986).

It is therefore timely to ask the following questions. Under what conditions are women most able to be made complicit to militarization? Why is it that militarized men need women's complicity? Which women seem especially vulnerable to be 'militarized'? Is it possible for men to militarize their societies *without* women?

The Chilean case provides an interesting launching pad for the analysis and response to some of these questions. The success claimed by the Pinochet regime in 'militarizing' female supporters through programmatic indoctrination by the SNM has to be evaluated and explained in the context of the last thirty years of Chilean social and political history.

There are historical antecedents that account for the emergence of an army of women volunteers in Pinochet's Chile. The origin of Cema may be traced back to the time when upper-middle and upper-class women performed 'maternalistic charity' on behalf of the poor with an evangelical zeal triggered by the Catholic Church; the 'well-do-do' ladies distributed material goods—food, clothing and medicines to their pauperized working-class sisters. Charity was in exchange for their presence at Sunday Mass. The first mothers' centres were organized around sewing workshops in an effort to integrate them into the labour force. In 1954 a private organization started the 'Ropero del Pueblo' (The Poor People's Closet) and in 1962 the women's section of the Christian Democratic Party multiplied mothers' centres in an effort to root the party and its social reforms among the poor. During President Eduardo Frei's government, at the end of the 1960s, there were about 8,000 mothers' centres and around 400,000 organized women who had initially joined these centres to buy their own sewing machines but who thrived on their membership to these organizations because they became involved in neighbourhood activities.

The exchange of benefits for a specific ideology was also present during the Allende government, where mothers' centres were recreated under COCEMA (Confederación Nacional de Centros de Madres), where they became meeting places to discuss community affairs. Later these mothers' centres were incorporated into large organizations called JAP, government agencies in charge of regulating prices of commodities and distributing them fairly amongst the Chilean population at the time that the women of the opposition to the Allende government were producing a black-market fright.

With the advent of the junta, mothers' centres are given another image by the regime: 'apolitical' mothers identify themselves with the Fatherland through their links with their families, and they become 'docile and obedient patriotic mothers'.

In all of these cases, women's participation in volunteer work and in mothers' centres has been manipulated by a religious institution, a political party and lately the military. Women are not then the originators nor the creators of a new social order, but they become the propagandists and executors of an externally designed social project; their traditional supportive role and derived identity fall into place with the hierarchical mentality of the military and remain even more marginalized.

The campaign of terror unleashed by the military government against the citizens who oppose its policies is complex and makes conventional women more vulnerable to his dictatorial discourse. Pinochet contrasts revolutionary alternatives to social reform (which he despises and fears) with the advantages of order and offers the implementation of authority over participation. These words are constantly addressed to women.

Rapid and violent socio-cultural changes impinging on women's roles have marked the last thirty years of women's history. Conservative frames of reference defining women's place in society have been dropped, women have entered the labour force by the thousands and many of them are the official family breadwinners. According to Munizaga and Letelier, these multiple changes have produced anxiety and lack of orientation in many women who feel more at ease returning to their traditional familiar role, which is Pinochet's image of women and his strategy to make them complicit with the military government (Munizaga and Letelier, 1987). The SNM reinforces the traditional role of women as mothers and home-makers.

Lastly, but very important, is the issue of empowerment. Female supporters of the regime, especially the volunteer corps, are proud of their spirit of sacrifice and their selfless commitment to a cause. In exchange for their admiring support of Pinochet, they can wear a uniform that makes them proud. As one of them said, 'We have to obey orders and work hard to deserve this uniform, which marks our membership to this institution'.

CONCLUSION

We have seen how the same cultural model of womanhood has been used in Chile by two very different categories of women from two opposing political programmes. Mujeres por la Vida have tried to alter the power structure of militarized Chilean society by unbalancing patterned mechanisms of oppression; the women in 'pallet' colours, on the contrary, derive their identity from Pinochet and have become his staunch supporters.

We should learn more about the structural vulnerability of women who ally themselves with military governments and keep in mind, as Cynthia Enloe has pointed out, that all women are affected by the military's need to exploit and yet ideologically marginalize women, and that women will remain society's camp followers *so long as the military as an institution and militarism as an ideology are widely accepted as guarantors of the social order* (Enloe, 1983: 17).

ACKNOWLEDGEMENT

I would like to acknowledge the constructive criticisms of the final draft of this chapter offered by Cynthia Enloe, as well as Giselle Munizaga's insightful analysis of Pinochet's discourse.

REFERENCES

Bunster, Ximena (1984), 'Overcoming Death: Chilean Women's Resistance to Pinochet's Junta and Their Struggle for a Return to Democracy', *Cultural Survival* 8 (2).

(1985), 'Surviving Beyond Fear: Women and Torture in Latin America', in June Nash and Helen Safa (eds.), *Women and Change in Latin America* (New York: J.F. Bergin).

Enloe, Cynthia (1983), *Does Khaki Become You? The Militarization of Women's Lives* (London: Pluto Press, 1983).

Koonz, Claudia (1987), *Mothers in the Fatherland: Women in Nazi Germany* (New York: St Martin's Press).

Lechner, Norbert and Levy, Susana (1984), *Notas Sobre La Vida Cotidiana III. El Disciplinamiento de la Mujer* (Santiago: Flacso, Numero 57).

Munizaga, Giselle, and Letelier, Lilian (1987), 'Mujer y Regimen Militar', unpublished manuscript, Santiago, Ceneca.

Valdés, Teresa (1986), 'Las Mujeres Bajo La Dictatura Militar en Chile', unpublished manuscript, Santiago.

PART 5

WOMEN AS CREATORS OF WORLD PEACE

14

Warriors and Saints: Dilemmas in the History of Men, Women and War

Elise Boulding
Professor Emerita, Dartmouth College, Hanover, NH, USA

War as women have experienced it throughout recorded history from the times of the earliest city-states, has been an organizing principle involving the domination of the weak by the strong, and the domination of women by men in a variety of political and social forms which bear the common label of patriarchy. We will assume that the reproductive roles of women had something to do with the asymmetric power situation that arose in every society, creating a gender-based division of labour that did not correspond to any physical or mental differentiation in capacity beyond reproduction itself. In spite of a number of explanatory theories, it remains a continuing intellectual puzzle to understand how this asymmetric division of labour, based on a continuing exercise of brutality, violence and war, was apparently so stable over so many centuries, given the many other potentialities of the male and the female of the species.[1]

In the nuclear era, the stability of the war system is finally coming to an end. However, the nature of the reconstruction process that needs to take place in order to replace a stable war system with a stable system of peaceful conflict resolution is not well understood. In this paper we will explore the similarity of the peace- and war-making endowments of women and men, the nature of women's adaptations that have made the continuance of the war system possible, women's repeated efforts to create non-traditional roles which could break that cycle, and finally the prospects for system change as we enter the twenty-first century.

WOMEN'S DOUBLE CAPACITY: THE WARRIOR AND THE SAINT

It is first necessary to establish the point that women are not inherently any more peaceful than men. They have made splendid warriors throughout history, and women can thrill to sword-brandishing as much as men. How else can one explain the recurring theme in women's literature of amazons, and the present-day US social movement (complete with several newsletters) of the Guild of the Free Amazons? These 'wiry, agile, lean-hipped and flat-breasted' women have taken the Amazon, or Renunciates Oath, wear distinctive leather jackets, boots and riding trousers, live together in Guilds and have highly developed fighting skills.[2] While not featured in most history books, the red-haired Celtic Queen Boudicca, who fell with her two daughters while fighting to repel Roman invaders of Britain; the warrior Queen Isabel, who led her troops on horseback to turn warring kingdoms into a united Spain; and Rani Lakshmi Bai of Jhansi, a warrior in the great Maratha tradition, who unsuccessfully led her troops against the British in India; not to mention Joan of Arc, who fought to defend France—are just the tip of the iceberg in a generally unsung record of heroic women soldiers of every century. Most women soldiers fought disguised as men and remained undiscovered unless killed on the battlefield. Readers of the historical record thrill to the same qualities in these war heroines that they thrill to the best of the war heroes—courage, self-sacrifice for a righteous cause, love of one's people.

It is not only the warriors who evoke the thrill reaction, however, it is also the heroically good, the peacemaker, the 'saint'. 'Saint' is used here metaphorically to refer to a class of women who have heroically striven to break the historical cycle of recurring wars and to replace it with a new order of human caring. Some examples: Mary of Egypt, who left the luxuries of dissolute Alexandria for a life of hardy solitude in the desert in the fifth century, becoming a living legend in her own lifetime; Rabi'a, a tenth-century Moslem slave revered throughout Islam as a mystic, a servant of the needy and teacher of the ways of love; the Beguine women, who dared to open communes for single women of the labouring class in medieval urban Europe at a time when unmarried women were only allowed to live in cities as prostitutes, assigned to a special district; Clare of Assissi, who defied conventions to follow St Francis and found a radical women's order vowed to singlehood, simplicity and service; the Maryknoll Sisters of our own time, who are serving humanity in situations of war and extreme danger on all continents, and whose ranks of martyrs are growing. We find the same heroic transcendence of self, the courage, vision, love and disciplined capacity for action in these activist women saints that we find in St Francis, in Gandhi, in Martin Buber, in Martin Luther King.

What I am suggesting is that the heights of heroism, both violent and non-violent, have been reached repeatedly in history by both men and women; we respond to that heroism in instinctive recognition of the distilled essence of our own capacity as human beings. Violent heroism has been accepted as a part of how society works, but so has non-violent heroism. Our task now is to reconstruct our understanding of heroism so as to move away from violence towards non-violence, harnessing the same energies to peace-building behaviour that were formerly harnessed to war. With the tools of destruction now available, we can no longer accept the situation of arrested development of the species that has kept us pegged at the levels of violence history has taught us to expect. At this historical moment, we either enter a period of social learning that enables us to manage conflict more creatively, or the social order degenerates from the previous unsatisfactory but relatively stable war system to an unstable, chaotic and regressive situation of a world of warring camps. That new social learning is not only necessary for men, however, it is also necessary for women.

THE GENDER TRAP

The recognition of the heroic element in war, the defence of one's 'people', has been an element in keeping women willing to bear the next generation of soldiers, however reluctantly or despairingly. Loyalty to a patriarchal regime is not induced by force alone. Rarely do Lysistratas arise to question the 'us versus them' theme of the nation-state. On the one hand, then, we have the continuing destructiveness of a system of domination that depends on recurring warfare to feed the greedy drives for accumulation of goods and power (totally non-heroic drives!), and on the other hand we have the continuing willingness of women to buffer the destructiveness of that system by bearing children, procuring food and conducting the variety of maintenance activities that enable society to continue in spite of its self-destructive character. The basic energies common to all human beings have been redirected so that men seek power and women protect men from the consequences of power-seeking.

In order to protect men from those consequences, women have been called to a ceaseless reconstruction of the social infrastructure that provides the health, education and human services required for society not to fall apart, as well as a ceaseless tending of the rural resources of the land in order that there be an uninterrupted supply of food. Because we tend to think of health, education and welfare as specialized services, we overlook the fact that these services are provided within and between households by women at every level of societal complexity from tribal societies, city-states and ancient empires to modern states. Each society has depended on the basic level of education initially offered by its women to its children, on the healing skills of women, and on their capacity to forage and to share food and emergency help in times of crisis. None of these activities are confined within individual households. They are all inter-household activities, operating at the community level.

As urbanism developed, these services became more visible; women's religious orders provided hospitals and schools and services to the poor, but the difference from earlier times was only one of scale. Today, professionalized services still account for only a small fraction of these basic services, which are still rendered primarily by women within and between households. Even within the professional sectors, nursing, teaching and social work are primarily women's work. Every war has put renewed pressure on women to maintain these services under great difficulties. They have not only maintained household and community as such, but they have provisioned and nursed mobile armies. At the close of every war, destroyed communities have been rebuilt, and much of the physical labour of rebuilding has been women's work.

Another activity traditionally expected of women is conflict resolution, since it is troublesome to go to war all the time. The old practice of marrying the daughters of one village to the sons of the next was a war-avoidance strategy, as was the practice of marrying royal daughters to the sons of potential adversaries (Boulding, 1977: 429–43). Much community peacemaking goes on between the women of households in conflict, and this is as true for societies practising purdah as in non-purdah societies. In Moslem countries, women's bathhouses are important conflict-resolution centres.

In addition to family-based roles, there is another type of traditional wartime role filled by women: as camp followers, disparagingly called prostitutes, who forage for food, cook it, nurse the wounded and help with a variety of battlefield jobs including handling ammunition and firearms. (Their modern-day counterparts work in munitions factories or directly in the armed services.)

Each of the activities described can be interpreted as being protective of the war system, in that they enable society to go on within existing frames of reference and are not specifically directed at changing the social order. But women can and have taken up other roles besides those of system-maintenance, as we shall see. A critical interim step that women must take before entering into social-change roles is to reposition themselves outside the gender trap which keeps them in system-maintenance roles. The awareness of victimage that must develop in order for that repositioning to take place, will now be explored.

GETTING OUT OF THE GENDER TRAP: AWARENESS OF VICTIMAGE

One of the important things the nineteenth- and twentieth-century women's movements have done is to make women aware of themselves as victims of a historical patriarchal order which regularly generates warfare and violence as well as forms of oppression specific to women. Attention has understandably focused on violence against women in the home—wife beating—and on women's vulnerability to rape both in peace and war. It has also focused on the structural violence of forced domesticity, of limited opportunities in the political and economic domains and limited personal freedom of choice. Making the connections between violence against women and the war system itself is a relatively recent development in the women's movement. The unhappy situation which has prevailed until now, that the women's peace movement has not paid much attention to women's problems, and that the women's rights movement has not paid much attention to war problems, should come to an end. During the first International Women's Decade, of the three themes of equality, development and peace, very little attention went to peace. The Decade programme overlooked the fact that the requirements of militarism so thoroughly distort the economy and the polity that no goals of social justice, be they for women, children, other minorities or the poor in general, can be achieved. It is now time to put the same kind of energy into changing the war system itself that until now has gone into combating victimage *per se*. What might this involve?

WOMEN AS SYSTEM-CHANGERS

The alternative for women to being system-maintenance victims is to become system-change activists. The system changes required are far-reaching, involving a re-examination of the scale and degree of centralization of industrialized and industrializing societies, types of capitalization of the economy, occupational structures, use of natural resources, patterns of civic involvement in decision-making, type of education and other arenas. It is therefore appropriate to think of the changes that lie ahead as revolutionary in nature, and of women system-changers as revolutionaries. There are two types of revolutionaries: violent and non-violent. The same qualities that turn women into warriors and saints, can also turn them into violent or non-violent revolutionaries. We will examine both types of revolutionaries, beginning with the non-violent ones.

Non-violent Revolutionaries

Non-violent women revolutionaries are not well recorded in mainstream history, partly because women's activities are rarely thought of in those terms. The women who responded to the urban migrations toward the end of the feudal era in Europe by founding urban women's communes, were revolutionaries because they created new social roles, new occupational structures and a new educational system for women and for the children they taught in their schools. So were the women cathari and anabaptists who travelled around Europe teaching other women to read, who translated the Bible into the vernacular, thereby demystifying Church authority, and who worked with men to create forms of community organization with full equality for men and women (Boulding, 1977, Ch. 9).

One of the best-documented stories of non-violent women revolutionaries in the past century and a half is the story of the women leaders of the independence movement in India (Kaur, 1985; Kamaladevi, 1986). Well before Gandhi was calling on women to practise *satyagraha*, the grandmothers, mothers, wives and daughters of the educated classes in India were forming organizations providing education and action-training for other women, in order to rebuild an Indian society freed from colonial structures. Mother and daughter Kristo and Kumudini Mitter, mother and daughter Swami Kumari and Sarla Devi, and Madam Bhikaiji K.R. Cama, all belonged to that earlier generation of leaders. Their groundwork helped make Gandhi's achievements possible. There was a continuing leadership of successive generations of women into the immediate pre-independence years. Swaroop Rani, wife of Pandit Motilal Nehru and her daughter Vijaylakshmi Pandit, were among several generations of Nehru women to lead in this struggle. Together with Sarojini

Naidu and Kamaladevi, they are the best known of women leaders. However, the teenage Kanak Lata Barua, and the 73-year-old Manangini Hazra, both shot by the British on separate independence marches in 1942, can stand for thousands of lesser-known women who provided the leadership which helped village women all over India take the courage to engage in civil disobedience against the salt tax and other indignities, face English gunfire unarmed and accept martyrdom in the hundreds, imprisonment in the thousands. Schools, village industries, craft co-operatives, political education and massive non-cooperation with the authorities, were the tools for the non-violent revolution which eventually won India's independence. In Europe, many have known first hand the non-violent women leaders in the underground resistance movements of the Second World War. Today we are witnessing the non-violent leadership of women for revolutionary change in the Philippines, in Central America and in other less well-recorded struggles on other continents.

Some of the women who began as non-violent revolutionaries turned to violence because non-violence did not appear to be achieving results. They are therefore in many respects similar to their non-violent sisters, and deserve special attention if we are to understand the problems of shifting from war-engendering dominance structures to a more egalitarian problem-solving type of social order.

Violent Revolutionaries and the Symbolic Use of Terror

Violent revolution and terrorism are not synonymous. Terrorism is a special form of revolutionary violence. Since papers elsewhere deal with women's roles in fighting wars of independence, I will focus here only on the use of symbolic violence, or terrorist action, to achieve important social goals.

Two important historical eras of terrorism give us insight into today's terrorist activities. The first is the revolutionary movement in the Russia of Alexander II, the second the revolutionary movement in the India of the early 1900s. The women's movement in Russia in the second half of the nineteenth century became strongly involved first in reform, then in non-violent revolution, and finally in the 1870s in symbolic terrorism. As a student of this process has written:

> The transition to terrorism did not come easily to Russian revolutionaries. Most of them had to overcome a deep resistance to violence, which involved them in a painful inner struggle. If they did join the new organization, it was only because they saw no other way of advancing the cause of political freedom in Russia. They argued that in killing the tsar they would be eliminating not a human being but an abstract principle—the autocracy. But they remained reluctant assassins and repeatedly expressed their revulsion from bloodshed.
>
> (Broido, 1977: 181)

Vera Zasulich shot and wounded General Trepov in protest against his brutality to prisoners, and the prison system generally. At her trial she said, 'I could find no other way of drawing attention to what had happened. . . . *It is a terrible thing to lift a hand against a human being*, but I felt I had to do it . . . I fired without aiming . . . [she had then immediately thrown the revolver down] I was afraid it might go off again . . . I did not want this' (Broido, 1977: 146). She was acquitted and hailed by the populace as a saint.

Sofya Perovskaya, who was to die at 27 for having organized the assassination of the Tsar, is described as a 'small graceful, ever-laughing girl [who] possessed a fearlessness that amazed the bravest of men'; as one who had taken a lot of persuading before joining the revolutionaries, but who pursued her course of action with absolute single-mindedness once decided, who was moved by a deep sense of duty, and by a 'divine spark which flowed so richly in her and which women possess in a much greater measure—let us admit it—than men', which is 'why the Russian revolutionary movement owes its almost religious fire above all to them, and why, as long as there are women in it, it will remain invincible'.[3]

Vera Figner, who joined the movement in spite of her dislike of terrorism, is described as a 'young woman of a strong and silent, almost nunlike type . . . [combining] high intelligence and great energy with warm responsiveness to human suffering . . . she understands sorrow, she has a truly great heart'[4] (Broido, 1977: 187). She survived twenty years of solitary confinement and lived to write her memoirs.

Similar descriptions come to us from the terrorist movement in India at the turn of the century. Madama Cama, who began as a leader of the independence movement and an apostle of unity among Hindus, Muslims and Sikhs, said in 1908 that 'Three years ago it was repugnant to me even to talk of violence as a subject of discussion but owing to the heartlessness, the hypocrisy and the rascality of the liberals that feeling is gone'. She called on Indians studying in Europe to learn to shoot straight so they could 'shoot the English out of the land we love' (Kaur, 1985: 102). She died at the age of 75 revered by the people as the reincarnation of the goddess Kali.

A group of five women university students in the early 1930s joined the revolutionary movement and carried out assassinations on behalf of independence. Bina Dass can be taken as representative of the five. At the convocation at which Bina was to receive the BA degree, she stood up and shot the governor as he rose to speak. To the court she said:

> I fired at the governor impelled by my love of the country which is being repressed. I thought that the only way to death was by offering myself at the feet of my country and thus to make an end of all my suffering. I invite the attention of all to the situation created by the measure of the Government which faced even a frail woman like me, brought up in all the best tradition of Indian womanhood. I can assure all that I have no personal feeling of animosity against Sir Stanley Jackson, the man who is just as good as my father and the Honourable Lady Jackson who is as good as my mother. But the Governor of Bengal represents the system which has kept enslaved three hundred million of my countrymen and countrywomen.
>
> (Kaur 1985: 174)

A leading Punjab woman who was also a terrorist, Lado Rani Zutshi, said of the English, 'These people are wild beasts and devoid of humanity. Their civilization is only temporary. They have come into power only temporarily, and have forgotten what humaneness is. They are now to learn to what extent this tyranny can go' (Kaur: 1985: 176). Zutshi also spent some years in prison.

It is less painful to talk of past terrorism than to consider terrorism of the present. For women who live more protected lives it is difficult to realize how fine the line between violence and non-violence can become for highly motivated social activists. In the United States we have witnessed the same transition from non-violence to violence in the service of high ideals in the personal development of some women members of the Weathermen, an underground group which left the original SDS (Students for a Democratic Society) in 1970. Some terrorists keep their character intact and re-emerge as accepted public leaders. (It is frequently noted, for example, that some prominent public leaders in Israel today took part in terrorist activities aimed at achieving statehood for Israel in their youth.) For other terrorists, personality deterioration sets in. This deterioration is an important theme explored by Herrick in his novels based on a study of documents relating to European terrorism (Herrick, 1981 and 1983). We are in fact witnessing in our time a mutual deterioration of terrorists and of the peoples terrorized. It is not a pretty sight, and may be one of the most compelling arguments for maintaining strategies of non-violence under conditions of oppression.

Common to both violent and non-violent revolutionaries, as to warriors and saints, is a capacity for vision, self-transcendence and self-discipline, qualities necessary to initiate social change in the world. It can be used for good or ill. The task of transforming and redirecting that energy towards creative non-violent action, in both sexes, is a tremendous one.

SYSTEM-CHANGE ROLES AND SOCIAL LEARNING

The commitment to a peaceful reconstruction of the social order is a commitment to a continuous process of social learning-cum-action. Non-violent change is only possible when oppression is met by non-compliance and a refusal to co-operate with traditional dominance behaviour. This requires an egalitarian spirit, and a transformation of leadership from domination to an interactive, dialogic process between the more and the less articulate members of a group. All leadership has an element of role modelling, but interactive leadership is based on a process of social learning which goes on between leader-followers and follower-leaders, to paraphrase Paolo Freire's characterization of dialogic education (Freire, 1979).

This social learning is in fact a resocialization away from the oppressive old order and a preparation for the new more egalitarian order, for leaders as well as followers. It helps bring the new society into focus, and clarifies the new social roles that will be called for in the new order. At its best, it begins the transformation process which enables the movement members to begin living now according to 'new rules'. This type of interactive leadership is very characteristic of the non-violent revolutionary. It may also continue to describe the leadership of those who have crossed the line from non-violent to violent action, at least in the short run. Violence itself, however, tends to create conditions antithetical to social learning, and reduces interactions to a blind power-struggle.

MYTHS AND REALITIES OF GENDER-BASED ROLES

While the transition from the historic military/patriarchal order in all its forms to a peaceable egalitarian order has been seen as a move away from the rule of men, we must reject any simplistic gender equations here, for the reasons pointed out: women and men both have the capacity for violence and for peaceableness, whether at the heroic or the ordinary, everyday level. What we need to do now is to examine carefully the actual behaviours of women and men in different settings and see what moving toward the post-military society actually involves. Recent work on the 'genderization of science' (Keller, 1978 and 1985; Harding and Hintikka, 1983; Bleier, 1986; Ruddick, 1987) reveals to us the extent of the problems we face in discovering the objective thereness of the phenomenological world in which we live. These authors point out that because most scientists are male, they view empirical phenomena with the biases of a male world-view and therefore fail to describe the phenomena accurately. Men are socialized to see hierarchical ordering principles and cause–effect relations in short-term time spans, where women are socialized to see complex interdependencies over longer time spans. (For women's perceptions, see Chodorow, 1974;

Miller, 1976; Gilligan, 1982; Belenkey *et al.*, 1986; Brock-Utne, 1985; Reardon, 1985). Women's ways of seeing apply whether they are addressing physical, biological or social systems.[5]

There is in fact a double falsity in the male bias in science. It not only distorts descriptions of phenomena in general, but it distorts descriptions of the actual role behaviour of men as well as women. Male behaviour tends to be *coded* as masculine, women's behaviour as feminine. If we insist on accurately describing behaviour as it takes place, independently of whether that behaviour is engaged in by a man or a woman, we will find that there is a significant amount of reality-falsifying gender-role stereotyping in most behavioural descriptions. The heavy value-loading on male power, dominance and authority roles, the glorification of the male warrior and the male athlete and male manipulative competence in turning the natural world into raw materials for a science and technology-based social order inevitably produces more of a gender dichotomy than exists in reality. Everything is couched in terms of woman the nurturer and man the warrior.

In short, there is a gap between the image of the male built into our cultural constructs and institutional forms, and the behaviour of a substantial number of males. We should call attention to that gap and make use of it in correcting the historical record as well as in our reporting of the present. The task of creating a more humane and peaceful social order should not be seen as one in which women have to bear the burden of a complete transformation of the consciousness of men, or of being the carriers of nurturance skills for the species, with perhaps a little help from some enlightened males. That view ignores the complexity of the developmental experience of men as well as women. It ignores the social formation experience of the St Francises, the Martin Bubers, the Gandhis, the U Thants, the Dag Hammarskjolds, whose public as well as private roles were characterized by nurturant behaviour. It ignores the many gentle, tender men who struggle with the social forms imposed on them. It also ignores the social formation of the combative women leaders of history, from Queen Boudicca to Margaret Thatcher, and ignores the not insignificant number of women who do not enjoy childrearing but who are 'condemned' to it.

While the institutional and behavioural supports for patriarchy are strong, they are obsolete, without survival value in the nuclear age. In order for the transition to a post-patriarchal society not to seem impossibly difficult, the existing behavioural supports for the post-patriarchal, post-military society both historically and in the present need to be made visible through a more careful coding by social scientists of the behaviour of both men and women. Making the actual institutional changes are a complex and difficult matter, but available non-traditional behavioural repertoires help set the conditions for change.

DE-LINKING GENDER AND SEX-ROLE ORIENTATION

We know that everyone has both 'masculine' and 'feminine' components (as coded in terms of traditional expectations) in their behaviour. However, the significance of the empirical fact that some men have a high 'feminine' score on sex-role orientation tests and some women have a high 'masculine' score on the same tests, has not been adequately explored in relation to potential shifts in the performance of both public and private roles in contemporary society by men and women. Recent research on the negotiating behaviour of men and women makes it clear that biological sex is a poor predictor of negotiating skill, but that the sex-role orientation of the negotiator is a good predictor. This suggests that negotiation needs to be studied in terms of actual behaviour, not in terms of the sex of the participants.[6]

Negotiating behaviour is an important test case in the gender-based division-of-labour argument, since negotiation is the most pacific and least power-oriented of all public role behaviours. It is also the most pervasive form of everyday interaction available to us, as Strauss (1978) has shown in his study of the negotiated social order. We all negotiate our way through every day of our lives, dealing with the different perceptions and preferences of those around us in situations, however trivial, where co-operation is necessary to get a job done. History could well be rewritten in terms of successful negotiations—that is, wars not fought. This could provide a different self-image for the human species.

Another change in self-image for the species could come with the rewriting of the history of parenting. The image of the stern patriarchal father and the submissively nurturant mother is etched on our brains, as are the studies of the 1960s and 1970s that suggested children were only discovered *as beings requiring special care* quite recently (Aries, 1965; De Mause, 1974). At the same time, the feminist movement has offered parenting as a model of all human interaction (Chodorow, 1974; Dinnerstein, 1977; Ruddick, 1980 and 1985) for a future more gentle, egalitarian society. It therefore comes as good news from more recent research that there have been people in every century who have been aware of the special characteristics of the child, and that tender nurturing fatherhood has similarly always been present, although perhaps more the exception than the rule (Pollack, 1983). Phyllis Mack's (1986) study of feminine behaviour among radical non-violent activist males, looking at Franciscans, Quakers and Gandhians, makes clear the existence of pronounced male public nurturance behaviour in these groups; the words 'mothering' and 'fathering' are repeatedly used to describe the behaviour of men. George Fox, one of the founders of Quakerism, was often referred to as a 'Mother in Israel' by his followers. Awareness of and celebration of nurturant fathering so that its incidence may increase, is an important step towards resocialization away from patriarchy.

CULTURAL VARIABILITY IN SEX-ROLE ORIENTATIONS OF CULTURES

Anthropology has made us aware of the cultural patterning of men's and women's roles, with the nurturant and feminine sometimes being valued in men, the aggressive and masculine sometimes valued in women (see Mead's classic 1950 study). We are less sensitive to these cultural variations in industrial societies, but examples abound of subcultures where men adopt gentle, peaceable social roles, and gender-based division of labour does not lead to strong structures of dominance. The men in each of the historic peace Churches, like Mennonites, Brethren and Quakers, provide one set of examples; the gay subculture another, and the men's awareness movement[7] still another. The peace movement has a mixed record in this regard, so do the 'Green' political parties in the countries where they exist, but there is a self-conscious effort on the part of some men in each of these movements to turn towards a more interactive, less dominating style of public role-taking. Such shifts need to be noted and recorded, because they are steps in the resocialization process required to achieve and maintain the post-military society.

THE DANGERS OF MASKING AND DOUBLING

False nurturance, the masking of violence by the use of pseudo-nurturant language, is a serious problem for both men and women. Patriarchy has thrived on such masking: there is the image of the father who 'protects' his household, however cruel the whip he uses, and the image of the gentle, docile wife who is actually acting out rage in her pseudo-submission.

The practise of doubling so vividly described by Lifton (1986) is equally dangerous. It involves keeping two identities completely separate in one's mind—a responsible healing-oriented medical doctor identity, for example, and a ruthless experimenter-torturer identity, as in the case of the German doctors who worked in the Nazi death camps. Women find it harder to double than men, but the increased participation of women in the armed forces and in public life has shown that under certain circumstances they are capable of the same maintenance of double identities. Military discipline is in itself a training in doubling; as much as women soldiers may struggle against it, it affects them. The institutional Church has provided many historical examples of doubling, in every religious tradition, as heretics have ruthlessly been pursued in the name of God. The use of military violence to maintain and/or expand the nation-state has been elevated to a high moral plane by religious legitimation. Even today, many of the wars being fought on various continents are perceived by each side as a 'holy war' against the enemy. The capacity for doubling runs deep.

THE GROUNDS FOR HOPE

We do not have to despair, because every civilization, no matter how warlike, has generated and kept alive images of a future in which former warriors live together in peace, equality and physical abundance. The Jewish image of Zion—the holy mountain where none shall hurt nor destroy, the Greek image of the Elysian Fields, the Viking image of Asgard in Walhalla, the Islamic vision of the peaceable garden in the desert, the Chinese image of the peace of 'the land under heaven' all point to a basic human capacity for both picturing and desiring a state of peace. History skips over these images and concentrates on wars.

Feminist history needs to bring out these other, culturally obscured images of human aspirations, as well as records of actual peacemaking behaviour. It needs to show that the adventurous spirit informs not only the warrior but the 'saint'—that is, the peacemaker. It needs to introduce new metaphors for describing social process, replacing the language of winning with the language of the 'positive sum game' which has good outcomes for everyone. It needs to bring out more multidimensional meanings for games and play, recovering playfulness from the deadly competition of professional sports. It needs to rescue computers, the tools used by more and more people in the new information age, from the programmers who use the language of killing for ordinary problem-solving protocols. The old metaphor for learning, 'mastery', needs to be replaced with the metaphors of dialogue, exploration and connected knowing. In short, we need to begin describing everything we do in the language of adventurous connections rather than dominance. Since language shapes both behaviour and culture, it is no accident that some of the important new work in semiotics is being done by women (Coward and Ellis, 1977; Harding and Hintikka, 1983; Bleier, 1986).

Most of all, we need to begin picturing the new order in our minds, fantasying it, playing with possibilities. If we want an egalitarian, sharing, joyful society in which human beings of both sexes can develop their best potentialities, what kind of social infrastructure would maintain such a society? We have some wonderful images presented by women science fiction writers that can help to stimulate the imagination.[8] An exercise in first stepping into a desired future in imagination, then consciously elaborating the structures needed to maintain it, and finally imagining the future history that would get us there, is a very liberating experience for people who feel trapped in an unyielding present.[9] As Polak (1961), the recently deceased Dutch historian-sociologist told us, societies move toward what they image. If we remain frozen in the present as we have done since the Second World War, society stagnates. Imaging the future gives us action ideas in the present.

I have suggested that women and men have always had the same basic capacities for both violence and reconciling nurturance, and that the apparent stability of the patriarchal structures of dominance by violence in recorded history has now come to an end. Women can speed that ending and help society avoid a long period of regressive chaos by discontinuing the war-maintaining gender-based division of labour that has kept the system going for so long, and shifting toward more direct social-change roles. Women cannot do this alone. History provides male and female role models for the saints as well as the warriors, for the peaceable revolutionary as well as the conquering hero. The peaceable models need to be studied, celebrated and utilized. Sliding towards violence when structures of domination appear to be unyielding is a continuing danger, however. The peacemakers must give conscious attention to the basics of the skills of non-violence, and to a continuous resocialization for everyone that fosters adventurous and assertive interaction on behalf of human well-being without violence. Each of us has something of the warrior and something of the saint/peacemaker inside. Dealing with those potentialities is a lifelong challenge.

We have more going for us than we think. There is less violence and more nurturance practised by men than the cultural mirror allows us to see, and more capacity for assertive leadership for change on the part of women than the mirror reflects. A combination of a more observant stance towards the empirical reality of how men and women actually behave in private and public settings, more attention to imaging the outlines of the kind of world we would like to see and to the skills of crafting that world, will empower us to find the action strategies we need.

NOTES

1. Gerda Lerner's recent study, *The Creation of Patriarchy*, is very illuminating but still leaves questions about the relationship between patriarchy and war unanswered.
2. This description of the Free Amazons, and the text of the Renunciates Oath, are to be found in the introduction to Bradley (1985).
3. These descriptions come from the writings of Kravchinsky, quoted in Broido (1977: 184–5). For other sources on women revolutionaries in this period, see Engel and Rosenthal (1975).
4. This description comes from Uspensky, quoted in Broido (1977: 187).
5. This is not to suggest that men's perceptions are biased and women's perceptions are not, but to point to the importance of the scientist's awareness of the effect of his/her socialization on what is observed.
6. The Gilkey-Greenhalgh (1984) study of negotiation styles of men and women provides a striking example of the inadequacy of biological sex *per se* as a predictor of conflict-resolution skills, an area where women are stereotypically considered to have a basic advantage because they are women. The study looks at second-year MBA students to compare men and women on their management of negotiation procedures in terms of the variables of time perspective (is the negotiation seen as continuous or discrete), empathy, willingness to compromise, eschewing of short-term gains through interruptions and tricky behaviour. The findings based on the sex of the participants were weak, inconclusive. When data was analysed according to the sex-role orientation of each participant (using the BEM scale), a strong relationship emerged between negotiating style and that orientation. For our purposes the significant fact is that among the forty-one men in the study, eleven, or 27 per cent, had a predominantly feminine sex-role orientation; among the twenty-three women, ten, or 43 per cent, had a predominantly masculine sex-role orientation. Since MBAs are generally known as fairly aggressive go-getting types, 43 per cent women with masculine sex-role orientation is not surprising, but 27 per cent of men with feminine sex-role orientation is.

7. An analysis of the role changes taking place in the three gender-articulated communities, women with women, men with men, and women with men, is found in E. Boulding's 'Changing Gender Roles in Familial, Occupational and Civic Settings', in Benne and Tozer (1987). Special attention is given in this study to different parts of the men's movement, although the data is drawn primarily from the United States.
8. In the United States women science fiction writers run the gamut from the Free Amazon world of Marion Zimmer Bradley to the gentle androgynous society of Ursula LeGuin's *The World for World Is Forest*, with Marge Piercy's *Woman on the Edge of Time* somewhere in-between. See the issue of the University of Colorado journal, *Frontiers*, on women writers of fantasy (Vol. 2, no. 3, Fall, 1971). LeGuin's most recent book is a stunning recreation of a more androgynous society very far into the future, after the landscape of earth has changed considerably, *Always Coming Home* (1985). Charlotte Perkins Gilman's *Herland*, a nineteenth-century women's utopia, has already been mentioned. The following paper in this volume will give us a broader international picture of feminist utopias (Isaksson).
9. For several years, Warren Ziegler and I and a number of associates have been conducting workshops in imaging a future without weapons which follow the protocol described here in such abbreviated fashion. A fuller description of the process can be found in E. Boulding (1987b). I have noted during these workshops that women often enter into the imaging process more easily than men.

REFERENCES

Aries, Philippe (1965), *Centuries of Childhood*, trans. from French by Robert Baldick (New York: Vintage Books, Random House).

Belenky, Mary, Blythe, M., Goldberger, Nancy and Tarule, Jill (1986), *Women's Ways of Knowing: Self, Mind and Voice* (New York: Basic Books).

Bleier, Ruth (1986), *Feminist Approaches to Science* (New York and Oxford: Pergamon Press).

Boulding, Elise (1976), *The Underside of History: A View of Women Through Time* (Boulder, Colo.: Westview Press).

(1987a), 'Changing Gender Roles in Familial, Occupational and Civic Settings', in K. Benne and S. Tozer (eds.), *Society as Educator*. Published as the National Society for the Study of Education 1986 Yearbook (Chicago: University of Chicago Press).

(1987b) 'The Image-Action Nexus', *Journal of Social Issues*, in press.

Bradley, Marion Zimmer (ed.) (1985), *Free Amazons of Darkover* (New York: DAW Books).

Brock-Utne, Birgit (1985), *Educating for Peace: A Feminist Perspective* (New York: Pergamon Press).

Broido, Vera (1977), *Apostles into Terrorists, Women and the Revolutionary Movement in the Russia of Alexander II* (New York: Viking Press).

Chodorow, Nancy (1974), 'Family Structure and Feminine Personality', in M.Z. Rosaldo and L. Lamphere (eds.), *Women, Culture and Society* (Stanford: Stanford University Press).

Coward, Rosalind, and Ellis, John (1977), *Language and Materialism* (London: Routledge & Kegan Paul).

de Mause, Lloyd (1974), *The History of Childhood* (New York: Psychohistory Press).

Dinnerstein, Dorothy (1977), *The Mermaid and the Minotaur* (New York: Harper & Row).

Engel, Barbara and Clifford Rosenthal (ed.) (1977), *Five Sisters: Women Against the Tsar* (New York: Schocken Books).

Freire, Paolo (1979), *Pedagogy of the Oppressed* (New York: Continuum).

Frontiers: A Journal of Women's Studies (1977), Fantasy and Futures Section, vol. 2, no. 3 (Fall).

Gilman, Charlotte Perkins (1979), *Herland: A Lost Feminist Utopia* (New York: Pantheon).

Gilkey, Roderick and Greenhalgh, Leonard (1984), 'Developing Effective Negotiating Approaches Among Professional Women in Organizations', paper presented to the Third Annual Conference on Women and Organizations, Simmons College, August 1984. Faculty Working Paper, Amos Tuck School of Business Administration, Dartmouth, Hanover, N.H.

Gilligan, Carol (1982), *In A Different Voice* (Cambridge, Mass.: Harvard University Press).

Harding, Sandra and Hintikka, Merrill B. (eds.) (1983), *Discovering Reality, Feminist Perspectives on Epistemology, Metaphysics, Methodology and Philosophy of Science* (Dordrecht, Holland: D. Reidel).

Herrick, William (1981), *Love and Terror* (New York: New Directions).

(1983), *Kill Memory* (New York; New Directions).

Kamaladevi (Challopadhyah) (1986), *Inner Recesses Outer Spaces, Memoirs* (New Delhi: Navrang).

Kaur, Manmohan (1985), *Women in India's Freedom Struggle* (New Delhi: Sterling.

Keller, Evelyn F. (1978), 'Gender and Science', *Psychoanalysis and Contemporary Thought* 1: 409–33.

(1985), *Reflections on Gender and Science*. New Haven: Yale University Press.

LeGuin, Ursula (1972), *The Word for World is Forest* (New York: Berkley).

(1985), *Always Coming Home* (New York: Harper & Row).

Lerner, Gerda (1986), *The Creation of Patriarchy* (New York, Oxford: Oxford University Press).

Lifton, Robert J. (1986), *The Nazi Doctors: Medical Killing and the Psychology of Genocide* (New York: Basic Books).

Mack, Phyllis (1986), 'Feminine Behaviour and Radical Action: Franciscans, Quakers and the Followers of Gandhi', *Signs* 11 (3), 457–77.

Mead, Margaret (1950), *Sex and Temperament in Three Primitive Societies* (New York: New American Library).
Miller, J.B. (1976), *Toward a New Psychology of Women* (Boston: Beacon Press).
Piercy, Marge (1976), *Woman on the Edge of Time* (New York: Knopf).
Polak, Fred (1972), *The Image of the Future*, 1 vol., condensation by Elise Boulding (San Francisco: Jossey-Bass/Elsevier).
(1961), *The Image of the Future* 2 vols., trans. Elise Boulding (New York: Oceana Press).
Pollack, Linda (1983), *Forgotten Children: Parent–Child Relations from 1500 to 1900* (Cambridge: Cambridge University Press).
Reardon, Betty (1985), *Sexism and the War System* (New York: Teachers College Press, Columbia University).
Ruddick, Sara (1980), 'Maternal Thinking', *Feminist Studies* (Summer): 342–67.
(1987), 'Remarks on the Sexual Politics of Reason', Eva Kittay and Diana Meyers (eds.), *Women and Moral Theory* (Totowa, NJ: Rowman & Allenheld).
(1985), 'Preservative Love and Military Destruction: Reflections on Mothering and Peace', in Joyce Tribilcot (ed.), *Mothering and Feminist Theory* (Totowa, NJ: Littlefield, Adams).
Strouss, A. (1978), *Negotiation Varities, Contexts, Processes and Social Order* (New York: Jossey Bass).

15

Visions of a Peaceful Future: War and Peace in Feminist Utopias

Eva Isaksson
University of Helsinki,
Finland

Saint Hildegard of Bingen was a remarkable German abbess, scientist and composer of music who lived in the eleventh century. She published several works on theology, natural sciences, medicine and cosmology. Hildegard saw heavenly 'visions', revealing the structure and working of the whole universe to her.

In Hildegard's model of the universe, war and famine had their causes in the interconnection of macrocosm and microcosm. According to her, the macrocosm is a layered mechanism composed of four elements and forces that keep the mechanism in motion. From each layer of matter, a wind blows, setting the universe in eternal motion. This motion exerts influence over the microcosm, that is human beings with their environment on earth. The microcosm, in its turn, can exert influence over the macrocosm. Thus hate, jealousies and wars between human beings will set the nature into violent motion, ultimately causing floods and famine.

Hildegard asks, 'What remains to be done when war after war is being fought among people?' She calls upon heavenly virtues to transform human bodies, so that we will no longer be able to raise our weapons anymore. The most important among these virtues will be Temperance, which promises to take away all bitterness and divisions among people, regardless of their positions and strengths relative to each other.

Hildegard's 'virtues' which are to break the chain of cause and effect in a turbulent, ultimately androcentric universe, could perhaps be interpreted in our terms as a collective choice to change destructive social patterns. Yet Hildegard is just one historical heroine among many women visionaries. Several truly remarkable visions of future have been formulated by women.

For the purposes of this paper, a number of alternative scenarios for the future will be called visions. Visions of the past can be seen as alternative scenarios as well, particularly when the particular past is a utopian society. Thus, a variety of women's utopias, dystopias (reverse utopias), works of fantasy and futurology will be grouped together to form a larger category of feminist visions. These visions are either descriptions of a society in which there is no sex hierarchy, or descriptions of societies which challenge this hierarchy by being a distorted yet true picture of the world we live in.

SEPARATE FUTURES IN A WASTED WORLD

Charlotte Perkins Gilman's utopian novel *Herland* was published in 1915, during the First World War. Three men start a journey as an exploration of an unknown part of the world and end up finding themselves intruders in an all-female society. Herland has once been just another hierarchically structured society with its own army, king and slaves. An earthquake has destroyed most of the army, the slaves killed the rest, and finally women kill the male slaves:

> This succession of misfortunes was too much for those infuriated virgins. There were many of them, and but few of these would-be masters, so the young women, instead of submitting, rose in sheer desperation and slew their brutal conquerers.

Women of ancient Herland found themselves protected by high mountains on every side. Then nature herself solved their procreation problems by making parthenogenetic conception possible. Herland becomes a country of peaceful mothers, who are, paradoxically, daughters of women who had once killed. Being neither in need of protection against the rest of the world, nor in a position to invade their surroundings, Herland women obviously do not need an army, yet they develop their own technology:

> They had had no wars. They had had no kings, and no priests, and no aristocracies. They were sisters, and as they grew, they grew together—not by competition, but by united action. . . . The land was fair before them, and a great future began to form itself in their minds.

It should be noted that in the visionary feminist literature, there are no utopian societies which consist of men only, while several exist which are all-female. Among these, Herland is an exception. Its women are not defending their existence against a hostile patriarchal society, as is usually the case.

Suzy McKee Charnas has imagined in *Walk to the End of the World* (1974) and in *Motherlines* (1978) a post-holocaust world, divided into a male-dominated stronghold called Holdfast and into tribes of wild horsewomen who have adapted themselves genetically to be able to breed with horses. According to the history of Holdfast,

> it was a Black female's refusal to sit in the back of the bus that sparked the rebellion of Blacks, female Gooks fought against our troops in the Eastern Wars; female terrorists made bombs side by side with our own rebel sons.

After the holocaust ('wasting'), women were excluded by men from all decision-making processes and told 'to mind their own business, which was reproduction'. When some of the women opposed this policy, 'the men heard, and they rejoiced to find an enemy they could conquer at last'.

The men of Holdfast have organized themselves into a highly military homosocial structure. Women's work consists of doing the heavy manual and routine labour and of giving birth to more soldier sons and to more worker daughters. In the Holdfast society, implications of masculinity and femininity no longer have subtle sides to them. Instead, the new, post-holocaust military will no more defend men against other men, but against women as a threat to the existing male hierarchy.

In the end, Holdfast is destroyed in a struggle and only the wild horsewomen remain: 'These were not warriors, destroying enemies who had treated them unjustly, but wild women brawling over prizes.' Yet they are prepared to kill, but only men who try to penetrate into their territory, and they let 'fems', escaped women from Holdfast, live.

Monique Wittig has imagined a more open confrontation between a romanticized women's culture and a society of men in her classic, radical feminist work *Les Guérillères*:

> The women say they have learned to rely on their own strength. They say they are aware of the force of their unity. They say, let those who call for a new language first learn violence. They say, let those who want to change the world first seize all the rifles. They say that they are starting from zero. They say that a new world is beginning.

The women's culture in Wittig's book glorifies battle and killing of men. Only a few men who accept the new feminist principles are allowed to live.

Yet another battle is fought in Donna Young's *Retreat: As It Was*! between women and men. Men are described as a genetic mutation, an inherently violent species. Women arm themselves against men but are defeated. On the ruins of their utopian society, the new patriarchy which we will ultimately inherit, is built.

Sally Miller Gearhart's *Wanderground* is again a society of women, built outside a hostile patriarchal society, since 'the male of the human species is too violent to be lived with'. The Wanderground women have replaced technology with magical skills and allied themselves with nature in the struggle to save the life on earth. Some men try to adopt a new approach, calling themselves 'gentles' and attempting to develop non-violent psychic powers despite the distrust and suspicion of women, who do not believe in men's ability to become non-violent.

Gearhart has made a suggestion which is based on the supposed inherent or at least deeply rooted violence of males. According to her, 'the ratio of men to women must be radically reduced so that men approximate only ten percent of the total population'. This would be achieved by one half of the female population reproducing by ovular merging, a technique yet to be developed to make sperm superfluous. The rationale in reducing the number of men would be, according to Gearhart, to break male bonding, and consequently, to reduce men's possibilities to give expression to their violent capabilities. In Gearhart's opinion, 'either the future is female or the future is not'.

These visions, of either past or future, all represent a sex-segregated or separatist society. In some visions, women are fighting a just cause against men, or they choose the stance of 'moral motherhood' to rid the world of war as another patriarchal burden, by the strength of their femaleness.

AMAZONS: REWRITING OR REVISITING OUR PATRIARCHAL PAST?

The popular amazon/swordswoman genre is another expression of feminist visionary imagination. The original Amazon mythology recorded by male writers and historians show Amazons as strong women who are ultimately conquered by victorious men. They are women just beyond the known frontiers of our world, to be tamed, subdued and made into wives. Alternatively, Amazons have become feminist wishful thinking, something that must have existed because we need it.

There is some historical fact behind the myth. Women of defeated geographical areas must have joined each other to defend themselves against mobile, well-armed nomad tribes after men had been killed.

Male writers have been especially thrilled by the idea of an Amazon as a sexual object to be conquered and convinced of the military and sexual prowess of her male opponents. Amazon fantasies by women usually picture, instead, a community of women which exists inside a male-dominated society. Amazons might be living somewhere in-between areas controlled by patriarchal societies, or they might be just another part of the population, working as swordswomen either in groups or separately. The social background is often feudal, or the stage is set at a time when state structures were being formed. Amazon stories can be regarded as one way to revisit the past during which patriarchy was establishing itself, and as a way to envision women's realities and strategies during a time of social change.

Marion Zimmer Bradley has created in a whole long series of novels a planet called Darkover. Its inhabitants are descendants of the crew of a space colonizers' wrecked survey ship. They have forgotten long ago their origins and lost their former technological and social knowledge. The Darkover society is feudal and strictly patriarchal. There is, however, a way for women to escape their destinies as wives and mothers. A class of women called 'Renunciates', or more popularly 'Free Amazons' live and work together in all-women communities by their own rules.

Marion Zimmer Bradley has herself said that among her vast production, novels containing Amazons have become immensely popular with women readers. In *The Shattered Chain* (1976), the oath of the Free Amazons is introduced. According to it,

> I swear that I am prepared to defend myself by force, if I am attacked by force, and that I shall turn to no man for protection. . . . I shall owe allegiance only to my oath-mother, to my sisters in the Guild and to my employer for the season of my employment.

Marion Zimmer Bradley reports that there actually exist contemporary women who are trying to live according to a modernized version of the Amazon oath in their 'guild houses', and who are learning martial arts and self-defence in the style of the Darkover Free Amazons.

The Renunciates are forbidden to wear a sword but are instead permitted the use of a long knife for self-defence. They are not exclusively swordswomen but practise other professions as well. In contrast to segregated communities envisioned by other writers, Darkovan Amazons can freely choose their sexual relationships and partnerships, as long as these are not in conflict with the oath, which forbids them to be subordinate to men's wills and wishes.

Free Amazons remain a collective heroine, living and working together in non-hierarchical ways. There is, however, an ever-increasing amount of literature about women as solitary swordswomen. An early foremother was *Jirel of Joiry* by C.L. Moore (1934), a solitary fighter who once defeated the male warrior whom she loved without herself realizing it.

Her life then became punishment for and in spite of her own admirable strength.

Jessica Amanda Salmonson has contributed a distinct touch of his own in a whole series of solitary women fighter images. Salmonson is a trans-sexual (male to female). His heroines are in no way embodiments of a feminist vision, but in spite of that they are illuminating for an analysis of masculinity and femininity. *Tomoe Gozen* is a female samurai living in Naipon, a parallel world to the past feudal Japan in another universe. She is more fierce than most of her male counterparts. Her excellence, however, is the cause of her downfall. She is able to kill practically everyone, including both friend and foe. As the number of dead around her grow, she becomes an outlaw and a vagabond. In her final battle, she kills another swordswoman, whose love and friendship she wants to win but cannot have.

Salmonson's heroines are confused and cruel, incapable of comradeship. They are not the typical Amazons, but have instead absorbed essentially masculine traits, which makes their sexual identities become distorted. Their only remaining choice is to kill as long as they can, having no allegiances either to men or to women.

An increasing amount of Amazon stories is being written both by men and by women. The role of women in this genre is continuously changing and evolving. The swordswomen are becoming stronger and handier in the use of their weapons, their personalities fuller. At the same time the social analysis in the stories is becoming increasingly sophisticated. We need to ask whether this is just another form of ever-spreading militarization, or whether there is a more complex message to be uncovered. What do stories about Amazons tell about our visions of alternative social developments in the history of early societies? What do they reveal about our changing definitions of masculine and feminine behaviour and the social and cultural frameworks behind them?

UTOPIA AT WAR WITH DYSTOPIA

Marge Piercy's utopian novel *Woman on the Edge of Time*

(1976) has become a classic. The heroine, Connie Ramos, is a middle-aged Chicana woman sent by her male relatives to a mental institution on false charges of child battery and violent behaviour. In the institution she is subjected to a medical experiment to control emotions by electrodes that have been implanted in the brain.

Connie, seemingly an extremely helpless and powerless woman, manages to make an escape into future, to the year 2137 in a utopian society called Mattapoisett. She is told that the strange future she is experiencing, will happen only if she can make it happen by fighting against her own oppression.

Mattapoisett is a decentralized, egalitarian society in which men and women are finally equal. Women no longer have the original power to give birth. Babies are instead conceived out of test tubes. Men have become co-mothers with an ability to breastfeed. Technology is at a sophisticated enough level. Ecological balancing and maintaining self-sufficiency of local communities are, however, priorities that limit the application of technological and biological innovations to a sensible minimum.

Mattapoisett is not a society at complete peace, though. All inhabitants serve a time at doing defence. There is a war going on against another society, which is quite different from the idyllic Mattapoisett. The enemy society is a nightmare populated by half-mechanical men and women, whose bodies have been adapted into weapons or into sex toys. Connie is introduced to this other future during a period of having an implant in her brain. She learns that she has power in the decision, which of the two alternative futures will become true. After she manages to make doctors remove the implants, she regains her ability to visit Mattapoisett again. This time her gentle friends are at the frontlines, fighting and occasionally being killed. Someone explains to her:

> The enemy is few but determined. Once they ran this whole world, they had power as no one, even the Roman emperors, and riches drained from everywhere. Now they have the power to exterminate us and we to exterminate them. They have such a limited base—the moon, Antarctica, the space platforms—for a population mostly of androids, robots, cybernauts, partially automated humans, that the war is one of attrition and small actions in the disputed areas, raids almost anyplace. We live with it. It's the

tag end. We fear them, but we've prevailed so far and we believe we'll win . . . if history is not reversed. That is, the past is a disputed area.

Connie is in the process of realizing that it is she whose task is to reverse the course of history. Her act of war on the side of Mattapoisett is one of violence. She succeeds in killing almost the whole group of doctors experimenting with her and other patients. Connie remains institutionalized, but she has been able to alter the course of future so that, as she is told:

Someday the gross repair will be done. The oceans will be balanced, the rivers flow clean, the wetlands and the forests flourish. There'll be no more enemies. No Them and Us. We can quarrel joyously with each other about important matters of idea and art. The vestiges of old ways will fade. I can't know that time—any more than you can ultimately know us. We can only know what we can truly imagine. Finally what we see comes from ourselves.

Mattapoisett is an example of a utopia that is 'necessary not because it is logically and historically necessary, but because we need it' (Sweickart). It is a society where science is used as a 'tool of the community to enhance the quality of life for each citizen' (Lee Cullen Khanna).

A NEW TECHNOLOGY OR NONE

Women writers of science fiction, fantasy and utopian literature are strongly divided on the role of technology in desirable feminist scenarios for the future. Some feminist thinkers have been content to conclude that in a patriarchal society, science and technology will automatically be used to control both women and nature. This conclusion is then used to justify alternative scenarios, in which most technology is wiped away and more or less magical capabilities are developed, as in *Wanderground*, where telepathy and telekinesis are everyday matters.

Scientific revolution began in the sixteenth century as a strengthening of the connection between cause and effect, between theory and experiment. New weapons were developed the accuracy of which required thorough knowledge of laws of motion of all matter. When soldiers fired cannons, they needed to know where their cannon balls would land.

The linearity of events, greater predictability and increasing accuracy became primary concerns for both scientists and soldiers alike.

This close connection between scientific research and military technology was established notably during a time when the male and female spheres were becoming strongly differentiated, both socially and philosophically. Women were losing some of the social ground they had been holding in the Middle Ages and were being left out of the new scientific societies and institutions that men were now forming. This exclusion of women lasted from the height of the scientific revolution in the seventeenth century far into the late nineteenth century, when women were at last beginning to gain access to men's institutions of higher learning.

The science and technology that had been developed to serve the modern world in the meantime, reflected largely the values and needs of a patriarchal society with strong sex and class segregation. For women, this means and has meant that their social and cultural roles are dominated by forces that they have not formulated themselves and which they feel themselves powerless to change. Women have become a reserve army of labour, increasingly controlled by military and economic institutions that serve no other purpose than the continuation of the military-industrial, technological *status quo* based on a patriarchal view of the world as a place for conquest and control.

So how are these processes being reflected in feminist visions and scenarios? Mostly we see no processes at all, but instead frozen images of sex-dualistic dystopias, in which war and violence have become inseparable attributes of masculinity, while women are being identified as allies of the violated nature. Will the unavoidable next step then be to cancel the whole technological evolution and to return to a female future in the spirit of *Wanderground*? Or must we begin with what we now have, in which case we will have to learn far more about things technological than we perhaps ever imagined ourselves capable of.

IS THERE ANYBODY OUT THERE AND FIGHTING?

While women continue to envision ways into alternative futures, men have in fact gone on to plan the next steps into a world both strange and dangerous. The International Astronomical Union (IAU) now has a commission for the search of extraterrestrial life, under whose auspices even galactic colonization is being discussed as a real possibility. Some scientists maintain that the energy required for interstellar colonization is disproportionate compared with the energy required for planetary colonization, so that no intelligent civilization would proceed further than beyond their own backyards. Others, however, are happily making plans for 'the natural extension of the conquest of the space which our civilization initiated as soon as we had the necessary technology'. We are told that colonies will only need energy and raw materials, but we are given no explanations as to the reason (apart from 'natural extension of the conquest of the space') for colonization, the social structure of such colonies and the role of women needed to manipulate 'energy and raw materials'. What will be expected of those invisible women colonizers, except for giving birth to a new generation of settlers and participating in the transformation of energy and raw materials into food, shelter and technological tools? Will women continue to hold subordinate positions in these new societies that will probably be formed? Will women be able to contribute to decisions about technological priorities and applications on space stations and future settler ships on their way to deep space?

One of the explanations for there being no extraterrestrials that we have ever heard of, claims that the earth might be situated in a political no-man's-land, created to avoid military confrontation between two extraterrestrial colonies. To women, this might well sound as the ultimate irony. What use would our feminist visions be if there exist a multitude of patriarchal colonies, all prepared to enforce their domination over the rest of the galaxy, even if our own civilization could be converted.

Astronomer Margaret Burbidge has estimated that a civilization which has developed a certain technological level might have a relatively short lifetime, say fifty years, before it self-destructs in a nuclear holocaust. Her evidence is of experimental nature: so far, we have not been able to detect electromagnetic radiation of an undeniably civilized origin. From the discovery of radio to the development of nuclear weapons and the actual use of them, the civilization would emit radio waves for a relatively short time before disappearing from the electromagnetic universe that radio astronomers listen to. According to Burbidge's hypothesis, we are either alone, or human beings are doomed to ultimate destruction.

It is of course perfectly possible that there are no galactic colonies and that there will be no conquests of the space quite simply because there have been visions that have pointed to another direction. Maybe a truly advanced civilization seldom steps out of its native solar system, maybe there are no star wars on a galactic scale simply because our cosmic sisters have decided so.

FUTURE OR NO FUTURE

Elise Boulding has contributed much to our understanding of women's visions with her classic work 'Perspectives of Women Researchers on Disarmament, National Security, and World Order' (in the collection *Women in Futures Research*). Those women in her sample who could visualize a post-military world, saw it as a

> highly differentiated, localist, egalitarian world in which human needs would be met with appropriate technology at the local level and with minimally functioning international organizations handling residual redistributive requirements.

She also stressed that women researchers were prepared to be patient and sober; no one was expecting an overnight disarmament or a sudden earthquake to swallow the leading actors of the patriarchal theatre, while their roles would probably remain, simply because women are just as much socialized to maintain the military culture as men are.

Jan Zimmerman, who has written a woman's guide to tomorrow's technology which is both hilariously funny and deadly serious, has argued that women can, and indeed must gain control of new technologies in order to avoid being controlled by/with them. The technology is here and we cannot simply make it to go away by wishful thinking or political analysis. We must realize what is happening and then find our own ways to make the technology meet *our* needs: 'The future will be ours only if we create it'.

The women who answered Elise Boulding's questionnaire were stressing the need for more research on the concept of national security itself, on 'how militaries affect the allocation of resources within individual societies and thus shape the development strategy planned'. In the context of feminist visions, this means that we must begin to question how the military system functions in our utopias, in our alternative futures and in the scenes of our fantasy. Who will control the reproduction in our utopias and to what purpose? Who will assemble the weapons with which the imaginary dystopian armies will be fighting? And, ultimately, how can we take the initiative away from the military in planning for future, so that our future will not remain just that—solely a utopia.

SELECTED READING

Papagiannis, Michael D. (ed.) (1985), *The Search for Extraterrestrial Life: Recent Developments*. Proceedings of the 112th symposium of the International Astronomical Union, (Dordrecht: Reidel).

Rohrlich, Ruby and Baruch, Elaine Hoffman, (eds.) (1984), *Women in Search of Utopia. Mavericks and Mythmakers* (New York: Schocken Books).

Rothschild, Joan (ed.) (1983), *Machina Ex Dea: Feminist Perspectives on Technology* (New York: Pergamon).

Women in Futures Research (1981), Special issue of *Women's Studies International Quarterly* 4 (1).

Zimmerman, Jan (1986), *Once Upon the Future: A Woman's Guide to Tomorrow's Technology* (London: Pandora).

16

Women and Decisions on Nuclear Weapons

Scilla Elworthy McLean
Oxford Research Group, UK

WHY WOMEN, WHY NOW?

In November 1986, an international meeting of women parliamentarians, activists and researchers was held in Greece at the invitation of Margaret Papandreou and under the auspices of Women for a Meaningful Summit. This meeting was like a coming-of-age for women world-wide involved in work for disarmament because, although only a fraction of them could be present, their views, hopes fears and courageous actions were described to the world.

The common essence, the common strands which emerged from this meeting were the following:

1. An awareness that the social, economic and political crises facing the world today are interrelated and can be traced to technological investment in the war industry.
2. A determination to get down to the real reasons why the 'arms control' process isn't working.
3. The realization that women are speaking out not only on their own behalf, but that they use the language and represent the fears of the vast majority of the world's population in their horror over the costs of continued arms escalation, and in their wish for genuine defence and real mutual security.

The following are all taken from messages to the International Assembly of Women for a Meaningful Summit, Athens, 1986:

To achieve real peace, it is not enough merely to desire peace. It needs the concrete efforts of people all over the world. Women who make up more than half the world's population are a vital force in safeguarding world peace.

(Mme Huang Gan Yin, All China Women's Federation)

Power remains in the hands of the minority regime which resists any pressure for participation by the majority and indigenous owners of the land, by force. The country is under a state of siege at the moment with the security forces in full occupation of South Africa's black communities, brutally killing innocent civilians and unarmed children [who are] merely protesting about inferior education. This is why peace means so much to us.

(Winnie Mandela, South Africa)

Images come to my mind. Two leaders holding our fate in their hands, turning away from each other on a cold, wet evening in Iceland. They may be leaders but they are pawns in the hands of the military industrial complex, of the hawks in their administrations. . . . As women from many countries we should be taking control of our own lives . . . we have the imaginative vision. We can turn things around in unity—East, West, North and South.

(Meg Beresford, General Secretary, British Campaign for Nuclear Disarmament)

Women's Actions for Peace

Throughout this century women have been more and more active on issues of peace and disarmament. But it is in the last ten years that womens' actions have mushroomed, both in numbers and in imagination, in all parts of the world.

In the following we have listed some of them:

1975 International Women's Day Conference Mexico City—launching of a petition calling on UN General Assembly to organize a world disarmament conference.

1976 Women for Peace marches in Northern Ireland.

1978 Women march against the neutron bomb in all Nordic countries, 3,000 demonstrate in Stockholm and Gothenburg.

First Special Session on Disarmament—1,000 women gather in New York from all over the world.

Women Strike for Peace organize demos in San Francisco (2,000 women) Hollywood Bowl (14,000 women), New York (15,000 women). Hundreds of Japanese women affected by Hiroshima and Nagasaki attend.

1979 Soviet Women's Committee organize a conference 'A Peaceful and Secure Future for All Our Children'.

1980 Women and Life on Earth USA organize a conference on eco-feminism in the 1980s—700 women present.
UN Mid-Decade Women's Conference held in Copenhagen, 70,000 signatures presented by women from FRG and 500,000 signatures from Scandinavian women demanding an end to the arms race.

1981 Scandinavian Women's Peace March, Copenhagen to Paris.
Japanese Women's Peace Rally in Tokyo, 5,000 women attend.

1982 First major NVDA by women at Greenham—seven-gate blockade.
WILPF launch 'Stop the Arms Race' campaign for 1 million signatures in the United States.
May 24th International Women's Day for Disarmament, 100 actions in Iceland, Germany, Spain, Italy, Austria, Nigeria, Australia and UK.
Scandinavian Women's Peace March from Stockholm to Minsk, 300 women.
Women's Pentagon Action in Washington, 2,000 women encircle the Pentagon.
Embrace the Base at Greenham, 30,000 women present.

1983 La Ragnatella Women's Peace Camp set up in Comiso, Sicily.
2,000 women link arms between Greenham and Burghfield.
May 24th, 700 events with 1 million women world-wide involved.
Greenham women stand for Parliament.
Women's Peace March—Berlin to Geneva.
Seneca Women's Peace Camp set up.
Greenham Women Against Cruise take Reagan to court in New York and 102 peace camps set up by women all over UK.
Pine Gap Women's Peace Camp set up in Australia at US base.

1984 Five Nations Women's Delegation to Washington and New York.
Danish women set up Peace Camp at NATO Northern Command in Jutland.
International Women's Peace Camp at Stockholm set up.
Women's National Conference Against Nuclear War—Washington.
Resistance Internationale des Femmes à la Guerre organize conference 'Feminism and Pacifism' in Paris, 300 women attend.
Cockburn Sound Women's Peace Camp set up in Australia, fifteen-day camp, 500 women.

1985 Women's Peace March through Central America.
Conference on Women and Peace held in Geneva to prepare for Nairobi.
Great Peace Journey initiated by Swedish women.
UN Decade for Women Conference, start of women's global network, 1,000 copies of WPA Special International Newsletter handed out to women attending the conference.
Women's Peace Camp set up opposite UN during US and Soviet arms control negotiations.

Women for Peace Brussels organize 'Women Working for a Peaceful World' conference, women from France, UK, Holland attend.
May 24th, publication of 'Detente from Below', open letter from women in deployment countries East and West, endorsed by women in GDR and Czechoslovakia.
'Women's Alternatives for Negotiating Peace' conference held in Halifax, Nova Scotia, 350 women attend.
Women's 'No' days in Netherlands, rejecting missiles and arms race, 29 Jan., 26 March, 18 June, 22 Oct.
'Many Visions, Many Hands' weekend in Manchester, 700 women and 150 children attend.
Icelandic women go on strike for twenty-four hours demanding their men stop waging war.

1986 Nuclear-free and Independent Pacific (WFIP) French Testing international telephone tree set up.
Women for Peace in Europe launch a block-bridging letter and signature initiative in Eastern and Western Europe.
4,000 Finnish Women refuse to bear children unless their government closes the nuclear power stations by 1990.
2,000 women in Netherlands demonstrate against nuclear testing.
Women for a Meaningful Summit organize international symposium in Athens—400 women from 36 countries attend.

(I am indebted to Sue Scott of the Women's Peace Alliance, UK, for this list.)

It is clear from gatherings of women all over the world that women share a powerful, urgent anxiety about the arms race, and feel that they must act to avert global war. The language women use to express their sense of urgency, their feelings about increased militarism, about the misuse of power, is common to women from East and West, North and South. It is clear also that women have particular experience and a particular approach which equips them to act effectively to bring about a safer world.

Women now want to know where they can best focus their energy. The Oxford Research Group has spent four years researching how decisions are made on nuclear weapons, East and West. This paper is intended to supply insight, in the light of that research, into how women can act to change nuclear decisions. It is necessary first to describe briefly how the nuclear weapon decision-making system works. Then we can look more closely at the key areas of decision-making. One detailed example is given on p. 268 below. The next step is to examine the assumptions shared by these decision-makers—their view of the world, their discourse. Only then are we in a position to discuss various options for change and finally to review the detailed example in terms of how change can be brought about.

WHAT ARE WOMEN UP AGAINST?

The production of a modern nuclear weapon is an exacting task, even for an advanced industrial state. Typically, it takes ten to fifteen years, from concept, through assembly line, to deployment. The warhead, delivery vehicle and platform will usually be developed separately, and brought together to form the new weapon.

Weapons scientists and rocket engineers, in their laboratories and design bureaux, create the concepts for new weapons. The military may indicate their requirements, and defence ministry officials may select which projects to approve, but the creative urge lies in the technical inventiveness of the weapons scientists, and the ability of the weapons laboratories to apply basic advances in pure branches of science to weapons purposes.

The scientists also act as advisers to defence ministries and military services; in the Soviet Union they sit on Scientific-Technical Committees of the Defence Ministries and Armed Services, which screen and evaluate concepts for new weapons.

In the United States, Britain and France, the defence contractors who manufacture the missiles, aircraft and submarines are key actors in the decision-making system. Dependent on military contracts for their corporate survival, they compete for business by seeking to out-perform one another in military technology. The competition between contractors such as Boeing, General Dynamics, Grumman, Lockheed, McDonnell Douglas and Northrop is a powerful engine of weapons innovation. They employ ex-military personnel to anticipate new military requirements; they lobby Congress and provide political funds to senators; they exchange personnel with the military services, the Defense Department and the weapons laboratories in order to maintain a leading edge in both technology and business.

In the Soviet Union and Cuba, such firms have no equivalent; the functions they perform are carried out by the Defence Industry Ministries and the Ministry of Medium Machine-Building respectively. Their targets are set by central planners and the Politburo. There is, however, deliberately fostered competition between the several design bureaux which design and build Soviet missiles.

The armed services of the five powers are the customers for, and often the driving force behind, new nuclear systems. In the case of the United States, the Soviet Union, Britain and France, nuclear weapons are fully integrated into the weaponry and war-plans of each service. The armed services of the United States and the Soviet Union have their own weapons-procurement sectors, and inter-service rivalry provides a considerable momentum in the selection of new weapons. In France and Britain the civilian officials in the ministries of defence dominate procurement decisions. In China the Strategic Missile Force is accountable to the People's Liberation Army, the Ministry of Defence and the Central Military Commission, which takes all the crucial decisions.

The ten to fifteen year gestation period of a weapons system is significantly longer than the lifespan of a government or administration in the Western democracies. Ministers of defence have short tenures, (Britain has had five over a ten-year period), are technologically ill-equipped and devote only a small part of their time to nuclear weapons policy decisions. Consequently, the defence bureaucracies have won considerable control over defence decisions. In principle, their activity is directed by ministers. In practice it is not feasible for ministers to involve themselves in all the decisions, and in any case they are briefed and presented with options developed by their officials. The permanent unelected officials within the defence ministries may be in their posts long enough to manage most or all of the life of a weapons project. As a result they often hold more real power and decision-making ability than ministers. The defence bureaucrats inhabit a world of shared values and assumptions, reinforced in France by the domination of the Grandes

Ecoles, and in Britain by shared educational backgrounds and the secretive subculture of the British civil service.

In the centrally planned countries, however, continuity of leadership has been remarkable. Until Deng Xiaoping's reform of the Chinese leadership, the majority of the Politburo had been together, sharing in decision-making, since the days of the Long March. The major nuclear weapons decisions in China probably rest in the hands of less than fifty individuals, most of whom occupy two or more positions. Determination to build and sustain a nuclear arsenal has been a long-held preoccupation since the split with the Soviet Union.

Similarly, in the Soviet Union, there is a remarkable concentration of decision-making over nuclear decisions at the top, together with continuity of leadership in the Politburo. When Brezhnev was in charge of heavy industry in the 1950s, his office is said to have been

> a kind of staff where the most important problems of rocket-building were solved, and meetings held with the participation of the most notable scientists, designers and specialists from different fields of science, technology and production.

Almost all the leading figures with responsibilities for the development of nuclear weapons are also members of either the Politburo or the Central Committee. There is thus, ironically, much greater political control of nuclear weapons development in the Soviet Union and in China than in the Western democracies, where the transitory nature of political control vests real power with the permanent bureaucracies.

In the United States, the role of the presidency is more analogous to that of a major piece in a game of chess. Other even more major pieces constantly manoeuvre with one another and engage in strategies, combinations and calculated sacrifices in a constant struggle for position. The air force, the navy, the National Security Council and the Pentagon often behave like rival power groups, with Congress as an occasional additional player, between which the president sometimes arbitrates. Decisions over nuclear weapons policy involve power struggles between these groups, and the outcome is often more a matter of internal politics than rational planning. It is possible, almost unexceptional, for deployments to be ordered or weapons produced which no one wanted, simply as a result of inter-agency struggles.

If, in the United States, inter-agency committees and trade-offs are the highest source of decision-making power, in Britain and France this position is held by the Financial Planning and Management Group and the Conseil de Défense respectively, little-known bodies which bring together the most senior defence, foreign policy and military officials. Within the alliances, little-known bodies such as the High-Level Group in NATO and *ad hoc* groups of defence officials drawn from different states, wield very considerable influence.

In order to reach the stage at which it is a candidate for deployment, a new nuclear weapon in the West must have won the approval of some or all of these groups. It must be technically 'sweet', it must have the backing of a defence contractor, it must be accepted as militarily useful by one of the services, it must win the approval of defence officials, and the high-level agencies must endorse it. Having reached this stage, a weapon will have had a considerable amount of money invested in it, and will have built up an enormous momentum through the support of vested-interest groups.

For a government to decide to kill the development of a weapon at this stage would take exceptional determination and the investment of much political capital. Yet, in Britain and France this is the only stage in the weapon's development in which democratic mechanisms are engaged. In Britain, for example, the Chevaline warhead for Polaris was developed for thirteen years at a cost of £1,000 million before Parliament was even informed. Indeed, no major nuclear weapons system has ever yet been conclusively terminated by an elected representative assembly, even in the United States.

Nuclear weapons represent the most awesome concentration of power at the disposal of any human group. Control over their development lies mainly in the hands of men for whom the development of nuclear weapons is either a *raison d'être* or an overriding priority.

(This brief summary is based on the introduction to the second Oxford Research Group book, *Nuclear Weapons:*

Who's in Charge? by Dr Hugh Miall, published by Macmillan, April 1987.)

WHY THE NUCLEAR ARMS RACE DOESN'T STOP

1. *Arms control, far from being a restraint, has frequently been a rationale for new weapons*. Cruise and Pershing II, for example, were deployed in order to be able to 'negotiate from strength' over SS20s. The same rationale has been used in the case of Trident, MX and MIRV; there are indications of a similar military influence over arms control policy formulation in the Soviet Union, prior to August 1985 when Secretary Gorbachev introduced the Soviet moratorium on nuclear weapon testing.
2. *Democracy, when it comes to nuclear weapons, doesn't work*. None of the five major nuclear weapons states consulted their respective parliamentary institutions before acquiring nuclear weapons. In Britain, France, the Soviet Union and China representative bodies still exercise negligible influence over nuclear weapons decisions. Only the US Congress exercises a measure of power, and even its decisions are frequently circumvented by the Pentagon and weapons corporations.

   The people of these nations, in whose name nuclear weapons have been built, have had no direct say in the decisions. Only in the UK and the US have nuclear weapons been the subject of a sustained public debate, but this debate has had remarkably little practical effect on all but a few decisions.
3. *Politicians aren't the real decision-makers on nuclear weapons*. Weapons now take so long to be built and are so complex that politicians are no longer in control of their development. Key decisions on the design, strategy, targeting, funding, building and deployment of the weapons are taken by much less visible groups of men.

Nuclear Weapons Decision-Makers

At the moment the men who make the real decisions on nuclear weapons are largely unaccountable. They carry on their work out of the public eye. Often, their power is used illegitimately. Whether they work in the West or in the East, they tend to share the same basic assumptions and speak the same language.

After four years' research, the Oxford Research Group has identified key groups of decision-makers in each of the nuclear weapons nations. Below is a list of some of the most accessible of these groups:

1. Weapons scientists and physicists who design new possibilities for nuclear warheads.
2. Intelligence analysts who are the sole source for assessment of the enemy threat.
3. Strategic planners in think tanks who devise nuclear war scenarios.
4. Defence contractors who design and make the missiles and other 'delivery systems' for nuclear weapons.
5. Military strategists who have operational control and strategic direction of nuclear weapons.
6. Officials in defence bureaucracies who decide how the budget is spent.
7. Foreign-policy and arms-control policy formulators who adapt foreign policy to defence policy.

We have chosen one particular example: weapons scientists and physicists who design new lethal possibilities for nuclear warheads. We have indicated very briefly why this group is important, to whom these people are officially responsible, whether they are under control or not. There are similar examples in all countries with powerful defence industries. (For more information on other groups and other countries, contact Oxford Research Group, 1 High Street, Woodstock, Oxon OX7 1TE, UK.)

Example: Weapons Scientists and Physicists Who Design New Lethal Possibilities for Nuclear Warheads

In the United States:

- at Lawrence Livermore National Laboratory, Livermore Valley, near San Francisco.
- at Los Alamos National Laboratory, near Santa Fé, New Mexico.
- at Sandia National Laboratory, Kirtland Air Force Base, Albuquerque, New Mexico.

Why these people are important

The startling innovations, the new ideas for weapons that the military have not asked for, come from the laboratories.

Their professional pride and team spirit is totally invested in the continuation of nuclear programmes and nuclear testing. In the early months of 1978, it was quite clear that the president was willing to pull out all the stops for a total test ban. On 20 May, Carter signed Presidential Decision Memorandum 38 instructing US negotiators to pursue a five-year total test-ban treaty. In August, however, both Donald Kerr (Director of Los Alamos) and Michael May (Associate Director of Livermore) appeared before the House Armed Services Committee to attack the five-year testing hiatus. Laboratory Directors Batzel and Agnew sent critical letters to key members of Congress. There was no five-year test ban.

Are they under control?

Current political leadership, (and for the past two decades) assumes that to encourage technical innovation and gain 'superiority', scientists must be allowed to have their heads. It has allowed scientists to dictate what *technically* will be the best way of defending us.

Who are they responsible to?

Los Alamos and Livermore are officially operated by the University of California, but ownership, control and funding are in the hands of the Department of Energy (DoE).

ONE DISCOURSE DOMINATES

All this, all these councils and committees and agencies and departments detailed in the past few pages, rest on one common set of assumptions shared by decision-makers West and East, one view of the world, one language, one discourse. I will attempt briefly to outline some of the basic notions which underlie this discourse:

1. That hierarchical structures are the only viable mode of human organization, involving vertical chains of command and the issuing and obeying of orders.
2. That extensive secrecy is essential for security. The higher up the hierarchy, the more an individual is privy to more secret information.
3. That competition is the 'natural' way in which people interact, and that conflicts can best be solved by superior force. This dualist and confrontational concept of *two sides* is deeply embedded in our society, and is the basis for assuming, possibly even requiring, an enemy.
4. That subordination to an opponent is worse than any alternative. Dr Stephen Kull of Stanford University has interviewed sixty defence professionals, including civilian and military officials of the Pentagon, and members of the National Security Council, in a study of beliefs about winning a superpower war. He concludes:

> Resistance to subordination, per se, underlies the resistance to arms control much more than any real fears about suddenly ending up in a significantly inferior military position. This fear of subordination is also the deepest source of motivation towards war-winning strategies. Oddly, it appears that this fear is, in some cases, deeper than the fear of nuclear war. Many are more willing to make threats of nuclear war buttressed by expanding arsenals, and to even intentionally raise the risks of nuclear war than to move in the direction of mutual subordination with the Soviet Union.

5. That a crisis or threat from outside demands a military response. Betty Reardon, in her book *Sexism and the War System*, put it thus: 'Militarisation—the process of emphasising military values, policies, and preparedness, often transferring civil functions to military

authority—assumes that when a society is in crisis or threatened, the crisis or threat can best be weathered by strengthening the military.

6. That the 'technological fix' is the most modern and effective way of solving defence problems.
7. That people who refuse to use the language of technologists and strategists have nothing valuable to contribute to the defence debate.

Carol Cohn was one of forty-eight college teachers (one of ten women) attending the MIT/Harvard Summer Programme on Nuclear Weapons and Arms Control, an intensive, two-week crash course in the technology of nuclear weaponry and the subtleties of nuclear strategic doctrine, taught by some of the most distinguished experts in the field. When at the end of the programme she was invited to be a Visiting Scholar at MIT's Center for International Studies, she jumped at the opportunity, and spent the next year of her life immersed in the world of defence intellectuals. The story is told in her own words in the next paper in this book, 'A Feminist Spy in the House of Death'. Carol Cohn's experience, and her lucid, thoughtful description of it epitomises the experience of countless women and men who have been perplexed and confused in their efforts to discuss their concerns about nuclear war with the 'experts'.

Defence professionals have their own basic assumptions and their own discourse, which rules out most of the things ordinary people want to say. Take 'threat assessment' for example. In the defence professionals' view (whether Russian or American) threat assessment means assessment of enemy threat. It does not assess the threat felt by people from the nuclear weapons stationed on their own soil. Nor does it assess children's fear of the threat of nuclear war. Women understand what the defence professionals never will.

The problem can be summed up as follows. The language women use about nuclear weapons, and the kind of questions put, is the same as 99 per cent of the population of the world: simple, straightforward and commonsensical. Yet the 'serious' discourse on nuclear weapons, world-wide, is dominated by a tiny percentage of men who speak one particular language, peculiar to them, and see the problems in one particular and exclusive way. All the decisions about nuclear weapons are taken by them.

HOW CAN THIS BE CHANGED?

There are a number of options.

Option 1: Join the system

One obvious option would appear to be to bring more women into positions of power over nuclear weapons. In the five nuclear nations, there are approximately 800 key decision-making positions. Of these, five are currently occupied by women. Some biographical details of these women are presented below, to enable you to evaluate the influence that they have had.

Rozanne LeJeanne Ridgway

Position: Assistant Secretary of State for European and Canadian Affairs.
Address: State Department, 2201 C Street NW, Washington, DC 20520, USA.
Tel.: 202–655–4000
History: Born in 1935, she graduated in 1957 with a bachelor's degree in political science. Her career followed a classic State Department pattern rising through the ranks until 1977 when she was named Ambassador to Finland, the first woman career officer to get a European ambassadorship. In 1980 she became the State Department's Counsellor—'a utility infielder among the department's senior officers'—where she worked on the Madrid human rights conference and helped co-ordinate policy on Poland. In 1983 she was sent to East Berlin to head an embassy that was first established in 1974. She took up her new post, of which she is known to have been the personal choice of the Secretary of State George Shultz, in 1985.
Outlook: Unlike others who have held the post previously she is not conspicuously identified with specific policy positions.

Rather, as a career diplomat she brings with her a reputation of a clear-eyed administrator, a problem solver, a no-nonsense way of doing business and a mordant wit.

Amoretta Hoeber

Position: Principal Deputy Assistant Secretary of the Army.
Address: Department of Defense, The Pentagon, Washington DC 20301.
History: Ever since she graduated from Stanford University in 1963 with a degree in political science, specializing in Soviet studies, she has been convinced that the Soviet threat is real. Born in 1942 her career has been built around that belief. She began studying chemical warfare in 1975 while researching Soviet defence strategy in Europe for the System Planning Corporation, a defence analysis firm in Arlington, Virginia. Her findings took her to the CIA in search of information, but only two or three people could tell her anything. Outside the CIA, she found even less. Until 1981, she was one of scores of defense analysts (called 'Beltway Bandits' for the highway that encircles Washington, DC) shuttling between think tanks and writing papers about nuclear strategy and poison gas. She wrote a book, published in 1981, *The Chemistry of Defeat*, which outlines the analysis of the Soviet Union's chemical warfare programme and her belief that America is lagging behind. She is now one of a handful of experts on a subject no one wants to talk about.
Responsibilities: Now supervises army's research, development and acquisition of weapons, and the Pentagon's controversial chemical modernization programme. That programme consists of working out ways to prevent the protective rubber suits (called 'nightmare drag' by one lieutenant colonel) from frying the soldiers inside them, writing manuals about how to fight a chemical war, and integrating chemical weapons into other battle plans. She also works on the development and testing of binary weapons, and talks to members of Congress, the press and the public about why the army thinks the United States needs better chemical weapons. History shows, she will tell her audience, that nations have used chemical weapons only against countries

that could not retaliate in kind. Under this theory, she explains, the best way to keep the Soviets at bay is to produce binary weapons, which they don't have.

Outlook: Perhaps as a result of her total immersion in her subject, she is impatient with what she considers an 'uninformed 'view of defence on the part of the public, particularly women. She refers to the 'uninformed' as 'peaceniks'. A member of the National Women's Political Caucus, Hoeber was asked last year by Caucus chair Kathy Wilson to argue for the Reagan defence programme at the Caucus convention in San Antonio. Hoeber bar-graphed her audience into exhaustion with a slide talk comparing Soviet and American ratios of anti-tank missiles, interceptor aircraft, and other vehicles. 'I felt like it was 3,000 peaceniks and me', she said later. What does she consider the most important issue for women? 'Defence', answers Hoeber immediately. 'If we can't do that well, the rest doesn't matter much'. Her supreme confidence is a necessary attitude for administrators, in that an admission of problems in a programme could make Congress think twice about its funding. It is the product of a personality that Saul Hormats, former Development Director of the Army Chemical Corps, believes is almost evangelical: 'There is a knee-jerk reaction in defence to what we think the Soviets are doing. It's like discussing religion. Hoeber believes it and it colours everything she does'. Even one of Hoeber's supporters says, 'She is not willing to examine with an open mind evidence that might prove her wrong'.

Rt Hon. Margaret Thatcher

Position: Prime Minister and First Lord of the Treasury (since 1979) Conservative Member of Parliament for Finchley (since 1959).
Address: 10 Downing Street, London SW1, UK.
Tel.: 01–445 4292

History: Born October 1925. Educated: Kesteven and Grantham Girls School, Somerville College, Oxford (MA, BSc). Became third woman president of Oxford University Conservative Association, 1946. Research chemist 1947–51; called to the Bar, Lincoln's Inn, 1954; elected to Parliament for

Finchley 1959, Joint Party Secretary, Ministry of Pensions and National Insurance 1961–4; Secretary of State for Education and Science 1970–4; Leader of the Opposition 1974–9; first woman prime minister 1979. Co-chair Women's National Commission, 1970–4.

Responsibilities: As prime minister, she has ultimate decision-making power on all major issues in British defence and foreign policy. She chairs the key cabinet sub-committees—the Defence and Overseas Policy Committee, MISC 7 and others concerned with secret defence and intelligence matters. She is one of the very few, if not the only, cabinet minister to know the basis on which US nuclear weapons sited in the UK can be fired. She holds the ultimate power to order the firing of British tactical and strategic nuclear weapons.

Outlook: She has been described as the back street Tories' crusading Joan of Arc, who listens to her own inner voices and the monetarist and libertarian voices of Friedman and Hayek; 'the best man the Conservatives have got' (Harold Wilson); a conviction politician and radical critic of the Old Establishment fuddy-duddies, vested interests and consensus-style top civil service mandarins; inclined to divide the domestic and overseas world into the goodies and baddies—those who are 'with us' and those 'against us'; an 'Iron Nanny' trying to destroy the 'nanny state'; a 'radical populist', 'she cannot see an institution without hitting it with her handbag' (Julian Critchley). She is in favour of wealth-creating entrepreneurs, more effective competition through lower wage levels, nuclear power, equal treatment for working women, hanging, Anglicized Gaullism, NATO and Ronald Reagan; she is against work-shirkers, trade-union militants, European federalism and Russians (except Gorbachev).

Gloria Franklin

Position: Head of Policy Studies Secretariat, MoD.
Address: Ministry of Defence, Main Building, Whitehall, London SW1A 2HB.
Tel.: 01–218 2617

History: Read Modern Languages at Oxford University specializing in Russian studies. When finished, faced problem of what to do with this, tried several openings and finished up working for GB–USSR Society for a year. Then offered opening into civil service in 1970 (FCO of MoD) and 'since there were so few women in defence', opted for that. (She has given a speech recently at Leeds on 'Women in Defence'.) Entered 'fast stream', being promoted to rank of assistant secretary in 1985. (According to 1985 figures, there are currently 129 women as opposed to 1,892 male assistant secretaries.) Also coded grade 5.

Responsibilities: Now she heads the Policy Studies Department, woefully understaffed with two senior people only (at principal level) and five juniors, to tackle the following:

1. Preparation of annual Defence White Paper (Defence Estimates).
2. Writing of speeches for ministers.
3. Supervision of six MoD lectureships at universities in UK (Lancaster, Kings College, Edinburgh, etc.) and links with academics.
4. Think-tank role (future policy).

One of her principals is busy six months of the year on the White Paper, and the other is full-time on the defence lectureships; she herself finds she spends most of her time on administration, writing speeches and the only very occasional paper or talk of her own. Wishes she had more time for this, and for the think-tank side which she regards as seriously under-attended to.

She deplores the lack of knowledge of the Soviet Union—says the few qualified people go off to the United States—and there are so few coming up (John Simpson told her that in all Hampshire only two high schools did Russian A-level)—she holds the view that the Soviet leadership (as distinct from the Soviet people, whom she likes) do still hanker after world leadership, and if you make any concessions, they take terrible advantage of you—they behave like hagglers in an Eastern bazaar. She is lobbying for a new defence lectureship in foreign studies, as well as the money they have just given to Chatham House. Interestingly, she deplored the fact that public opinion in the Soviet Union plays no part in how policy is made, and Soviet citizens cannot ask questions or get information on defence matters.

Regarding being a woman in defence, one of the chiefs of staff objected to her, because she was a woman: 'It's getting much better though'.

Mme Chen Muhua
(Chen is the surname.)

Position: Minister of Foreign Economic Relations and Trade, State Councillor
Address: Minister, Ministry of Foreign Economic Relations & Trade, Beijing, People's Republic of China.
History: Chen Muhua is 63. She has spent her entire career working in China's economic bureaucracies, dealing mainly with foreign economic relations. Starting, after 1949, as a division chief in the State Planning Commission, she subsequently worked in the unit dealing with imports of complete plants in the General Bureau of Economic Relations with Foreign Countries, becoming a bureau chief after this body was made a ministry-level commission. Subsequently, she rose to be the minister of the Commission for Economic Relations with Foreign Countries, and finally, was made head of the Ministry of Foreign Economic Relations and Trade. Because of the huge size and broad foreign economic responsibilities of this ministry, its head is a key individual in the foreign affairs field, and Chen meets regularly, as will be noted below, with State Councillor Ji and Foreign Minister Wu to deal with foreign policy issues. (Some observers, both Chinese and foreign, speculate that a stronger individual may soon be appointed to this position.)
Responsibilities: Mme Chen is not only a member of the Politburo but also a member of the State Council's fifteen-member 'inner cabinet'. The recent reforms in China are all in the direction of increasing professionalism and lessening the decision-making power of the party, making State Council membership much more important than it was, possibly more important than Politburo membership. She is also Minister of Foreign Economic Relations and Trade, and participates in the core membership of the select 'Foreign Affairs Small

Group' of the party. This group, first referred to by Premier Zhao in 1984, meets fairly frequently and assembles key party and government leaders and other experts most directly responsible for and best informed about the conduct of foreign policy specifically for the purpose of advising the Secretariat.

She is noted as one of a triumvirate who are in top charge of foreign affairs in China, under the State Council, along with the current and former foreign ministers. When there are problems they cannot solve, they raise them with the State Council. In this capacity Mme Chen is undoubtedly of key influence on China's arms control and disarmament policy, as well as on her relations with the Soviet Union and US.

The experience of these five women, limited though the data is, indicates highly conventional career patterns. There is little or no indication that they have questioned the assumptions underlying the policies on which they work, or of any awareness on their part of structural violence within their societies. From the details available, there is little or no discernible difference in their approach to their responsibilities or in their outlook, from those of their male colleagues. In other words, these five women have not brought to their work any qualities or attitudes identifiable with them as women.

They have accepted the values and assumptions of the defence professionals' world without challenge; they have adopted its norms, as Carol Cohn so quickly found herself doing (see Ch. 17 below). In order to become *insiders*, they have 'become men'. So the system has not, in my view, been affected or changed.

Option 2: Develop 'the Opposing Virtues'

We should not think that because we are less brutal, less violent, less inhuman than those we are confronting, that we will prevail. Brutality, violence and inhumanity have immense prestige. . . . The contrary virtues, so as to have equivalent prestige, must be exercised in a constant and effective manner. Whoever is only *incapable* of being as brutal, violent and inhuman as the adversary, *yet without exercising the opposite virtues* is inferior to this adversary in both inner strength and prestige; and they will not hold their own against them.

(Simone Weil)

Most women have been trained and educated not only to undervalue but to devalue their virtues. 'I'm afraid I don't think very clearly—I can't explain it', meaning: I don't think about it in the *normal* way, and if I described how I think about it, you'd laugh. 'No, I don't work, I only look after the children', meaning: all the care and responsibility and compassion that goes into this exhausting eighteen-hour-day job doesn't count as work. 'Oh, we didn't do much, we just talked', meaning: the care and sustaining of this relationship and the regeneration of strength through sharing don't rate time allocated to them.

So the first step is to spell out and recognize and marvel over the virtues, the assets, associated with women.

But developing power is certainly not simply a question of having assets. It is a combination of the *recognition* of those assets with a *willingness to use them*. Most powerlessness stems not from having less assets, but from an unwillingness to use them. For most women, this is because in a competitive and materialistic culture, willingness to use assets is equated with willingness to beat or control others. But we are talking about a different kind of power, where the assets are different and the willingness to use them is vital.

Starting at the level of self-awareness, a key fact emerges: *the illegitimate use of power depends for its success on a lack of awareness on the part of the powerless*. As long as a slave is unaware of the extent of his bondage, slavery continues. When a person becomes self-aware, she begins to recognize her own nature: she no longer has to struggle to convince others, and particularly herself, that she is what she is not. She begins to *own* her own language and norms, and is less easily convinced that she ought to be able to communicate with a set of expressions which are foreign. She will therefore be less easily patronized by 'experts'. She will refuse jargon which she doesn't understand, or which appears to mean something horrific if said in plain English. As she begins to have the confidence to exercise this self-awareness and insist on talking in ordinary terms which ordinary people can understand, she will begin to have an impact on one key aspect of control, where the professionals set the agenda.

A second asset consists, strangely enough, in taking

personal responsibility. We are *all* responsible for the arms race, we have *all* allowed our world to come to the brink of extinction, we *all* have to change. There is nobody we can blame. So a person accepts, in some specific way, his or her own responsibility for doing something about some tangible part of it. It is *only consequent upon this act, that a person can effectively ask others* who have distinct and evident responsibility for decisions affecting the arms race *to recognize their responsibility*. Most of those who shape weapons decisions do not feel responsible for them: the system, being 'right', removes responsibility from them. They are shielded. Pointing fingers at them has no effect, and only makes them creep further behind their shield. Accepting personal responsibility for something is a very adult, mature thing to do; it requires coming out from behind the shield, and that requires courage.

A third asset lies in thinking holistically, in thinking about an issue as a whole, not reducing it to parts. When a person comes to the level of thinking holistically she/he will insist on *discussing the arms race as a whole system*. With her there will no longer be the possibility of diving down convenient, argumentative rabbit-holes of the technical capacities of this or that missile; she will constantly bring conversations back to the larger implications of weapons deployment, and the very fact that the complexity of the arms race is so great that it demands new ways of thinking to deal with it. Ways of thinking which will accommodate and take account of complexity and interconnections, rather than severing connections in order to simplify.

Another asset lies simply in numbers of people, and using them. As we have seen, one of the ways in which decision-making has been kept to an élite holding similar views, is by keeping them physically and emotionally distanced from the impact of the weapons they build and from the reactions of the public. The findings of the Oxford Research Group shows that there is more in common between nuclear weapon decision-makers in, say, Russia and Britain than there is between British nuclear weapon decision-makers and those who oppose them in their own country. 'The gulf is no longer between East and West, or even between North and South, but between the defence élites and the public of the world' (Professor Anatol Rappaport).

Analysts in NATO and in Moscow are paid to spend their time counting and assessing the European peace movements; decision-makers in the Kremlin and the Pentagon read the articles, but they never go down to demonstrations, far less listen to those who oppose their ideas. So the conversation has to be brought to them, in any one of a myriad of ways.

1. For example, since women surrounded the base at Greenham Common five years ago, they have had endless and fascinating conversations with officers and enlisted soldiers, although this is officially forbidden.
2. Groups in Britain and America have 'adopted' individual decision-makers, writing to them constantly, arranging meetings, pursuing a dialogue.
3. Motions have been tabled in the British Parliament to ensure that NATO decisions are debated in Parliament *before* Britain agrees to the decision, not after. All this is to *widen* the debate, to bring in different views.
4. In New Zealand a Defence Commission has been set up, actively inviting the views and defence proposals of non-government organizations and researchers, to incorporate them into policy-making.
5. Two English musicians on tour in China invited a Chinese nuclear weapon decision-maker to one of their concerts to discuss ways in which China could make a further move in multilateral disarmament talks.

Another asset lies in using the positive strength of some of the powerful institutions which already exist. Parliament, for instance, exists to ensure democratic decision-making in Britain. It has substantial powers, but they have not caught up with the nuclear age. They need to be changed, for instance so that MPs know *which weapons systems* they are voting money for. They need to be changed so that MPs can debate and decide whether Britain should be party to a NATO decision, *before* that decision is taken by the government. They can be changed, so that the formidable strength of Parliament can be used to implement the will of the people.

Existing structures can also be made to work by the public introduction of self-regulating mechanisms. These are most powerful if the assertions and stated intentions of the industry, council or department, are taken at face value. For example, a publicity campaign to oblige the directors of Sellafield publicly to eat fish caught next to the discharge pipeline every week might ensure quite quickly that excessive radioactive discharges cease. On a larger scale, the leaders of the two superpowers could be obliged to prove that their stated peaceful intentions are true, to send their children to live in the opposing country. The famous button which has to be pressed in order to start a nuclear war could be implanted inside a baby: the national leader would then be obliged to kill a baby before he could start the war.

Option 3: Changing the Discourse

We have seen earlier in this paper that the 'serious' discourse on nuclear weapons, world-wide, and all the decisions about nuclear weapons, are dominated by a tiny percentage of men who speak one particular language, peculiar to them and see the problem in one particular and exclusive way. However, a whole system, which has been designed and built up over years to achieve certain goals, cannot be changed by using its own language. Because its own language doesn't allow the real questions to be put: the real challenge to its goals.

If you want to change apartheid, for instance, you can't do it in the language of apartheid, because apartheid doesn't concede the notion of rights for blacks. Democracy to white South Africans does not *mean* one person one vote. So if you want to make radical changes, you have to use a *different language*.

Women's great strength is that they are not steeped in the male twentieth-century system. They generally find themselves *outsiders* when it comes to large establishments. They don't share the same view of the world, the same language, as those who have climbed the hierarchies. They are not part of the club. And they are now beginning to realize this, thanks to the staggering statistics which emerged from the United Nations Decade for Women—that women are one-third of the world's paid workforce, performing two-thirds of the world's work, at one-tenth of its average wages and controlling 1 per cent of its wealth.

Therefore they find it easier to think in a different way.

Here we have large numbers of people who have listened and watched and understood what's happening to the planet, who have shouldered their own personal responsibility for it, and who have grasped the problem in holistic terms—they see the extent of the crisis, and the implications of what is being done today. They are in touch with the high energy of their own anger, but because they are self-aware, they don't use that anger to *blame*. They use it to *name what's happening*.

Here is an example. A group of women from Woodstock obtained an interview with a senior civil servant in the Foreign and Commonwealth Office responsible for formulating British policy on arms control. The women were by this time extremely knowledgeable about the problems of verification of nuclear weapons tests, and the British position that this was the major obstacle in the way of a Comprehensive Test Ban Treaty. Their questions dealt with the complexity of the issues internationally, and were met with rather terse, didactic, school-masterly answers. Eventually, one woman's anger rose and she said: 'Why do we need to test more weapons when we already have enough to kill every man, woman and child twelve times?' The official refused to respond, and was clearly angered. The essential characteristics are that the statement must be totally accurate, and expressed as an adult, not as a child (as in a complaint).

The statement must show clearly and briefly that the given picture is either nonsense, a gross distortion or based on false assumptions. It should be said as loudly as possible, preferably in the media. Generally, the less emotion contained in the statement, the better, because the emotion will follow, as a response. The nuclear establishment hate to have their pretences and illusions pointed out, and the more furious the response, the more the nail has been hit on the head.

Here are a few examples:

1. Defence is not about armies any more. It's our armies who, in NATO's own words, *need defending by nuclear weapons*. This is crazy.

2. People are as afraid of nuclear weapons on their own soil as they are of those of the opponent, so 'defence' is making people feel afraid instead of making them feel safe.
3. The Soviet government uses the Western threat as a reason for not being accountable to its people, not giving them information on defence. The United States uses the Soviet threat in order to get money for new weapons through Congress.

You will be able to think of many more.

The powerful thing about this is that it is telling the truth, and the public can always recognize that. Nuclear weapon decision-makers recognize it too, with great discomfort. It is the most effective way of countering information which you know to be distorted, attitudes which are patronizing and 'expert', and carefully maintained fictions and secrets. When it invokes the emotions of the nuclear establishment, it can be the beginning of change. It requires courage.

How Could This Work in Practice?

First, women should *name* what's going on, in public. They should make sure the public knows, in simple, straightforward language, exactly what goes on behind the weapons; the real reasons why they are produced, how the money is spent, how they are sold to the public. For this they need short, basic, factual statements and brief examples, backed up by solid research.

Women are good at taking their questions, their simple straightforward questions that ordinary people all over the world ask, to their elected leaders. They should insist on answers. Politicians probably won't be able to answer them at first because they have become caught up in the discourse of nuclear weapon decision-making. But women will find that if they keep putting the questions, loudly, the politicians will respond, because they understand the need to talk in the language of the masses of the people.

But politicians aren't the real decision-makers on nuclear weapons. In order to stop the escalation of the arms race, women have to go straight to the root of the problem, to those less visible groups of men who are responsible for key decisions on the design, strategy, targeting, funding, building and deployment of the weapons.

Earlier in this paper we gave an example about weapons scientists and physicists in the United States who design new lethal possibilities for nuclear warheads. In the following are suggestions as to what can be done to change this particular situation. (More information about other cases is again available from Oxford Research Group.)

1. *Public opinion*: By the public being made aware of these facts—through local interviews with these scientists, newspaper articles, good ethical questions put to them, in public.
2. *Personal approach*: By talking directly to them—arranging discussions, writing, calling them.
3. *Changing the discourse*: Ask the real questions, for example:
   - Why aren't you designing real defensive weapons?
   - How does it feel to have spent your professional life designing things to kill people?
   - Does it matter that there is no end in sight to the growing cost of nuclear weapons, mainly because their design is more sophisticated?
4. *Making existing structures work*: Use the legislative and financial powers of Congress to deny funding to any DoE research which does not have a clear and precise political mandate, spelling out exactly how the research is to fulfil exclusively defensive and non-offensive aims.

CONCLUSION

It is my deep belief that the arms race can and will only be changed when the values and assumptions which underpin it are challenged and replaced by the values and assumptions which women are now beginning to express on behalf of the vast majority of humankind. The nuclear weapons decision-making system is extremely resistant to having its values, its power, challenged.

In these pages I have tried to break this system down into

pieces, manageable pieces, to pinpoint the different forces which drive the arms race forward, and to indicate ways in which women can use their particular skills and experience to change it.

There is clearly room for the talents of each and every one. You do not need to become a defence expert to be effective in this work. You do not need to be a strategist or to argue numbers of missiles. You do need to concentrate your efforts on one particular area; you need to focus. Only then can you put your finger on the core of the problem in that area—on the fundamentally invalid things that are being said or assumed there. When you have uncovered that, you need to say it loudly and clearly. To say it to those directly involved and to say it to the media. We cannot predict *how* these actions will change the arms race, but change it they will. Try it and tell us.

17

A Feminist Spy in the House of Death: Unravelling the Language of Strategic Analysis*

Carol Cohn
Center for Psychological Studies in the Nuclear Age, Cambridge, MA, USA

'I can't believe *that*,' said Alice.

'Can't you?' the Queen said in a pitying tone. 'Try again: draw a long breath, and shut your eyes.'

Alice laughed. 'There's no use trying,' she said: 'one *can't* believe impossible things.'

'I daresay you haven't had much practice,' said the Queen. 'When I was your age, I always did it for half-an-hour a day. Why, sometimes I've believed as many as six impossible things before breakfast. . . .'

(Lewis Carroll, *Through the Looking Glass*)

My close encounter with nuclear strategic analysis started in the summer of 1984. I was one of forty-eight college teachers (one of ten women) attending a summer workshop in nuclear weapons, nuclear strategic doctrine and arms control, taught by distinguished 'defence intellectuals'. Defence intellectuals are men (and, indeed, they are virtually all men) who, in Thomas Powers's words, 'use the concept of deterrence to explain why it is safe to have weapons of a kind and number it is not safe to use'.[1] Moving in and out of government, working sometimes as administrative officials or consultants, sometimes in universities and think tanks, they create the theory that informs and legitimates American nuclear strategic practice.

For two weeks I listened to men engage in dispassionate discussion of nuclear war. I found myself morbidly fascinated—not by nuclear weaponry, or by images of nuclear

* Adapted from Cohn 'Sex and Death in the Rational World of Defense Intellectuals', *Signs* 12 (1987), pp. 687–718,

destruction, but by the extraordinary abstraction and removal from what I knew as reality that characterized the professional discourse. I became obsessed by the question, 'how can they think this way?' At the end of the summer programme when I was offered the opportunity to stay on at the university's centre on defence technology and arms control (hereafter known as 'the Center'), I jumped at the chance to find out.

I spent the next year of my life immersed in the world of defence intellectuals. I attended lectures, listened to arguments, conversed with defence analysts and interviewed graduate students throughout their training. I learnt their specialized language, and I tried to understand what they thought, and how they thought. But as I became more and more engaged with their information and their arguments, I found that my own thinking was changing. Soon I could no longer cling to the comfort of studying an external and objectified 'them'. I had to confront a new question: how can *I* think this way? How can any of us?

Throughout my time in the world of strategic analysis, it was hard not to notice the ubiquitous weight of gender, both in social relations and in the language itself; it is an almost entirely male world (with the exception of the secretaries), and the language contains many rather arresting metaphors. There is, of course, an important and growing body of feminist theory about gender and language.[2] In addition, there is a rich and increasingly extensive body of theoretical work exploring the gendered aspects of war and militarism, which examines such issues as men's and women's different relations to militarism and pacifism, and the ways in which gender ideology is used in the service of militarization. Some of the feminist work on gender and war is also part of an emerging, powerful feminist critique of ideas of rationality as they have developed in Western culture.[3] While I am indebted to all of these bodies of work, my own project is most closely linked to the development of feminist critiques of dominant Western concepts of reason. My goal is to use critical feminist perspectives as part of an analysis of the nature of the nuclear strategic project itself.

This article is the beginning of an analysis of the nature of nuclear strategic thinking, with emphasis on the role of a specialized language that I call 'techno-strategic'.[4] I have come to believe that this language both reflects and shapes the American nuclear strategic project; that it plays a central role in allowing defence intellectuals to think and act as they do; and that all of us concerned about nuclear weaponry and nuclear war must give careful attention to the language we and others choose to use—with whom it allows us to communicate and what it allows us to think as well as say.

STAGE I: LISTENING

'Clean Bombs' and Clean Language

I had previously encountered the extraordinary language used to discuss nuclear war in my reading, but somehow it was different to hear it spoken. What hit me first was the elaborate use of abstraction and euphemism, of words so bland that they never forced the speaker or enabled the listener to touch the realities of nuclear holocaust behind the words.

Anyone who has seen pictures of Hiroshima burn victims may find it perverse to hear a class of nuclear devices matter-of-factly referred to as 'clean bombs'. These are weapons which are largely fusion, rather than fission; they release a somewhat higher proportion of their energy as prompt radiation but produce less radioactive fallout than fission bombs of the same yield.[5] Clean bombs may provide the perfect metaphor for the language of defence analysts and arms controllers. This language has enormous destructive power, but without the emotional fallout that would result if it were clear one was talking about plans for mass murder, mangled bodies, human suffering. Defence analysts don't talk about incinerating cities: they talk about 'countervalue attacks'. Human death, in nuclear parlance, is most often referred to as 'collateral damage'. While Ronald Reagan's renaming the MX missile 'the Peacekeeper' was the object of considerable scorn in the community of defence analysts, some of these same analysts refer to the missile as a 'damage limitation weapon'.[6]

These phrases, only a few of the hundreds that could be

discussed, exemplify the astounding chasm between image and reality that characterizes techno-strategic language. They also hint at the terrifying way in which the existence of nuclear devices has distorted our perceptions and redefined the world. 'Clean bombs' as a phrase tells us that radioactivity is the only 'dirty' part of killing people.

It is hard not to feel that one function of this sanitized abstraction is to deny the uncontrolled messiness of the situations one contemplates creating. So that we not only have 'clean bombs' but also 'surgically clean strikes' ('counterforce' attacks that can purportedly 'take out'—that is, accurately destroy—an opponent's weapons or command centres, without causing significant injury to anything else). The image is unspeakably ludicrous when the surgical tool is not a delicately controlled scalpel, but a nuclear warhead.[7]

White Men in Ties Discussing Missile Size

Feminists have often suggested that an important aspect of the arms race is phallic worship; that 'missile envy' is a significant motivating force in the nuclear build-up.[8] I have always found this an uncomfortably reductionist explanation and hoped that my research at the Centre would yield a more complex analysis. But still, I was curious about the extent to which I might find a sexual subtext in the defence professionals' discourse. I was not prepared for what I found.

I think I had naïvely imagined myself as a feminist spy in the house of death—that I would need to sneak around and eavesdrop on what men said in unguarded moments, using all my cunning to unearth sexual imagery. I had believed that these men, at least in public, would appear to be aware of feminist critiques. If they had not changed their language, I thought that at least at some point in a long talk about 'penetration aids',[9] someone would suddenly look up, slightly embarrassed to be caught in such blatant confirmation of feminist analyses.

I was wrong. There was no evidence that such critiques had ever reached the ears, much less the minds, of these men. American military dependence on nuclear weapons was explained as 'irresistible, because you get more bang for the buck'. Another lecturer solemnly and scientifically announced 'to disarm is to get rid of all your stuff'. (This may, in turn, explain why they see serious talk of nuclear disarmament as perfectly resistible, not to mention foolish. If disarmament is emasculation, how could any real man even consider it?) A professor's explanation of why the MX missile is to be placed in the silos of the newest Minuteman missiles, instead of replacing the older, less accurate ones, was 'because they're in the nicest hole—you're not going to take the nicest missile you have and put it in a crummy hole'. Other lectures were filled with discussion of vertical erector launchers, thrust-to-weight ratios, soft lay downs, deep penetration, and the comparative advantages of protracted versus spasm attacks—or what one military adviser to the National Security Council has called 'releasing 70 to 80 percent of our megatonnage in one orgasmic whump'.[10] There was serious concern about the need to harden our missiles, and the need to 'face it, the Russians are a little harder than we are'. Disbelieving glances would occasionally pass between me and my one ally in the summer programme, another woman, but no one else seemed to notice.

But if the imagery is transparent, its significance may be less so. The temptation is to draw some conclusions about defence intellectuals themselves about what they are '*really* talking about', or their motivations. But the temptation is worth resisting. Individual motivations cannot necessarily be read directly from imagery, which originates in a broader cultural context. The history of the atomic bomb project itself is rife with overt images of competitive male sexuality, as is the discourse of the early nuclear physicists, strategists and SAC commanders.[11] Both the military itself and the arms manufacturers are constantly exploiting the phallic imagery and promise of sexual domination that their weapons so conveniently suggest. *Air Force Magazine*'s advertisements for new weapons, for example, rival *Playboy* as a catalogue of men's sexual anxieties and fantasies. Consider the following, from the June 1985 issue of *Air Force Magazine*: emblazoned in bold letters across the top of a two-page advertisement for the AV–8B Harrier II—'Speak Softly and Carry a Big Stick.' The copy below boasts 'an exceptional thrust to weight ratio', and 'vectored thrust capability that makes the . . . unique rapid response possible'.[12] An ad for the BKEP (BLU–106/B) reads:

The Only Way to Solve Some Problems is to Dig Deep.
THE BOMB, KINETIC ENERGY
PENETRATOR

(format and emphasis in the original)

'Will provide the tactical air commander with efficient power to deny or significantly delay enemy airfield operations.' 'Designed to maximize runway cratering by optimizing penetration dynamics and utilizing the most efficient warhead yet designed'.[13] (In case the symbolism of 'cratering' seems far-fetched, I would point out that I am not the first to see it. The French use the Mururoa Atoll in the South Pacific for their nuclear tests, and assign a woman's name to each of the craters they gouge out of the Earth.)

Another vivid source of phallic imagery is to be found in descriptions of nuclear blasts themselves. Here, for example, is one by journalist William Laurence, who was brought to Nagasaki by the air force to witness the bombing:

> Then, just when it appeared as though the thing had settled down into a state of permanence, there came shooting out of the top a giant mushroom that increased the size of the pillar to a total of 45,000 feet. The mushroom top was even more alive than the pillar, seething and boiling in a white fury of creamy foam, sizzling upward and then descending earthward, a thousand geysers rolled into one. It kept struggling in an elemental fury, like a creature in the act of breaking the bonds that held it down.[14]

Given the degree to which it suffuses their world, that defence intellectuals themselves use a lot of sexual imagery does not seem especially surprising. Nor does it, by itself, constitute grounds for imputing motivation. The interesting issue is not so much the imagery's possible psychodynamic origins as how it functions—its role in making the work-world of defence intellectuals feel tenable. Several stories illustrate the complexity.

During the summer programme, a group of us visited the New London Navy base where nuclear submarines are home-ported, and the General Dynamics Electric Boat boatyards, where a new Trident submarine was being constructed. At one point during the trip we took a tour of a nuclear-powered submarine. When we reached the part of the sub where the missiles are housed, the officer accompanying us turned with a grin, and asked if we wanted to stick our hands through a hole to 'pat the missile'. *Pat the missile*?

The image reappeared the next week, when a lecturer scornfully declared that the only real reason for deploying Cruise and Pershing II missiles in Western Europe was 'so that our allies can pat them'. Some months later, another group of us went to be briefed at NORAD (the North American Aerospace Defense Command). On the way back, our plane went to refuel at Offut Air Force Base, the Strategic Air Command headquarters near Omaha, Nebraska. When word leaked out that our landing there would be delayed because the new B–1 bomber was in the area, the plane became charged with a tangible excitement that built as we flew in our holding pattern, people craning their necks to try to catch a glimpse of the B–1 in the skies, and climaxed as we touched down on the runway and hurtled past it. Later, when I returned to the Centre I encountered a man who, unable to go on the trip, said to me enviously, 'I hear you got to pat a B–1'.

What is all this 'patting'? What are men doing when they 'pat' these high-tech phalluses? Think about what else men pat. Patting is an assertion of intimacy, sexual possession, affectionate domination. The thrill and pleasure of 'patting the missile' is the proximity of all that phallic power, the possibility of vicariously appropriating it as one's own. But patting is not only an act of sexual intimacy. It is also what one does to babies, small children, the pet dog. The creatures one pats are small, cute, harmless—not terrifyingly destructive. Pat it, and its lethality disappears.

Much of the sexual imagery I heard was rife with the sort of ambiguity suggested by 'patting the missiles'. The imagery can be construed as a deadly serious display of the connections between masculine sexuality and the arms race. But at the same time it can also be heard as a way of minimizing the seriousness of militarist endeavours, of denying their deadly consequences. A former Pentagon target analyst, in telling me why he thought plans for 'limited nuclear war' were ridiculous, said, 'Look, you gotta understand that it's a pissing contest—you gotta expect them to use everything they've got.' This image says, most obviously, that this is about competition for manhood, and thus there is tremendous danger. But at the same time it says that the whole thing is not very serious—it is just what little boys or drunk men do. The image diminishes the contest and its outcomes by representing it as an act of boyish mischief.

Domestic Bliss

Sanitized abstraction and sexual imagery, even if disturbing, seemed to fit easily into the masculine world of nuclear war planning. What did not fit was another set of words that evoked images which can only be called domestic.

Nuclear missiles are based in 'silos'. On a Trident submarine, which carries twenty-four multiple warhead nuclear missiles, crew members call the part of the sub where the missiles are lined up in their silos ready for launching 'the Christmas tree farm'. In the ever-friendly, even romantic world of nuclear weaponry, enemies 'exchange' warheads; weapons systems can 'marry up'. 'Coupling' is sometimes used to refer to the wiring between mechanisms of warning and response or to refer to the psycho-political links between strategic and theatre weapons. The patterns in which a MIRVed missile's nuclear warheads land is known as a 'footprint'.[15] These nuclear explosives are not dropped; a 'bus' 'delivers' them. These bombs are called 're-entry vehicles', or 'RV's' for short, a term not only totally removed from the reality of a bomb but also resonant with the image of the 'recreational vehicles' of the ideal family vacation.

These domestic images are more than simply one more way to remove oneself from the grisly reality behind the words; ordinary abstraction is adequate to that task. Calling the pattern in which bombs fall a 'footprint' almost seems a wilful distorting process, a playful, perverse refusal of accountability—because to be accountable to reality is to be unable to do this work.

The images evoked by these words may also be a way to *tame* the uncontrollable forces of nuclear destruction. Take the fire-breathing dragon under the bed, the one who threatens to incinerate your family, your town, your planet, and turn it into a pet you can pat. Or domestic images may simply serve to make everyone more comfortable with what they are doing. 'PAL' (permissive action links) is the carefully constructed, friendly acronym for the electronic system designed to prevent the unauthorized firing of nuclear warheads. The President's Annual Nuclear Weapons Stockpile Memorandum, which outlines both short- and long-range plans for production of new nuclear weapons, is benignly referred to as 'the shopping list'. Carrying the culinary image farther, the National Command Authorities choose from 'a menu of options' when deciding among different targeting plans. The 'cookie cutter' is a phrase used to describe a particular model of nuclear attack. Apparently, it is also used at the Department of Defence to refer to the neutron bomb.[16]

The imagery that domesticates, that humanizes insentient weapons, may also serve, paradoxically, to make it alright to ignore sentient human bodies, human lives.[17] Perhaps it is possible to spend one's time thinking about scenarios for the use of massively destructive technology, and to have human bodies remain invisible in that technological world, precisely because that world itself now *includes* the domestic, the human, the warm and playful—the Christmas trees, the RVs, the affectionate pets. It is a world that is in some sense complete unto itself; it even includes death and loss. But it is weapons, not humans, that get 'killed'. 'Fratricide' occurs when one of your warheads 'kills' another one of your own warheads. There is much discussion of 'vulnerability' and 'survivability', but it is about the vulnerability and survival of weapons systems rather than people.

Male Birth and Creation

There is one set of domestic images that demands separate attention—imagery that suggests men's desire to appropriate from women the power of giving life, and that conflates creation and destruction.[18] The bomb project is rife with images of male birth.[19] In December 1942 Ernest Lawrence's telegram to the physicists at Chicago read, 'Congratulations to the new parents. Can hardly wait to see the new arrival.'[20]

At Los Alamos, the atom bomb was referred to as 'Oppenheimer's baby'. One of the physicists working at Los Alamos, Richard Feynman, writes that when he was temporarily on leave after his wife's death, he received a telegram saying, 'The baby is expected on [such and such a] day.'[21] At Lawrence Livermore, the hydrogen bomb was referred to as 'Teller's baby', although those who wanted to disparage Teller's contribution claimed he was not the bomb's father, but its mother. They claimed that Stanislaw Ulam was the real father; he had the all important idea, and inseminated Teller with it. Teller only 'carried it' after that.[22]

Forty years later, this idea of male birth and its accompanying belittling of maternity—the denial of women's role in the process of creation and the reduction of 'motherhood' to the provision of nurturance (apparently Teller did not need to provide an egg, only a womb)—seems thoroughly incorporated into the nuclear mentality, as I learnt on a subsequent visit to US Space Command in Colorado Springs. One of the briefings I attended included discussion of a new satellite system, the not yet 'on line' MILSTAR system.[23] The officer doing the briefing gave an excited recitation of its technical capabilities, and then an explanation of the new Unified Space Command's role in the system. Self-effacingly, he said, 'We'll do the motherhood role—telemetry, tracking and control—the maintenance.'

In light of the imagery of male birth, the extraordinary names given to the bombs that reduced Hiroshima and Nagasaki to ash and rubble—'Little Boy' and 'Fat Man'—at last become intelligible. These ultimate destroyers were the progeny of the atomic scientists—and emphatically not just any progeny, but male progeny. In early tests, before they were certain that the bombs would work, the scientists expressed their concern by saying that they hoped the baby was a boy, not a girl—that is, not a dud.[24] General Grove's triumphant cable to Secretary of War Henry Stimson at the Potsdam conference, informing him that the first atomic bomb test was successful read, after decoding, 'Doctor has just returned most enthusiastic and confident that the little boy is as husky as his big brother. The light in his eyes discernible from here to Highhold and I could have heard his screams from here to my farm.[25] Stimson, in turn, informed Churchill by writing him a note that read, 'babies satisfactorily born'.[26] In 1952 Edward Teller's exultant telegram to Los Alamos announcing the successful test of the hydrogen bomb, 'Mike', at Eniwetok Atoll in the Marshall Islands, read, 'It's a boy'.[27]

The nuclear scientists gave birth to male progeny with the ultimate power of violent domination over female Nature. The defence intellectuals' project is the creation of abstract formulations to control the forces the scientists created—and to participate thereby in the scientists' world-creating/destroying power. The history of the bomb project is permeated with imagery that confounds man's overwhelming technological power to destroy nature with the power to create—imagery that inverts men's destruction, and asserts in its place the power to create new life and a new world; imagery that converts men's destruction into their rebirth.

William L. Laurence witnessed the Trinity test of the first atomic bomb, and wrote, 'The big boom came about a hundred seconds after the great flash—as the first cry of a new-born world. . . . They clapped their hands as they leaped from the ground—earthbound man symbolising the birth of a new force'.[28] Watching 'Fat Man' being assembled the day before it was dropped on Nagasaki, he described seeing the bomb as 'being fashioned into a living thing'.[29] Decades later, General Bruce K. Holloway, the commander-in-chief of the Strategic Air Command from 1968 to 1972, described a nuclear war as involving 'a big bang, like the start of the universe'.[30]

God and the Nuclear Priesthood

The last thing one might expect to find in a subculture of hard-nosed realism and hyper-rationality, is the repeated invocation of religious imagery. For surely, given that Western science's identity was forged by its struggle for freedom from the constraints of religion, the only thing as unscientific as the female, the subjective, the emotional, would be the religious. And yet, the first atomic bomb test was called Trinity. Robert Oppenheimer thought of Krishna's words to Arjuna in the *Bhagavad Gita*: 'I am become Death, the shatterer of worlds'.[31] Defence intellectuals, when challenged on a particular assumption, will often duck out with a casual 'now you're talking about matters of theology'. Perhaps most astonishing of all, the creators of strategic doctrine actually refer to members of their community as 'the nuclear priesthood'. It is hard to decide what is most extraordinary about this: the arrogance of the claim, the tacit admission that they really are creators of dogma, or the extraordinary implicit statement about who, or rather what, has become God.

STAGE II: LEARNING TO SPEAK THE LANGUAGE

Although I was startled by the combination of dry abstraction and counter-intuitive imagery that characterizes the language of defence intellectuals, my attention was quickly focused on decoding and learning to speak it. The first task was training the tongue in the articulation of acronyms.

Several years of reading the literature of nuclear weaponry and strategy had not prepared me for the degree to which acronyms littered all conversations, nor for the way in which they are used. Formerly, I had thought of them mainly as utilitarian. They allow you to write or speak faster. They act as a form of abstraction, removing you from the reality behind the words. They restrict communication to the initiated, leaving all others both uncomprehending and voiceless in the debate.

But being at the Center revealed some additional, unexpected dimensions. First, in speaking and hearing, a lot of these terms can be very sexy. A small supersonic rocket 'designed to penetrate any Soviet air defence' is called a SRAM (for short-range attack missile). Submarine-launched cruise missiles are referred to as 'slick'ems', and ground-launched cruise missiles as 'glick'ems'. Air-launched cruise missiles are magical—alchems (ALCMs).

Other acronyms work in other ways. The plane in which the president supposedly will be flying around above a nuclear holocaust, receiving intelligence and issuing commands for the next bombing, is referred to as Kneecap (for NEACP—National Emergency Airborne Command Post). Few believe that the president really would have the time to get into it, or that the communications systems would be working if he were in it—hence, the edge of derision. But the very ability to make fun of a concept makes it possible to work with it rather than reject it outright.

In other words, what I learnt at the programme is that talking about nuclear weapons is fun. I'm serious. The words are quick, clean, light; they trip off the tongue. You can reel off dozens of them in seconds, forgetting about how one might interfere with the next, not to mention with the lives beneath them. Nearly everyone I observed—lecturers, students, hawks, doves, men, and women—took pleasure in using the words; some of us may have spoken with a self-consciously ironic edge, but the pleasure was there none the less. Part of the appeal was the thrill of being able to manipulate an arcane language, the power of entering the secret kingdom. But perhaps more importantly, learning the language gives a sense of control, a feeling of mastery over technology that is finally not controllable, but powerful beyond human comprehension. The longer I stayed, the more conversations I participated in, the less I was frightened of nuclear war.

How can learning to speak a language have such a powerful effect? One answer discussed earlier is that the language is abstract and sanitized, never giving access to the images of war. But there is more to it than that. The learning process itself removed me from the reality of nuclear war. My energy was focused on the challenge of decoding acronyms, learning new terms, developing competence in the language—not on the weapons and wars behind the words. By the time I was through, I had learnt far more than an alternative (if abstract) net of words—the content of what I could talk about was monumentally different.

Consider the following descriptions, in each of which the subject is the aftermath of a nuclear attack:

> Everything was black, had vanished into the black dust, was destroyed. Only the flames that were beginning to lick their way up had any colour. From the dust that was like a fog, figures began to loom up, black, hairless, faceless. They screamed with voices that were no longer human. Their

screams drowned out the groans rising everywhere from the rubble, groans that seemed to rise from the very earth itself.[32]

[You have to have ways to maintain communications in a] nuclear environment, a situation bound to include EMP blackout, brute force damage to systems, a heavy jamming environment, and so on.[33]

There is no way to describe the phenomena represented in the first with the language of the second. The passages differ not only in the vividness of their words but in their content: the first describes the effects of a nuclear blast on human beings, the second describes the impact of a nuclear blast on technical systems designed to assure the 'command and control' of nuclear weapons. Both of these differences may stem from the difference of *perspective*: the speaker in the first is a victim of nuclear weapons; the speaker in the second is a user. The speaker in the first is using words to try to name and contain the horror of human suffering all around her; the speaker in the second is using words to ensure the possibility of launching the next nuclear attack.

Techno-strategic language can be used only to articulate the perspective of the users of nuclear weapons, not the victims.[34] Speaking the expert language not only offers distance, a feeling of control and an alternative focus for one's energies; it also offers escape—escape from thinking of oneself as a victim of nuclear war. I do not mean this on the level of individual consciousness; it is not that defence analysts somehow convince themselves that they would not be among the victims of nuclear war, should it occur. But no matter what one deeply knows or believes about the likelihood of nuclear war, and no matter what sort of terror or despair the knowledge of nuclear war's reality might inspire, the speakers of techno-strategic language are positionally allowed, even forced, to escape that awareness, to escape viewing nuclear war from the position of the victim, by virtue of their linguistic stance as users, rather than victims, of nuclear weaponry.

Finally, then, I suspect that much of the reduced anxiety about nuclear war commonly experienced by both new speakers of the language and long-time experts, comes from characteristics of the language itself: the distance afforded by its abstraction; the sense of control afforded by mastering it, and the fact that its content and concerns are those of the users, rather than the victims of nuclear weapons. In learning the language, one goes from being the passive, powerless victim to the competent, wily, powerful, purveyor of nuclear threats and nuclear explosive power. The enormous destructive effects of nuclear weapons systems become extensions of the self, rather than threats to it.

STAGE III: DIALOGUE

It did not take very long to learn the language of nuclear war and much of the specialized information it contained. My focus quickly changed from mastering technical information and doctrinal arcana, to attempting to understand more about how the dogma was rationalized. Since underlying rationales are rarely discussed in the everyday business of defence planning, I had to start asking more questions. At first, although I was tempted to use my newly acquired proficiency in techno-strategic jargon, I vowed to speak English. I had long believed that one of the most important functions of an expert language is exclusion—the denial of a voice to those outside the professional community.[35] I wanted to see whether a well-informed person could speak English and still carry on a knowledgeable conversation.

What I found, however, was that no matter how well-informed my questions were, no matter how complex an understanding they were based upon, if I spoke English rather than expert jargon, the men responded to me as though I were ignorant, simple-minded or both. A strong distaste for being patronized and a pragmatic streak made my experiment in English short-lived. I adapted my everyday speech to the vocabulary of strategic analysis, speaking of 'escalation dominance', 'pre-emptive strikes' and, one of my favourites, 'sub-holocaust engagements'. This opened my way into long, elaborate discussions that taught me a lot about techno-strategic reasoning and how to manipulate it.

But the better I became at this discourse, the more difficult it became to express my own ideas and values. While the language included things I had never been able to speak about before, it radically excluded others. I could not use the language to express my concerns, because it was conceptually impossible. This language does not allow certain questions to be asked, certain values to be expressed. To pick a bald example, the word 'peace' is not a part of this discourse. As close as one can come is 'strategic stability', a term that refers to a balance of numbers and types of weapons systems—not the political, social, economic and psychological conditions implied by the word 'peace'. Moreover, to speak the word is to immediately brand oneself as a soft-headed activist instead of a professional to be taken seriously.

If I was unable to speak my concerns in this language, more disturbing still was that I began to also find it hard even to keep them in my own head. No matter how firm my commitment to staying aware of the reality behind the words, over and over I found that I could not keep human lives as my reference point. I found I could go for days speaking about nuclear weapons without once thinking about the people who would be incinerated by them.

It is tempting to attribute this problem to the words themselves—the abstractness, the euphemisms, the sanitized, friendly, sexy acronyms. Then one would only need to change the words, make them more vivid: get the military planners to say 'mass murder' instead of 'collateral damage', and their thinking would change.

The problem, however, is not only that defence intellectuals use abstract terminology that removes them from the realities of which they speak. There *is* no reality behind the words. Or, rather, the 'reality' of which they speak is itself a world of abstractions. Deterrence theory, and much of strategic doctrine, was invented to hold together abstractly, its validity judged by internal logic. These abstract systems were developed as a way to make it possible to, in Herman Kahn's phrase, 'think about the unthinkable'—not as a way to describe, or codify, relations on the ground.[36]

So the problem with the idea of 'limited nuclear war', for example, is not only that it is grotesque to refer to the death and suffering caused by *any* use of nuclear weapons as 'limited', or that 'limited nuclear war' is an abstraction that obfuscates the human reality beneath any use of nuclear weapons. It is also that 'limited nuclear war' is itself an abstract conceptual system, designed, embodied and achieved by computer modelling. In this abstract world, hypothetical, calm, rational actors have sufficient information to know exactly what size nuclear weapon the opponent has used against which targets, and adequate command and control to make sure that their response is precisely equilibrated to the attack. In this scenario, no field commander would use the tactical so-called 'mini-nukes' at his disposal in the height of a losing battle. Our rational actors would be free of emotional response to being attacked, of political pressures from the populace. They would act solely on the basis of a perfectly informed mathematical calculus of megatonnage. To refer to limited nuclear war is to enter a system that is *de facto* abstract and removed from reality. In fact, I am tempted to say that the abstractness of the entire conceptual system makes descriptive language nearly beside the point.

This realization helped make sure of my difficulty in staying connected to human lives, as well as of some of the bizarre and surreal quality of what people said. But there was still a piece missing. How is it possible, for example, to make sense of the following:

> The strategic stability of regime A is based on the fact that both sides are deprived of any incentive ever to strike first. Since it takes roughly two warheads to destroy one enemy silo, an attacker must expend two of his missiles to destroy one of the enemy's. A first strike disarms the attacker. The aggressor ends up worse off than the aggressed.[37]

'The aggressor ends up worse off than the aggressed'? The homeland of 'the aggressed' has just been devastated by the explosions of, say, a thousand nuclear bombs, each likely to be ten to one hundred times more powerful than the bomb dropped on Hiroshima, and the aggressor, whose homeland is still untouched, 'ends up worse off'?

I was only able to make sense of this kind of thinking when I finally asked myself the question that feminists have been asking about theories in every discipline: what is the reference point? Who (or what) is the subject? In other disciplines, we have frequently found that the reference point for theories about 'universal human phenomena' has actually been privileged Euro-American white men. In techno-strategic discourse, the reference point thus ends up worse off than the aggressed because he has fewer weapons left; any other factors, such as what happened where the weapons landed, are irrelevant to the calculus of gain and loss.

The fact that the subjects of strategic paradigms are weapons has several important implications. First, and perhaps most critically, there simply is no way to talk about human death or human societies when you are using a language designed to talk about weapons. Human death *is* collateral damage—collateral to the real subject, which is the weapons themselves.

Understanding this also helps explain what was at first so surprising to me: most people who do this work are on the whole nice, even good, men, many with liberal inclinations. While they often identify their *motivations* as being concern about humans, in their work they enter into a language and paradigm that precludes people. Thus the nature and outcome of their work can, I believe, utterly contradict their genuine motives for doing it.

In addition, if weapons are the reference point, it becomes in some sense *illegitimate* to ask the paradigm to reflect human concerns. Hence questions that break through the numbing language of strategic analysis and raise issues in human terms can be dismissed easily. No one will claim that the questions are unimportant; but it is inexpert, unprofessional, irrelevant to the business at hand to ask. The discourse among the experts remains hermetically sealed. The isolation of this technical knowledge from social or psychological or moral thought, or feelings, is all seen as legitimate and necessary. The outcome is that defence intellectuals can talk about the weapons without actually asking if they *can* do it, or if they are the best *way* to do it, or whether they may even damage the entities they are supposedly protecting. These are separate questions.

This discourse has become virtually the only response to the question of how to achieve security that is recognized as legitimate. If the language of weaponry was one competing voice in the discussion, or one that was integrated with others, the fact that the referents of strategic paradigms are only weapons might be of less note. But when we realize that the only language and expertise offered to those interested in pursuing peace refers to nothing *but* weapons, its limits become staggering. And its entrapping qualities—the way in which, once you adopt it, it becomes so hard to stay connected to human concerns—become more comprehensible.

STAGE IV: THE TERROR

Within a few weeks, what had once been remarkable became unnoticeable. As I learnt to speak, my perspective changed. I no longer stood outside the impenetrable wall of technostrategic language, and once inside, I could no longer see it. I had not only learnt to speak a language: I had started to think in it. Its questions became my questions, its concepts shaped my responses to new ideas. Like the White Queen, I began to believe six impossible things before breakfast—not because I consciously believed, for instance, that a 'surgically clean counterforce strike' was really possible, but because some elaborate piece of doctrinal reasoning I used was already predicated on the possibility of those strikes, as well as on a host of other impossible things.[38]

My grasp on what *I* knew as reality seemed to slip. I might get very excited, for example, about a new strategic justification for a no-first-use policy and spend time discussing the ways in which its implications for our force structure in Western Europe were superior to the older version.[39] After a day or two I would suddenly step back, aghast that I was so involved with the *military* justifications for not using nuclear weapons—as though the moral ones were not enough. What I was actually talking about—the mass incineration of a nuclear attack—was no longer in my head.

Or I might hear some proposals that seemed to me infinitely superior to the usual arms-control fare. First, I would work out how and why these proposals were better, and then ways to counter the arguments against them. Then, it might dawn on me that even though these proposals sounded different, they still shared a host of assumptions that I was not willing to make. I would first feel as though I had achieved a new insight. And then all of a sudden, I would realize that these were things I actually knew before I ever entered this community—and had since forgotten. I began to feel that I had fallen down the rabbit hole.

CONCLUSIONS

The language issues do not disappear. The seductions of learning and using it remain great, and as the pleasures deepen, so do the dangers. The activity of trying to out-reason nuclear strategists in their own games gets you thinking inside their rules, tacitly accepting all the unspoken assumptions of their paradigms.

Yet the issues of language have now become somewhat less central to me. And my new questions, while still not precisely the questions of an insider, are questions I could not have had without being inside; many of them are more practical: which individuals and institutions are actually responsible for the endless 'modernization' and proliferation of nuclear weaponry, and what do they gain from it? What role *does* techno-strategic rationality play in their thinking? What would a reasonable, genuinely defensive policy look like? Others are more philosophical, having to do with the nature of the 'realism' claimed by the defence intellectuals for their mode of thinking, and the grounds upon which it can be shown to be spurious. What would an alternative rationality look like?

My own move away from a focus on the language is quite typical. Other recent entrants into this world have commented that while the cold-blooded, abstract discussions are most striking at first, within a short time you get past it and come to see that the language itself is not the problem.

However, I think it would be a mistake to dismiss these early impressions. They can help us learn something about the militarization of the mind, and they have, I believe, important implications for scholars and activists who seek to create a more just and peaceful world.

Mechanisms of the mind's militarization are revealed through both listening to the language and learning to speak it. *Listening*, it becomes clear that participation in the world of nuclear strategic analysis does not necessarily require confrontation with the central fact about military activity—that the purpose of all weaponry and all strategy is to injure human bodies.[40] In fact, as Elaine Scarry points out, participation in military thinking not only doesn't require confrontation with, but actually demands the elision of, this reality.[41]

Listening to the discourse of nuclear experts reveals a series of culturally grounded and culturally acceptable mechanisms that serve this purpose, and that make it possible to 'think about the unthinkable', to work in institutions that foster the proliferation of nuclear weapons, to plan mass incinerations of millions of human beings for a living. Language that is abstract, sanitized, full of euphemisms; language that is sexy and fun to use; paradigms whose referent is weapons; imagery that domesticates and deflates the forces of mass destruction; imagery that reverses sentient and non-sentient matter, that conflates birth and death, destruction and creation—all of these are part of what makes it possible to be radically removed from the reality of what one is talking about, and from the realities one is creating through the discourse.[42]

Learning to speak the language reveals something about how thinking can become more abstract, more focused on parts disembedded from their context, more attentive to the survival of weapons than the survival of human beings. That is, it reveals something about the process of militarization—and the way in which that process may be undergone by man or woman, hawk or dove.

Most often, the act of learning techno-strategic language is conceived of as an additive process: you add a new set of vocabulary words; you add the reflex ability to decode and use endless numbers of acronyms; you add some new information that the specialized language contains; you add the conceptual tools that will allow you to 'think strategically'. This additive view appears to be held by defence intellectuals themselves; as one said to me, 'Much of the debate is in technical terms—learn it, and decide whether it's relevant later'. This view also appears to be held by many in the opposition, be they critical scholars and professionals attempting to change the field from within, or public-interested lobbyists and educational organizations, or some feminist anti-militarists.[43] Some segments of the opposition believe that our nuclear policies are so riddled with irrationality that there is lots of room for well-reasoned, well-informed arguments to make a difference; others, even if they don't believe that the technical information is very important, see it as necessary to master the language simply because it is too difficult to attain public legitimacy without it. In either case, the idea is that you add the expert language and information, and proceed from there. However, I have been arguing throughout this paper that learning the language is a transformative rather than an additive process. When you choose to learn it you are not simply choosing to add new information, new vocabulary, but to enter into a mode of thinking—a mode of thinking not only about nuclear weapons but also, *de facto*, about military and political power, and about the relationship between human ends and technological means.

Thus those of us who find US nuclear policy desperately misguided appear to face a serious quandary. If we refuse to learn the language, we are virtually guaranteed that our voices will remain outside the 'politically relevant' spectrum of opinion. Yet, if we do learn and speak it, we not only severely limit what we can say, but we also invite the transformation, the militarization, of our own thinking.

I have no solutions to this dilemma, but I would like to offer a couple of thoughts in an effort to reformulate its terms. First, it is important to recognize an assumption implicit in adopting the strategy of learning the language. When we assume that learning and speaking the language will give us a voice recognized as legitimate and will give us greater political influence, *we are assuming that the language itself actually articulates the criteria and reasoning strategies upon which nuclear weapons development and deployment decisions are made*. I believe that this is largely an illusion. Although I do not have space to support this argument here, I want to suggest that techno-strategic discourse functions more as a gloss, as an ideological curtain that hides the actual reasons these decisions get made. That rather than informing and shaping decisions, it far more often functions as a legitimation for political outcomes that have occurred for utterly different reasons.[44] If this is true, it raises some serious questions about the extent of the political returns we might get from using it, and whether they can ever balance out the potential problems and inherent costs.

I do not, however, want to suggest that none of us should learn the language. I do not believe that that language is well-suited to achieving the goals desired by anti-militarists, yet at the same time, I, for one, have found the experience of learning the language useful and worthwhile (even if at times traumatic). The question for those of us who do choose to learn, I think, is what use are we going to make of that knowledge?

One of the most intriguing options opened by learning the language is that it suggests a basis upon which to challenge the legitimacy of the defence intellectuals' dominance of the discourse on nuclear issues. When defence intellectuals are criticized for the cold-blooded inhumanity of the scenarios they plan, their response is to claim the high ground of rationality; they are the only ones whose response to the existence of nuclear weapons is objective and realistic. They portray those who are radically opposed to the nuclear *status quo* as irrational, unrealistic, too emotional. 'Idealistic activists' is the pejorative they set against their own hard-nosed professionalism.

Much of their claim to legitimacy, then, is a claim to objectivity born of technical expertise and to the disciplined purging of the emotional valences that might threaten their objectivity. But if the smooth, shiny surface of their discourse—its abstraction and technical jargon—appears at first to support these claims, a look just below the surface does not. There we find strong currents of homoerotic excitement, heterosexual domination, the drive towards competency and mastery, the pleasures of membership in an élite and privileged group, of the ultimate importance and meaning of membership in the priesthood, and the thrilling power of becoming Death, shatterer of worlds. How is it possible to point to the pursuers of these values, these experiences, as paragons of cool-headed objectivity?

I do not wish here to discuss or judge the holding of 'objectivity' as an epistemological goal. I would simply point out that when defence intellectuals rest their claims to legitimacy on the untainted rationality of their discourse, their project fails according to its own criteria. Deconstructing strategic discourse's claims to a monopoly on rationality is, then, in and of itself, an important way to challenge its hegemony as the sole legitimate language for public debate about nuclear policy.

I believe that those who seek a more just and peaceful world, have a dual task before us—a deconstructive project and a reconstructive project that are intimately linked.[45] Our deconstructive task then, is to pay close enough attention to techno-strategic discourse that we might begin to know how to dismantle it. The dominant voice of militarized masculinity and decontextualized rationality speaks so loudly in our culture, it will remain difficult for any other voices to be heard until that voice loses some of its power to define what we hear and how we name the world—until that voice is delegitimated.

Our reconstructive task is a task of creating compelling alternative visions of possible futures, a task of recognizing and developing alternative conceptions of rationality, a task of creating rich and imaginative alternative voices—diverse voices whose conversations with each other will invent those futures.

NOTES

1. Thomas Powers, 'How Nuclear War Could Start', *The New York Review of Books*, 17 January 1985, p. 33.
2. For useful introductions to feminist work on gender and language, see Barrie Thorne, Cheris Kramarae and Nancy Henley (eds.), *Language, Gender and Society* (Rowley, Mass.: Newbury, 1983), and Elizabeth Abel (ed.), *Writing and Sexual Difference* (Chicago: University of Chicago Press, 1982).
3. For feminist critiques of Western rationality, see: Nancy Hartsock, *Money, Sex and Power* (New York: Longman, 1983); Sandra Harding and Merrill Hintikka (eds.), *Discovering Reality: Feminist Perspectives on Epistemology, Metaphysics, Methodology and the Philosophy of Science* (Dordrecht, Holland: Reidel, 1983); Evelyn Fox Keller, *Reflections on Gender and Science* (New Haven, Conn.: Yale University

Press, 1985); Jean Bethke Elshtain, *Public Man, Private Woman: Woman in Social and Political Thought* (Princeton, NJ.: Princeton University Press, 1981); Genevieve Lloyd, *The Man of Reason: 'Male' and 'Female' in Western Philosophy* (Minneapolis, Minnesota: University of Minnesota Press, 1984), which contains a particularly useful bibliographic essay: Sara Ruddick, 'Remarks on the Sexual Politics of Reason', in Eva Kittay and Diana Meyers (eds), *Women and Moral Theory*, (Totowa, NJ.: Rowman & Allenheld, 1987).

Some of the growing feminist work on gender and war is explicitly connected to critiques of rationality. See: Virginia Woolf, *Three Guineas* (New York: Harcourt, Brace, Jovanovich, 1966); Nancy C.M. Hartsock, 'The Feminist Standpoint: Developing the Grounds for a Specifically Feminist Historical Materialism', in Harding and Hintikka, pp. 283–310; Nancy C.M. Hartsock, 'The Barracks Community in Western Political Thought: Prologomena to a Feminist Critique of War and Politics', in Judith Stiehm (ed.), *Women and Men's Wars* (Oxford: Pergamon Press, 1982); Jean Bethke Elshtain, 'Reflections on War and Political Discourse: Realism, Just War and Feminism in a Nuclear Age', *Political Theory* 13(1): pp. 39–57; Sara Ruddick, 'Preservative Love and Military Destruction: Some Reflections on Mothering and Peace', in Joyce Trebilcot (ed.), *Mothering: Essays in Feminist Theory* (Totowa, NJ.: Rowman & Allenheld, 1984), pp. 231–62; Genevieve Lloyd, 'Selfhood, War and Masculinity', in E. Gross and C. Pateman (ed.), *Feminist Challenges* (Boston: Northeastern University Press, 1986).

There is a vast and valuable literature on gender and war which is somewhat aslant of what I'm doing, but indirectly informs my work. See, for example: Cynthia Enloe, especially *Does Khaki Become You?: The Militarization of Women's Lives* (Boston: South End Press, 1984); Judith Hicks Stiehm (ed.), *Women and Men's Wars* (Oxford: Pergamon Press, 1983); Jean Bethke Elshtain, 'On Beautiful Souls, Just Warriors, and Feminist Consciousness', in Stiehm, pp. 341–8; Sara Ruddick, 'Pacifying the Forces: Drafting Women in the Interests of Peace', *Signs* 8 (Spring 1983): pp. 471–89; Sara Ruddick, 'Drafting Women: Pieces of a Puzzle', in Robert K. Fullinwider (ed.), *Conscripts and Volunteers: Military Requirements, Social Values, and the All-Volunteer Force*, Maryland Studies in Public Philosophy (Totowa, NJ: Rowman & Littlefield, 1983); Amy Swerdlow, 'Women's Strike for Peace versus HUAC', *Feminist Studies* 8(3) (Fall 1982): 493–520; Mary C. Segers, 'The Catholic Bishops' Pastoral Letter on War and Peace: A Feminist Perspective', *Feminist Studies*, Vol. 11 (3): 619–47.

4. I have coined the term 'techno-strategic' to represent the intertwined, inextricable nature of technological and nuclear strategic thinking. The first reason is that strategic thinking seems to change in direct response to technological changes rather than political thinking, or some independent paradigms that might be isolated at 'strategic'. (On this point, see Lord Solly Zuckerman, *Nuclear Illusions and Reality* (New York: Viking Press, 1982).)Even more importantly,strategic theory not only

depends upon and changes in response to technological objects, it is also based on a kind of thinking, a way of looking at problems—formal, mathematical modelling, systems analysis, game theory, linear programming—that are part of technology itself. So I use the term 'techno-strategic' to indicate the degree to which strategic language and thinking are imbued with, indeed constructed out of, modes of thinking that are associated with technology.

5. Fusion weapons' proportionally smaller yield of radioactive fallout led Atomic Energy Commission Chairman Lewis Strauss to announce in 1956 that hydrogen bomb tests were important 'not only from a military point of view but from a humanitarian aspect'. Although the bombs being tested were 1,000 times more powerful than those which devastated Hiroshima and Nagasaki, the proportional reduction of fallout apparently qualified them not only as clean, but as humanitarian. Lewis Strauss is quoted in Ralph Lapp, 'The "Humanitarian" H-Bomb', *Bulletin of Atomic Scientists* 12 (7): 263.
6. Since the MX would theoretically be able to 'take out' Soviet land-based ICBMs in a 'disarming first strike'. The Soviets would have few ICBMs left for a retaliatory attack, and thus damage to the United States would theoretically be limited. However, to consider the damage that could be inflicted on the United States by the remaining Soviet bombers and sub-based missiles 'limited' is to act as though words have no meaning.
7. US government conservative assessments of the number of deaths resulting from a 'surgically clean' counterforce attack vary widely. The Office of Technology Assessment projects between 2 million and 20 million immediate deaths. See James Fallows, *National Defense* (New York: Random House, 1981), p. 159. A 1975 Defense Department study estimated 18.3 million fatalities, while the US Arms Control and Disarmament Agency, using different assumptions, arrived at a figure of 50 million, as cited by Desmond Ball, 'Can Nuclear War Be Controlled?' Adelphi Paper No. 169 (London: The International Institute for Strategic Studies, 1981).
8. The phrase is Helen Caldicott's, *Missile Envy: The Arms Race and Nuclear War* (Toronto: Bantam Books, 1986).
9. For the uninitiated, 'penetration aids' refers to devices that help bombers or missiles get past the 'enemy's' defensive systems; e.g. stealth technology, chaff or decoys. Within the defence intellectual community, they are also familiarly known as 'penaids'.
10. General William Odom, 'C31 and Telecommunications at the Policy Level', in *Incidental Paper: Seminar on Command, Control, Communications and Intelligence*, Spring 1980, Center for Information Policy Research, Harvard University, p. 5.
11. This point has been amply documented by Brian Easlea, *Fathering the Unthinkable: Masculinity, Scientists and the Nuclear Arms Race* (London: Pluto Press, 1983).
12. *Air Force Magazine* 68 (6): p. 77–8.
13. *Ibid.*, p. 114.

14. William L. Laurence, *Dawn Over Zero: The Study of the Atomic Bomb* (London: Museum Press, 1974), pp. 198–9.
15. MIRV stands for 'multiple independently targetable re-entry vehicles'. A MIRVed missile not only carries more than one warhead; its warheads can be aimed at different targets.
16. Henry T. Nash, 'The Bureaucratization of Homicide', in *The Bulletin of Atomic Scientists* (April 1980), reprinted in E.P. Thompson and Dan Smith (eds.), *Protest and Survive* (New York: Monthly Review Press, 1981), p. 159. The neutron bomb is notable for the active political contention that has occurred over its use and naming. It is a small warhead that produces six times the prompt radiation but slightly less blast and heat than typical fission warheads of the same yield. Pentagon planners see neutron bombs as useful in killing Soviet tank crews while theoretically leaving the buildings near the tanks intact. Of course, the civilians in the nearby buildings, however, would be killed by the same 'enhanced radiation' as the tank crews. It is this design for protecting property while killing civilians along with soldiers that has led people in the anti-nuclear movement to call the neutron bomb 'the ultimate capitalist weapon'. However, in official parlance the neutron bomb isn't called a weapon at all; it is an 'enhanced radiation device'.

    It is worth noting, however, that the designer of the neutron bomb did not conceive of it as an anti-tank-personnel weapon to be used against the Russians. Instead, he thought it would be useful in an area where the enemy *did not have* nuclear weapons to use. (Samuel T. Cohen, in an interview on National Public Radio, as reported in Fred Kaplan, 'The Neutron Bomb: What It Is, the Way It Works', *The Bulletin of Atomic Scientists*, October 1981, p. 6.)
17. See Elaine Scarry, *The Body in Pain: The Making and Unmaking of the World* (New York: Oxford University Press, 1985), Ch. 2, for further discussion of language that reverses sentient and insentient matter, that 'exchange[s] idioms between weapons and bodies' (p. 67).
18. For further discussion of men's desire to appropriate from women the power of giving life and death, and its implications for men's war-making activities, see Dorothy Dinnerstein, *The Mermaid and the Minotaur* (New York: Harper & Row, 1977).
19. For further analysis of male birth imagery in the atomic bomb project, see Evelyn Fox Keller, 'From Secrets of Life to Secrets of Death.' Paper delivered at The Kansas Seminar, Yale University, 20 November 1986; and Easlea (note 12 above).
20. Lawrence is quoted by Herbert Childs in *An American Genius: The Life of Ernest Orlando Lawrence* (New York: Dutton, 1968), p. 340.
21. Feynman writes about the telegram in Richard P. Feynman, 'Los Alamos from Below', in Lawrence Badash, Joseph O. Hirshfelder and Herbert P. Broida (eds.), *Reminiscences of Los Alamos 1943–1945* Dordrecht, Holland: Reidel, 1980), p. 130.
22. Hans Bethe is quoted as saying that 'Ulam was the father of the hydrogen bomb and Edward was the mother, because he carried the

baby for quite a while', in J. Bernstein, *Hans Bethe: Prophet of Energy* (New York: Basic Books, 1980), p. 95.

23. The MILSTAR system is a communications satellite system which is jam resistant, as well as having an 'EMP-hardened capability'. (This means that the electromagnetic pulse set off by a nuclear explosion would theoretically not destroy the satellites' electronic systems.) There are, of course, many things to say about the sanity and morality of the idea of the MILSTAR system and of spending the millions of dollars necessary to EMP-harden it. The most obvious point is that this is a system designed to enable the United States to fight 'a protracted nuclear war'—the EMP-hardening is to allow it to act as a conduit for command and control of successive nuclear shots, long after the 'initial exchange'. The practicality of the idea would also appear to merit some discussion—who and what is it going to be communicating to and from after the 'initial exchange'? And why bother to harden it against EMP when all an opponent has to do to prevent the system from functioning is to blow it up, a feat certain to become technologically feasible in a short time? But, needless to say, exploration of these questions was not part of the briefing.
24. Robert Jungk, *Brighter than a Thousand Suns*, trans. James Cleugh (New York: Harcourt, Brace, 1956), p. 197.
25. Richard E. Hewlett and Oscar E. Anderson, *The New World, 1939/46: A History of the United States Atomic Energy Commission*, 2 vols. (University Park: Pennsylvania State University Press, 1962), Vol. 1, p. 386.
26. Winston Churchill, *The Second World War*, Vol. 6, 'Triumph and Tragedy' (London: Cassell, 1954), p. 551.
27. Quoted by Easlea, p. 130.
28. William L. Laurence, *Dawn Over Zero: The Story of the Atomic Bomb* (London: Museum Press, 1947), p. 10.
29. Laurence, p. 188.
30. From a 1985 interview in which Holloway was explaining the logic of a 'decapitating' strike against the Soviet leadership and command and control systems—and thus how nuclear war would be different from the Second World War, which was a 'war of attrition', in which transportation, supply depots and other targets were hit, rather than a 'big bang'. Daniel Ford, 'The Button', Part II, *The New Yorker* 61 (7): 49.
31. Jungk, p. 201.
32. Hisako Matsubara, *Cranes at Dusk* (Garden City, New York: Dial Press, 1985). The author was a child in Kyoto at the time the atomic bomb was dropped. Her description is based on the memories of survivors.
33. General Robert Rosenberg, formerly on the National Security Council Staff during the Carter administration, speaking at the Harvard Seminar on C31. 'The Influence of Policy Making on C31', in *Incidental Paper: Seminar on Command, Control, Communications and Intelligence*, Spring 1980, Center for Information Policy Research, Harvard University, p. 59.

34. Two other writers who have remarked upon this division of languages between the 'victims' and the professionals (variously named) are Freeman Dyson, *Weapons and Hope* (New York: Harper & Row, 1984) and Glenn D. Hook, 'Making Nuclear Weapons Easier to Live with: The Political Role of Language in Nuclearization', *Journal of Peace Research* 22 (1): 67–77. Dyson notes that there are two languages in the current discussion of nuclear weapons, which he calls the language of 'the victims' and the language of 'the warriors'. He sees the resulting problem as being the difficulty the two groups have in communicating with each other, and thus in appreciating each other's valid concerns. His project, then, is the search for a common language, and a good portion of the rest of the book is directed toward that end. Hook follows Camus in naming the two groups 'the victims' and 'the executioners'. He is more explicit than Dyson about naming these as perspectives, as coming from positions of greater or less power, and points out that those with the most power are able to dominate and define the terms in which we speak about nuclear issues, so that no matter who we are, we find ourselves speaking as though we were the users rather than the victims of nuclear weapons. Although my analysis of perspectives and the ways in which language inscribes relations of power is similar to his, I differ from Hook in finding in this fact one of the sources of the experts' relative lack of fear of nuclear war.
35. For an interesting recent discussion of the role of language in the creation of professional power, see JoAnne Brown, 'Professional Language: Words that Succeed', *Radical History Review* 34 (1986): 33–51.
36. For a detailed accounts of the development of strategic doctrine, see Fred Kaplan, *The Wizards of Armageddon* (New York: Simon & Schuster, 1983), and Gregg F. Herken, *The Counsels of War* (New York: Knopf, 1985).
37. Charles Krauthammer, 'Will Star Wars Kill Arms Control?' *The New Republic*, issue 3, 653, 21 January 1985): 12–16.
38. For an excellent discussion of the myriad uncertainties that make it ludicrous to assume the targeting accuracies posited in the notion of 'surgically clean counterforce strikes', see Fallows, Ch. 6.
39. 'No first use' refers to the commitment to not be the first side to introduce nuclear weapons into a 'conventional' war. The Soviet Union has a 'no first use' policy, but the United States does not. In fact, it is NATO doctrine to use nuclear weapons in a conventional war in Western Europe, as a way of overcoming the Warsaw Pact's supposed superiority in conventional weaponry and troop strength.
40. For an eloquent and graphic exploration of this point, see Scarry, p. 73.
41. Scarry catalogues a variety of mechanisms that serve this function (pp. 60–157). The point is further developed by Sara Ruddick, 'The Rationality of Care', forthcoming in Jean Bethke Elshtain and Sheila Tobias (eds.), *Thinking About Women, War, and the Military* (Totowa, NJ.: Rowman & Allenheld, 1987).
42. My discussion of the specific ways in which this discourse creates new

realities is in the next part of this project, entitled, 'The Emperor's New Armor'. I, like many other social scientists, have been influenced by post-structuralist literary theory's discussion of deconstructing texts, point of view and narrative authority within texts, and take the language and social practice of the defence intellectuals as a text to be read in this way. For a classic introduction to this literature, see Josue Harari (ed.), *Textual Strategies: Perspectives in Post-Structuralist Criticism* (Ithaca, NY: Cornell University Press, 1976); and Jacques Derrida, *Of Grammatology* (Baltimore: Johns Hopkins University Press, 1976).

43. Perhaps the most prominent proponent of this strategy is Sheila Tobias, 'Demystifying Defense: Closing the Knowledge Gap', *Social Policy* 13 (3): 29–32; and Sheila Tobias, Peter Goudinoff, Stefan Leader and Shelah Leader, *What Kinds of Guns Are They Buying for Your Butter*? (New York: Morrow, 1982).
44. I develop this argument at greater length in a work currently in progress: 'The Language of Peace or a Piece of the Language?'
45. Sandra Harding and Merrill Hintikka articulate the model of the deconstructive and reconstructive projects of feminist philosophical inquiry in Harding and Hintikka, pp. ix–xix, esp. p. x.

PART 6

MILITARIZATION OF WOMEN—CURRENT TRENDS

18

Denmark

Birgitte Siert, Cynthia Loft, Birgitte Andersen, Ingrid Sandholdt, Tine Forchhammer, Hanne Klein and Bitten Forchhammer
Denmark

This paper has been worked out by a group of grass-roots peace activists. Our contact with the Centre of Peace and Conflict Research at the University of Copenhagen, where you find only male researchers, turned out to be rather negative—although they had to admit that they didn't have piles of material on the particular subject of this volume, 'women and the military system'. Our approach has largely been guided by an urge to obtain direct contact with women who are in some way involved in the Danish military system, that is in Denmark's total defence system, instead of focusing on the more theoretical part.

Denmark is a small country, with a population of some 5 million, a high standard of living, a well-developed system of education and extensive social services—even today under a conservative coalition cabinet. Denmark is a monarchy; the legislative power is invested in the king or queen, who acts through the cabinet and the Parliament jointly. The Danish Parliament has only one chamber of 179 members, elected for four years by proportional representation. The present situation in Parliament seems to be rather confusing, with nine different political parties represented—but it is not all that confusing after all, for they seem to split more or less evenly, one half leaning to the right and one half leaning to the left.

Right up to 1948, Denmark's foreign policy was one of neutrality. At that time, Denmark became a member of NATO (The North Atlantic Treaty Organization). The majority of the Danish people consider this membership an advantage—even if a doubtful one—but in spite of this fact, ever since the start of NATO it has been difficult to make the Danes live up to their obligations, economically as well as when it gets to the point of agreeing to mutual decisions. Denmark is known to its NATO colleagues for various footnotes to NATO communiqués, in connection with nuclear weapons and lately SDI (Space Defence Initiative). Although the majority of the Danish population is for continuing the membership of NATO, you will also find a majority against use of nuclear weapons.

In 1985 the majority of Danish women connected with the military system were organized on a voluntary basis in the Home Guard. There are three women's services: the Women's Royal Air Corps, the Women's Royal Naval Service and the Women's Royal Air Force, numbering just less than 12,000 women in all, between one sixth and one-seventh of the total strength of the Home Guard.

When you get around to the military system proper—the army, the navy and the air force—you will find only 718 women altogether out of a total strength of 37,500. All these women have joined the forces under some kind of contract, as no such thing as compulsory conscription for women is in force, or is likely to become so in the near future in Denmark, according to the Ministry of Defence. Women have so far been excluded from combat units (but various experimental arrangements have been started up) as has been the case in other NATO countries. A great number of women are involved with the civil defence system.

As early as 1962, a law regarding personnel of the defence forces made it possible for women to join the forces as volunteers. At that time, apparently, nobody in the armed forces was very interested. It lasted until 1965, before a committee was appointed, and slow-working as such committees often are, a report didn't appear until 1968, resulting in a set of administrative rules in 1971 for accepting women in certain areas, strictly ruling out combat units. From then on, the system gradually loosened up. From 1974 women were allowed into officers' training courses. In 1978 the Law on Equal Rights was passed, but that didn't have a significant effect—dispensations were of course obtainable, and the Ministry of Defence saw to it that a dispensation was asked for. About three years later it was decided that certain experimental arrangements admitting women into combat units into the army, as well as into the navy and air force were to take place, 'in order to obtain a solid base for a long-term strategy, which on one side ensures the forces living up to the intentions of the law on equal rights, but on the other hand does not jeopardize the efficiency level of the armed forces'. The aim of these experiments was an evaluation of equal treatment for men and women in certain combat units. If the evaluation turned out positive, women might have the same possibilities of advancement as men in the same fields.

WOMEN IN THE ARMY

In 1985 a small number of women, fifty in all, aged between 17 and 26 were 'invited' into four types of army units that are typical combat units, like tank units, armoured infantry divisions and artillery batteries.

Who were these women applying for these new jobs in the army? Some came from other parts of the army, where they might have served in the ranks, or as sergeants or officers. Some came from the civil life, and some came with a Home Guard background. This experiment is expected to last until end of 1987; so far only a partial report on the project has been made, and that has been kept classified. But it wouldn't be surprising if the report on the army experiment will give more or less the same results as the one already available from the navy, where the experiment was over in 1984, and the report was issued in 1985.

Through the headquarters we managed to get through to a young woman who was willing to come and see us and tell us about her impressions. Although she turned up—as she said herself—with a far from favourable picture of these peace-women, she soon relaxed, and a vivid exchange of questions and answers followed. One of our first questions was: what made her join? She told us how frustrated she had felt in a small town, having lost her job. Bored stiff, she soon got to a point where something exciting had to happen. In her family there had been a close contact with the Home Guard, and she was taking part herself. So she found that it was just 'it' when she heard about the experiment that was to be carried out in the forces in the so-called combat units. She applied, was taken through various tests and was accepted—and accepted again—which boosted her confidence a little. Then the daily, often physically hard work in the training camp started. These women, the first ever in combat units, were of course the centre of much attention, both good and bad. For the first five months they were in their own company, only women together, apart from their instructors. They found life rather fun and challenging, they had good comradeship and so on. But after the first basic training they were posted out, a few women with a far greater number of men. Then their troubles seemed to start. It was not that they themselves felt they couldn't cope with the tasks, it was rather that the whole atmosphere of negative expectations was weighing heavily on them. In her own case, she reached a point feeling depressed and fed up with being called 'a stupid woman' all the time. In order to retain her self-esteem and integrity as a woman, as she expressed it, she decided to resign. When she was asked how much they were instructed in the strategies of NATO and so on, we got the impression—not surprisingly—that these questions were not so much in the minds of the ranks. We see her as a typical bright young person, male or female, who enters the forces mostly out of tradition, not having thoroughly considered what they are there for, looking at their job with the forces as any other job in the civil world. Some just come to terms with the system, while others object.

WOMEN IN THE NAVY

From 1962 women have been accepted in the navy, although in restricted numbers. In July 1981 a trial period was introduced for women taking active part in combat units. This lasted until 1984, and a report was presented in 1985.

Approximately 400 women responded to the advertising of the project, and ninety-nine were accepted; but as approximately 18–20 per cent gave up or withdrew, more were accepted in order to keep the quota. There were fewer disciplinary problems with women than men, but women had a slightly higher percentage of absence due to ill health. It was concluded that comradeship between men suffered due to the presence of women, that 'women were more sensitive to rough speech, noisy behaviour and gender-related attitudes', and that 'women were motivated for the work, showing great interest and hard work. This resulted in better performance in units comprised of both genders than in purely male units'. Moreover, the report stated that 'women showed some nervousness in loading and firing cannons, resulting in mistakes being made', and that 'many women could not refrain from closing their ears and eyes to the firing blast'.

The final evaluation was that it would be possible to use women in the majority of the jobs on board. However, it would not be advisable to employ too many women, nor should they be given jobs on submarines. The latest news about the navy experiment is that the Ministry of Defence has just officially recommended the evaluation and the way is open for women to join the navy on equal terms with men—with the few mentioned exceptions.

WOMEN IN THE AIR FORCE

1986 statistics show there are 273 'career' women in the air force, excluding the office personnel from the Women's Auxiliary Air Corps.

A collective interview with three women from a rocket base showed no desire from their part for an increase in women applicants and that they felt there were equal opportunities for advancement and a satisfactory work atmosphere was prevailing (as opposed to the army). No discrimination was reported. Motivation for their joining the service had been a definite preference for working with men in an 'exciting' male job.

The typical auxiliary woman had a family background within the air force. None of the three women wanted war nor the use of atomic weapons, Star Wars and so on, but they felt that a *deterrent element* was essential for preserving peace—and that an increase of funds was necessary for this as the superpowers were not interested in arms reduction.

They were not unduly disturbed by the atomic race, as they believed that atomic tests, underwater or underground, were not responsible for the destruction of nature; this was instead, in their opinion, due to industrial pollution. The idea of the existence of an alternative protection for their country was unacceptable for them. They found their work satisfactory, although leaving no time for discussions, reading, nor individual thinking outside of their daily duties.

WOMEN'S AUXILIARY CORPS: THE HOME GUARD

The Women's Auxiliary Corps was created in 1946 with the motto 'Serve Your Country'. The Women's Naval Corps was started in the same year. In 1951 an agreement was drawn up between the Ministry of Defence and the two organizations whereby the two corps became part of the national defence via the Home Guard. The agreement included financial state support, decision-making for training, service and uniform. In 1953 the Women's Air Force was started. In 1973 the Women's Corps Staff as such was disbanded as a result of the creation of the Home Guard Command.

In order to be accepted as a member of the Home Guard, one has to be found worthy by a unanimous local committee. Following acceptance and signing of a contract, the new member is sent on a training course (unless having previously received military training). This course consists of orientation into the Home Guard, use of radio, First Aid and weapons.

Women can become instructors in the use of weapons, radio, ABC-weapons and they can also be posted to various units to replace men. Many of the younger women are demanding an equal status with men.

According to the Ministry of Defence's report (October 1985) there are 75,000 members of the Home Guard, 11,172 of which are women, that is between 14 and 15 per cent. Unofficially, however, the numbers are considerably smaller, as many of the registered women are inactive, and therefore could not be of use if called up; thus the percentage of active women is approximately 10 per cent.

The Women's Auxiliary Corps is at present a branch of the Home Guard but in a few years is expected to cease as an individual unit. The women will then carry out the same functions as men. Today women are mainly used in the sanitary, radio and accounting sections. Among its other tasks the Home Guard will help the police with various duties during the so called state of emergency.

Women's motivations for joining the Home Guard can be one of the following: a tradition in the family or a wish to share the responsibility of protecting home and children, or taking on an untraditional challenge.

We shall end this section by quoting a female officer: 'A woman's spirit is different from a man's in a battle situation—perhaps we are not sufficiently coldblooded (or hot-blooded)! Perhaps women will find it difficult to shoot down another human being? I'd be kicked out for suggesting that women might not obey orders!'

CIVIL DEFENCE

Civil defence is a part of Denmark's total defence and as such in close co-ordination with NATO's superior committee for the area.

The Danish Civil Defence, which falls under the Ministry of the Interior, has—according to the Civil Defence law—the following aims:

1. By means of preventive and remedial measures to provide a civilian protection of life and property from the consequences of acts of war.
2. In times of peace to give assistance in cases of catastrophe and other corresponding situations which necessitate public intervention.

Civil Defence comprises both civilian staff, officers on military service and privates in the Civil Defence, together with various volunteers in different corps and federations.

Everyone who is resident in Denmark and is between 16 and 65 years of age can be ordered to serve in the Civil Defence, should special circumstances make this necessary.

Moreover, the law decrees that whoever is employed by the state, by a municipality or by a concessionary company (e.g. a power station) should carry out the civil defence duties that are imposed upon him/her.

In a Civil Defence pamphlet it is stated that civil defence is humanitarian aid that comprises warning, shelters, evacuation assistance, rescue work, and the like.

> Civil Defence helps to prevent war! By protecting ourselves we show the world that we value our lives and are not indifferent to suffering and death. The majority of the Danish population can survive a modern war! But we need a larger and better Civil Defence to be able to solve the task.

The Civil Defence war effort is closely co-ordinated with the military, and in the case of war Civil Defence is transferred to the defence command, which means that it is the military that evaluates questions concerning evacuation.

A Civil Defence statement from 1982 contains the following: in case of war:

> the efforts of the military forces depend on the damages a war will inflict upon the civilian community being dealt with rapidly and convicingly. If the Civil Defence cannot carry out effective 'first aid on a national level' the military threat facing Denmark will be more serious than otherwise.

Sections of the Danish peace movement have a negative attitude towards Civil Defence. Strengthening it will mean a continued militarization of all sections of society. It leads to a false sense of security, since if a war breaks out, Civil Defence can all the same do nothing. At worst it can mean that it is easier for politicians to balance on the brink of an atomic war. Civil Defence studied in connection with an offensive strategy will appear to the adversary to be an offensive measure. Preparations are being made to be able to protect the civilian population from a retaliating attack. Seen in this light, Civil Defence will simply be another loop in the vicious spiral of rearmament.

Jan Øberg, in his book *Myter om vor sikkerhed* (Myths about Our Security), says that Civil Defence is a military appendix that in reality has other aims than those of assisting the civilian population.

If a war were to break out, civilians would rush onto the

streets, take their cars and try to escape, perhaps considerably impeding the military advance. In reality the first days of the war could be a fight against the civilian population in order to prevent it from creating problems for the military. The civilian population must be forced to remain where it is.

All the aforesaid is to demonstrate that Denmark's Civil Defence not only removes oil from tourist localities, and deals with fires and floods (as it does so admirably in times of peace), but that it also has a task that is closely related to the military.

Where do women come into all this? Part of the Danish Civil Defence is made up of volunteers, both men and women. The women volunteers are organized in the *Danske Kvinders Beredskab*—DKB (Danish Women's Reserve). DKB started its organization in 1940. Its aim is first and foremost enlistment of volunteers and information to and about Civil Defence.

DKB has an effective hierarchical structure command and attaches importance to the qualitative characteristics of leaders on each level. DKB carries out training both for a preparedness section and special sections: signalling service, billeting/provisioning and ambulance service. DKB recruits both women who are conscious NATO adherents and thus support NATO policies as being right for Denmark, and also women who wish to carry out humanitarian work and do not see any problems with regard to DKB's/Civil Defence's participation in the total defence.

DKB has been so effective in its training that men have demanded to take part—not in DKB's training, but by having the whole training section transferred to the men's voluntary organization, 'Civilforsvarsforbundet' (Civil Defence Federation), or CFF. They did not succeed, however, and male volunteers can now be admitted to DKB's courses.

DKB/CFF—*Civilforsvarsforbundet* (Civil Defence Union) had at the end of 1985, 12,900 members. There were in all 18,000 Civil Defence volunteers. Volunteers received quite a large indirect subsidy to a budget of 420 million Danish Crowns (60 million US dollars).

WOMEN AND THE MILITARY INDUSTRY/ ONE ASPECT

From an article in a socialist paper the *Weekly* regarding 'a closed meeting, a "summit" between Danish and American industry and military discussing co-operation', we extracted a list of thirteen firms. We phoned the personnel managers and asked how many female employees they had. The reason we gave for the call was our attending the 'Women and Military System' symposium, during which we would be discussing reconversion.

All the personnel managers were polite, even kind. Two of them regretted they can only sell to NATO, which is, right now, not buying. The industry has its 'ups and downs', so unfortunately they did not receive any orders.

One of them said, 'People are pragmatic, they have to earn a living'. This particular firm, when receiving a military order, always tried to find/plan an alternative civil product from the technique used. He said he would like to receive some material from our conference and was glad the peace movements exist.

At another firm the personnel manager—a woman—had started the job the day we phoned, so we called her back a week later. She then told us that the firm did not want to give us any information. We rather admire her for having the guts to ask.

MILITARIZATION

We don't know enough about the reasons for war, or so some men say. From various research projects, some conclusions can be drawn: 'Wars must be explained by theories and models concerning real politics, the arms race, power, development, economic development and imperialism'.

These conceptions are not what women are usually concerned about; could this be a hint as to why so few women participate in the debate about disarmament and security politics? Neither do discussions about sex-roles as a cause of war meet great enthusiasm from women.

WOMEN AND DEFENCE POLITICS

In our opinion, the women's movement—although strong in some fields, has never really participated in defence and security discussions. When the topic was suggested, the answers were 'none of our business', 'men's wars', or 'these discussions belong in the political parties'.

The Danish section of the old peace organization WILPF has not directly taken part in the new women's movement, but has worked with 'Women for Peace' from the start of this movement in 1979. Some in 'Women for Peace' and women from other peace organizations have also been active in the women's movement. They have, however, not succeeded in—or even tried to—looking at defence and security politics from a feminist angle. Their viewpoints have been as a whole absorbed in the policies of mixed peace movements and in futile discussions about which movement to join, or in party politics.

The Women's Peace Camp at Ravnstrup, the NATO command centre in Mid-Jutland, was the most revolutionary rising in Denmark, but it had to stop after fourteen months due to lack of participants.

EQUALITY

In a report from the 'Defence Centre for Leadership' psychologist Susan Schlüter has ventured the following on the experiment with women in combat units:

> The Military looks at the integration of women within the military world from a male point of view, i.e. that women should respond and react as a man would. This leads to the women attempting to live up to this picture, and therefore they lose any influence to change this norm. A total integration in the masculine milieu cannot be achieved, unless there is a complete acceptance of the female presence.

Another 'development' in this field, and again in the name of equality, was the follow-up of the Nairobi meeting in 1985. All Danish ministries had to work out suggestions as to how they will live up to the Nairobi plan of action for equality, development and peace.

In September 1986 the proposal of the Ministry of Defence—based on the experiment in the combat units—was made public. It is recommended in vague terms, with due respect to certain exceptions, that women should be accepted in the forces on equal terms with men. This proposal was going to be presented to the Danish Parliament on the 20 January 1987, together with the proposals from the other ministries.

At a conference held by the Council of Equality with participation of female politicians from five political parties, we asked two questions: (1) Do you believe that women would plan the Danish Defence in the same way as it is today, or in other words, how are we going to use our equality? (2) Do we wish for compulsory service for women? (a) in a Danish defence system of today, (b) in a so-called alternative defensive system, or (c) in a defence system, planned by women? The answers were (we were all very short of time):

Conservatives	Women ought to participate in the debate, although they would not agree on one kind of defence policy.
The Socialist People's Party	Being an anti-militaristic party they don't want compulsory service, neither for men nor for women. They view defence issues as not divided between men and women, but rather between political parties.
The Liberals	Do not want compulsory service for women; women are handicapped enough!
The Social Liberals	As the Socialist People's party.
Social Democrats	As the Socialist People's Party, and the Social Liberals; compulsory service for women is not of current interest.

One tends to get the impression that the politicians did not really want to talk about women and/in the military system.

The Danish peace organizations are using a lot of precious time discussing individual priorities—work could have been done by one 'side', or together when there had been an agreement. Some individuals and smaller groups analyse and publish good leaflets and magazines. Peace research is 'in'. However, in terms of material reaching the population as such, the results are meagre. Pollution is considered the immediate danger and the main issue just now, not militarization.

Right here at the end we would like to ask a question: Could it be that women have (though perhaps not quite acknowledged) a need for defence and still quietly accept 'the warriors', because confessing the need would mean accepting co-responsibility for the arms race?

If your answer is No why is it that women do not protest more loudly against the way they are 'protected'/defended? If your answer is Yes—what about suggesting women take over the defence, and that compulsory service should be for women only, and only for women who have passed the age of 50?

19

Federal Republic of Germany

Astrid Albrecht-Heide
Technische Universität Berlin, FRG

HISTORICAL ASPECTS OF WOMEN IN THE MILITARY AND PARAMILITARY ORGANIZATIONS, BOTH DURING WAR AND IN PEACETIME

First of all I would like to make a remark with respect to the term 'peacetime': a number of peacetimes just have been prewar-times; this may also be the case now (Christa Wolf, 1981)—but this time it may be pre-extermination-time.

The Nineteenth Century and the First World War

During the nineteenth century women in Germany were involved into welfare activities for soldiers, especially medical care (Seidler, 1978). For the First World War Ursula von Gersdorff (1969) distinguishes between two phases: improvised female military service (labour) and organized female military service (labour). The following passages are based on v. Gersdorff's findings:

1. Up to summer 1916 women's military service was dominantly improvised. It centred around medical care and welfare activities; and it was based on war experiences of the nineteenth century. Thus, as the First World War was the first 'modern' industrialized war, a war of attrition, female service was inadequate.
2. After this, and while a planned war economy was executed, female military service was becoming increasingly organized, mainly with respect to war- and

arms-production, and activities in the field of communication:

(a) The organizational basis was, for example, a centre for female labour (Frauenarbeitszentrale) within the State Secretariat for the Organization of War (Kriegsamt).

(b) Women in the communication zones were working as reserve labour for male draftees in this field. They were active in quite a number of areas: in clerical jobs; as leaders of transports; in reserve activities in fulfilling the duties of sergeants; in sapper-activities in the direct front lines (especially at the French–German front line). Since 1918, the last year of the First World War, there existed a Female Signals' Unit (Weibliches Nachrichtenkorps).

Between the Wars and the Second World War

Between the two World Wars, up to 1933, women sewed, tailored and cooked for the reduced military; some were working within the air-raid-warning department of the Reichswehr. Female telephonists were hired for the military in 1932.

National socialists had already conceptualized the service of men and women during wartime in 1935. In these plans they were included for direct and indirect military activities. From 1936/7, at the latest, war preparations were executed by, among other things, a mobilization plan which included female military activities. Female labour within the arms' industry became a vital—or rather, lethal—factor. From October 1938 women could be drafted into an emergency service. In spring 1939 female service within the air force and air-raid-warning was precisely formulated. From 1941 it was possible within the obligatory labour service (one year) to send young women to militarily relevant services.

The majority of women did not wear military uniforms, although quite a number wore the uniforms of the Nazi mass organizations. (The most useful introduction in this field in German is Kuhn *et al.*, 1982; in English, see Stephenson, 1975 and 1981). Nevertheless, in terms of actual numbers, quite a few women adopted military uniforms (Gersdorff, 1969: 74) as Wehrmachtshelferinnen (Helpers of the Wehrmacht) (Seidler, 1979) and female SS (Seidler, 1978: 175–202).

CURRENT TRENDS

Degree of Militarization of the FRG

In order to give some impression of the degree of militarization—though only in terms of the tip of the iceberg—I shall quote from an official White Paper those paragraphs which describe the density and amount of military presence in the Federal Republic of Germany:

> No other country of the North Atlantic Alliance has stationed more troops and weapons on its soil than the Federal Republic of Germany . . . The Federal Republic of Germany is a host country to troops of six Allied states, for
>
> —233,000 American soldiers
> — 65,000 British soldiers
> — 50,000 French soldiers
> — 32,000 Belgian soldiers
> — 6,700 Dutch soldiers
> — 5,400 Canadian soldiers . . .
>
> No other Western country is being used by the military on such restricted space as intensively as the Federal Republic of Germany. A total space of 402,800 ha is military zone. . . .
>
> Nowhere is the airspace more intensively used than that over the Federal Republic of Germany. Four Million flights take place annually, 580,000 of which are military flights, . . . 110,000 are executed as low-level flights. Low-level flights are permitted in more than two-thirds of the airspace of the Federal Republic of Germany.
>
> In no other Western country are there more exercises/manoeuvres than in the Federal Republic of Germany. Annually 5,000 exercises/manoeuvres over three to four days with up to 2,000 soldiers take place. Eighty manoeuvres include more than 2,000 soldiers and take more than four days.
>
> (Der Bundesminister, 1983: 129–30)

Female Military Service with Weapons: Counter-constitutional

On the basis of the experiences of National Socialism in the Constitution of the Federal Republic of Germany, female service in the military with weapons is qualified as counter-constitutional. This was obviously the result of a controversial discussion and not an overwhelming *a priori* unity (Albrecht-Heide and Bujewski, 1982: 30). While it may sound fairly safe that female armed service in the military qualified as counter-constitutional, the basis of this safety seems to be somewhat shaky. Whenever you start to ask a jurist about the meaning of law texts (in the Roman tradition) they will start to interpret. Because of developments in military technology, some claim that the precise nature of a 'weapon' is open to dispute. The discussion has been started and there exists an unpublished report with respect to the legal question of a female armed military service ('Gesamtgutachten', 1982); it ends with a fairly restrictive interpretation which nevertheless does not completely resolve the issue.

Current Status of Women in the Military of the FRG

As in all other countries of the world, women in West Germany serve as wives and mothers of soldiers, a force which (re)produces military manpower.

About one-quarter of all civilian workers within the military are women; and they are doing jobs which are done in other militaries (e.g. in the United States, the Netherlands or Israel) by female soldiers. In the Federal Republic of Germany accurate numbers and details about the jobs of these women are generally treated as if they were classified military information. We do not have a Freedom of Information Act, which allows access to all data that are not classified as secret, as in the United States. Therefore my figures are dated and limited. Nevertheless they may give an idea of the type of work women are doing. An indicator of the readiness of the present (and previous) government to have a public and democratic discussion on the issue of 'Women in the Military' is that the last White Paper of the Ministry of Defence (1985) did not include a single sentence on the matter. In the official press conference, on 19 June 1985, when asked why this was so, the Minister of Defence (Wörner) stated that it was because he did not want any new discussions.

The newest data I could get hold of are from 1980 and give

Table 19.1 Female civil employees in the West German military (1980)

Activity/job specification	Number	%
Language service	523	1.1
Clerical jobs	10,412	21.5
Telephone, telecommunication	3,192	6.6
Parachute laying	9	0.0
Drivers of electro-carts	2	0.0
Medical doctors	68	0.1
Nurses	1,008	2.1
Different types of assistants within the medical field	1,153	2.4
Cooks	62	0.1
Kitchen personnel	10,379	21.4
Aircartographers	22	0.1
Information on	26,830	55.4
Total number of female civil employees in the military	48,463	100.0
No information on	21,633	44.6

Source: Tabellen zu Frauen, 1980.

details on the jobs of 55.4 per cent of female civil employees within the Federal Armed Forces (Table 19.1).

Since an amendment to the Soldiers' Law (Soldatengesetz) in 1975, Parliament has permitted women in uniform as medical officers on a voluntary basis. While male medical officers can get their medical qualifications while paid as soldiers in the military, women must qualify at their own cost. This is probably one of the reasons that numbers have stayed very low.

In 1980 there existed only forty-five female medical officers (thirteen of them specialists.) Their ranks were as follows: sergeant-majors, fifteen (ten specialists); regimental medical officers, twenty-three (three specialists); medical officers, seven ('Tabellen zu Frauen', 1980). According to an essay published in 1985 by a member of the Social Research Institute of the Federal Armed Forces (Sozialwissenschaftliches Institut der Bundeswehr)—without referring to any sources—at that time there existed about 100 female medical officers (Lippert, 1985: 145).

FUTURE TRENDS

Since the mid-1970s repeated discussions about low birth rates and their consequences for the military have taken place; in official politics, possible reductions in troops have never been discussed. One of the proposals has always been to open further military careers in voluntary service, for women, but for several reasons it does not seem to have had first priority. In a report from a commission on long-term planning for the Federal Armed Forces we can read of manpower shortage:

> Possible counter-measures essentially are:
> —increase in long-term voluntary service [for male soldiers] and at the same time an extension in the average length of service;
> —prolongation of service (of draftees);
> —reduction in the number of exceptions from military service;
> —reduction in the amount of manpower used in the police, frontier defence service (Bundesgrenzschutz), service in developing countries, services with respect to catastrophies and emergency cases;
> —voluntary service of women in the armed forces.
> Beyond this it has to be examined whether—and if so, under which conditions—foreigners (foreign workers) may serve within the armed forces.
>
> (Kommission, 1982: 34)

Some of these measures have been executed in the meantime (e.g. draftees' service has been prolonged from fifteen to eighteen months, and exceptions from the draft have been reduced). Discussions on a women's service go on and there is no evidence (but just hints from people 'who generally know') on specific plans.

The general tendency in the very slow and creeping process of open militarization of women in the FRG (there exists a lot of 'hidden' militarization) was first to open services which seem to be in harmony with 'the female social character' in our culture. I presume that this bias will not be changed too quickly. Therefore I assume that during the 1990s there will be further opportunity for women to enter careers which are characterized by:

1. lack of male manpower
2. an affinity to the female social character.

Unfortunately, it is not possible here to go into greater detail to make more explicit my hypothesis that 'affinity to the female social character' in the context of the military might be a superficial and ultimately unrealistic approach.

WOMEN IN PARAMILITARY ORGANIZATIONS

While, due to German history, especially between 1933 and 1945, open militarization has been extended to women, rather reluctantly, paramilitary organizations, especially the mobile police (Bereitschaftspolitzei) have been less reticent. Here, as in normal police forces, women are all given weapons training. There has yet to be a thorough investigation of this area.

PUBLIC OPINION

Almost no group in our society is not divided on the issue of whether more women should become soldiers. In (the quite manifold and pluralistic) women's movement there are those who, mainly on the grounds of equality and emancipation, seek a female service, at least on a voluntary basis, if not as draftees as well; at the fringes of this group there is the prominent feminist, Alice Schwarzer, who argues in a number of articles or discussions that the Federal Armed Forces should draft men and women equally—and she would, of course, personally resist such a draft. Her main argument is that she does not want to be patronized with respect to her (emancipated) 'No' (see, in particular, Schwarzer 1978, 1979 and 1980). Other women in the women's movement are explicitly anti-militaristic and/or pacifist. The majority of publications are produced by feminists who are in favour of these opinions (see Albrecht-Heide *et al.*, 1982, v. Bothmer, 1982; Brändle-Zeile, 1983; Janssen, 1980/3; Quistorp, 1982; Randzio-Plath, 1982; Schenk, 1983; Sölle, 1981). Besides these books there exist numerous articles and publications not on the official book market.

The majority of the political parties represented in our

parliament (CDU—Christian Democratic Union; CSU—Christian Social Union; SPD—Social Democratic Party of Germany; FDP—Free Democratic Party, or Liberals; Grüne Partei, or Green Party) are also split on this issue, including the women supporters of these parties. Without any compromises, only the Greens are in opposition to female soldiers. The Liberals (FDP) and their women are most akin to the equality/emancipation arguments. Their arguments are developed either along the line of Alice Schwarzers' or, on the male side, as an argument against injustice to young men, who (they blindly argue) have to serve in the public interest, while young women are free of any such obligation and can go ahead with their professional career.

REFERENCES

Albrecht-Heide, Astrid and Bujewski, Utemaria (1982), *Militärdienst für Frauen*? (Military Service for Women?), Frankfurt and New York: Campus (Anti-militaristic social researchers.)

Bothmer, Lenelotte van (1982), *Ich will nicht Krieg* (I Don't Want War), Stuttgart: Radius. (Former, anti-militaristic, Social Democratic Member of Parliament).

Brändle-Zeile, Elisabeth (1983), *Frauen für Frieden* (Women for Peace), Stuttgart: Windhueter Druck-und Verlagskollectiv (Collection of biographies edited on behalf of the Green Party in Baden-Württemberg.)

Der Bundesminister der Verteidigung (The Ministry of Defence) (1983), *Weissbuch 1983: Zur Sicherheit der Bundesrepublik Deutschland* (White Paper 1983: on the Security of the Federal Republic of Germany), o.O. (Bonn) o.J.

Gersdorff, Ursula von (1969), *Frauen im Kriegsdienst 1914–1945* (Women in War Service 1914–1945), Stuttgart: Deutsche Verlagsanstalt. (Historian at the Research Institute of Military History, specialist in important pro-military documentation.)

'Gesamtgutachten über die im Zusammenhang mit der Verwendung weiblicher Soldaten in den Streitkräften stehenden Rechtsfragen' (Judgment on Legal Questions Related to the Utilization of Female Soldiers in the Armed Forces), Stand, 26 July 1982.

Janssen, Renate (1980), *Frauen ans Gewehr*? (Women to the Guns?), Köln: Pahl-Rugenstein. Pro-Workers-Movement and Anti-militaristic Publishing House, Pahl-Rugenstein (new edn 1983).

Kommission für die Langzeitplanung der Bundeswehr: Bericht (Commission on the Long-Term Planning for the Federal Armed Forces: Report) (1982), Bonn.

Kuhn, Annette and Rothe, Valentine (1982), *Frauen im deutschen Faschismus* (Women inside German Facism), 2 vols, Düsseldorf: Schwann. (Historian; best selection of documents, with an excellent commentary.)
Lippert, Ekkehart (1985), *Frauen und Militär. Ein Überblick über den Stand der gegenwärtigen Diskussion* (Women and the Military: A Survey of the State of the current Debate) in *Anstösse* 4: 143–4. (Well-informed liberal member of a social research organization of the Federal Armed Forces.)
Quistorp, Eva (ed.) (1982), *Frauen für den Frieden* (Women for Peace), Bensheim: päd.-extra-Buchverlag. (Green Party Member of Parliament.)
Randzio-Plath, Christa (ed.) (1982), *Was geht uns Frauen der Krieg an*? (What Do We Women Have to Care about War?), Reinbek: Rowohlt (Former anti-militaristic, Member of the European Parliament for the Social Democrats.)
Schenk, Herrard (1983), *Frauen kommen ohne Waffen* (Women Come Without Weapons), Munich: C.H. Beck (Social researcher and poetess.)
Schwarzer, Alice (1978), *Frauen ins Militär*? (Women into the Military?) in *Emma* 6.
(1979), *Frauen ins Militär*? in *Emma* 10.
(1980), *Frauen ins Militär*? in *Emma* 12.
Seidler, Franz W. (1978), *Frauen zu den Waffen*? (Women into Combat?) Koblenz and Bonn: Wehr und Wissen. (Military-Oriented publisher, 'Defence and Knowledge'.)
Seidler, Franz W. (1979), *Blitzmädchen. Die Geschichte der Helferinnen der deutschen Wehrmacht im Zweiten Weltkrieg* (Blitzmädchen: History of Female Helpers of the German Wehrmacht Through the Second World War) Koblenz and Bonn: Wehr und Wissen.
Sölle, Dorothee (1981), *Im Hause des Menschenfressers* (In the House of the Man-Eater), Reinbek: Rowohlt (Feminist, theologian, poetess.)
Stephenson, Jill (1975), *Women in Nazi Society*, London: Croom Helm.
(1981), *The Nazi Organization of Women*, London: Croom Helm/ Totowa, New Jersey: Barnes and Noble.
'Tabellen zu Frauen in Uniform und zivilen Mitarbeiterinnen' (1980), (Tables on Women in Uniform and Civil Female Employees), Ms, o.O. June.
Wolf, Christa (1981), in Berliner Begegnung zur Friedensförderung (Berlin Meeting for the Support of Peace), Protokoll, 13/14 Dezember, o.O. Berlin, DDR, o.J., pp. 47–8. (East German author of *Kindheitsmuster*—A Model Childhood.)

20

Finland

Eeva-Liisa Tuominen
General Secretary,
Council for Equality between the sexes, Finland

MILITARIZATION OF WOMEN BETWEEN 1918 AND 1945

After the First World War in many countries the women's military organizations and women workers in the war industry were demobilized. In Finland the trends were quite different; the voluntary women defence organizations were formed. The Finnish voluntary conscriptive women organization, Lotta Svärd, was established in 1921. The name of the organization, Lotta Svärd, is taken from one of the most famous figures created by the national poet, J.L. Runeberg. Lotta Svärd was a soldier's wife, following the troops and selling food and drinks as well as helping wounded soldiers.

In the beginning the Lotta Svärd organization was mainly run by women themselves and its work consisted of many activities typical of women's organizations. Little by little it became an integral, supporting and assisting part of the military forces. Its members in practice took orders from outside their organization.

During the war, in 1939, legislation was implemented to guarantee women work in the war industries. In the same year the so-called 'voluntary work service' for women between 18 and 35 years was also established. The members of Lotta Svärd were also involved in many technical tasks supporting the army, even in the firing line.

There were 232,000 members (lottas) in 1944 when the organization was demobilized as a part of the Peace Treaty.

About 90,000 lottas had taken part in the active service, 72,000 women worked in the war industries. Some 62.5 per cent of nurseries were mobilized in the military services.

The mobilization percentage in Finland was extremely high, 14 to 15 per cent of the whole population; if Lotta-activists are taken into account, the figure is between 16 and 17 per cent. It is quite obvious that civil life, the civilian economy as well as the war industries employed women. There have not been any proper studies of the subject; the first one has just been begun in the Department of Political Sciences at the University of Helsinki.

WOMEN IN TODAY'S FINNISH SOCIETY

Nearly half of the labour force of Finland consists of women, who work mainly full time. Women's total hours of work (i.e. the time spent in gainful employment and domestic work) is longer than men's because the latter take very little part in domestic work and care of the children.

The educational level of women and men is equally high. Ever since the 1940s the majority of the secondary-school graduates have been girls.

A sharp differentiation according to sex still prevails, however, regarding both education and occupations. Also, the income level of women has remained essentially lower than that of men. Over 80 per cent of employees are organized in trade unions, and women now slightly outnumber men. Thirty-two per cent of MPs are women.

1. The quantitative growth of labour has been due mainly to women's increased participation in working life.
2. The industries with predominantly female labour have been expanding but their growth has discontinued.
3. Women no longer withdraw from the labour market to care for their children.
4. Women no longer act as a flexible part of the labour force, giving way to the pressures of economic trends, and the unemployment rate of women has grown in the 1980s to the level of male unemployment, about 5 or 6 per cent.

5. The income level of women has approached that of men only quite slowly.

The social demands for improving the status of women in working life in general and regarding their wages and salaries in particular have gained force in the early 1980s. Sectors with predominantly female labour, such as health care, business employees and office employees of industrial establishments and the state sector have organized strikes to support their salary requirements. The strikes organized in sectors with predominantly female labour was a phenomenon typical of the early 1980s.

There are increasing demands for better co-ordination of working life with family life. Accordingly, the statutory maternity leave has been extended to eleven months and 'parental leave' has been introduced. In the public sector, both parents have the right to take time off to care for a sick child, whereas in most of the private sector only the mother has that right.

The problem of children's day-care is still difficult, but there have been stronger demands for increasing the places of municipal day-care to meet the requirements.

The rising level of part-time employment (12 per cent among women) has been experienced by women as impairing their work status, and accordingly, it has met with strong and extensive opposition.

THE CURRENT TRENDS IN THE MILITARIZATION OF WOMEN

The Finnish UN Peace Corps: Equality for Women

In 1984 the legislation concerning the Finnish UN Peace Corps was modified so that it is possible to recruit women into service too. The parliamentary Council for Equality between Men and Women was unanimously against the modification; the Council argued that it was the first step to the militarization of women; women will be under military orders and they should be ready to handle arms. The UN Peace Corps serves in war zones.

The Council pointed out that the modification was not one of the prerequisites in ratifying the UN Convention on the Elimination of All Forms of Discrimination Against Women. There was not a question of implementing human rights and fundamental freedoms. The Council is a body which should be contacted when arguing that legislation reforms are promoting equality between men and women.

In 1987 the Ministry of Defence gave a decree on the implementation of the modification to realize the recruitment of women in the UN Peace Corps. The Ministry argued that women in the UN Peace Corps couldn't leave military jurisdiction. Before that, senior representatives of the Ministry were invited for talks with the Council. During the discussion, it became very clear that they did not share the same conception of equality. The Council opposed the decree as such and demanded that the Ministry of Defence open a full public debate: what does it mean to be a woman in the UN Peace Troops. After some months of silence, in the beginning of June 1987 there was a piece of news—there had been a working group in the Ministry of Defence, to consider the practical problems of accepting women into the UN Peace Corps. The need for further consideration was not reported in the state council when the decree, mentioned above, was introduced.

The working group had come to the conclusion that it is not possible to send women into war zones without giving them training in arms, at least for self-defence. The working group states that UN Peace Corps mainly operate in war zones and, as such, their activities are generally of a military nature. All these conclusions are, as the Council of Equality correctly argued, consequences of the 'equalization' of the legislation concerning the Finnish UN Peace Corps.

WOMEN AND THE PERIOD OF CRISIS

In 1970 the state committee gave its report on the measures to be taken to make possible the mobilization of women during the period of emergency or crisis. The committee proposed special legislation to allow the recruitment and training of women in peacetime in military or supporting roles. It is estimated that the demand on the female workforce would be about 112,000 during a period of emergency.

The proposals were not carried out.

In February 1986 the Minister of Defence proposed that training women as a reserve for the period of emergency could be taken as a part of the emergency legislation under preparation. The modification of emergency legislation has since been removed from the Ministry of Defence to the Ministry of Justice. There hardly is the word 'women' in the report concerning the modification, but the groups which it states to be needed during the period of emergency are largely female dominated sectors in the economy.

In 1986 a female MP from the Conservative Party introduced an initiative in the Parliament concerning voluntary conscriptive women. In 1986, in the report of the so-called Women's Group attached to the Delegation of 'Defence Teaching' in the Ministry of Defence, there were several proposals on how to improve women's knowledge in security policy questions. The members of this Women's Group were individually chosen by the Ministry of Defence. The Council for Equality publicly demanded that the report should be sent for comment to the women's organizations.

There is a lot of public-relations work aimed at encouraging the involvement of women in the military system. The arguments used are, 'because of the equality', 'in all other civilized countries women can be soldiers', and so on. 'Women's issues' are even discussed in the military magazines; there are special 'friend campaigns' with female-dominated areas of interest like nurseries. Increasing numbers of women are invited to the élite defence courses to 'share the responsibility'; women are interviewed about how useful it is to participate, how it is part of the promotion of women's status in Finland, and so on. The Council for Equality is not consulted. Members of the Council are accused of being 'conservative'.

It is thanks to the activities of the Council that the Finnish Law of Equality specifically states that the fact that only men are conscripted is not based on any principle of sex discrimination.

FEMINIZATION AND CIVILIANIZATION OF JOBS IN THE ARMY

In 1986 the Parliamentary Defence Committee stated that the decline in the male population will diminish available reserves of men by about 100,000 by the year 2000 and it is necessary to encourage the deployment of women in military-assisting activities; this means a move towards the 'civilianization' of the work which is not purely military.

However, women in the several sectors of the Defence Department already comprise over half of the so-called civilian personnel: 26 per cent of women are in the office work, 20 per cent in the canteens, 16 per cent are cleaners and 14 per cent work in the military hospitals. Women as well as other civilian personnel can be members of the trade unions.

A national opinion poll also shows that supposedly over half of the population is in favour of militarization of women. Needless to say, the questions asked are themselves quite suggestive.

The interests of women and family and the interests of the Ministry of Defence conflict. The military expenditure plans are based on parliamentary committee reports and child-care service expenditure plans are based on the demand announced by the local authorities. The military expenditure proposals are considered to be at a minimum and are approved as such in the state budget. Child-care services in the state budget are, however, always a question of political negotiation.

21

France

Nicole Gabriel
University of Paris, France

'A WOMAN WITH A GUN COULD KILL A MAN WITH AN AXE': 'MODERN' WOMEN IN A MODERNIZED ARMY

As in most Western armies, there has been an increasing tendency towards the recruitment of women ever since the early 1970s. However, the trend in France is less noticeable than in the US army, where the number of women has been multiplied by nearly four times since 1972, so that they today represent 10 per cent of the total force. (In 1940 there was not one woman in the US army.) The slower progression in France is probably due to the fact that there still is—and for a long time will be—compulsory military service for men over 18. None the less, womanpower in the French land, air and naval forces, and in the 'gendarmerie' which is in charge of local defence, has been increasing in a continuous, although less spectacular way. There were 7,880 women in 1972; there are over 18,700 today, representing 6 per cent. This increase of women soldiers has taken place in peacetime and corresponds to a process of slow but uninterrupted integration.

Women in the army have seen their status change several times since the end of the Second World War and their situation is very gradually becoming equal to that of men. Here are a few important dates:

1951: A decree laid down the first personal status of women in the army and created a female hierarchy, parallel to the male one.

1973: There was a twofold and slightly contradictory movement: on the one hand a distinctive female corps was set up; on the other there was a tendency towards integrating women in the normal hierarchical structure. The foundation of a military academy for women (in Caen, Normandy) consolidated the first trend, the opening of the prestigious Ecole Polytechnique to female students the second.

1975–6: There was a renewed effort towards integrating women in mixed units, although access to certain positions of responsibility—especially in the naval forces—remained limited.

In 1982, under a Socialist government, the second tendency predominated and there was a growing trend towards incorporating female recruits in a mixed army, starting from the beginning. Thirty measures for women soldiers were issued,[1] the first being the dissolution of the military academy for women of Caen-Carpiquet: professional training is now mixed in all the four army corps. The main lines of this policy stipulate that women are to have access to a much wider range of posts. Units for women only are gradually being phased out. Even in the most reluctant corps, the navy, experiments in accepting and embarking women are to be undertaken. In nearly all units—except certain commando units—7 per cent, sometimes 10 per cent, of the posts are to be opened to women, this limit offering, in fact, quite a substantial opening. Lastly, the uniform will henceforth be identical for men and women (except for the cap).

However, the actual men–women ratio in the French army (6 per cent women) is still no more than a token gesture. There are very few women generals, the best-known being General Valérie André, an army doctor. The admission of women corresponds to the general evolution of a society where women make up 46 per cent of the active population. The slow response is that of a masculine universe *par excellence*.

In most European armies, women have always had a role to play, albeit a gender-defined one, ranging from Mother Courage to Florence Nightingale and Mata Hari. As nurses, cleaning-women, canteen-workers or -keepers, laundresses, prostitutes or secret agents, sometimes paid, sometimes volunteers, they provided men with food and care. In contrast, the movement we have been witnessing recently can be described as a progression from the periphery to the centre, women's roles tending no longer to correspond to their sex role.

This process goes hand in hand with radical changes in the military institution, partly because the army is progressively losing its leadership in our 'nuclear monarchy', with decision-making in the hands of a civilian élite, partly because '*the great mute*', as the army is called in France, is undergoing drastic modifications and is turning into a white-collar army. Aggression, aggressiveness, physical strength and courage remain ideologically leading values but are in fact no longer essential in a soldier's everyday life, except in a few hot spots where special units are being sent in. Even conventional warfare is becoming an increasingly technological process since the soldiers push buttons or sit behind computers. The era of tussle, hand-to-hand fighting, and ambushes belongs, in effect, to the colonial past.

The actual process of feminization of the armies has been accompanied by the fading away of traditionally 'virile' virtues. But is the soldier becoming a bureaucrat? On the contrary, the fighter-type is still wanted in those corps responsible for peacekeeping rather than offensive work—the gendarmerie and the police, whose role is to maintain public order. Their aggressive presence in the streets of big cities, in the vital areas of transit, such as certain underground or railway stations, in suburbs with a high percentage of immigrants and in some overseas territories such as New Caledonia, is intended to deter through fear. Fear becomes an element of everyday life in certain districts. As it has been noticed in recent years, police forces have been bolstered up by the presence of virile young women, a tendency also to be observed in fascist regimes. However, it is a mere (deterrent?) presence, since the recent measures aimed at the feminization of the gendarmerie explicitly forbid the use of women in cases of active maintenance of public order.

Indeed, the militarization of everyday life is becoming

clear, especially since the return of a Conservative government to power. Even when basic democratic rights such as strikes and demonstrations are being exercised, the police tend to react as if it were confronting serious social unrest. One example was the behaviour of the police during the recent university and high school movement. Minister Pasqua sometimes spoke as if he was fighting a civil war. But this violence was only the tip of the iceberg, looked upon with horror by worried parents. Daily violence against the immigrant population, the hunt for the enemy within, enforced through the campaign against terrorism and the rhetoric of 'insecurity' (actually due to the growing unemployment rate and to poverty) do indeed indicate possible vacillations in a democracy.

'IL FAUT DES CIVILS POUR FAIRE DES MILITAIRES'[2]

Therefore I don't think the process of militarization of society which is in progress in France can be reduced to a mere increase of womanpower either in the army or police. In my opinion, this amounts to a mere adaptation to ruling standards. The militarization of civilian society is not to be confused with its consequence: a more self-assertive presence of the forces of order. It is a much more global process which has been in operation since the end of the 1970s, corresponding to the change in US foreign and domestic policy, the mounting spiral of the arms race and the deployment of new missiles and domestic policy.

However, the international situation is only one side of the problem. The French military-industrial complex reacts as such and requires *so-called* consensus on questions of national defence. France needs national cohesion for three main reasons: as a nuclear power, both civil and military, responsible for one of the most ambitious programmes in the world; as an imperial power with vital economic and strategic interest in the Middle East, in Africa, in the Pacific; and last but not least, as an arms producer and exporter. Concerning the French *force de frappe*, consensus is, I am sorry to say, solid. The idea of an autonomous deterrence belongs to the Gaullist legacy and a French patriot thinks it is his perfect right to have his own Bomb so as to be independent both from the US and the Soviets, and to have enough nuclear energy so as not to depend on the Arabs, the oil-producing countries. Resentment, envy of the superpowers as well as of the '*nouveaux riches*', and national pride all mingle in quite an explosive mixture. Yet this consensus has to be enforced from above for it may come under threat. For instance, it is becoming more fragile on the question of nuclear energy. In spite of the blackout decided by the French government after Chernobyl, an opinion poll published last October by the weekly *L'Express* revealed that 52 per cent of the French population were not in favour of the construction of any more nuclear plants. The keystone to this consensus is essentially ignorance. There is not nor has there ever been any public debate on French nuclear policy. When the military budget is voted in Parliament, discussions last for a short afternoon. This is the consequence of the complex and unaccountable decision-making process in French nuclear policy which actually functions without democratic control. The same thing can be said of the closely intertwined armaments policy which works (or rather used to)[3] through three essential components, as one general put it: hierarchy, secrecy and the high professionalism of all the parts concerned. Hence the qualification of French cohesion as a 'pseudo-consensus'.[4]

Now, how does this specifically affect women? Let us look back at the past five or six years under a Socialist government. Very soon after May 1981, President Mitterrand and the Socialist politicians disappointed the expectations of both pacifist and anti-nuclear militants. On the contrary, they flattered the feminists, created a Ministry for Women's rights which indeed supported feminist projects.

But above all, the Socialist government stressed the esprit de défense (spirit of defence). It aimed explicitly at symbiosis between the nation and the army, as Defence Minister Hernu, the most popular minister despite the *Rainbow Warrior* scandal, repeatedly said. This concept of symbiotic cohesion was emphasized by the use of rhetoric partly borrowed from Gaullism, partly claiming its origins in the French

Revolution and in the idea of a nation in arms. It is not surprising if Jean-Pierre Chevènement, once a left-wing socialist, decided when he was Minister of Education that the text of the French national anthem should be taught in class and that every schoolchild should know it by heart. As a sign of the reappropriation by the left of what had long been an emblem of the right, the cadence of *La Marseillaise* was slightly slowed down.

Were women the target of all these efforts? Not primarily. They were addressed as citizens, like the rest of the population. But the ideological campaign was essentially directed towards youth, of both sexes. A number of agreements were signed between several ministries (Research, Culture, Sports and Youth) and the Ministry of Defence. Although the first two are important (the Hernu–Lang agreement, for instance, made it possible for the Parisian public to watch, several times a week in January and February 1987, 'a tribute to the Army Cinémathèque' at the Musée du Cinéma), I should like to concentrate on the Hernu–Savary agreements, Savary being the first (and unfortunate) Minister of Education in the Socialist government.

Education, especially at primary and secondary level, is a stronghold of feminine activity. Women were not targets, but they had to be allies. These agreements brought the army into the classroom and familiarized young people with uniforms,[5] initially in their outdoor or extracurricular activities. Several examples of this may be given, especially from rural areas where unemployment is severe. The efforts of the army in the direction of youth have no bellicist, or even aggressive overtones. The army presents itself as a useful realm of society in peacetime: officers visit schools and make speeches about the opportunities offered by the army; sometimes children are invited to visit barracks, inspect material, video-installations, and if they are lucky, they can even take driving lessons. They usually go with their masters and the headmaster (if the latter is reluctant, pressure can be applied). The local press reports the event.

When *lycées* are involved, particularly in big cities, the penetration of the 'spirit of defence' is less obvious. In fact, the army hardly appears at all. But those who are addressed are the history teachers: in the final classes of secondary and high school, *The World since 1945* is on the Syllabus; moreover, civilian instruction, which had gradually been dropped, has been reintroduced. In order to improve information on subjects in which teachers have had little training, lectures are organized at district level on topics such as nuclear bombs and weapons, deterrence, world conflicts, European security and terrorism. These lectures (to which members of the army and of the Ministry of Defence are sometimes invited) are organized on a voluntary basis. However, it has not been demonstrated that the presence (or the absence) of a teacher is without effect on his/her career. There seems to be some resistance, passive resistance at least, especially amongst women: they just won't go! This attitude does not necessarily mean opposition, for one has to consider that this is extra and unpaid work and that these lectures take place on Wednesdays when children are at home.

In an experiment conducted in the district of Créteil (near Paris), the organizer, a woman, loudly lamented the fact that there were only fifteen women (out of sixty participants) at the seminar, the men–women ratio being in inverse proportion to that in the educational system at secondary school level.[6] Yet these lectures are organized at a high hierarchical level, and this simple fact has a deterrent function. Even those teachers who claim to laugh at this tutoring and say they would never go and listen to someone from the army, are on their guard in class and try not to express their opinion too clearly. Some of them won't broach the subject of nuclear policy for instance, arguing that they have too little information. They could perfectly well obtain this information, but a taboo is being created. Here again, fear and ignorance have a role to play in establishing and consolidating consensus.

Yet I maintain that there is resistance. A newsletter written and edited by teachers is published several times a year. It collects and presents all the information on the applications of the Hernu–Savary agreements.[7] There are instances of rebellion and repression which are hardly ever reported in the normal media, like the case of a philosophy teacher in Villeurbane (the town of which Hernu is the mayor) who was revoked for having written 'French army out of Lebanon and

Chad' on the blackboard. There are also many less heroic deeds, often performed by female primary school teachers.

Another, perhaps less evident channel of militarization in schools is the massive introduction of data-processing. This is certainly more subtle since the usefulness of computers is an obvious fact. Still, we know that the next war will be waged—or even decided—by artificial intelligence. And that most computer games are war games. This aspect was never taken into account by pedagogues. On the contrary, it was masked by the rhetoric of *modernization*, the key-word used by young Prime Minister Fabius. This necessary modernization was expressed in terms of vital interest and economic survival for France.

The language of power is never openly gender specific. It is characterized by very little stress on the person of the woman as such. There are no talks of compulsory military service for women, for instance, whereas there is in other European countries. The image of a woman with a gun is not likely to appeal to the French imagination, which does not seem to be ready for the idea of conscription as a necessary rite of passage for the female population. Yet non-specific does not mean neutral. Even though the discourse is not specifically gender-articulated, the consequences of actual militarization affect women first and foremost, along with cuts in the education or health sector and reductions in subsidies to the unemployed.

In this connection, I would like to point out a very recent example which also stresses French continuity in spite of the change of government in March, 1986. An agreement was signed between two ministers, both women, in the new Conservative majority, Michèle Barzach (Family and Health) and Cécile Alliot-Marie (State Secretary for Education): 100 school doctor posts are to be done away with and filled by young doctors doing their military service. This means an obvious economy for the state, it enhances the presence of the army in schools and makes increased social control possible (laws are already being prepared to track down young drug addicts and impose quite an energetic cure on them, in prison if necessary). Such a measure is by no means gender-neutral since nearly all school doctors (who don't need initial capital to open a practice and have convenient working hours) are in fact women.

As a (in the original sense of the word) 'panic' system, the military-industrial complex tends to penetrate and permeate the whole social body. As far as the women's question is concerned, it seems to be treated in two different ways. In an explicit discourse, women are neither segregated nor sorted out, but they are looked upon as gender-neutral citizens. On the other hand, the system still uses women in their traditional fields: as mothers and/or educators, in charge of the social 'buffering' (Elise Boulding), as an echo chamber tending to the consolidation of consensus and the reinforcement of the social fabric. Still dancing according to Man's flute. This happens, however, without their knowing exactly the ins and outs of a policy they are helping to spread.

Military-industrial complexes appear as containing left-overs of the Old and seeds of the New. They are based upon the order of patriarchy but could probably do without it; for these two different treatments, one restricted to the technocratic élite, the other to the vast majority of the population, correspond to a more general conception of a dual society, not necessarily divided according to gender.

NOTES

1. *Trente mesures pour les femmes militaires*, NCC 84, October 1982.
2. 'One needs civilians to make militaries', a sentence pronounced by François Mitterand, very often quoted by his collaborators (very recently by Chevènement, Mermaz) and assumes different meanings: one of them is a demographic interpretation; another stresses the necessity of national cohesion and of a popular army. (One has to remember the fact that long after the colonial wars, the army was still perceived by many as putschist and dangerous.)
3. The French armament industry has found great difficulty in opening new markets lately. See, for instance, 'Monsieur Serge Dassault cherche des clients', *Le Monde*, 18–19 January 1987.
4. Agnès Bertrand, 'Le Pseudo-consensus', *Nouvelles Questions féministes* 11–12 (Winter 1985).
5. 'Protocole d'accord, signé entre le ministère de la défense et le ministère de l'éducation nationale', *Bulletin* 43, 25 October 1982.
6. See: Marie-Lucy Dumas-Soula, 'Témoignage: les enseignants et la défense', *Défense nationale*, October 1986.

7. 'Ramassis d'infos sur la militarisation et l'enseignement', ARMS, Maison des Associations, route de Bordeaux 16000 Angoulême. For information, see also l'Union Pacifiste.

22

The Netherlands

Annemiek Bolscher
University of Nijmegen, the Netherlands
and Ine Megens
Scientific Office of the Pacifist Socialist Party, Amsterdam, the Netherlands

THE HISTORY OF WOMEN IN THE MILITARY: A SHORT REVIEW

During the Second World War the foundation was laid for the military auxiliary women's corps. In 1943 the auxiliary women's corps, the Vrouwen Hulp Korps (VHK) was founded from Great Britain. This corps aided evacuees, assisted with food distribution and took part in the organizing of the transportation of children. The strength of the force amounted to about 200 women. After the war the VHK remained. In particular, it became a reservoir of administrative personnel.

In 1944 the women's section of the navy (Marva) was established. In view of the so-called 'liberation' of the Dutch Indies, it was thought that too few men would be available for the navy. Accordingly, women were recruited with the slogan 'Free a man for the fleet'. In 1948 the strength of the Marva was about 700 women. Within the navy they were employed in the administrative section, as cooks, tailors and drivers.

Although women had entered the army during the Second World War, it was not until 1951 that a political decision was made that the participation of women in the army had to become permanent. From 1955 the Dutch army had three female corps: the Marva (women's section of the marines), the Milva (the military women's section) and the Luva (women's section of the air force). Although the corps had military status, separate legal rules were applied to them with respect to the training and career. The reasons for discharge were different too: marriage and pregnancy involved dismissal. The possibilities of women in the military were limited. Most women were employed in the adminstrative, social or nursing sections. A few were drivers. Women constituted only 1 per cent of the total amount of military personnel. The work of women was considered to be temporary and supporting. In advertisements to recruit women for the corps it was said, 'the only weapons of the female soldier, her accuracy and charm—weapons we should call "disarming" ' and 'here women are not trained in readiness to fight but to fulfil a useful function'.

The position of military women in this period was essentially different from that of men. Most of the jobs remained closed to women. The jobs they fulfilled were of a traditional female character. The unequal position of women is an accepted fact in this period, about which nobody seems to care. At the end of the 1970s, however, the policy changed.

THE INTEGRATION POLICY

In 1978 the Netherlands decided to dissolve the women's corps, to give women access to all jobs in the military and so integrate them completely. It was intended that in future all functions, including combat functions, would be open to women. As professional soldiers, men and women could take part on an equal base in the Dutch military. With this decision the Netherlands has a unique position in the world. Military conscription for women, however, was not opportune. The integration policy has been under development now since 1978; in these eight years a lot of experiments have been held; a dozen or more reports have been written and several enquiries have been held. A definite policy concerning women and the military still has to be approved by the Parliament.

From 1 January 1979 new legal rules for women came into force. Women who now joined the army were given the same contracts as men and went through the same training. The women's corps were slowly dissolved and completely abolished in 1982. From that date on there were no longer separate functions for men and women: officially, women have the same right and duties as men. Still, in the early 1980s one could not speak of any real equality. First of all, there were several 'practical' problems to be solved, like the adaptation of barrack and ship accommodation and the apposition of physical requirements. These were still totally attuned to men. Often it was not possible for women to satisfy these requirements. After a few years of experimenting it appeared that more was needed to bring about actual integration than just formal admittance. The interest of women in the army seemed to diminish more than to increase. In the beginning of 1983 there were about 1,450 women employed within the army; a small 3 per cent of the total numbers of professional personnel. Because of this small number of women, the risk of an isolated position was very high. The physical requirements remained a problem and so did the acceptance of women by their male colleagues. The decision to integrate women was mainly a political decision, one which many men and women in the military itself were not very pleased with. Many prejudices against women and doubts concerning the integration policy were expressed.

The defence administration considered a change in policy. They asked for advice from the Public Council for the Military Forces (Maatschappelijke Raad voor de Krijgsmacht, MRK). The MRK is an official advisory council consisting of representatives of trade unions, churches, women's and youth organizations and scientists. Council gave firm support for the policy of integration. Furthermore, they made several recommendations to put an end to the neglect of women. Their ideas and proposals were supported by the Emancipation Board. The most important measures proposed were:

1. More attention to a change of mentality.
2. No compulsory service but a right to join the army (*dienstrecht*).
3. Preferential treatment for women.
4. Horizontal flow in and a vertical flow through.
5. Adjustment of the physical requirements.
6. Measures of quota system.[1]

The defence administration looked convinced. In December 1985 the note on policy 'Women in the Military' came out.[2] In that paper the policy regarding the integration over the next few years is outlined. The policy put forward can be briefly summarized as follows:

1. Continuing on the same road: all jobs must in principle be open to women. Exceptions: the marine corps and jobs on submarines.
2. Similar entrance requirements for men and women.
3. No compulsory service now or in the near future.
4. Active recruitment aimed at women.
5. Measures to encourage a change of attitude.
6. Preferential treatment for women in individual cases.
7. A new short-term contract for women to get to know the army for the duration of two to three years.

THE INTEGRATION POLICY IN PRACTICE

A formal policy of equal rights and duties does not mean that in practice all women had equal chances. In 1979 the integration of women in the military forces was started cautiously. One can speak of a formal admittance to all jobs. In practice this meant that many training schools still had their doors closed to women. Hardly any effort was made to interest more women in a job in the army. A sex-neutral recruitment policy was followed, to that effect that the usual 'M/F' was added to advertisements. The attempts to facilitate access to the army for women were rather different for each of the military forces. The navy decided on a large experiment with women in jobs on ships. The land forces distinguished all jobs according to their physical demands, within functional groups. The integration policy did not lead to a great increase in the number of women in the military forces (Table 22.1).

The year 1984 meant the end of the four-year contract for the first draft of women who entered the army under the integration policy. A lot of them decided to leave and not to re-enlist for a new period and pursue a military career. Unfortunately, no figures are available. Since then a slight increase in the total number of women soldiers has again taken place. There is a small growth in the army, but it is especially in the navy that numbers have increased. This is all

Table 22.1 Numbers of women in the military forces

	1978	1981	1982	1983	1984	1986
Royal Navy	257	486	551	591	585	676
Royal Army (incl. Mil. Police)	+450	491	541	543	514	534
Royal Air Force	304	354	364	324	307	290
Total numbers		1,331	1,456	1,458	1,406	1,500

the more striking if we look at the percentages and not at total numbers (Table 22.2).

If one looks at the percentages, one has to remember that next to the professionals there are about 40,000 military conscripts. From the total military forces women comprise about 2 per cent. This is not a very impressive result of the integration policy. Especially not if compared to the numbers of the former auxiliary women corps in 1978. In spring of 1986 a big advertising campaign was started. In the newspapers and women's magazines whole-page advertisements were published. A lot of women responded—about 12,000—but in the end the number of women who applied for a job stayed low.

Of course it is not a question of total numbers only; until now, especially in case of the army, most of the women end up in lower-ranking jobs. The demands for combat jobs in the infantry, cavalry, artillery and the Royal Engineers are too

Table 22.2 Women in the Dutch army, July 1986

	Navy	Army	Mil. Police	Air Force
Officers	61	100	1	49
Non-commissioned officers	61	128	5	105
Others	456	82	100	136
In training	98	69	49	?
Total	676	379	155	290
% professionals	4.6%	1.5%	4.2%	2.3%

high to be met by most women. The idea that women can enter combat jobs is a myth, a myth that is carefully kept up by pointing at the few women who have managed to become a Battery Commander Operator or even a fighter pilot. These women are always good enough for some publicity. This policy—similar requirements for men and women—is not directed towards change. In this respect it is restricted to formal equality.

INTEGRATION WITHOUT RESERVE

We would like to stress two points which are important for understanding the background and range of the integration policy. First of all, there is the issue of combat functions, and second, we want to restore something about the discussion of military service in the Netherlands.

Most Western NATO countries where the integration policy took shape in the 1970s made some kind of reservation. But not the Netherlands. From the beginning there were no formal limitations: no combat jobs were closed to women. With this policy the Dutch army seems to affirm its image as an institution open to social influences—an army in which the 'new leadership' and 'socialization of the army' made a great impression. Elsewhere I have hypothesized that because of this, the Dutch army may have been used by NATO as a test case for the integration of women in the army.[3] After careful examination of the internal information of several ministries however, we have now come to the conclusion that the decision to open combat function to women was probably not the intended result of a formal decision ten years earlier.

The Netherlands made no reservation regarding the army when they signed the Treaty of New York (1953) in which the political rights of women are guaranteed. Article 3 of the Treaty reads as follows: 'Women are entitled to hold public office on an equal footing with men and occupy all public positions which are instituted in accordance with the national law, without any distinction.'

The Netherlands did not sign the treaty until 1971. At that time the civil servants at the Ministry of Defence stated that making a reservation for the army was attracting attention in an unwanted way. Some thought that the treaty still offered opportunities for a 'reasonable discrimination', such as the exclusion of women from fighting man to man. The treaty, it was said, 'couldn't be meant to correct the job of God'.

It took some time, but in 1979, eight years later, the complete integration of women in the Dutch army was formally launched. Whether the ideas about 'reasonable discrimination' had changed by that time is an open question. The fact that there was no legal possibility to limit the jobs of women in the army had to be taken into account. A lack of manpower or the more technical way of fighting, reasons which in other countries contributed to the growing part of women in the military, did not have a decisive influence on Dutch policy-makers. In the back of their minds they may have thought of the declining birth rates, but in the Netherlands that will not be an acute problem until the 1990s, probably even later. Moreover, manpower problems are more of a problem with conscripts than with the professionals. Introducing compulsory service for women is the only way to increase the number of women in the army on a larger scale. Using women as a reserve army because of manpower problems would probably meet with difficulties in society. In the Netherlands only 35 per cent of the women between 15 and 65 are active on the labour market, which is far less than in other countries in Western Europe. The issue of military service for women has not been debated in public, but it gave rise to a new discussion between policy-makers.

MILITARY SERVICE: A RIGHT TO GAIN OR A DUTY TO FULFIL

In a situation where there is compulsory service only for men, women will always keep a special position. Because they can only take part as professionals, they are always in a minority position and have to prove themselves as leaders of male soldiers.

Women themselves miss the experience as ordinary soldiers. It was for this reason that the MRK introduced the idea of *dienstrecht*. The MRK wanted to encourage women to get to know the army. Girls are not confronted with the military in the way boys are and therefore it doesn't occur to them to pursue a military career, was their argument. *Dienstrecht* is a kind of adjustment in which women are allowed to fulfil the jobs of conscripts under the same conditions and for the same period. During this time the women can find out if the army is suited to them, and then make a well-considered choice about a military career. Although it would not necessarily enlarge the number of women soldiers as a whole, it would create the opportunity for separate basic training because the turnover is much higher. For women officers, that would mean that they don't always have to drill male soldiers but can gain experience with a women-only company. As a final argument for *dienstrecht* the MRK said that this adjustment for women would make it possible for professional soldiers—men and women—to serve as ordinary soldiers first 'which in the opinion of the Board is a very useful measure for future officer personnel'.

The Secretary of Defence objected to many of the suggestions by the MRK. Concerning the idea of *dienstrecht* he felt that this kind of agreement seemed too similar to military service. In a letter, as in other reports, the Secretary of Defence stressed the importance of the operational readiness and the maintenance of the fighting-strength of the military. The word *dienstrecht* was also rejected by the Emancipation Commission. To them this adjustment seemed a sneaky introduction of military service. Nevertheless, they supported the idea of creating special contracts for women of two to three years, which is less than the minimum for male professional soldiers but far more than the sixteen to twenty months a conscript has to serve. This suggestion has been accepted.

Military conscription for women is out of the question for all policy-makers. In pursuance of the Treaty of New York of 1979 concerning the banishment of all discrimination of women, this policy was explicitly formulated. Perhaps they learnt wisdom after the experiences with the first Treaty of New York, or they just wanted to be sure and so made a reservation regarding military service. Women will not be obliged to follow military service because they have less opportunities in society, the official argument goes. Military service usually means a break in a career and hampers men in their development. For women this would mean an extra problem because of their backward position.

The Dutch government also saw some more practical problems: introducing military service for women would enlarge the amount of potential candidates. Making an objective selection which distributes the weight justly and equally will become much harder. The load of work, the financial consequences and the expected mass of exemptions from military service for women all lead to the conclusion that military service for women is not desirable. One of the reasons for freedom from military service probably would be pregnancy. Military service might then become an undesirable pressure to become pregnant—a very curious argument.

THE INTEGRATION POLICY AS A POLITICAL ISSUE

For more than eight years now the integration policy has been under debate. In these years a load of papers and reports have been produced by the military and policy-makers at the Defence Ministry. There has also been rather wide media coverage of the issue. The first woman helicopter pilot or the first woman on board a minesweeper is always good for a picture in the newspapers. Women are still considered curiosities. Some newspapers also gave attention to rumours and scandals concerning women on board. An action committee of concerned wives of (male) marine personnel against the presence of women on board received much attention.

Outside the military and the defence bureaucracy the issue has not raised a lively political discussion, neither in the women's movement nor in the (women's) peace movement. When asked, a lot of women personally reject the idea of being a military servant, but if other women want to go into the military they feel that they should have the opportunity to do so. A questionnaire about the integration policy in 1982 showed that 52 per cent of the Dutch people were of the opinion that women should be able to fulfil combat functions.

In the beginning of the 1980s a few small anti-militaristic women's groups were formed which took up the issue of women in the army, sexual harassment and pornography. They got a lot of publicity, and the issue of sexual violence is under investigation now. More and more information is becoming public and incidental cases are brought to the military courts. No women were involved in these cases, which of course does not mean that women are not troubled by sexual harassment. The actions of anti-militaristic groups seemed to have been successful in highlighting these problems. To stimulate a political debate on the integration policy as such, has failed. Therefore we need to discuss not only the actual measures but also the nature of the military.

We are of the opinion that we cannot speak of any real integration of women in the military forces. There are still a lot of problems to be solved. The defence administration describes the factors which obstruct the integrations as follows:

1. The lack of interest shown by women in a military career.
2. The high ratio of women that don't pass the examinations and selections.
3. The isolated position of women.
4. The lack of acceptance of women as colleagues by male soldiers.

Nowhere are the problems with the integration connected with the specific task and the resulting characteristics of the armed forces. The army resembles a mainly male-oriented society. This expresses itself, for example, in requirements for job performances, communications structures and in a general cultural environment. Women are expected to adapt and to adjust to this *status quo*. It was never intended to change the traditional organization in this respect. On the contrary, the integration of women must not be on the cost of the operational readiness and war-fighting capability of the armed forces; it is 'only' a personnel problem. But even from the point of view of efficiency and management, we see that few attempts or adjustments are made to optimize the new situation. The best reason we can think of for this is the fact that the integration was introduced mainly for political motives and was more or less forced on the military.

NOTES

1. De vrouw in de krijgsmacht, Rapport van de Maatschappelijke Raad voor de Krijgsmacht. The Hague, 1984. Kanttekeningen bij het advies 'De vrouw in de krijgsmacht. Brief van de Emancipatie Raad, The Hague, 8 January 1985.
2. Vrouw in de Krijgsmacht. Beleidsnota van de Staatsssecretaris van Defensie, W.K. Hoekzema, The Hague, Ministry of Defence, December 1985.
3. Ine Megens, 'Vrouwen en het leger', *Socialistisch Perspektief* 4(1): 28–39. See also Cynthia Enloe, 'NATO's Interest in Women: The Lesson Machine' in W. Chapkis (ed.), *Loaded Questions: Women in the Military* (Amsterdam, 1981), pp. 65–71.

Unfortunately almost all material is in Dutch. Official documents can be applied for at the Ministry of Defence, Defensievoorlichting, Postbus 20701, 2500 ES Den Haag, The Netherlands. Other information is obtainable from one of us:

Annemiek Bolscher
Evertsenstraat 46
6512 JN Nijmegen
The Netherlands

Ine Megens
Scientific Office PSP
Pacifist Socialist Party
Postbox 700, 1000 AS Amsterdam.

23

Norway

Ellen Elster
Folkereisning mot Krig, Norway

In this paper, I will concentrate on women's participation in the military, as it is here that the militarization of women clearly happens. Though there are not many women involved—a little more than 1 per cent of the total forces—we cannot deny the general significance that opening of the military gates to women has for the public in general and women in particular. This is also the area which has been most closely followed in the last decade.

We know, however, less about other areas of militarization and their impact on women, for example, the military economy, prostitution, military wives and so on. Military expenditure per head is fairly high in Norway compared to other countries. On a ranking scale among 142 countries in the world, Norway is number 15. But expenditure on health services and education is even higher. On the same scale, Norway ranks 3 and 2 respectively (Sivard, 1983, Table III). These two sectors take about one-third of the Gross National Product each, while the military takes about 3–4 per cent. As in most other countries, women are mostly employed in the health services and education.

In the following I begin by looking at the situation for women in the military today. Then I make a jump back into history. Having been under foreign rule for 400 years, the question of women's relation to the military is fairly recent. I have also taken a look at women's anti-militarist involvement as I know it. I see two political directions: the military one and the anti-military one, or the work for a peaceful world. I then return to the present situation, but this time exploring more the subjective experiences of the military life for women and the debate about women's participation in the military, concluding with alternative ways forward, such as women's participation in the peace movement.

The current trends in Norway are very much like those we find in other Western industrialized countries and especially within the NATO countries. I hope, however, that by giving Norwegian examples Norwegian cultural trends will be clarified.

THE PRESENT SITUATION AND RECENT DEVELOPMENTS

About 500 women are today directly engaged in the Norwegian military forces, and about sixty women are joining the forces every year. The number of women participating has been doubled since 1977, when the military first opened its gates for women. The Tables 23.1 and 23.2 show the distribution within the various military fields.[1]

Because of the Law of Equality in Norway there are no upper limits on the ratio of women in the military. In 1986 there were less women applying for the military training than in 1985. The number was reduced by one-third. Military planners feel that their publicity has been inadequate, and that it lately has become easier to get into civil training schools and work. A representative for the women soldiers thinks, however, that the informal network has been working very

Table 23.1 Total number of women in service and in training, 1 July 1985

	Army	Navy	Air force	Home guard	Sanitary	Total	Total, Nov. 1986
Officers	157	41	69	–	25	292	331
Soldiers	20	–	8	–	–	28	69
Enlisted	20	15	31	–	–	66	59
Trainees	30	30	28	–	–	88	84
All in service	227	86	136	–	25	474	543

Table 23.2 Total number of women not in service/reserves, 1 July 1985

	Army	Navy	Air force	Home guard	Sani-tary	Total
Officers	226	60	58	132	700	1,176
Soldiers	248	123	118	545	–	1,044
All reserves	474	183	176	677	700	2.220

effectively, so that women with negative experiences in the military have shared this with other women outside.[2]

The service is based on voluntary participation. At first only limited tasks were open to women, and only non-combat positions. This is not so today. In principle, all positions are open to women, and today women are doing military service together with and on equal terms with men. The only difference is that women join the service voluntarily while men are conscripted.

Women can, however, be conscripted to do civil defence service. This applies to women between the ages of 28 and 40 who have no children under 16 years old. It is illegal to object, but women can easily be freed for social or health reasons. Women can be used within all branches of the civil defence, though physically demanding services are voluntary.

There are no upper limits to the ratio of women in the civil defence forces. By 1 January 1986, 4,006 women (9 per cent of the total forces) had done their service. This is an increase since 1982, which was 6 per cent of the total forces.[3]

This development in Norway is not an isolated phenomenon. After all, Norway is a member of NATO and parallels developments in other NATO countries. In the early 1970s military leaders and planners were worried about future recruitment: the birth rate was falling dramatically. The introduction of modern technology would also require higher educational standards.

Women officers within NATO countries have been meeting each other since 1961 in order to exchange experiences and discuss how women might achieve greater responsibility within the military. They were first taken seriously by the male military leaders in 1976, and their meetings were, from that time, given formal status directly under the authorities of the NATO's military committee (Enloe, 1981).

This was a time when the echo from the women's liberation struggle for equal rights sounded throughout the North and the West of the world. Clearly, the military planners knew how to make use of the general development in the society in order to fill their military needs: 'In accordance with the general development in the society it is an aim to give men and women the same job opportunities. The Defence Department will also give women the same job opportunities within the military'.[4]

This does not sound right knowing that the military is the most patriarchal institution we know of. We shall later see that the military is not giving the women the most hearty welcome.

However, Figure 23.1 shows the development of available 18-year-old male recruits between 1980 and 2000 in Norway.

Figure 23.1 Conscription from 1980 to 2000, (net available 18-year-old males)

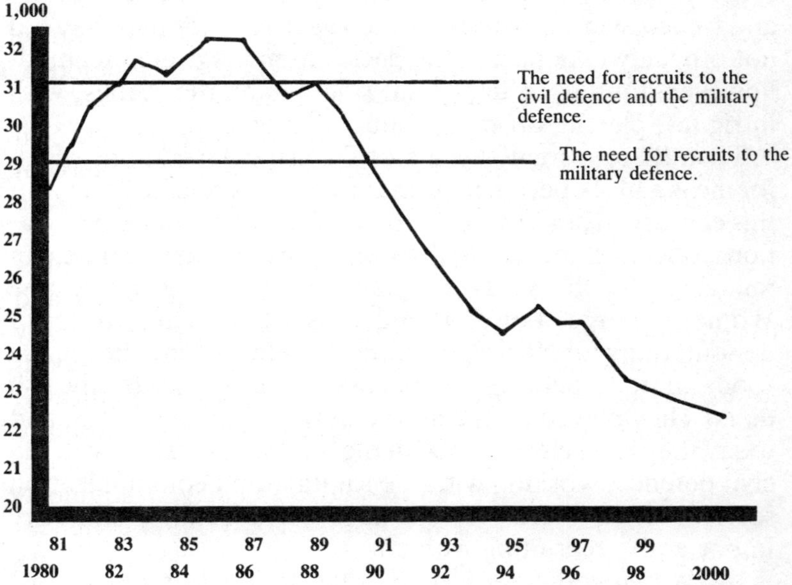

Source: The figures are based on Norwegian Statistic Bureau predictions.

It shows that there will be a shortfall of 8,000 male conscripts, in terms of the military level deemed necessary by the politicians.[5]

AN HISTORICAL PERSPECTIVE

Women's participation in the military did not start when women stopped producing enough boys. It has been a slow development through history, a giving and taking along with other tendencies in society. History shows us that there is nothing in women's nature which makes women more peaceful. Very much depends on the society into which we are socialized.

Military Women

Norwegian written history goes back to the age of the Vikings. That was a time of constant war, and the women took an active part in the socialization of the young men to become tough and strong, to endure hardship and strain, to compete and to be a winner (Brock-Utne, 1985: 77). Though they did not officially take part in the decision-making, they seemed, however, to play an important role behind the scenes, with intrigues, playing off men against each other.[6]

Then there were 400 years of Danish colonization, which for me is a black period in terms of women's role in society. In this century, from 1889 to 1896, there was a women's association collecting money to buy weapons for the Norwegian military. In 1928 'Norwegian Voluntary Conscriptive Women' (Norges Lotteforbund) was established in order to do something for Norwegian military defence, and they made food, knitted stockings and arranged social events for the soldiers. They played a certain role during the war 1940–5, and today they have closer ties with the military as well as with the civil defence, working with the sanitary and communication services when there is a shortage of personnel, and very importantly, recruiting women.

In 1951, together with nine other national organizations, 'Norwegian Voluntary Conscriptive Women' formed

'Women's Voluntary Emergency', whose main function is to recruit women for service. Its main tasks are (1) providing information about total defence, (2) supporting the civil defence and the civil society's ability to meet crises, national catastrophes, incidences and so on, (3) co-ordinating female recruits in case of war and informing women generally about tasks they will be required to do in the event of war. Today, co-operation with military defence has become closer, and the organization is heavily funded by the Defence Department.[7]

Norway was not directly involved in the First World War, while during the Second World War women were conscripted for service both in Great Britain and in Sweden, working in auxiliary positions.[8] The reason was the need for soldiers. In 1945 the women were immediately demobilized only to be conscripted the next year in connection with the occupation of West Germany. About 500 women were trained for this mission. Massive protests from peace and women's organizations resulted in a decision from the Parliament to discontinue the service in 1947.

The emergency laws came in 1950 and give the right to conscript women to the military in times of war or in an emergency situation. This just happened. There was no debate in the women's organizations, perhaps because there were no consequences for women during peacetime, with no training immediately involved. The same thing happened with the Civil Defence Law 1953 and which can in principle be used to conscript both men and women for service, but few women seem to be aware of the fact.

A women's service has, however, existed since 1951. Women had the possibility to sign an agreement with the military to meet for service in case of war or mobilization. The women were given some training. This service was looked at closer in the beginning of the 1970s and appeared to be unsatisfactory and the recruitment did not go very well. The service was purely supportive with no military status and therefore held little attraction to women. In 1954 four positions as women inspectors were established to co-ordinate the service. They have still the same function today, but are now of higher officer rank.[9]

Women for Peace

But we also know of another history of women, a history of peace. Also in Norway there have been women who have talked and worked against war and for a peaceful society, for example Camilla Collet during the eighteenth century.[10] In 1915 a group of women from Norway joined the international meeting in The Hague in protesting against the Great War, and took part in the activities of the Women's International League for Peace and Freedom in its efforts to stop the war, to get an international League of Nations established, arranging international disarmament conferences and warning about the growing fascism in Europe during the 1930s (Gjermoe, 1983).

Around the turn of this century we also had a growing labour movement. Along with working men, working women also organized themselves. They saw clearly that there would be no socialism without women being liberated not only from the ruling class but also from men's oppression, which happened in all classes. The peace question was also central. As long as there was any kind of oppression, there would be no peace. Johanne Reutz Gjermoe, a woman who worked actively within the labour movement and in organizing working women, has written that the women's organization met opposition from the men within the movement. She had worked for co-operation with other women's groups but felt that this was not wanted by the leading men. After the Labour Party were elected to government in 1936, the party changed its anti-militarist attitude completely. The neutrality policy was undermined, and the party wanted working women to go together with the bourgeois women's organizations in order to mobilize women for a work-service in case of war. 'During war we are allowed to co-operate, but not during peace', Gjermoe commented. However, the plan was never put into practice. The Second World War was about to reach Norway (Gjermoe, 1983: 53).

No one has pictured the relation between women's liberation, socialism and an anti-war point of view better than Nini Roll Anker in her novel, *The Woman and the Black Bird* (Anker, 1945). She finished her book in 1942, just a few months before she died. Because of the war it was published in 1945 but was rejected by the critics. It expressed a strong pacifist message, which was not popular so soon after the war.

The book analyses potential historical impact of the role of women, describing an imprisoned woman who has helped her son to desert the war. She looks back at her life, her marriage and her sons. Her world has been the home and the children. Meanwhile, the outside world is full of armament and preparations for a new war. An insidious fear takes her and brings her into conflict with her husband, who is 'realistic'. The war comes and takes her sons. But what has she—or any other woman—done to prevent it? Have they not just continued as a crowd wave without any will between the active men:

> The men are giving us phrases and assurance about peace, and all the earth's mothers are helping them. The mother-love is their best ally and they know it. But a mother never dare think such a thought, because then she cannot only be a mother, or only a woman. Then she would have to be human. Then she would have to raise herself against the man without whom she cannot live, then she would have to raise her children against him, the maintainer. Then she would have to tell them the truth, the bloody truth about life!
>
> (Anker, 1977: 130)

A well hidden part of our history is the part women played, especially the many housewives, during the last world war. Although many acted heroically, very little is known. Their activities became part of everyday life. They used an untraditional network in spreading news, or they rather used the network they always used. Of course, there were few victims among them, few accused them of doing anything out of the ordinary, and of course their activities have more or less remained hidden. Helga Stene, a teacher and a historian, has for many years applied for research money to dig into this unknown history, without much result. One example she gives concerns the Nazi's attempt to establish a youth service in 1942. We all have heard about the teachers' and the clergies' protests. But who knew that women mobilized a nation-wide petition within a short time during which about 200,000 protest letters were sent to the central office and created chaotic conditions, and nothing could be done about it because it was impossible to find out who was behind it (Stene, 1959 and 1984). When the war ended, the men did not want the women they had been fighting alongside in the underground movement to celebrate the victory. Nor did any women who got killed get any memorial erected in their honour as men did (Brock-Utne, 1985: 63).

Ever since 1945, women's groups have been working courageously in the name of peace. In 1946 they stopped conscripting women who were to be sent to West Germany (Elster, 1976); they protested in 1949 when Norway became a member of NATO—not without complications (Gjermoe, 1983: 117); they worked actively against the nuclear threat in the 1960s and again in the 1980s with the establishing of Women for Peace (Brock-Utne, 1985: 47–50).

MILITARIZATION OF WOMEN

Women in the military

A survey in 1981 (Stenvik, 1982) shows that women joining the Norwegian forces were young and unmarried. They had not been employed before, and often came directly from college to the military. More than half of them had fathers or other close relatives already working in the military. The reasons for women joining the military were mainly practical, that is, educational and economical, rather than ideological in nature, according to Stenvik, who conducted the survey.

'The level of consciousness was amazingly low', a woman who spent four months in the air forces told the paper *Ikkevold* (Nonviolence).[11] 'Most of the women thought that this was fun and unconventional. Few knew what their future would be like, only that the military gave an exciting opportunity, not really knowing what the military was about'. In other words, many of the women joined the army more by chance than anything else. They knew they would get a training without having to take up a loan[12] and even get paid, and they would get a safe and stable job (Oltedal and Walle, 1984–5).

Women are found among the professionals, but not among the leaders. They are few and very scattered throughout the organization, which means that they have little opportunity to develop a community with other women and few possibilities for developing common understanding of what is or can be their short and long-term interests (Stenvik, 1982).

Two women, who have completed their training in the navy carried out a study among women in the navy, and what they thought about it (Oltedal and Walle, 1984–5). They spent a long time interviewing the women in order to get as honest answers as possible. The study shows that the military is not ready to receive women, both on the practical and on the psychological side. It shows that women are treated as special cases in a negative way, because they are a minority. Women are made invisible in the sense that the men will not listen to them while giving orders, or the men repeat in a female voice. The men may laugh at a woman who is overweight; women in the military should be 'pretty' and 'delicate'. The men blame the women for destroying the good atmosphere among the men. They are also blamed for taking jobs from the men. And they are blamed for joining the forces in order to find a man. The study says nothing about whether there is any sexual harassment.

The military is based on competition. Right from the beginning there is both physical and intellectual competition, and those who do it the best are well rewarded. It is not easy to be a woman competing with men. If a woman does better than a man, she risks being harassed in various ways by the men. According to the women in the study, the men on the same level in the hierarchy are the worst, while the older male officers seem to be quite positive towards the presence of women.

Being very few women among many men and in environments which are built up by and for men, many of the women in the study feel lonely, they miss the presence of other women. In order to be accepted and to manage this situation, they accept the men's premises, join the men in their dirty, sexist jokes, their tough way of talking, they go into rash exercises to prove that they are just as 'tough' as the men. The authors conclude that the most serious problem the women meet in the military, is to be forced into this male ideal-model and to be judged according to male criteria (Oltedal and Walle, 1984–5).

In the 1981 survey most of the women believed that the women's service in the military would open up areas previously closed to women. Few of them were, however, concerned about women's issues and the question of women's equality. It was clear that conditions for women were not always well suited for them and that they consequently did not function as 'equals' with the male soldiers (Mathisen, 1986: 206–7; Stenvik, 1983: 38–49).

Grethe Værnø, the chairwoman of 'Women's Voluntary Emergency', former Conservative Member of Parliament and eager spokesperson for the women's service in the military, points out that equality in the military is important. More women have to be recruited, otherwise the women already in the military will never experience equality, and the equality policy in the rest of the society will fail. Værnø thinks that the military is creating male chauvinists and that working for equality within the military has been neglected. But she also thinks that those women who want to join the military have been counteracted by other women who are opposed to the military. She goes as far as to say that the opposition has ruined the solidarity between women.[13]

Will women be conscripted?

From time to time we have had eager debates about conscription of women. Those in favour have always argued for equality, but often from different points of view. From a military point of view, the armed services do in fact play the most important role. By the year 2000 it is thought there will be too few male recruits. Nowadays they talk about the 'time not being right', the need for changes in the physical requirements. As I see it, public opinion must get used to the idea of women in uniforms. The military planners might be frightened of the opposition that this suggestion might cause: 'It is a question of whether society is able to accept conscription both for men and women'.

There is an awareness among military personnel that in order to reach full equality in the military, women will have to be conscripted. Some think that a solution might be near, while others see it as a very difficult and big step to take.[14]

According to the Constitution of 1814, all citizens were obliged to 'defend their country'. But at that time the word 'citizen' meant men. This is even clearer concerning the right to vote; all citizens above 25 years old could vote, but women first won this right some 100 years later in 1914. The Constitution does not, however, justify conscription for women; on the contrary, there is nothing in the Norwegian legislation to prevent it either.[15]

I think that military authorities might as well find other solutions to military conscription, for example preserving the voluntary service by making it more attractive for women. This is what they have tried to do by opening all positions to women. Or they could widen the concept of conscription to include a kind of civil and/or social service. These proposals have been discussed. In this way they can control the intake of women to the military. The military can pick the people it needs for its purposes from all youths at a certain age, and the rest will do the service in other parts of the total defence and/or within the health and social services. I do not think that sufficient consideration has been given to the implications of connecting health and social services with the military system (Elster, 1984).

A more totalitarian point of view is presented by a small but very loud group of women, representing the Marxist-Leninists, once inspired by Mao's China. Conscription of women means for them full equality. Also women must be able to defend themselves and their country. This will increase the opportunity for equality elsewhere in the society, and they refer to the examples from liberation wars where women have participated in the army.

In between we find Grethe Værnø to whom I already have referred. She has been one of the foremost Conservative spokeswomen on this issue, though she is not always representative. It is her opinion that women should not have any more duties until the worst inequalities in society have been dealt with. Today women have attained some equalities on the labour market, but only to find that they have a double task, both at home and at work, since men do not share in the housework. Shall the next 'victory' for equality be that women are burdened threefold? Grethe Værnø asks.

During the past few years radical feminists have engaged themselves in the debate about conscription of women and women's relation to the military more generally. They differ between equality and liberation. Going into the military will mean a mechanistic equality based on men's assumptions, when in fact they want liberation from patriarchy and other oppressive structures, and this liberation must occur on women's premises. The way forward should not mean accepting the men's world. It should be nonviolent, and the goals should be realized through daily activities. Against this background conscription is totally irrelevant. So is the proposal on social conscription, as this has to be seen as part of the total defence system. Social service or community service is seen as a way to reinforce women's feelings of guilt since they are not able to do their duties imposed by the society. Feminists see that the lack of mutual caring particularly for the elderly, has something to do with the way we organize our society. This means that a highly industrialized and technological society, where effectiveness is the measure of how well-functioning you are, is not the answer. This is also interrelated with the type of defence we have got. Our military defence has developed to defend the type of society we have got today. A change of society will also demand a change of defence, a defence which will be a reflection of the good society (Elster, 1984).

Among the Norwegian peace organizations, the Norwegian section of Women's International League for Peace and Freedom and FMK, the Norwegian section of War Resisters' International, have participated actively in the discussion and spoken out against any kind of conscription. WILPF considers that women's primary societal duty is to care for children, while FMS is against conscription of men as well as women. Both organizations feel that conscription of women will lead to greater militarization of the society, and consequently to an escalation of armaments in the world. Disarmament, to them, implies that less and less people get involved both directly and indirectly in military activities (Elster, 1982, 1983 and 1985; Mathisen, 1986).

WOMEN AND THE PEACE MOVEMENT

I have already mentioned that there exist women's groups working for peace today (e.g. Women for Peace and WILPF) and that radical feminists have during the past few years developed an analysis where they see the links between feminism and nonviolence. They say that we cannot have a peaceful world without women and other groups being liberated from all oppression.

There was a rise of the consciousness and of the activities by women against war in the early 1980s. Activities today, however, seem to be at a lower level. Whether they really are at a lower level, or whether there is just less media interest, I do not know. I would think it is a combination of the both.

There are also women participating in mixed-sex peace groups and organizations. There the women are often a minority. Their work is often not visible. Bett Romstad (1983) had compared in a paper a mixed-sex organization, No to Nuclear Arms (NTA), with Women for Peace, a women-only peace group. She points to the differences in goals, slogans, activities, ways of organizing and writing pamphlets. For example, women in NTA do most of the tedious work, while men have a leading position doing the so-called serious work, making speeches at meetings, getting interviewed on TV and so on. In Women for Peace, however, women do the whole range of work, from the tedious work to taking responsibilities, leadership, public speaking and writing. Through this work they get the chance to acquire the necessary training and experience for political work, which they need to be able to participate in a real democracy (Brock-Utne, 1985: 66–8; Mathisen, 1986: 205–6). I would like to mention here that in smaller mixed-sex groups like FMK, the tasks are more equally distributed among the activists, only that there are very few women participating. About 5 per cent of the membership are women.

In Norway there is also much debate about the front-line role women can take in furthering world peace. For that women must win power. We have, however, seen what happens to women when they get into positions of power. In Norway we currently have a woman prime minister. But she would never have been elected if she had chosen a more feminist stand (Brock-Utne, 1985: 34). It is of course true that about half of her government consists of women, and many of them have been fairly radical in their policies, though many think they are not radical enough. Over the past ten years there has also been a kind of women's revolution, with many more women being elected to local councils around the country. However, many resign after one period of four years and the parties have had difficulties in finding new women willing to accept a further period. The job is something you have to do on top of everything else, evening meetings without providing for child-care, reading through piles of papers in addition to full-time work, children and housework, husbands' protesting because they never see their wives and because they have to do more housework.

Things have to be done differently. Power must be reached through different channels. How, is difficult to say. Maybe we ought to talk about different kinds of power. Meanwhile, women can offer a different perspective on the world, a women's perspective: a new history, promoting awareness of the oppression of women, the effects on women of militarization, trying to look at the traditional peace work in different ways—feminist perspectives on conscription, conscientious objection, disarmament, reconversion and so on. The strength women gain from women's groups can be used to introduce other approaches and perspectives to the more male-dominated sections of society. If not, I am afraid that the 'peace' will remain inside the house and hardly reach the outside world, in Norway and elsewhere.

NOTES

1. *Fakta*, no. 0685, August 1985 (newssheet from the Defence Department), about women in the defence forces. The figures from 1986 are given directly from Lieutenant-Colonel and Woman Inspector of the Norwegian Army, Elisabeth Sveri, December 1986.
2. *Forsvarets Forum* no. 21, 11 October 1986, p. 7 (defence political magazine).
3. Information given by secretary within the Directorate of Civil Defence, December 1986.

4. St.meld. no. 62 (1974–5). *Kvinnetjenesten i Forsvaret* (an official document from the Defence Department to Parliament on the women's service in the military), p. 6.
5. *Forsvarets Forum*, 11 October 1982, on changes in the defence: less 8,000 men in year 2000! Can women be used?)
6. Vera Henriksen, a Norwegian author, has written several books about powerful Viking women.
7. From an article on the voluntary organizations' place in an emergency situation. *Sivilt Beredskap*, no. 4/83, pp. 26–8.
8. In Britain the troops were called the Auxiliary Territorial Service (ATS).
9. The information for this part is taken from NOU 1973: 37. *Kvinnetjenesten i Forsvaret*, pp. 10–12, 45–7.
10. Camilla Collet (1813–95), Norwegian author, working for women's rights.
11. *Ikkevold* (Nonviolence), no. 6, December 1986, pp. 4–5. Interview by Christine Amadou.
12. In Norway young people can take up a cheap loan from the state to finance their training.
13. *Forsvarets Forum*, March 1986.
14. In Norway young men are conscripted at the age of 18.
15. NOU 1979: 51. *Verneplikten*, pp. 76–8 (an official document looking at the conscription system. A few pages are also devoted to the question of the conscription of women. The proposals fall against this for the time being).

BIBLIOGRAPHY

Amadou, Christine (1986), 'Forsvaret: Mer enn en jobb!' (Defence: More than a Job), *IKKEVOLD* (Nonviolence) 6: 4–5.

Anker, Nini Roll (1945), *Kvinnen og den svarte fuglen* (The Woman and the Black Bird), Oslo: Aschehoug, 1977.

Brock-Utne, Birgit (1985), *Educating for Peace: A Feminist Perspective*, The Athene Series, Oxford: Pergamon Press.

Elster, Ellen (1976), 'Si det apent som det er—om K-soldatene' (Say It as It Is—About the Women Soldiers Going to West Germany), *IKKEVOLD* 5–6: 7.

—— (1982), 'Kvinner i det militaere i Norge' (Women in the Norwegian Military), unpublished.

—— (1983), 'Den norske debatten om verneplikt for kvinner', (The Norwegian Debate on Conscription of Women), in V. Mathisen (ed.), *Kvinner, militarisme og nedrustning* (Women, Militarism and Disarmament) PRIO Report 13, pp. 50–8.

—— (1984), 'Samfunnstjeneste' (Community Service), *IKKE-VOLD* 5 and 6.
—— (1985), *Conscription of Women*, paper written for symposium on youth and conscription, Finland.
Enloe, Cynthia (1981), 'NATO's Interest in women: The Lesson Machine', in W. Chapkis (ed.), *Loaded Questions: Women in the Military*, Amsterdam/Washington, DC: Transnational Institute.
Fakta (1985), no. 0685, August.
Forsvarets Forum (1982), October.
—— (1986), March.
—— (1986b), October.
Gjermoe, Johanne Reutz (1983), *For likeverd og fred* (For Equal Worth and Peace), Oslo: Forum Boktrykkeri.
Mathisen, Vigdis (1986), 'A Report from the Seminar on "Women, Militarism and Disarmament" in Norway, Nov. 11–12, 1982', Appendix in Brock-Utne, B., Traylor, J. and Aas S. (eds.), *Women, Militarism and Disarmament*, PRIO Report 6, pp. 202–13.
NOU (1973), *Kvinnetjenesten i Forsvaret* (Women's Service in the Military), p. 37.
—— (1979), *Verneplikten* (Conscription), p. 51.
Oltedal, Ane Trude, and Walle, Anne-Siri (1984–5), 'Kvinner i marinen' (Women in the Navy), a paper delivered at Sjøkrigsskolen (the Navy high school).
Romstad, Bett (1983), 'Trenger vi en egen kvinneorganisering for fred?' (Do We Need Our Own Women Organizing for Peace?), V. Mathisen (ed.), *Kvinner, militarisme og nedrustning* (Women, Militarism and Disarmament) PRIO Report 13, pp. 20–8.
Sivard, Ruth Leger (1984), *World Military and Social Expenditures 1983*, Norwegian issue, FMKs fredspolitiske skrifter, Oslo.
Sivilt Beredskap (1983), no. 4.
Stene, Helga (1959), 'Norske kvinner i hjemmefronten' (Norwegian Women in the Homefront), from Frederika Bremer Association's 75-years anniversary publication, *Kvinnovärld i vardande*, Stockholm.
—— (1984), 'Hva med kvinnenes innsats under krigen?' (What about the Women's Activities during the War?), in *Helga Stene 1904–1983*, (in memoriam) published by the Norwegian section of WILPF. Weberg Boktrykkeri A/S. The article has earlier appeared in *Forskningsnytt* 1/21.
Stenvik, Anne-Grethe Backe-Hansen (1982), 'En "reserve-armé" av kvinner? *Kvinner i Forsvaret*. (A 'Reserve Army' of Women? Women and Defence), thesis in sociology, Working Paper no. 193, Institute of Sociology, University of Oslo.

—— (1983), 'Kvinner i det norske Forsvaret' (Women in the Norwegian Defence), in V. Mathisen (ed.), *Kvinner, militarisme og nedrustning* (Women, Militarism and Disarmament), PRIO Report 13, pp. 38–49.

Stort.meld.no. 62 (1974–5), *Kvinnetjenesten i Forsvaret* (The Women's Service in the Military.)

24

Switzerland

Stella Jegher
Schweizerischer Friedensrat and Christlicher Friedensdienst/ Frauenstelle, Switzerland

PRELIMINARY REMARKS

Condition of Women in Switzerland

Militarization cannot be considered without looking at the especially late achievement of the right to vote for women in Switzerland: only in 1971 did women win this right on national level, and in one of the cantons (political districts in the federal system) it has still not been introduced.

Also the law on equal rights for women and men came rather late: in 1981 (and one of the reasons for this was to stimulate discussion of compulsory service for women).

Some basic rights for women have still not been achieved; for instance, effective maternity rights, equal job protection and so on. In higher political and even more in economical positions women are highly underrepresented.

The Swiss Defence System

In accordance with the concept of *Gesamtverteidigung*, in 1973 Switzerland developed a system of complete defence, trying to integrate all sections of the society. Women's integration must be seen in this context too. *Gesamtverteidigung* includes the following departments: army (including a women's section), civil protection (with participation of women), economic and social security, co-ordinated services (involving war-preparation courses for certain professions, such as sanitary staff and physicians), information and protection of state and foreign policy.

In discussing the militarization of women, we cannot consider the army alone; we must take into account the whole defence system, which is in itself very militaristic and totalitarian. This plays an important part in the discussion of women's conscription in particular. *Gesamtverteidigung* has met with active resistance from the pacifist movement and others, particularly when further compulsory service is asked for.

Last but not least let's remark that in Switzerland, there's no right to conscientious objection. Several initiatives to introduce such a right have been rejected by the Swiss population. Only those objectors who have 'strictly ethical' reasons will presently have the right to do their service in civil institutions. But they remain integrated within the General Defence System.

REVIEW OF WOMEN'S PARTICIPATION IN NATIONAL DEFENCE

There is no legal base for compulsory service for women: the Constitution imposes an obligation upon all *men* only. But the government has the extra-constitutional right to call up women in case of threat of a war. (However, the proposal for a new constitution elaborated in 1977 includes compulsory service for women as well—but it has not (yet) been introduced in full.)

Actually, women can serve in the defence forces in three areas:

1. In the Women's Military Service (Militärischer Frauendienst, MFD), a section of the army. It is *voluntary* (ages 18 to 35 years). Twenty-eight days of initial introduction is followed by at least thirteen weeks of complementary courses. In the event of a general mobilization, the service becomes compulsory. The MFD is mainly used for the following services: cooking, care for refugees and wounded people, early warning services, communication services, carrier-pigeons, transports. About 2,500 women are in the MFD. This is three-quarters of the number the army considers necessary.

2. Women's service in the Red Cross (Rotkreuzdienst, RKD) (national Red Cross). This is voluntary (ages 18 to 35 years). There is a thirteen-day introduction plus a follow-up course of thirty-nine days. Service is compulsory in the event of mobilization. About 4,000 women (physicians, chemists, sanitary staff as well as girl-guides) participate—only two-fifths of the staff needed.
3. Women's civil defence. This is a voluntary service (ages 16 years on), with the obligation to serve for five years (can be renewed). The introduction course is five days' long. The service can be convocated for no more than two days per year, and can be made compulsory in times of national crisis. Today, about 20,000 women are active in the service, which is thought by those responsible to be one-fifth of the number necessary in an emergency.

The above-mentioned women's services are based on particular laws. In return, there exists no law for women's integration into other sections of the General Defence System such as co-ordinated sanitary services or national economic supply services.

The General Defence Office (Zentralstelle für Gesamtverteidigung) is seeking an extension of compulsory service in these fields, claiming that there are large staff shortages in the war-economy administration, in the information services, in the sanitary services and so on: 'About 45,000 more people are needed to assure the medical supplies in the event of war' (Bericht zur Vernehmlassung betr. die Mitwirkung der Frau in der Gesamtverteidigung, 1982).

Women can be conscripted at the cantonal level. The cantons are, for instance, responsible for the organization of civil defence and as well for some 'co-ordinated services'.

NEW PROPOSALS AND ADVANCES FOR WOMEN'S PARTICIPATION IN DEFENCE

The first discussion of compulsory service for women in civil defence took place in 1957: the intention was to introduce a new article in the Constitution, instituting women's conscription as part of national defence. It was largely rejected by the population, and so much the more by the large women's organizations, since women did not even have the right to vote at this time.

The discussion started again with the introduction of this right (in 1971). In 1970 the leading women's organization, the so-called 'Bund Schweizerischer Frauenorganisationen' (BSF) nominated a commission with the task of examining the possibilities for women's participation in defence. They worked out four models: (1) general conscription (army and civil protection); (2) general conscription in the reserve system; (3) voluntary cadre organizations (preparation to tasks within the *Gesamtverteidigung*); (4) voluntary social service. The second model found the greatest support. It meant mainly a compulsory service for women in the event of a national catastrophe (the idea of a special instruction appears then for the first time, and this remains an important element in the discussion).

Several advances in Parliament concerning the participation of women in defence led in 1976 to the nomination of a government commission to consider the question. The commission, under the former chief-MFD Madame Andrée Weitzel, elaborated eighteen models for possible services, ten of them for compulsory service. The report met great opposition, since it was not only militaristic but even anti-feministic. The result of this was the institution of a second, new commission in 1981, under the chair of the sociologist Madame Ruth Meyer. The commission was composed of six men (with the exception of one, from each of the defence bodies) and five women (one of them the new chief of the Women's Military Service). They suggested eight models:

1. Voluntary service as it is (MFD, RKD, civil defence).
2. Widened voluntary service (including service in the national economic supply services and co-ordinated services, i.e. sanitary services, information).
3. Voluntary instruction (survival in case of war and crisis, protection from chemical and atomic weapons, life in the shelter, etc.).
4. Compulsory school-teaching for girls and boys.
5. Compulsory instruction for women.
6. Compulsory service for women in certain professions

(public-health services, national economic supply services, public administration).

7. General conscription for women with one service only for basic instruction.
8. General conscription with several services (as is the case for men).

The report of the commission was submitted for public consultation (as usual in Switzerland for new law-proposals). There was an enormous reaction from all quarters, from women's organizations to pacifist organizations, from parties to trade unions and to employers organizations: about 4,400 answers were sent back, from organizations, political bodies and individuals. (A postcard action of an anti-militaristic women's organization alone brought 2,000 answers, rejecting all participation of women and asking for equal rights in better fields).

The results show clearly that a compulsory service for women is overwhelmingly rejected. Only the Conservative Party (Liberal-Democratic Party, one of the biggest) supported the idea of compulsory service. But neither one of the voluntary-basis models was clearly preferable. The Socialist Party rejected all models because none of them provided participation outside the *Gesamtverteidigung*. Numerous pacifist organizations pointed out that women's participation should not be realized by integrating them in a system based on enemy-images and military security, but rather on constructive contributions to a non-violent society on a national and international level. But such answers, which did not follow the items in the official questionnaire sent out with the report, were unfortunately scarcely taken into consideration by the report on the results of popular consultation.

Anyway, it was difficult for the government and for the people willing to push women's integration to go forward with it after the consultation. On the other hand, many complained of a general lack of information about the *Gesamtverteidigung* system. Consequently, the plans for women were put aside somewhat and a big information campaign started (TV-spots, information booklets and so on) about *Gesamtverteidigung*.

On the other hand, the Meyer Commission was slightly

broadened (with further women members) and entrusted with the further consideration of new possibilities for women's involvement on a voluntary base within civil defence, the co-ordinated health-service and the national economic supply services. The government hopes in the meantime to recruit about 100,000 women volunteers to make up the shortfall.

While public discussion of the subject (in the mass media), has almost disappeared, this does not mean that attempts to integrate women in the militaristic defence system have stopped—they continue in a furtive way, for example, on a cantonal level.

UNOFFICIAL, CANTONAL AND INSIDIOUS INTRODUCTION OF WOMEN'S SERVICES

Several cantons have started to introduce compulsory service, or at least compulsory instruction courses for sanitary staff 'not yet conscripted'—which means mainly women. It is not yet certain whether there is a legal basis for such proceedings—some women's organizations are trying to clarify this.

The national Red Cross, as a sister organization of the Co-ordinated Services, starts this year with the introduction of a new subject in nursery schools (which are under the official control of the Red Cross), twelve hours of compulsory instruction in *Katastrophenschutz* (protection from catastrophes). By 'catastrophe' they mean first of all war, and the instruction is consequently concentrated on health-protection in the event of war.

One negative side of 'co-ordinated services' is of course also the automatic registration of people working in certain professions, which can have well-known negative consequences at different fields (inner control, war-society).

There is a quite widespread opposition to such developments, both in pacifist and in feminist circles. The most difficult problem is that almost all legal conditions seem to have been considered before proceeding slowly with the integration of women into defence structures. On the other hand, it is also difficult to argue against the general defence system, which appears so 'harmless' and is generally quite popular.

Women for Peace started recently with an 'instruction for women' project, offering a critical, but as far as possible non-ideological, view of what *Gesamtverteidigung* means and explaining why women could be much more 'useful' in other fields of political and social life, based on greater justice and a non-violent concept of relations between nations and within societies.

BIBLIOGRAPHY

Frauen und Militär ed. Christine Perren, Schweizerischer Friedensrat, 1979.

Wir passen unter keinen Helm, Kurzfassung des Weitzel-Berichts und Kritik, SFR, 1980.

Kein Ort für Frauen: Argumente gegen den Einbezug der Frauen, Frauenstelle für Friedensarbeit des Christlichen Friedensdienstes, September 1983.

Unsere tägliche Gewalt, Frauen für Frieden Basel, 1983.

For regular information about current trends, see *Friedenszeitung*, Postfach 6386, 8023 Zürich.

From the 'official' side, see *Bericht zur Vernehmlassung betreffend die Mitwirkung der Frauen in der Gesamtverteidigung and Kurzfassung der Resultate*, ed. der Zentralstelle für Gesamtverteidigung, 3003 Bern.

For information about the activities and background of the peace movement, see *Handbuch Frieden Schweiz*, 1986 ed. Forum für praxisbezogene Friedensforschung, Pf. 508, 4021 Basel.

25

United States

Cynthia H. Enloe
Clark University
Worcester, Mass., USA

In all of our countries today it is a challenge to map the military system: its boundaries seem fuzzy and rapidly expanding. Let's take just a few instances:

1. In many of our countries the police—or some arms of the police—are under the direct or indirect control of military commanders: in those countries shouldn't women's relationships to the police be mapped? (In the 1980s US police are under local town and state authority, but many police forces since the 1960s have adopted increasingly militarized modes of operation; in addition, many men joining police forces have served in the military, though we don't know how this may have shaped their notions of a policeman's standards of 'masculinity', their attitudes towards women or towards violence and weaponry.)
2. In many countries today the energy industry and/or public policy concerning energy are viewed by officials as auxiliaries to military planning: many women opposed to nuclear dependence are making this link in their own organizing. (In the United States today, the federal Energy Department's budget is increasingly devoted to military missions, though that is not counted as 'defence expenditures'. Some women's anti-nuclear organizing, but not all, makes the connection between weapons and energy policy.)
3. In some countries one or more domestic ethnic or racial communities feel as though they are living under military occupation, with their organizing treated by central

officials as if it were a threat to 'national security'. For women in these communities 'the military system' may seem far more pervasive than it does to women in the politically dominant communities. (Presently, in the United States, probably native Americans living on reservations and Hispanics along the south-western borders feel most immediately the militarization of their lives, though the agencies involved may be the militarized arms of the police or of the federal Border Patrol, an arm of the Justice Department.)

4. In many countries, universal male conscription is justified in part as supplying the country's 'youth' with literacy, citizenship training, even civilian job skills: what does this mean for young women's relationship to the civilian job market, where literacy in the dominant language and veterans' benefits may be denied to many or most women? (In the 1980s in the United States there is no conscription, though there is male-only 'registration' in preparation for a future draft for men on their eighteenth birthdays. However, there are education, health, housing and civil service entrance benefits for military veterans, and since men currently comprise 95 per cent of living veterans, the overwhelming majority of American women are excluded from those benefits.)

In other words, where any country's military system begins and ends is problematic. It does not usually have boundaries that are neatly coterminous with the country's uniformed soldiery or with the central government's current 'defence' budget. Nowhere do these caveats seem more timely than in the United States in 1987.

Perhaps the most striking thing about the present military system in this country is the porousness of its boundaries. This in turn is reflected in the subtleties and multiple dimensions of white women's and women of colour's relationships to that system. It affects their parenting of young boys and young girls; it affects their choices of entertainment; it shapes their schooling alternatives and their perceptions of job possibilities; it affects their relationships to their husbands, since so many men work in economic sectors reliant on government secrecy and defence spending; it has an impact on how they view their own and other women's sexuality, since today the US military takes wide-reaching public stands on homosexuality and sexually transmitted diseases such as AIDS. Not all of these realities, however, have been transformed by women into self-conscious political issues.

HISTORICAL PATTERNS

Militarization hasn't always been this high. From the late eighteenth century until the early twentieth century, the military system in this country had much narrower social, political, cultural and economic boundaries. While women were affected by each of those dimensions—especially if they were native American women or colonized Filipino or Puerto Rican women—their compliance was not sought so persistently in so many areas of their lives.

Partly this may have been due to the fact that the military did not hold out the promise of high social prestige to most American men (neither, incidentally, did the state's civil service). Civilian commerce was the site for proving one's American 'manhood' and climbing the social ladder. At the same time—or maybe partly because of that relatively modest social prestige—the government's public spending on military pay, clothing, construction and weaponry was a very small proportion of the economy; thus, while 'winning a military contract' did show up on a popular nineteenth-century parlour board-game, military monies did not have the capacity to direct entire sectors of the economy (an exception here might be the construction of waterways and irrigation systems in conquered western territories; the army corps of engineers and geographers employed by the War Department played crucial roles).

This is *not* to say that notions of femininity and women's labour were not used to sustain even the relatively modest military system of the eighteenth and nineteenth centuries. They were. To keep the military a masculine preserve, however, women's contributions either were camouflaged or denied (e.g. by defining their roles as spies, or nurses as 'civilian' and 'temporary'), or they were squeezed into conventional ideological categories such as being a 'good mother' or a 'faithful wife'—or a 'typical camp-follower'.

It is these deceptions that have made it difficult for many American women until now to recognize that women and concepts of femininity have played *any* role in the earlier military systems. But new feminist research on the roles women played—and the forms of resistance they encountered—in the Revolutionary War, the Civil War, the so-called Indian Wars, the Spanish–American and Philippines Wars, are not only exposing the ways in which previous military systems relied on women; they are also raising questions for many American women about what exactly *is* new about today's militarized condition and what is a continuous, if expanded, pattern. We know far more, though, about white American women's experiences—especially white women from Christian and longer-resident communities—than we do about the militarized experiences of Black, native American, Hispanic (Cuban, Puerto Rican, Mexican), Hawaiian, Filipino, Japanese, Chinese or Jewish women during the nineteenth century and first decade of the twentieth century.

Until we have information about *these* women's relationships to the military system, we really can't say with confidence that we know precisely what the pre-First World War military systems were like in the United States.

The military system began expanding by quantum measures during the First World War, despite this government's late entry into that conflict, and especially with the advent of the Second World War. Women began to be enlisted directly in the uniformed ranks, though usually amid public and official debates, first in the medical corps, then in the clerical and administrative staffs and only last in operational field units (the latter always carefully defined as 'non-combat' regardless of the actual physical dangers involved).

Women served in all-women units. There was much public concern expressed about preserving their 'respectability'. Until the very end of the Second World War, Black women were compelled to serve in segregated units and were more restricted than white women in serving outside the United States. By the end of the Second World War, there were 4,000 Black women in the US army's women's corps. But, despite government promises to Black leaders that Black women would be recruited in numbers so as to comprise 10 per cent of all military women, they never did reach that proportion.

Both of these wars—but, again, especially the 1940–5 war—were conceptualized as 'total wars' by American officials, thus making military intrusions into what conventionally was deemed the 'civilian' sphere more extensive and palatable. Women's mothering, women's wifely duties, women's paid labour and women's sexuality—government agencies (many of them staffed by civilian women during the Second World War) tried to influence all of these so that they would serve what they saw to be the war effort.

Thousands of Japanese and Japanese–American women on the West Coast suffered internment during the Second World War. They are today starting to analyse what this repressive experience has meant for the relationships of Japanese–American women to men within their own communities. But few of these women argue that the Second World War was good for women. By contrast, many other American women still in the 1980s are debating whether the First and Second World Wars 'liberated' women. Some older lesbian women are recalling how joining the military in what were then all-women's units not only gave them their first chance to live in essentially all-women communities but also gave them the chance to leave what they saw as the socially stifling atmospheres of conservative families and small towns across the countries. Other women, now in their sixties and seventies, remember the First and especially the Second World War as having given them their first chance to get a paid job or to earn decent wages (though women's wartime wages remained less than those given to men). Black women suffered discrimination in and out of the military during these periods of intense militarization, but for many Black women shortages imposed by these sorts of wars allowed them to escape poorly paid and socially oppressive conditions of domestic service work and agricultural work.

Thousands of women were pushed out of their relatively well-paying civilian jobs to make way for returning male veterans at the end of the Second World War. The women's corps of the military were cut back sharply and deliberately as well. But, still, the sorting out of the Second World War's benefits and liabilities for American women of different classes and communities goes on today. And any reassessment of the Second World War—'the Good War' in US mythology—which transforms women's memories, is likely to have profound impacts on women's present-day willingness to fill those roles that the military sets out for them.

The Vietnam War (which for most Americans is conceived of as being from 1965 to 1975, though actual US military involvement began in 1945) has been much less analysed from a feminist perspective. There are films and novels about women—as wives and as mothers—who have had to cope with their husbands and sons, scores of whom came back from military service in Vietnam with acute emotional and health problems.

Approximately 10,000 American women served in military capacities in the Vietnam War. Women who have served as military nurses in the US forces in Vietnam in the 1980s are finding their collective voice and are becoming politically organized to force the government to acknowledge their 'post-Vietnam' health problems. Many women, especially women now in their thirties and forties, came of age politically as part of 1960s and early 1970s anti-war activism; it was here—as well as in the civil rights movement—that many women first learnt how sexism could marginalize women and women's concerns in the name of allegedly progressive causes. Thus there are several legacies for American women of the Vietnam War: it helped dispel the Second World War presumption that war was liberating for women; it taught many women that anti-militarism that lacked a feminist content could be almost as sexist as militarism itself.

The violence with which the Vietnam War ended in Vietnam created thousands of homeless and stateless people. Today there are large numbers of Vietnamese, Kampuchean and Laotian women in the United States. *Their* experiences of the US military system have not yet been integrated into other American women's perceptions. Once again, our understanding of a past—in this case, recent past—military system is incomplete. Charting the stubborn persistence of some memories and transformation of other memories that

American women of different generations and ethnic communities hold and use may be as important in understanding present-day relationships of American women to their military system as charting numbers of women in uniform or on weapons assembly lines.

THE 1980s: MILITARY 'MANPOWER'

The present era in American society is being referred to by the popular media and by many public officials as the 'post-Vietnam' era—that is, it seems, an era when Americans can push aside nasty or uncomfortable memories of the Vietnam War and get on with being the international moral policeman. Yet it's more confusing than that. For a national post-Vietnam psychology is defensive as well as amnesic: the post-Vietnam American not only wants to go back to the Second World War, the 'good war'; he wants to invade Grenada or send arms to Angolan or Nicaraguan counter-revolutionaries in order to *prove* that 'we were right' in Vietnam after all. But most of the memories captured in the phrase 'post-Vietnam' are *men*'s memories. Because we don't yet have a sharp portrayal of women's memories of the Vietnam War, the very notion of this era we are living in and coping with its deeply masculinized.

In the midst of this confusion of militarized memories has come the largest, most calculated voluntary enlistment of American women into the regular uniformed forces. It was begun in 1972 to compensate for the end of the male conscription (and probably to forestall reliance on poor Black men for filling the new military 'manpower' needs). In order to 'end' what were seen by officials as the anomalous social condition called 'the Second World War', laws and administrative policies were changed so as to remasculinize the US military ranks: women's presence was sharply cut back from the mid-1940s through the Vietnam War. But with the end of the Vietnam War, politicians agreed that demobilizing anti-war sentiment at home called for the end of male conscription. It was precisely at this juncture that the Pentagon and the Congress decided once again to alter their women-in-the-military policies; now, in the early 1970s, however, the change was intended to drop the quotas on women and to actively enlist more women in order to help compensate for the men they were losing by ending the draft. Married women, pregnant women and women with children now may all enlist in, and stay in the US military (though, as of 1985, the military started actively denying enlistment to single mothers). While women are excluded from 'combat' posts (e.g. all infantry), they are allowed to be trained in the uses of firearms. Though the military recruitment advertisements stress the military as a place for women to learn 'non-traditional' skills, still the majority of military women are assigned to posts in medical, administrative and communications units.

Adding to the ideological confusion is the fact that this first-ever large-scale recruitment of women into the ranks of a supposedly 'peacetime' military started just as the second wave of the women's movement began in the United States. Many women, therefore, see the 'opening up' of the military as one more step towards American women's 'first-class citizenship'. The military's advertisers and recruiters have taken up the same theme.

As of June 1986, 9.5 per cent of the US regular uniformed forces were women. This is the highest proportion among all the NATO and Warsaw Pact forces (Canada is second with 8.9 per cent). This amounts to 214,152 women in the regular forces *at any one time*. Some 59,179 of these uniformed women were Black women.

Black women are only approximately 11 per cent of all American women; but they comprise 27.6 per cent of all the women presently in the US military. Hispanic women are approximately 8 per cent of all American women; they comprise 3.1 per cent of all women in the military today. Taken together, all Black, Hispanic, native American and Asian–American women comprise 34.2 per cent of all women in the present US military. Black women's proportion of all military women has been growing slowly but steadily since the beginning of the 1980s. This trend may say more about the prospects a young Black woman has in the civilian sector for a job that can pay the rent and provide health care for herself and her children than it does about the support of young Black women for militaristic values or for US foreign policies. We do not know. What we do know is that the Defence Department has concluded from their survey of current secondary school girls that young Black women are three times more likely than young white women to *say* that they presently are considering military enlistment.

There are significant variations according to military branch. These variations may be due not only to specific job descriptions or to young women's own enlistment choices; rather, they may be due to the varying ideologies of militarized masculinity guiding each branch's recruitment and promotion practice. Below are Defence Department figures for June, 1986:

Army: Women are 10.4 per cent of all uniformed personnel; 43.4 per cent of all enlisted (i.e. non-officer) women are Black women; 2.5 per cent of all enlisted women are Hispanic women.

Air Force: Women are 12.0 per cent of all air force personnel; 20.8 per cent of air force enlisted women are Black women; 3.0 per cent are Hispanic women.

Marines (bureaucratically, under the navy): Women are only 4.9 per cent of all marines personnel; 24.9 per cent of all non-officer, enlisted women are Black women; 3.9 per cent are Hispanic women.

Navy (minus marines): Women are 9.3 per cent of all navy personnel; 19.4 per cent of all enlisted women are Black women (i.e. less than one-half of the proportion in apparently less-exclusive army); 4.1 per cent are Hispanic women.

As in all militaries, one has to watch race/ethnicity at the same time as one monitors gender. Thus it might be useful to note that in June 1986, 21 per cent of all enlisted (non-officer) *men* in all branches were Black; while 4.0 per cent of all enlisted men were Hispanic. *But* for both most civil rights groups and most governmental officials, the racial figures that are watched and often watched with concern are those relating to Black men in the military, *not* Black women. Maybe this surprising (given the striking figures) political fact is a sign of American racism being less triggered with regard to

Black women. More likely might be the tendency of all women in the military to be lumped together as 'women' out of sexist concerns. Whatever the reason, this disproportion in political attention is a key feature of American women's relationship to the current US military system.

The above figures do *not* include women in the Reserves or in the military National Guard units of the fifty states. The National Guard units have played important roles in rescue work after natural calamities, but they also have been deployed to put down student and Black protests. In 1987 the National Guard is again the object of considerable controversy because of its growing role in Central America. Some state governors refused to permit the Guard units under their commands be sent by the Defense Department to Honduras for joint manoeuvres with Honduran troops. In December 1986 the Reagan administration signed into law a policy that would centralize the National Guard and undercut state governors' authority to keep National Guard units from being sent abroad. Thus those women who are serving in the National Guard, many of whom saw the Guard as a way of combining military benefits with family and career, may now be far more likely to take part in foreign-combat-supportive activities.

Today women in the regular armed forces are serving in the US Cruise missile installations in Comiso, Italy. They are also part of the regular troops now stationed in the US expanding bases in Honduras. Women also took part in the US military invasion of Grenada.

Some of the military women who took part in the Grenada invasion lobbied the Pentagon and Congress in order to do so, arguing that it was discriminatory for field commanders to so wield the concept of 'combat' as to exclude them. Other military women have waged internal bureaucratic battles so as to be able to serve on teams staffing missile silos, and have won: in 1987, women are serving on missile launch teams for the MX missile (renamed the 'Peacemaker' by the Reagan Administration), and the Minute Man missile.

Thus, defining 'combat' as a way to expand or restrict military women's access to certain military posts remains an area of controversy in the Pentagon, in Congress and in the public at large. Many of women's advocates in the military—led by the Secretary of Defense-appointed Defense Advisory Committee on Women in the Services, 'DACOWITS'—have spent enormous political energies in the last four or five years trying to keep the various services from expanding the definitions of 'combat'. Sometimes they have succeeded, sometimes they have not.

Other issues that women's advocates in the military and in such civilian groups as the Women's Equity Action League have brought to public attention are sexual harassment (by male superiors and by male co-workers), child-care inadequacies, promotion criteria and 'witch hunts' administered by male field commanders and intelligence units against women suspected of being lesbians.

This continuous lobbying—often with the aid of supportive Congressional representatives (some of whom are opposed to sexism; some of whom simply watch the declining numbers of young men in the US population and want the military to use more women so the US won't have to cut back its world-wide operations)—often may make it harder for most American women to tackle the less obvious relationships between women, sexism and militarism. That is, the efforts to 'open up' the military to women may take so much work and so much political skill that it *alone* looks like *the* issue for women. This distortion (or at least 'tilt') in political consciousness is reinforced when conservative opponents to the Equal Rights Amendment wield fears of 'women in combat' to frighten voters. A new pro-ERA campaign was being planned for 1987.

In 1982 a national opinion poll of women and men (with no gender breakdown, alas), showed that 93.7 per cent of Americans polled said they approved of women nurses being allowed to serve in combat zones; 83.4 per cent said they approved of women serving as military truck mechanics; 62.4 per cent approved of women piloting jet fighters; 57.4 per cent approved of women as crew members on a combat ship; but only 34.7 per cent said they approved of women serving as soldiers serving in 'hand-to-hand combat'.

THE 1980s: MILITARIZED CIVILIAN 'MANPOWER'

The Defense Department is one of the largest employers of federal civil service personnel. In 1984 the civil servants working for the Department totalled 1.06 million. Of these, 13.8 per cent were Black. Black women made up 6 per cent of all Defense Department civil service employees. They held nearly 30 per cent of all 'white-collar' jobs in the Department. Black women employed as secretaries in the Department probably see these jobs, paid at federal pay levels, as much better than most Black women can hope to obtain in the private business sector. Of course, many other jobs are as cleaners and custodial help. Virtually no women, Black or white, hold policy posts, presidentially appointed, and thus have minimal influence on military policy formulation.

What little policy influence any particular American women has on military operations is found among women who have been elected to Congress. But in the current Congress, women are a mere 5 per cent of the House of Representatives and 0 per cent of the Senate.

The Defense Department likes to refer to the military as a 'family'. At the same time, there are growing numbers of actual families in which one or both adults are in the military. The US military recently has been devoting more attention and resources to civilian women who are the wives of military men. This may be due to three converging but quite different trends: (1) as the pool of 18-year-old males has been dropping, the military officials have begun to worry more about *keeping* those men already in the services, and they seem to believe now that men are more likely to leave the military if their wives don't like the kind of life the military imposes on them; (2) social-science researchers for the military are beginning to conclude from their studies that men in combat are less able to perform well if they are under stress in their home life; (3) many 'military wives' (especially women married to officers, who have more access to policy-makers), military chaplains and social workers, have been pressing the Pentagon—and Congress—to improve the quality of life for 'military families'. Thus, while the latter may have women's needs as their primary concern, the former does not necessarily have women themselves as their priority but now see the *military* utility in supporting at least some of these family service demands.

There are over 2 million 'military dependents' in the United States at any one time today. If one subtracts the sons of military personnel and the relatively few military spouses who are men, then one is left with a very large number of young and middle-aged American women whose daily lives are directly controlled by military needs and assumptions. But to day, this fact has not been taken up as a political issue by the civilian women's movement.

In the army alone (the largest branch) in 1986, there were 400,000 civilian women married to army soldiers, 67 per cent of them married to enlisted (non-officer) men. In the 1950s, only 30 per cent of the US military personnel were married; in 1986 53 per cent were married. A growing number, according to the Defense Department are young (18 or 19 years old) enlisted men marrying women also in their teens. Soldiers are marrying younger than is the general US population. The army reports that in 1986 there were more than 260,000 children under the age of three in its families. It notes this figure in the context of the trend towards assigning more male enlistees to combat units which often require long and irregular hours and deployments away from home. This is leaving growing numbers of very young mothers to cope with young children on their own, with *their* mothers far away and with low enlistee pay supplemented usually by only a job at a nearby McDonald's.

Child abuse and wife beating both are believed, even by the Defense Department, to be higher among military families than in the US population at large. Some military officials have invited some civilian women experienced in violence against women to provide consultation or training programmes to the military. But while this has sparked some serious discussions among women in these fields, there as yet has been no national debate or consensus among anti-violence-against-women activists about if, or how, military wives and children could be served *without* civilian women's groups being co-opted or compromised.

'Civilianization' has been a policy during the Reagan

administration. It refers to transforming certain services to the military from Defense Department operations to civilian contract operations. Many of these services involve feminized occupations, like cleaning and food preparation. Thousands of women who never turn up on the Defense Department printouts of 'women in the military' actually service the military and depend on military contracts for these jobs. It may be, too, that, as these traditionally low-paid service jobs are 'civilianized' the women in them will lose whatever minimal protection a civil-service status offered them, since civilian entrepreneurs seeking these Defense service contracts will be encouraged to cut labour costs in order to come in with the lowest bids.

Other women who are directly touched by the military today (and on whom the military officials *depend* in order to achieve their own policy aims) are civilian women who are mothers of teenage boys and girls; those teenage girls themselves; guidance cousellors in secondary schools. All of these women are the objects of intense military recruitment campaigns. Military recruiters now regularly attend secondary schools to attract young people to enlist, either now or via what is called 'Delayed Entry' at the end of their secondary schooling. Two of the country's largest associations of school guidance/career counsellors have signed formal agreements with the Defense Department allowing military recruiters into the schools. Many school districts also have accepted the Defense Department's offer of its aptitude tests; they are administered to students and the results used by guidance counsellors, but the results also are shared with the talent-hungry military recruiters. In some school districts, parents' groups, often working with local peace groups, have protested against these policies and insisted that, minimally, groups with alternative views of the military be permitted to talk to students. One group took their case to the courts and, in Chicago, has won the right to come into the public schools and make alternative presentations.

Reserve Officer Training Corps (ROTC) are military units set up—with university administrators' permission—on university campuses. With the cutbacks in federal student aid and with the spiralling costs of both public and private university tuition (e.g. in 1987 some prestigious private universities have set their tuition fees at $10,000—or more—per year), the military's offer of ROTC university scholarships to young women and men seem very attractive. An ROTC student attends military classes taught by officers along with her/his regular classes; she/he attends special summer training programmes; upon graduation, the student is obliged to serve in the military for three years. During the Vietnam War, students campaigned to have many universities withdraw their permission to ROTC units on their campuses. Partly to compensate for those losses, the Defense Department opened up more ROTC units at largely Black colleges. But in the current post-Vietnam era, many universities have once again allowed ROTC units on campus. In 1986, 530 universities had ROTC units. These involved 110,872 students.

At Wellesley College, one of the most prestigious all-women's colleges, some students and faculty campaigned in 1985 to end ROTC's programme on their campus. They charged that, with its exclusion of lesbians (a policy of all branches of the US military), ROTC violated Wellesley's formal prohibition against discrimination on the basis of sexual preference. The campaign received widespread campus support. But when it finally reached the all-faculty assembly, it was defeated, perhaps in part because the college president—the first woman president of Wellesley to publicly identify herself as a feminist—spoke against the anti-ROTC measure, arguing that ROTC allowed some poorer women to finance their education at high-cost schools such as Wellesley.

Recently, the ROTC has moved down to the secondary schools. In 1986 the Junior ROTC existed in 1,375 high schools and involved 227,448 young people, both girls and boys. The Defense Department allocated $52.1 million in fiscal 1986, just for textbooks, uniforms and arms for these secondary school Junior ROTCs. Some girls join ROTC with future enlistment in the military in mind; but many join simply because it may be the best equipped 'extra-curricula' activity in their otherwise underfinanced local school. We do not know what sorts of long- or even short-range consequences participation in university or Junior ROTC units have on teenage American young women: does it alter their views of US foreign policy? Does it affect how they think about their bodies? Does it influence how they perceive boys or adult men? Does it shape how they contend with violence? Does it affect how they think about jobs or sexuality or marriage? We do not know. *And* we don't know how a son's or daughter's ROTC involvement affects their mothers' attitudes towards the US military, towards violence or towards mothering.

MOTHERING THE MILITARY IN THE 1980s

For all the alarm expressed by some military planners and congressional representatives about the declining pool of 18-year-old men available for military service, with or without a draft, there appears to be relatively little official expression of state-sponsored pro-natalism. This differs markedly from France, Romania and the Soviet Union. In these countries, government officials rationalize their support for policies which will encourage (or force) women to have more children with dire predictions of the nation's slide into military vulnerability. This does not as yet seem to be the mode of public discourse in the United States.

Certainly there now are constant efforts by conservative groups to cut back women's access to abortion. But perhaps an explicit appeal to more births per woman in the name of 'national security' is being tempered in the 1980s by some of these same conservative groups' (and their official supporters') anxieties about the rising numbers of teenage mothers, anxieties fuelled by the media portrayal of these young mothers as young Black women. Sometimes the large number of births to these mainly poor young women is treated by conservative, pro-military groups as if *it* were a threat to national security.

What does *not* seem to have much currency in public discussion presently is the suggestion that *if* indeed an effective military is especially dependent on a large pool of young men, and *if* that pool is shrinking largely due to choices being made by young women, *then* perhaps American policy-makers should radically rethink their notions of what is the US military's mission: maybe it would make sense to tailor the mission to fit the demography.

WOMEN IN A MILITARIZED ECONOMY

The defence budget in fiscal 1987 and fiscal 1988 takes up approximately one third of the total federal budget. This $312 billion, in turn, amounts to 6.5 per cent of the country's GNP (the West German defence budget amounts to 3.3 per cent of its GNP).

The principal approach to analysing women's relationship to this increasingly militarized economy has been to point to how high federal expenditures for the military in a time of high deficits has led to cuts in those federal health and welfare programmes that especially affect women and their children. The feminization of poverty (i.e. the growing proportion of America's poor who are women, and their dependent children) is directly related to the spiralling expenditures on the military.

We do not have accurate figures to show how many civilian women earn wages from companies whose executives have chosen to make them dependent on defence contracts. (But see Part 3 of this volume.) But it is probably safe to say that the numbers are growing. More and more companies outside the traditionally military-dependent and masculinized aerospace, armoured vehicle and shipbuilding sectors are today becoming reliant for their profitability on defence contracts. Most obvious is the electronics industry. Many electronics company executives, especially perhaps those losing civilian business to more advanced Japanese competitors, are seeking military contracts. An estimated 70 per cent of all assembly workers in the US electronics industry are women.

In 1986 more than 30,000 US companies are engaged in military production. This includes companies making uniforms and packaging food rations, not just companies making tanks and jet fighters. When a conference met in Boston in 1984 to discuss how more unions and executives could be persuaded to 'convert' to non-military products, some women participants introduced a statement taking issue with the common notion that 'defence workers' are all male. Some of the business sectors the military needs are feminized in their assembly ranks. Thus the 'conversion' movement, as well-intentioned as it may be, should, they said, beware of making sexist presumptions.

Relatively little explicitly feminist organizing has been directed towards women working in companies doing military contract work. But the 1983–4 Puget Sound Women's Peace Camp in Seattle, Washington, did address this issue directly. As reported in their book describing their actions and their discussions, *We Are Ordinary Women* (Seal Press, 1985), the women set up their camp outside the gates of Boeing, one of the major US airplane and missile manufacturers. One of the women actually worked at Boeing as a secretary. Her own conflicts between her need for a decent-paying job and her feminist values influenced other camp women as well, as they tried to fashion an approach to the women—and men—working at the plant which would be sensitive to those women's needs and worries.

Another dimension of the militarized economy for American women is research. In 1986 almost 70 per cent of every federal dollar allocated for research and development goes to the military—either directly to the military or to military-tailored research being done under the aegis of the Energy Department of the National Aeronautics and Space Administration (NASA). For young women just breaking into the previously masculine preserves of engineering and science, this has created a dilemma: either they can pursue their educational and professional goals and almost become involved in military-related research, or they can trim their professional sails and search out perhaps less-challenging or less-rewarding jobs that guarantee non-military work. This may in fact be a false choice; there may be exciting professional opportunities for women scientists and engineers that do not require military contract work. But to many young women at schools like MIT and Cal Tech, the picture looks bleak and compromise looks inevitable.

MILITARIZING THE GENDERED CULTURE

The American culture is mind boggling in its diversity (though it may not be *quite* so diverse as Americans think!). So it is dangerous to generalize about how far art, play, creativity and entertainment are being militarized in the United States today—or what that means for women in different social classes and ethnic communities. But here are just a few possible clues:

- In its first twenty-three days of commercial release, 'Rambo: First Blood' grossed $75.8 million dollars at the box office; only two other American films ever had made more.
- Twenty-five companies, by 1986, had acquired distribution rights for products carrying 'Rambo' identifications.
- 'GI Joe', made by the giant toy company Hasbro, was heralded by the *Wall Street Journal* as the biggest money-making toy of 1985.
- The Coleco Company, maker of the 'Rambo' plastic toys, was compelled in late 1986 to withdraw its 'Rambo-enemy' toy, 'Nomad', because peace groups charged that it was fostering anti-Arab racism among children.
- 'Women warrior' toys have now been developed for little girls. But most of them have the personas of fantastic princesses, not 'realistic' high-tech soldiers.
- There was a sharp drop-off in war toys in the United States in the mid-1970s, perhaps a reflection of the disillusionment with the military in the wake of US withdrawal from Vietnam. But by 1986, the toy industry was reporting that sales of war toys had increased 600 per cent over 1982, with more than 218 million war toys sold in 1985 alone.
- Adult 'war games' have been created in various regions of the country: men—and reportedly some women, usually taking part as companions of male players—can pretend to be guerillas or counter-insurgency troops in outdoor 'real life' settings, equipped with authentic weaponry.
- The racist organization, the Ku Klux Klan (whose national headquarters recently moved from its traditional

site in the South to Connecticut) reportedly is worried that it is being hindered in its efforts to compete for new conservative members with the newly emergent white supremacist groups. The latter seems more in tune with the generation in their twenties and thirties: the new white supremacist groups have as their uniforms military fatigues, eschewing the 'old-fashioned' religion-based white robes and hoods of the Klan. Both the Klan and the newer groups boast women's and childrens' auxiliaries.

- More and more American universities have activist anti-nuclear groups on their campuses. And there are growing numbers of formal courses offered on disarmament, nuclear war, peace studies and conflict resolution. Some of these courses are offered by or with faculty from women's studies; but some of the courses have very little gender consciousness, though sizeable numbers of women students may enrol.
- Several women-only peace encampments have thrived for several months or a year but have not been able to sustain themselves. The Seneca Peace Encampment in Seneca, New York, still exists and owns its own land.
- While the much-discussed 'gender gap' did not show up dramatically enough in the 1984 presidential election to alter the outcome, public opinion polls continue to show American women and men holding distinctly different opinions—sometimes separated by as much as 15 percentage points—on military-related policy issues such as US military involvement in Central America.

OTHER WOMEN AND US MILITARIZATION

Because the 1980s US military is so global in its operations, many women *outside* the United States are integrated into and/or subject to the workings of the US military system.

Honduran women, Grenadian women, Nicaraguan women, Canadian women, British women, West German women, Italian women, Spanish women, Greek women, Micronesian women, Australian women, Philippines women,

Japanese women, South Korean women, Kenyan women, Angolan women—these women and others have much to tell Americans about just how exactly the 'US military system' works in the late 1980s.

SOME USEFUL ADDRESSES

Women's Equity Action League, Women in the Military Project, 805 15th Street NW, Suite 822, Washington, DC, 20005 (Tel. 202–638–1961).

Militarism Resource Project, PO Box 13416, Philadelphia 19101–3416. (MRP has special reports on schools and recruiters, on sexual harassment, on Black women in the miiltary, among other topics.)

The Joint Center for Political Studies, Blacks in the Military Project, 1301 Pennsylvania Avenue, Washington, DC, 20004. (JCPS is a research organization devoted to issues concerning the Black community.)

Center for Defense Information, 1500 Massachusetts Ave, NW, Washington, DC, 20005. (This is an independent research organization.)

DACOWITS, Office of the Assistant Secretary for Defense for Personnel Department of Defense, The Pentagon, Washington, DC.

Military Family Resource Center, Office of the Assistant Secretary of Defense for Personnel, Ballston Centre Tower Three, Suite 903, 4015 Wilson Boulevard, Arlington, VA 22203.

Minerva, a quarterly report on women and the military, ed. Linda Grant De Pauw, 1101 S. Arlington Ridge Rd, 201, Arlington, VA 22202.

Center for Economic Conversion, 222C View Street, Mountain View, CA 94041. (CEC publishes *Plowshare*, which follows closely militarization of the economy, with specific articles about the electronics industry.)

Campaign Against Military Prostitution, c/o TW–MAE–W, PO Box SM 366, Manila, Philippines. (This is a feminist group with ties to Kenya, S. Korea and Honduras.)

Appendix: Women's Military Participation

Afghanistan	No statistics obtainable; a few women in service sector only.
Algeria	No statistics obtainable; women have obtained the rank of captain, but no higher.
Argentina	Forty women in each branch as 'auxiliary personnel'; marines accepted women cadets in 1979, infantry and air force in 1982 (1983).
Australia	(1986) 5,500 (7.9 per cent), non-combat roles only. Most women serve in traditional roles.
Austria	No statistics obtainable, but women in support roles (i.e. medical, clerical) only.
Belgium	(1984) 3,457 (3.8 per cent). A law of 1976 made possible recruitment of women officers and NCOs. There is in theory full equality in training and duties. All military posts are in principle open to men and women.
Brazil	(1980). Less than 1 per cent and only in unarmed service divisions.
Britain	(1984) 16,576 (5.1 per cent); (1981) air force 5,400, army 6,500, navy 3,900, largely in service sector. The Employment Equality Act (1977) makes discrimination on the basis of sex or marital status in employment or training illegal except in the military.
Bulgaria	A 1958 law makes possible recruitment of women.
Burma	(1980) 200 (0.1 per cent).
Canada	(1986) 9.1 per cent; three-quarters of non-combat classifications open to women. In 1979 a three- to five-year trial programme of women in near-combat positions was initiated; in 1987

	another programme of women in combat was announced by the Minister of Defence.
Chile	Women are not subject to a draft, although some are in the armed forces in civilian jobs, and in the auxiliary branch of the army, in the carabineros, civil police and the investigation service. (1980) 1,000 (1.2 per cent).
People's Republic of China	About 10 per cent of army, navy and air force personnel. Women are excluded from combat. Women are serving as medical staff, in communications, scientific/technological research, arms manufacture as well as in areas of culture and sport. There are only a few women reservists; some women serve in the permament militia.
Colombia	No statistics obtainable; women are not permitted in combat but are in the service sector.
Cuba	No statistics obtainable. Women age between 17 and 35 may volunteer for two years service but are not subject to the draft. Women were prominent in the militias during the early 1960s; a 1980 campaign aims to put more women in territorial militias.
Czechoslovakia	Women can be recruited into the army for a period of three years or more. No statistics obtainable.
Denmark	(1986) 718 (1.9 per cent). The three services have trial programmes for women in near-combat positions. The Danish Home Guard has a women's corps of 11,172 women (1985).
Ecuador	A few women in the armed forces.
Egypt	(1980) 700 (0.2 per cent). Women in service sector only. Women age 18 to 24 years can volunteer for a period of seven years (successive periods, five years). In times of emergency women have been used extensively.
El Salvador	Forty per cent of the commanders in the People's Revolutionary Army are women, as a large portion of the guerilla forces and local militias; none in the government forces.
Federal Republic of Germany	(1982) 48,895 women are employed by the Federal Ministry of Defence, of these 21,053 are civilian jobs in the armed forces; since 1975, women physicians can become medical officers

	(106 in 1984). Women are prohibited from bearing arms. In 1982 the Defence Minister proposed a plan to recruit 30,000 women because of the acute shortage of draft-age men.
Finland	(1986) 7,000 civilian women, of which 600 recruited, are employed by the armed forces.
France	(1986) 18,700 (6 per cent), including paramedical corps; women volunteers have been admitted into unarmed divisions since 1938.
German Democratic Republic	No statistics obtainable, but women have been admitted to all ranks since 1956, training is not as severe as for men, and women are not permitted in combat duty.
Greece	In January 1979 the first 1,500 female volunteers enlisted in the previously all-male military; most are in non-combat roles, although all receive combat training. In 1984 there were 1,618 (0.95 per cent) women soldiers.
Guatemala	No statistics obtainable; women serve in the government's military forces and are reportedly active in the country's opposition movement.
Honduras	Women in the armed forces, terms unknown; no statistics obtainable.
Hungary	No statistics obtainable; women are permitted in the military only as service workers (clerical etc.).
India	No statistics obtainable, but women serve as doctors and nurses.
Indonesia	(1980) 2,500 (1.0 per cent). Women are permitted in non-combat roles, including as paratroopers, and a few have reached the rank of colonel.
Iran	1983 legislation prohibits women serving in the military and police corps. Women are given military training in mobilization centres so as to be ready 'to defend their country should the occasion arise'.
Ireland	(1979) 300 women are in all the armed forces and can rise to ranked positions: the military forces are explicitly excluded from the employment equality act.
Israel	No general statistics obtainable; the 1959 Defence Service Law (Consolidated Version)

	makes military service compulsory for women aged 18 to 26 (18–34 for reserves) unless they are married, pregnant or receive conscientious or religious exemptions. In 1976–7 approximately 51.5 per cent of Jewish women were accepted; a large percentage of women failed educational requirements, which are reportedly more rigorous than those for men. Women are barred from combat roles. In 1980 women participated in 270 of 850 military categories, of which approximately 50 per cent were clerical; typing and parachute-folding are reserved for women. Women's basic training includes a course in cosmetics; the women's corps are called *Chen*—an acronym which translates into 'charm'. Twelve thousand women serve in the 100,000-member Civil Guard.
Italy	A 1981 court decision to exclude women from military service was in response to Diadora Bissani's attempt to enrol in the Naval Academy; despite a 1982 bill initiated by the Minister of Defence to accept women into military service on a voluntary basis, they are presently permitted only in civilian roles. In 1980 there were about 70,000 civilian women employees in the armed forces.
Japan	(1980) 2,900 (1.2 per cent), including 300 nurses, 600 medical workers, 1,900 enlisted women and NCOs and 100 officers. Women are not admitted to the Defence Academy but play a limited non-combat role in the military.
Jordan	No statistics obtainable, women serve in the armed forces but are excluded from combat positions.
Kenya	No statistics obtainable, but women are admitted to service on equal terms with men; only a few women are in the military.
Kuwait	Women are not permitted in the military.
Libya	No statistics obtainable; military service is compulsory for all women before marriage.
Luxembourg	There are no women in the small volunteer army. In 1979, twenty women were recruited for a three-year period.
Malaysia	(1980) 450 (0.7 per cent).

Mexico	No statistics obtainable; women are not permitted in combat but serve in clerical, medical and support roles.
Mozambique	Women are conscripted for military service.
The Netherlands	(1986) 1,500 (1.5 per cent)—navy 676, army 379, air force 290, military police 155. Since 1979 women can enlist in all branches of the armed forces with 'equal status and duties' to men. The special women's corps in each branch is being disbanded to effect integration, but military combat for women is not under consideration.
New Zealand	(1982) 8.55 per cent (army 5.9 per cent, navy 9.64 per cent, air force 11.26 per cent), non-combat roles only.
Nicaragua	As of 1983 women comprise 47 per cent of the militia, with 70 per cent of them in the health campaign; there are both mixed battalions and women's companies. In August 1983 the Nicaraguan government initiated compulsory military service for men but not women. Sandinista women's groups criticized this as discrimination, but commander Doris Tijeriano, the highest-ranking woman in the Sandinista army, responded by citing women's 'well-known biological and organic limitations'. Women were top-ranked commanders in the 1979 battles against Somoza, and by 1981 nearly 30 per cent of the Popular Sandinista Army were women; in 1982 over 90 per cent of the political instructors at the Carlos Aguero Military School were women.
Nigeria	No statistics obtainable; women can serve in the armed forces, terms unknown.
Norway	(1986) 543 (1.4 per cent) women in service and training. Women serve in civilian jobs (secretarial and medical) and since 1977 as reserve officers, in mobilization forces, and officer candidate courses. Women are barred from combat.
Pakistan	(1980) 5,500 (1.2 per cent). Women are not permitted in combat roles but serve as civilian medical personnel.
Palestine	No statistics obtainable; women are active in various guerilla forces.

Panama	Women in the armed forces, terms unknown, no statistics obtainable.
Peru	No statistics obtainable; virtually none, although a 1974 decree stipulates that military service is a responsibility of all citizens, and mandatory conscription of women aged 18 onto a service register was begun in 1975.
Philippines	(1980) 600 (0.6 per cent).
Poland	No statistics obtainable; women are not permitted to serve in the military but are allowed to work as civilians in service jobs; the only exceptions are female medical students who undergo military training (the same as male students) in the course of their studies.
Portugal	When Portugal's overseas wars ended, the number of the air force nurses were reduced. In 1984 there were only seven women, of which one was an officer. Women have not been permitted to serve in other military roles, although the first woman naval cadet was admitted to the academy in 1982.
Rumania	A 1972 law makes it possible for women to join the army as career officers and NCOs. All women attending college-level institutes are subject to military training during their school years.
Saudi Arabia	Women are prohibited from military service.
Senegal	No statistics obtainable; as of 1983, women may apply to the military-status Polytechnic School to train as civil engineers, and to the military School of Health. Nine women became the first female police officers and inspectors in the 1983 National Police School promotions.
Singapore	(1980) 3,500 (9.0 per cent).
Somalia	Women serve in the military along with men.
South Africa	No statistics obtainable; the South African Defence Force is recruiting more white women in attempts to strengthen the forces; some African women are guerilla fighters in the outlawed South-West African People's Organization (SWAPO) and other military units of groups fighting against apartheid and for national liberation.
Soviet Union	No definite statistics obtainable (one estimate is

	10,000), but women are present in near-combat and non-combat roles. Women with medical, veterinary and special training have to register and are subject to induction into the military reserve. They are obligated to undergo periodic training and are subject to recall in time of war.
Spain	Women are prohibited from service.
Sri Lanka	No statistics obtainable, but women serve in clerical, nursing (etc.) capacities.
Sudan	No statistics obtainable, but women can be trained for combat, although they are concentrated in support and service sectors.
Sweden	Women were first admitted into military in 1978 and may become officers but are not allowed in combat. Sixty-nine women volunteered in 1984.
Switzerland	(1986) 2,500 women serve in women's corps of the armed forces.
Taiwan	(1980) 12,500 (2.7 per cent).
Tanzania	No statistics obtainable. Women can serve in the armed forces; terms unknown.
Thailand	(1980) 4,460 (2.1 per cent). Women are not permitted in military schools, general ranks or combat duty; some women technicians have achieved high rank within the military.
Turkey	(1984) twenty-seven women serve as officers. From 1955 on female student officers have been accepted into colleges and universities of the Turkish Armed Forces. Women serve as rear service pilots and cartographic engineers as well as in traditional administrative and medical duties.
United States	(1986) 214,152 (9.5 per cent); army 10.4 per cent, navy 9.3 per cent, air force 12.0 per cent, marines 4.9 per cent. Women are not permitted in direct combat roles but serve mainly as clerical, communications and medical personnel.
Venezuela	No statistics obtainable; under the 1979 Law of Conscription, women must register for military service at age 18 and may enter all branches on the same terms as men.
Vietnam	No statistics obtainable. Women are not drafted but serve in local militias; women's military roles have become marginal after 1975.
Yugoslavia	(1980) 2,600 (1.0 per cent); the 1980 law permits women to volunteer for military service.

Zambia	No statistics obtainable; women are permitted in the military on an equal basis with men in all sectors, including combat, and a few serve as commissioned officers.
Zimbabwe	No statistics obtainable. Approximately half of the women soldiers in the liberation armies have been integrated into the national army.

Notes on Contributors

Elisabetta Addis teaches macroeconomics and monetary policy at the University of Abruzzi, Italy. She studied at Scuola Normale, Pisa and has been a Fulbright exchange student at Clark University, Worcester and Harvard University. She was a contributor to *Pace e Guerra*, a pacifist journal, and was a founder of the 10 March Group, a feminist group active in Rome and Perugia. She has published articles on monetary policy and central banking in Italy and this is her second article on women and war issues.

Astrid Albrecht-Heide Born 1938, married, two children, studied education, sociology, German and English language and literature in Hamburg and Berlin (West). PhD in the interdisciplinary field of socialization research. Assistant in the field of sociology of education at the Free University of Berlin, now Professor of Socialization Research at the Technical University of Berlin. Publications on adult socialization, female socialization, including (im)migrant women, and especially on Women and the Military (e.g. together with Utemaria Bujewski, *Militärdienst für Frauen*? [Military Service for women?]) Present project on social psychological and political-psychological implications of a female military service.

Birgitte Andersen, Bitten Forchhammer, Tine Forchhammer, Hanne Klein, Cynthia Loft, Ingrid Sandholdt, Birgitte Siert are a group of grass-roots feminist activists aged from 22 to 60. They have been active in peace movements and have a close contact with Ravnstrup, the Danish women's peace camp at a NATO base. They are engaged in polemic activities in the press and contribute to magazines issued by peace movements. The group continues its task of informing and activating women. *Contact*: Women and the Military System Group, c/o Bitten Forchhammer, 14 Rebild Hedevej, DK–9520, Skørping, Denmark.

Marion Anderson is the director of Employment Research Associates, an economist, and the author of a number of internationally distributed publications including *The Empty Pork Barrel: The Employment Cost of Military Build-up 1981–1985; The Impact of Military Spending on the Machinists Union; Neither Jobs Nor Security: Women's Unemployment and the Pentagon Budget*; and *Converting the Work Force: Where the Jobs Would Be*. Over 600,000 of these and other publications of Employment Research Associates have been sold. In addition to appearing on national television and before civic groups and college audiences across the United States, she has been invited to give expert testimony before numerous congressional committees, and has given briefings for US congressional staff members on the economic impact of the military budget.

Tsehai Berhane-Selassie has a BA in history from the University of Addis Ababa (1969) and a postgraduate diploma (1976) and a doctorate in social anthropology (1981), both from the University of Oxford. As a researcher at the Institute of Ethiopian Studies Addis Ababa University (1969–75), she has contributed several articles to the *Journal of Ethiopian Studies* and elsewhere. Her forthcoming publications include *Counting the Cost: Women, Politics and Production in Africa* and *Ethiopian Nationalism and Resistance to Italian Occupation*, both to be published by Zed Press. 'In Search of Ethiopian Women' has been published in *Change* in 1984. She has taught in the Department of Anthropology at Stanford University, California for a term (1982) and has been teaching anthropology at the Extra-Mural Studies Department of the University of London since 1983. She also worked at *Spare Rib* (1984–6) and since 1986 has been a research officer at the Institute for African Alternatives. She is a Fellow of the Royal Anthropological Institute.

Annemiek Bolscher and **Ine Megens** have worked together since September 1985 on the subject 'Women and the Military System'. They belonged to a working-group 'Vrouw en Leger'. Ine Megens studied history and peace research. She works at the Scientific Office of the Pacifist Socialist Party in Amsterdam. Annemiek Bolscher studied sociology of education. She has pursued research into the emancipation of women in the army.

Elise Boulding, Professor Emerita of Dartmouth College was Chair from 1978 to 1985, and previously was at the University of Colorado's Department of Sociology and Institute of Behavioral Science, from 1967 to 1978. She was born in Oslo, Norway; has a BA in

English; an MS in sociology and a PhD from the University of Michigan. She translated Fred Polak's *Image of the Future* from the Dutch. She has studied conflict and peace, development, family life and women; served on the governing board of the UN University, from 1980 to 1985; and was on the International Jury of the UNESCO Prize for Peace Education. She wrote *The Underside of History: A View of Women Through Time*. Her latest book, to be published in 1988, is *Building a Global Civic Culture: Education for an Interdependent World*.

Ximena Bunster has a PhD in anthropology from Columbia University. She was Professor of Anthropology at the National University of Chile until 1973. Since then, she has been Visiting Associate Professor at several US universities. She has focused her research on working women in Latin America, human rights and the effects of repression on women's lives. She is co-founder and director of Institute de Estudios Democraticos de la Mujer at Santiago, Chile, and active in organizing women and participating at women's mass mobilizations.

Wendy Chapkis edited and co-authored *Loaded Questions: Women in the Military* (1981), and co-authored (with Cynthia Enloe) *Of Common Cloth: Women in the Global Textile Industry* (1984). She worked for six years in the Transnational Institute, Amsterdam, the European centre of the Washington-based progressive think-tank. She is now working at the University of California, Santa Cruz. Her most recent book is *Beauty Secrets: Women and the Politics of Appearance*.

Carol Cohn is a senior research fellow at the Center for Psychological Studies in the Nuclear Age and a research associate in the Department of Psychiatry at the Harvard Medical School. She has both attended and taught in faculty training seminars on nuclear weapons and global security, and spent a year as a Visiting Scholar at the Defense Technology and Arms Control Programs of the Massachusetts Institute of Technology's Center for International Studies. She is currently writing a book on the language and thinking of nuclear defence intellectuals, under a grant from the John D. and Catherine T. MacArthur Foundation. For nine years she was on the faculty of the Seminar College of the New School for Social Research in New York, and for the last five years she has been doing faculty development workshops, focusing on the development and application of a pedagogical method designed to foster more active, complex and critical thinking in the classroom, with a particular emphasis on teaching about the issues raised by the nuclear threat.

Ellen Elster has been a grass-roots activist for a number of years within the Norwegian section of War Resisters International (WRI). Council member of WRI, 1979–85, she especially worked on the question of women and militarism, nonviolent movements in the Third World and nonviolent defence. She is also one of the initiators of the Norwegian Women for Peace. Numerous articles have appeared in the paper *Ikkevold* (Nonviolence), issued by the Norwegian section of WRI, where she has also participated on the editorial board. She is a trained social worker, now administering home helpers to elderly people living at home. Mother of three children.

Cynthia Enloe is Professor of Government and Women's Studies at Clark University, Worcester, Massachusetts. She is trying now to pull together the several strands of her interests and political concerns, in the workings of militarism, racism, sexism, bureaucracy and the international political economy in a book being written for Pandora Press (London and New York). Her previous books include *Does Khaki Become You? The Militarization of Women's Lives* (1983 and 1988); (with Wendy Chapkis) *Of Common Cloth: Women in the Global Textile Industry* (1984); *Ethnic Soldiers: State Security in Divided Societies* (1980). She currently is also North American editor of *Women's Studies International Forum*.

Nicole Gabriel lives and works in Paris where she teaches at the University Paris VII. She has written her doctorate on the organization of women in the German Social Democratic Party. Her interests lie mainly in comparative studies on the social movements in France and Western Germany and she currently works on the effects of militarization in Western societies and on pacifist and ecological issues.

Barten C. Hacker holds a 1968 PhD in history from the University of Chicago. He has alternated teaching at the University of Chicago, Iowa State University and Oregon State University with research for the US National Aeronautics and Space Administration, Massachusetts Institute of Technology, and US Department of Energy. His books include *On the Shoulders of Titans: A History of Project Gemini* (1978) and *The Dragon's Tail: Radiation Safety in the Manhattan Project, 1941–1946* (1987). His current research centres on interactions between military institutions, technology and political economy in three closely related areas: origins and development of the state, historical bases of women's social subordination, and development of engineering and engineering education.

Hermione Harris has been a lecturer in social anthropology in London, and has lived in Central America for several years co-ordinating a British technical assistance programme in Honduras and Nicaragua. She carried out research in Nicaragua for four documentary films shown on Channel Four television in 1986 and has researched and written on the position of women in the Revolution. She is currently living in London with her husband and two small children, working as a freelance writer and journalist. Recent publications include the introduction to *The Tiger's Milk: Women of Nicaragua* by A. Angel and F. Macintosh, published by Virago in 1987.

Marie-Aimée Hélie-Lucas Born in Algiers in 1939, the daughter and granddaughter of feminists. She studied philosophy and sociology in the University of Algiers and social anthropology at the London School of Economics and Political Science. She taught at the University of Algiers for more than ten years. From 1967 till 1982 she followed research in political sociology on the indicators of the making and reproduction of the new ruling class in the post-independence Algeria; since 1975 she has studied Algerian women and the state policy. She was a low-key participant in the Algerian liberation struggle from 1957 to independence in 1962 and has been a part of various critical currents in the left and participated in the first attempts of women to organize in the 1980s against new laws highly unfavourable to them. She was one of the founding members of AAWORD in 1975 (Association of African Women for Research on Development). After leaving Algiers in 1982, she lived in Holland, where she set up an international solidarity network 'Women Living Under Muslim Laws' through which women from Muslim countries and communities exchange information on the development of their situations, their struggles and their strategies, and generate support amongst themselves. She is now working full time for this network, whose co-ordinations are now established in Southern France, Pakistan and Nigeria. She has four children and often works in collaboration with her elder daughter Anissa Hélie-Lucas, who is also an active feminist.

Eva Isaksson has a degree in theoretical physics from the University of Helsinki. She is currently working at the University of Helsinki

Observatory and Astrophysics Laboratory; in her research work she has concentrated on the history of theories of gravitation. She has edited and written several books for the Society for the Promotion of Peace Literature (Finland): a collection of Einstein's writings on peace; the basic Finnish introduction to SDI; an exhaustive work of international scope about scientists' movements for peace and disarmament after the Second World War. Her most recent book is an overview on women, war and militarization. She has also written a book on women's work in exact sciences. She received a 1985 State Award for her publications on peace work. She has been active for a number of causes and is currently interested in women's work in science for both war and peace. She can be contacted at Hauhontie 8 F 34, 00550, Helsinki, Finland.

Barbara Jancar is Professor of Political Science at the State University of New York, Brockport. In the fall 1987, she was a fellow in the East European Program at the Wilson Center, Smithsonian Institution, Washington DC. From 1984 to 1987 she was co-director of the SUNY Paris Programme in the Social Sciences. She has travelled extensively in Eastern Europe and particularly Yugoslavia. In January 1981, as the guest of the Yugoslav women's association, she interviewed women veterans and national heroes who had fought in Yugoslavia's National Liberation War, 1941–1945. She has published articles and books on women in Eastern Europe. Forthcoming by Arden Press is *Women and Revolution in Yugoslavia.*

Stella Jegher Born in 1960, studied at the Geneva translators and interpreters school. She has worked in the secretariat of the Swiss Peace Council 1983–4 and in the East–West Commission of this council. Now working as a freelance translator and a freelance peace activist (mainly on East–West and women's issues) and since 1985, as secretary of the 'Forum for Practice-Oriented Peace Research' (Forum für praxisbezogene Friedensforschung) in Basel.

Scilla Elworthy McLean is director of the Oxford Research Group and research fellow of the University of Bradford. She has been a consultant on women's issues to UNESCO and research director of the Minority Rights Group in France. She is the author of studies on the role of women in international relations, in peace movements and on female circumcision.

The Oxford Research Group was established in 1982 to carry out research on how nuclear weapons decisions are made, and by whom they are made, in all the nuclear nations. The Group is currently analysing ways in which women can focus their efforts to halt the arms race. For further information contact Oxford Research Group, 1 High Street, Woodstock, Oxford OX7 1TE, UK (tel.: 0993 811293).

Ruth Roach Pierson teaches women's history and history of feminism at the Ontario Institute for Studies in Education, Toronto, Ontario, Canada. She is the author of *'They're Still Women After All': The Second World War and Canadian Womanhood* (1986) and editor of *Women and Peace: Theoretical, Historical and Practical Perspectives* (1987).

Judith Hicks Stiehm is Provost at Florida International University (University of Florida in Miami). She received her BA in East Asian Studies and a Teaching Certificate from the University of Wisconsin, her MA in American history from Temple University, and her PhD in political theory from Columbia University. Dr Stiehm was at the University of Southern California from 1970 to 1987 and was active in the Program for the Study of Women and Men in Society, serving as its director from 1975 to 1978 and Faculty Chair from 1979 to 1981. She has written or edited six books, including *Bring Me Men and Women, Mandated Change at the US Air Force Academy; Women and Men's Wars* (1982, ed.); *Men, Women and State Violence: Government and the Military* (1983); and *Women's View of the Political World of Men* (1984, ed.). Dr Stiehm has received the Dart Award for Academic Innovation and the Phi Kappa Phi Scholarly Book Award. She was also president of the Western Political Science Association in 1986.

Eeva-Liisa Tuominen Born 1945, has been deputy chief inspector in the Finnish Ministry of Social and Health Affairs and secretary-general of the Council for Equality since 1986. She has been working in a professional capacity with issues of equality between men and women in the workforce, and women and militarization. She is also interested in women's situation in the developing countries. She has been active in the Social Democratic Women's Organization and in trade-union politics. She has attended international meetings arranged by the UN, ILO, OECD and EEC, and also major international meetings of the women's movement.

Bibliography

BIBLIOGRAPHIES

'Bibliographical Essay', in Nancy Loring Goldman (ed.), *Female Soldiers—Combatants or Noncombatants? Historical and Contemporary Perspectives* (Westport, Conn.: Greenwood, 1982), pp. 290–5.

'Annotated Bibliography', in Ruth Roach Pierson, *'They're Still Women After All': The Second World War and Canadian Womanhood* (Toronto: McClelland and Stewart, 1986), pp. 221–36. Excellent feminist bibliography, particularly on women's wartime participation during the two world wars. Some items are cited here.

My Country Is the Whole World: An Anthology of Women's Work on Peace and War, compiled by Cambridge Women's Peace Collective (London: Pandora Press, 1984). Excellent collection including an ample bibliography. Illustrated.

Women in the Military: A Selective Bibliography, Washington, DC, Pentagon Library, November 1983. Books and periodicals mostly on American and British women, from the First World War to the present.

Hunter, E. *et al.*, 'Women in the Military: An Annotated Bibliography', *Armed Forces and Society* 4/4 (1978): 695–716.

Lippert, E. and Rössler, T., *Weibliche Soldaten: Bibliographie zu einem Reizthema* (Baden-Baden: Nomos Verlagsgesellschaft, 1981).

Ausgewählte Bibliographie zum Thema 'Frauen und Militär' (1985), descriptions from the essential publications in the German language. Available from the publisher: Evangelische Arbeitsgemeinschaft zur betreuung der Kriegsdienstverweigerer (EAK), Fachgruppe 'Frauen und Kriegsdienstverweigerung', Carl-Schurz-Str. 17. 2800 Bremen 1, FRG.

BOOKS AND ARTICLES

Publications in English: General

Allatt, Patricia, 'Men and War: Status, Class and the Social Reproduction of Masculinity', in Eva Gamarnikov *et al.* (eds.), *The Public and the Private*, London: Heinemann Educational, 1983, pp. 47–61. Armed forces educational programme in citizenship in England during the Second World War aiming at male solidarity.

Allen, Margaret, 'The Domestic Ideal and the Mobilization of Womanpower in World War II', *Women's Studies International Forum* 6/4 (1983): 401–12.

Amrane, Djamila, 'Algeria: Anticolonial War', in N.L. Goldman (ed.), *Female Soldiers* (Westport, Conn.: Greenwood, 1982), pp. 123–36. Classic work on women's participation in liberation struggle, derived from official statistics.

Anderson, Karen, *Wartime Women: Sex Roles, Family Relations and the Status of Women During World War II* (Westport, Conn.: Greenwood, 1981).

Anderson, Marion, *Neither Jobs nor Security: Women's Unemployment and the Pentagon Budget* (Lansing, Mich.: Employment Research Associates (474 Hollister Building, Lansing, MI 48933, USA)). A thorough analysis by an economist about the net job loss caused by military spending.

Berkin, Carol and Lovett, Clara (eds.), *Women, War and Revolution* (New York: Holmes & Meier, 1980). Women's involvement in wars and revolutions from the eighteenth to twentieth centuries in the Americas, Western and Eastern Europe and China.

Bérubé, Allan and D'Emilio, John, 'The Military and Lesbians During the McCarthy Years', *Signs* 9/4 (1984): 757–75. Contains historical documents on anti-lesbian sex education and purges in the American military of the 1950s.

Bevege, Margaret *et al.*, *Worth Her Salt: Women at Work in Australia* (Sydney: Hale & Tremonger, 1982). Includes several articles about women's wartime work and their participation in the armed services.

Bigland, E., *Britain's Other Army* (London: Nicholson & Watson, 1947).

Binkin, Martin and Bach, Shirley, *Women in the Military* (Washington DC: The Brookings Institute, 1977). Although outdated, still a good general introduction to women in the military, written just before the major surge of female participation in the US military. Appendix gives an overview of women in the militaries of NATO and the Warsaw Pact countries, Asia, Australasia and the Middle East.

Bloom, Anne R., 'Israel: The Longest War', in N.L. Goldman (ed.), *Female Soldiers* (Westport, Conn.: Greenwood, 1982), pp. 137–60. Detailed historical overview on women's military participation in Israel.

Bock, Gisela, 'Racism and Sexism in Nazi Germany: Motherhood, Compulsory Sterilization, and the State', *Signs* 8/3 (1983): 400–21. A sound feminist analysis of women's role in the militarized Nazi society.

Braybon, Gail, *Women Workers in the First World War: The British Experience* (London and Totowa, NJ: Croom Helm and Barnes & Noble, 1981). Feminist-socialist analysis of women's economic and social roles and women's status in British society around the time of the Second World War.

Brown, James and Safilios-Rotschild, Constantina, 'Greece: Reluctant Presence', in N.L. Goldman (ed.), *Female Soldiers* (Westport, Conn.: Greenwood, 1982), pp. 165–78. History of Greek women's military participation and their role in the modern army.

Brownmiller, Susan, *Against Our Will* (New York: Bantam, 1976). Includes a much cited chapter on rape in war.

Byles, Joan Montgomery, 'Women's Experiences of World War One. Suffragists, Pacifists, and Poets', *Women's Studies International Forum* 8/5 (1985): 473–87.

Cadogan, Mary and Graig, Patricia, *Women and Children First: The Fiction of Two World Wars* (London: Victor Gollancz, 1978).

Campbell, D'Ann, *Women at War with America: Private Lives in a Patriotic Era* (Cambridge, Mass.: Harvard University Press, 1984). Response of women in the United States to the Second World War in the armed forces, in nursing, in war factories, in volunteer work and in the home.

Cassin-Scott, J., *Women at War, 1939–1945* (London: Osprey, 1981). Summary of the historical background of British, American, German and Russian women in the Second World War.

Chaos of the Night: Women's Poetry and Verse of the Second World War, selected by Catherine Reilly (London: Virago, 1984).

Chapkis, Wendy (ed.), *Loaded Questions: Women in the Military* (Amsterdam: Transnational Institute, 1981). Fourteen papers presented at the 1981 conference on women in the military, especially in the NATO countries. Ideological and ethical questions in the context of international developments in women's military participation.

Conrod, W. Hugh, *Athene, Goddess of War: The Canadian*

Women's Army Corps, Their Story (Nova Scotia: Dartmouth, Writing and Editorial Services, 1983).
Costello, John, *Love, Sex and War: Changing Values 1939–1945* (London: Collins, 1985). Some aspects of sexual politics during the Second World War, rather from men's point of view.
Cottam, K. Jean, 'Soviet Women in Combat in World War II: The Ground/Air Defense Forces', in Tova Yedlin (ed.), *Women in Eastern Europe and the Soviet Union* (New York: Praeger, 1980) pp. 115–27.
Cottam, K.J. (ed. and trans.), *The Golden-Tressed Soldier* (Manhattan, Kansas: MA/AH Publishing, 1983).
Cottam, K.J. 'Soviet Airwomen in Combat in World War II' (Manhattan, Kansas: MA/AH Publishing, 1983).
Crosthwait, Elizabeth, ' "The Girl Behind the Man Behind the Gun": The Women's Army Auxiliary Corps, 1914–1918', in Leonore Davidoff and Belinda Westover (eds.), *Our Work, Our Lives, Our Words: Women's History and Women's Work* (London: Macmillan, 1986).
Daniell, Rosemary, *Sleeping with Soldiers: In Search of the Macho Man* (London: Grafton, 1986). One woman's search for her sexual identity.
Van Devanter, Lynda, *Home before Morning: The Story of an Army Nurse in Vietnam* (New York/Toronto: Beaufort, 1983). One of the best books about the war in Vietnam and its impact on lives of American women and men.
Dobrofsky, Lynne R., 'Women's Power and Authority in the Context of War', *Sex Roles* 3/2 (1977): 141–57.
Dobrofsky, Lynne R. and Batterson, Constance T., 'The Military Wife and Feminism', *Signs* 2/3 (1977): 675–84.
Duiker, William J., 'Vietnam: War of Insurgency', in N.L. Goldman (ed.), *Female Soldiers* (Westport, Conn.: Greenwood, 1982), pp. 107–22. An historical overview on women's role in the military history of Vietnam.
Elster, Ellen, 'Conscription of Women', in Kimmo Kiljunen and Jouko Väänänen (ed.), *Youth and Conscription* (Helsinki: Peace Union of Finland, 1987), pp. 78–90.
Enloe, Cynthia H., 'Women: The Reserve Army of Army Labor', *The Review of Radical Political Economics* 12/2 (Summer 1980).
—— *Does Khaki Become You? The Militarization of Women's Lives* (London: Pluto Press, 1983; Boston: South End Press, 1983). Describes how militaries have been for centuries dependent on women's services and on specific constructions of femininity. Best treatment so far of the relations between gender and militarism in the modern world.

—— 'Women in NATO Militaries: A Conference Report', in J.H. Stiehm (ed.), *Women and Men's Wars*, special issue of *Women's Studies International Forum* 5/3–4 (1982): 329–34. See Chapkis.
— 'Women and Militarization: A Seminar', *Radical Teacher* (special issue on Peace Studies) no. 26 (June 1984): 2–7. Excellent guidelines for teachers on the subject, with a good resource list.
—— 'Bananas, Bases, and Patriarchy: Some Feminist Questions about the Militarization of Central America', *Radical America* 19/4 (1985): 7–23.
Enloe, Cynthia, and Jordan, Harold, 'Black Women in the Military', *Militarism Resource Project News* 1/3 (Spring 1985). Militarism Resource Project, P.O. Box 13416, Philadelphia, PA 19101–3416, USA.
Ewing, Elizabeth, *Women in Uniform Through Centuries* (London: Batsford, 1975). From a fashion journalist's point of view. Amply illustrated.
Forcey, Linda Rennie, 'Making of Men in the Military: Perspectives from Mothers', *Women's Studies International Forum* 7/6 (1984): 477–86.
Gabin, Nancy, ' "They Have Placed a Penalty on Womanhood": The Protest Actions of Women Auto Workers in Detroit Area UAW Locals, 1945–1947', *Feminist Studies* 8/2 (Summer 1982): 373–98. Documents protest actions against the loss of wartime jobs during reconversion by women workers in the auto industry; describes systematic elimination of women workers in the postwar period and management strategies to achieve this goal.
—— 'Women Workers and the UAW in the Post-World War II Period: 1945–1954', *Labor History* 21 (Winter 1979–80): 5–30.
Gellhorn, Martha, *The Face of War*, 3rd ed. (London: Virago, 1986). War reports by a woman from the Spanish Civil War to the 1980s.
Gilbert, Sandra M., 'Soldier's Heart: Literary Men, Literary Women, and the Great War', *Signs* 8/3 (1983): 422–50. Describes role reversal in power relations between the sexes during the First World War period.
Goldman, Nancy, 'The Changing Role of Women in the Armed Forces', *American Journal of Sociology*, January 1973.
—— 'Women in the NATO Armed Forces', *Military Review* (1974): 72–82.
—— 'The Utilization of Women in the Armed Forces of Industrialized Nations', *Sociological Symposium* (Spring 1977): 1–23.
Goldman, Nancy Loring (ed.), *Female Soldiers: Combatants or Noncombatants? Historical and Contemporary Perspectives*

(Westport, Conn.: Greenwood, 1982). An important collection of papers from the 1980 international symposium by the Inter-University Seminar on Armed Forces and Society. Takes for granted the necessity for militaries; equals women's right to combat as a test of equal rights. Highly informative and detailed.

Goldman, Nancy Loring and Stites, Richard, 'Great Britain and the World Wars', in N.L. Goldman (ed.), *Female Soldiers* (Westport, Conn.: Greenwood, 1982), pp. 21–46. History of the British women's experience of war in the twentieth century.

Greenwald, Maurine Weiner, *Women, War, and Work: The Impact of World War I on Women Workers in the United States* (Westport, Conn.: Greenwood, 1980). Employment patterns of American women from 1870s to 1920s with particular attention to the war years: wartime changes in women's employment, scientific management and the work of social reformers.

Gregory, Chester W., *Women in Defense Work During World War II: An Analysis of the Labor Problem and Women's Rights* (New York: Exposition Press, 1974). Detailed history of American women's employment in defence production from 1941 to 1945.

Gregory-Lewis, Sasha, 'Lesbians in the Military', in Ginny Vida (ed.), *Our Right to Love: A Lesbian Resource Book* (Englewood Cliffs, NJ: Prentice-Hall, 1978), pp. 211–16.

Griesse, Anne Eliot, and Stites, Richard, 'Russia: Revolution and War', in N.L. Goldman (ed.), *Female Soldiers* (Westport, Conn.: Greenwood, 1982).

Hacker, Barton C., 'Women and Military Institutions in Early Modern Europe: A Reconnaissance', *Signs* 6/4 (1981): 643–71.

Hacker, Barton C. and Hacker, Sally L., 'Military Institutions and the Labor Process: Noneconomic Sources of Technological Change, Women's Subordination, and the Organisation of Work', *Technology and Culture* 28 (1987).

Hanley, Lynne, 'Her Story of War: De-Militarizing Literature and Literary Studies', *Radical America* 20/4 (1986): 17–29.

Hartmann, Susan, 'Prescriptions for Penelope: Literature on Women's Obligations to Returning World War II Veterans,' *Women's Studies* 5 (1978), 223–39.

Hartmann, Susan M., *The Home Front and Beyond: American Women in the 1940s* (Boston: Twayne, 1982). General study of changing social and economic patterns during the 1940s and of the extent to which dramatic changes precipitated by the Second World War were, in fact, 'only for the duration'.

Havens, T., 'Women and War in Japan, 1937–1945', *American Historical Review* 80 (October 1975).

Hietanen, Aki, 'Women in the Military System: Historical Myths and Contemporary Problems', in Kimmo Kiljunen and Jouko Väänänen (eds.), *Youth and Conscription* (Helsinki: Peace Union of Finland, 1987), pp. 99–106.

Higonnet, M.R., Jenson, J., Michel, S. and Weitz, M.C. (eds.): *Behind the Lines: Gender and the Two World Wars* (New Haven, Conn.: Yale University Press, 1987).

Hoiberg, Anne (ed.), *Women as New 'Manpower'*, special issue of *Armed Forces and Society* 4/4 (Summer 1978). Collection of fifteen articles, including results of research on women's experiences in sex-integrated military academies. Articles share the view that the military can be an opportunity for women.

Holm, Jeanne, *Women in the Military: An Unfinished Revolution* (Novato, Calif.: Presidio, 1982). Detailed, comprehensive, inside account of American women's military participation from 1778 to the present.

Honey, Maureen, *Creating Rosie the Riveter: Class, Gender, and Propaganda During World War II* (Amherst, Mass.: University of Massachusetts Press, 1984). Describes, how the postwar reaction flowed out of the war itself; women's recruitment into the US labour force was subordinated to the goal of welding the home front into an economic army.

—— 'The Working-Class Woman and Recruitment Propaganda during World War II: Class Differences in the Portrayal of War Work', *Signs* 8/4 (1983): 672–87.

Huston, Nancy, 'The Matrix of War: Mothers and Heroes', *Poetics Today* 6/1–2 (1985): 153–70.

—— 'Tales of War and Tears of Women', in J.H. Stiehm (ed.), *Women and Men's Wars*, special issue of *Women's Studies International Forum* 5/3–4 (1982): 271–82.

Jancar, Barbara, 'Yugoslavia: War of Resistance', in N.L. Goldman (ed.), *Female Soldiers* (Westport, Conn.: Greenwood, 1982), pp. 85–106.

Kamester, Margaret and Vellacott, Jo (eds.), *Militarism versus Feminism: Writings on Women and War* (London: Virago, 1987). A collection of writings by Catharine Marshall, C.K. Ogden and Mary Sargant Florence.

Keeva, Sally Hayton (ed.), *Valiant Women in War and Exile: Thirty-Eight True Stories* (San Francisco: City Light Books, 1986).

Keil, Sally Van Wagenen, *The Wonderful Women in Their Flying Machines: The Unknown Heroines of World War II* (New York: Rawson, Wade, 1979). The history of Women's Airforce Service Pilots (WASPS); 2,000 women trained as pilots on an all-female cadet air base in Texas from 1942 to 1944.

King, Alison, *Golden Wings: The Story of Some of the Women Ferry Pilots of the Air Transport Auxiliary* (London: C.A. Pearson, 1956).

Krippner, Monica, *The Quality of Mercy: Women at War, Serbia 1915–18* (Newton Abbot, Eng.: David & Charles, 1980).

Laska, Vera, *Women in the Resistance and the Holocaust: The Voice of Emptiness* (Westport, Conn.: Greenwood, 1983).

Lupton, Mary Jane, 'Images of Women and War in Literature', *Women: A Journal of Liberation* 8/1 (1981).

Marshall, Kathryn, *Combat Zone: An Oral History of American Women in Vietnam* (Boston: Little, Brown, 1987).

Marwick, Arthur, *Women at War 1914–1918* (London: Fontana, 1977).

May, Martha, 'The Historical Problem of the Family Wage: The Ford Motor Company and the Five Dollar Day', *Feminist Studies* 8/2 (Summer 1982): 399–424. Examines the ideology of male-earned family wage during World War I.

Mazrui, Ali A., 'Military Technology and the Masculinity of War: An African Perspective', *Impact of Science on Society* 26/1–2 (1976): 71–5.

Milkman, Ruth, 'Redefining "Women's Work": The Sexual Division of Labor in Auto Industry During World War II', *Feminist Studies* 8/2 (Summer 1982): 336–72.

—— *Gender at Work: The Dynamics of Job Segregation by Sex During World War II* (Chicago: University of Illinois Press, 1987).

Minns, Raynes, *Bombers and Mash: The Domestic Front 1939–1945* (London: Virago, 1985). Wartime life in nurseries, factories, women's auxiliaries, civil defence and women's forces in Britain. Detailed accounts of food rationing, cooking (with authentic wartime recipes), salvaging and women's volunteer work.

Mitchell, David, *Women on the Warpath: The Story of the Women of the First World War* (London: Jonathan Cape, 1966).

Morden, Col. B., *The Women's Army Corps, 1945–1978*, the US Army Historical Series, Washington, DC, Office of the Chief of Military History, Department of the Army, 1983.

Myles, Bruce, *Night Witches: The Untold Story of Soviet Women in Combat* (London: Panther/Granada, 1983).

Pierson, Ruth Roach, *'They're Still Women, After All': The Second World War and Canadian Womanhood* (Toronto: McClelland & Stewart, 1986). Excellent account by a feminist historian, including women's wartime work and women's services. One of the best books about women in the Second World War.

—— (ed.), *Women and Peace: Theoretical, Historical and Practical Perspectives* (London: Croom Helm, 1987).

Randall, Margaret, *Sandino's Daughters: Testimonies of Nicaraguan Women in Struggle* (Vancouver: New Star Books, 1981).

Reekie, Gail, 'War, Sexuality and Feminism: Perth Women's Organisations, 1938–1945', *Historical Studies* 21/85 (1985): 576–91.

Ridard, Bernadette, 'Women and Militarism', in Kimmo Kiljunen and Jouko Väänänen (eds.), *Youth and Conscription* (Helsinki: Peace Union of Finland, 1987), pp. 91–6.

Rogan, Helen, *Mixed Company: Women in the Modern Army* (New York: G.P. Putnam's Sons, 1981). Journalistic account based on the author's observations on women in training. Questions few assumptions about militarism, none about patriarchy.

Rowbotham, Sheila, *Women, Resistance, and Revolution* (London: Pelican Books, 1980). Traces the idea that women's revolutions might occur inside other revolts. She concludes that the connection between national and women's liberation are tenuous.

Royce, Marion, V., *The Effect of War on the Life of Women* (Washington, DC: World's YWCA, 1945). Results of a questionnaire investigating the impact of war situations on the lives of women in thirteen countries around the world.

Rupp, Leila J., *Mobilizing Women for War: German and American Propaganda 1939–1945* (Princeton, NJ: Princeton University Press, 1978). Comparative study of the ways in which prewar public images of women in American society and the prewar Nazi image of German women were made to accommodate the new wartime demands of women's labour.

Rustad, Michael, *Women in Khaki: The American Enlisted Woman* (New York: Praeger, 1982). Sociological investigation of women's experiences at an American military base in West Germany.

Sackville-West, Vita, *The Women's Land Army* (London: Michael Joseph, 1944).

Scars upon my Heart: Women's Poetry and Verse of the First World War, selected by Catherine Reilly (London: Virago, 1981).

Schaps, David, 'The Women of Greece in Wartime', *Classical Philology* 77/3 (1982): 193–213.

Segal, D.R., Kinzer, N.S. and Woelfel, J.C., 'The Concept of Citizenship and Attitudes Towards Women in Combat', *Sex Roles* 3/5 (1977): 469–77.

Segal, M.W. and Segal, R.S., 'Social Change and Participation of Women in the American Military', *Research in Social Movements, Conflicts and Change* 5 (1983): 235–58.

Settle, Mary Lee, *All the Brave Promises: Memories of Aircraft Woman 2nd Class 2146391* (London: Pandora Press, 1984). Mary Lee Settle was an American who volunteered for service in the ranks with the British Women's Auxiliary Air Force in 1942. Written twenty years afterwards.

Sexual Harassment in the Military: Militarism Resource Project Report 1/1 (1984). (PO Box 13416, Philadelphia, PA 19101–3416, USA.)

Shamgar-Handelman, Lea, *Israeli War Widows: Beyond the Glory of Heroism* (South Hadley: Bergin & Garvey, 1987).

Shepherd, Simon, *Amazons and Warrior Women: Varieties of Feminism in Seventeenth Century Drama* (New York: St Martin's Press, 1981).

Shute, Carmel, 'From Balaclavas to Bayonets: Women's Voluntary War Work, 1939–1941', *Hecate* 6/1 (1980): 5–26. Australian women's voluntary work in terms of the new social meaning and ideology with which it was endowed during the war years.

Sorensen, Henning, 'Denmark: The Small NATO Nation', in N.L. Goldman (ed.), *Female Soldiers* (Westport, Conn.: Greenwood, 1982), pp. 189–202.

Stewart-Smith, Natalie Jeanne, *The Women Airforce Service Pilots (WASP) of World War II: Perspectives on the Work of America's First Military Women Aviators* (Pullman, Wash.: Stewart-Smith, 1981).

Stiehm, Judith Hicks, *Bring Me Men and Women: Mandated Change at the US Air Force Academy* (Berkeley, Calif.: University of California Press, 1981). Study of an institution undergoing mandated change through women's integration into the US Air Force Academy following 1975 legislation. Excellent feminist analysis on the inside working of a formerly all-male institution and its strategies towards women.

—— (ed.), *Women and Men's Wars*, special issue of *Women's Studies International Forum* 5/3–4 (London: Pergamon Press, 1982). A challenging collection of papers from several important thinkers on the subject of women's analysis of war and their responsibility in the area of national security.

—— 'The Protected, the Protector, the Defender', in J.H. Stiehm (ed.), *Women and Men's Wars*, special issue of *Women's Studies International Forum* 5/3–4 (1982): 367–76. Analysis of defence and sex roles connected with it.

—— 'The Man Question'. in J.H. Stiehm (ed.), *Women's View of the Political World of Men* (New York: Transnational Publishers, 1984). The origins of mens' relationship with legitimate use of force.

—— 'A Feminist in Military Academy Land; or, Men and Their Institutions as Curiosities', in Paula Treichler, Cheris Kramarae and Beth Stafford (eds.), *For Alma Mater: Theory and Practice in*

Feminist Scholarship (Urbana,Ill.: University of Illinois Press, 1985), pp. 377–92. Author's experiences during her research (see Stiehm, *Bring Me Men and Women*, above).

—— 'The Generations of US Enlisted Women', *Signs* 11/1 (1985): 155–75. Cohort analysis of seven groups of American enlisted women who entered service between 1952 and 1976 at approximately the same time in their lives.

Stobart, Mabel St. Clair, *War and Women—From Experience in the Balkans and Elsewhere* (London: G. Bell, 1913).

Summerfield, Penelope, 'Women, Work, and Welfare: A Study of Child Care and Shopping in Britain in the Second World War', *Journal of Social History* 17/2 (1983): 249–69.

—— *Women Workers in the Second World War: Production and Patriarchy in Conflict* (London and Dover, New Hampshire: Croom Helm, 1984). Study of official policy towards working women in Britain in the war.

Tennyson-Jesse, F., *The Sword of Deborah: First-hand Impressions of the British Women's Army in France* (London: Heinemann, 1918).

Tobias, Sheila and Anderson, Lisa, *What Really Happened to Rosie the Riveter: Demobilization and the Female Labor Force* (New York: Mss Modular Publ., 1974).

Törnqvist, Kurt, 'Sweden: The Neutral Nation', in N.L. Goldman (ed.), *Female Soldiers* (Westport, Conn.: Greenwood, 1982), pp. 203–14.

Treadwell, Mattie, *The Women's Army Corps*, US Army in World War II, Special Studies (Washington, DC: Department of the Army, 1954). This voluminous official history of the WAC remains one of the best-documented works about women's military experience. Well-written and full of relevant details.

Truby, J. David, *Women at War: A Deadly Species* (Boulder, Colo.: Paladin, 1977).

Trustram, Myrna, *Women of the Regiment: Marriage and the Victorian Army* (Cambridge: Cambridge University Press, 1984).

Tuten, Jeff M., 'Germany and the World Wars', in N.L. Goldman (ed.), *Female Soldiers* (Westport, Conn.: Greenwood, 1982), pp. 47–60.

Tyrrell, Wm Blake, *Amazons: A Study in Athenian Mythmaking* (Baltimore, Maryland: Johns Hopkins University Press, 1984).

Urdang, Stephanie, *Fighting Two Colonialisms: Women in Guinea-Bissau* (New York and London: Monthly Review Press, 1979).

Vaught, Wilma L., *A Brief History of Women in Combat and War* (Washington, DC: Industrial College of the Armed Forces, 1973).

Wadge, D.C., *Women in Uniform* (London: S. Low Marston, 1947).

Wainwright, Hilary, 'The Women Who Wire up Weapons: Workers in Armaments Factories', in Dorothy Thompson (ed.), *Over Our Dead Bodies* (London: Virago, 1983), pp. 136–45.

Warner, Marina, *Saint Joan of Arc* (New York: Alfred A. Knopf, 1981).

West, Lois *et al.*, *Wife Abuse in the Armed Forces* (Washington, DC: Center for Women Policy Studies).

Wiegand, Karl L., 'Japan: Cautious Utilization', in N.L. Goldman (ed.), *Female Soldiers* (Westport, Conn.: Greenwood, 1982), pp. 179–88.

Willenz, June A., *Women Veterans: America's Forgotten Heroines* (New York: Continuum, 1983).

Women Against War: Personal Accounts of Forty Japanese Women, compiled by Women's Division of Soka Gakkai (Tokyo: Kodansha International, 1986). Distributed in the United States by Harper & Row. Excellent collection documenting Japanese women's experiences of war and its aftermath.

Women in the NATO Forces (Brussels: Public Information Advisor, International Military Staff, NATO) (1110 Brussels, Belgium), September 1982. Detailed information on women's situation, numbers, and terms of service in NATO countries.

Wood, Dorothea, 'Ethical Problems Related to the Conscription of Women', in Kimmo Kiljunen and Jouko Väänänen (eds.), *Youth and Conscription* (Helsinki: Peace Union of Finland, 1987).

Woolf, Virginia, *Three Guineas* (Harmondsworth: Penguin, 1982). First published in 1938, this book remains a classic analysis of women as 'outsiders' to the actual decision-making in matters of war.

—— 'Thoughts on Peace in an Air Raid', in *Collected Essays* (London: Hogarth Press, 1967), Vol. 4, pp. 173–7.

Yudkin, Marcia, 'Reflections on Woolf's *Three Guineas*', in J.H. Stiehm (ed.), *Women and Men's Wars*, special issue of *Women's Studies International Forum* 5/3–4 (1982): 263–9.

Yuval-Davis, Nira, 'Front and Rear: The Sexual Division of Labor in the Israeli Army'. *Feminist Studies* 11/3 (1985): 649–75. Feminist analysis of women in the Israeli military system. Explodes the myth of equality and shows how women serve in the rear and in subordinate roles.

Zeigler, Mary, *We Serve that Men May Fly: The Story of the Women's Division, Royal Canadian Air Force* (Hamilton, Ontario: RCAF (WD) Association, 1973).

Publications in English, with Special Emphasis on Feminist Perspectives for Creating a Peaceful World

Addis, Elisabetta, and Tiliacos, Nicoletta, 'Conflict, Fear, and Security in the Nuclear Age: The Challenge of the Feminist Peace Movement in Italy', *Radical America* 20/4 (1986): 7–15.

Boulding, Elise, 'Perspectives of Women Researchers on Disarmament, National Security and World Order', *Women's Studies International Quarterly* 4/1 (1981): 27–40.

Brock-Utne, B., *Educating for Peace: A Feminist Perspective* (New York: Pergamon Press, 1985).

Brock-Utne, B., Traylor, J. and Aas, S. (eds.), *Women, Militarism, and Disarmament*, PRIO Report 6/86, Oslo 1986. A report from the IPRA (International Peace Research Association) conference in Györ, Hungary, August 1983. With a number of contributions from Third World women.

Bussey, Gertrude, and Tims, Margaret, *Pioneers for Peace: Women's International League for Peace and Freedom 1915–1965* (London: WILPF, British Section, 1980).

Cataldo, M., Putter, R., Fireside, B. and Lytel, E., *The Women's Encampment for a Future of Peace and Justice: Images and Writings* (Philadelphia: Temple University Press, 1986).

Chalk, Rosemary, 'Women and the National Security Debate', *Bulletin of the Atomic Scientists*, August–September 1982, pp. 44–6.

Easlea, Brian, *Fathering the Unthinkable: Masculinity, Scientists, and the Nuclear Arms Race* (London: Pluto Press, 1983).

Elshtain, Jean Bethke, 'Women as Mirror and Other: Toward a Theory of Women, War and Feminism', *Humanities in Society*, 5, 2 (Winter–Spring 1982), 32.

Harford, Barbara and Hopkins, Sarah (eds.), *Greenham Common: Women at the Wire* (London: The Women's Press, 1984).

Jones, Lynne (ed.), *Keeping the Peace: A Women's Peace Handbook 1* (London: The Women's Press, 1983). Maps the new women's peace movement from the early 1980s from an international perspective. Guidelines for organising and action.

di Leonardo, Micaela, 'Morals, Mothers, and Militarism: Antimilitarism and Feminist Theory', *Feminist Studies* 11/3 (1985): 599–617. Review essay with a critical approach to women's peace movement and feminist analysis of studying the military system from a feminist perspective.

McAllister, Pam (ed.), *Reweaving the Web of Life: Feminism and Nonviolence* (Philadelphia: New Society Publishers, 1982). Collection of articles from the point of view of feminist non-violence.

For critical review, see di Leonardo (above).
McLean, Scilla, 'The Role of Women in the Promotion of Friendly Relations Between Nations', *Unesco Yearbook on Peace and Conflict Studies*, 1981, pp. 36–50.
—— (ed.), *The Role of Women in Peace Movements, in the Development of Peace Research, and in the Promotion of Friendly Relations Between Nations*, presented to World Conference for the United Nations Decade for Women, 1980.
Peterson, Abby, 'The New Women's Movement: Where Have All the Women Gone? Women and the Peace Movement in Sweden', *Women's Studies International Forum* 6/6 (1985): 631–8.
Piecing It Together: Feminism and Nonviolence (London: Feminism and Non-violence Study Group, 1983).
Reardon, Betty, *Sexism and the War System* (New York: Teachers College Press, 1985).
Roberts, Barbara, 'The Death of Machothink: Feminist Research and the Transformation of Peace Studies', *Women's Studies International Forum* 7/4 (1984): 195–200.
Ruddick, Sara, 'Pacifying the Forces: Drafting Women in the Interest of Peace', *Signs* 8/3 (1983): 471–89.
—— 'Preservative Love and Military Destruction: Reflections on Mothering and Peace', in Joyce Tribilcot (ed.), *Mothering and Feminist Theory* (Totowa, NJ: Littlefield, Adams, 1985).
Russell, Dora, *The Tamarisk Tree*, Vol. 3: *Challenge to the Cold War* (London: Virago, 1983). Roots of feminist peace movements in the 1950s and a woman's view of anti-nuclear activism.
Stanford, Barbara, 'Fear of Success and Hope for Survival: An Analysis of the Relationship Perspective in three US Peace Education Projects', paper prepared for the conference of IPRA (International Peace Research Association) in Györ, Hungary, August 1983.
Stephenson, Carolyn M., 'Feminism, Pacifism, Nationalism, and the United Nations Decade for Women', in J.H. Stiehm (ed.), *Women and Men's Wars*, special issue of *Women's Studies International Forum* 5/3–4 (1982): 287–300.
Strange, Penny, *It'll Make a Man of You: A Feminist View of the Arms Race* (Nottingham: Mushroom Books, 1983).
Thompson, Dorothy (ed.), *Over Our Dead Bodies: Women Against the Bomb* (London: Virago, 1983). Collection of articles against nuclear war. Critical review in di Leonardo (see above).
We Are Ordinary Women: A Chronicle of the Puget Sound Women's Peace Camp (Seattle: The Seal Press, 1985). Story of women's peace encampment outside the Boeing Cruise Missle Plant in Kent, Washington.

Wiltsher, Anne, *Most Dangerous Women: Feminist Peace Campaigners of the Great War* (London: Pandora Press, 1985). Passionate, detailed and exciting story of women's attempts at putting an end to the First World War. One of the best books ever written on peace work.

Women and Militarism, special issue of *Connexions* 11 (Winter 1984). Excellent international collection of articles; see also other issues of this publication. (Connexions, 4228 Telegraph Ave, Oakland, CA 94609, USA.)

Publications in German

Albrecht-Heide, Astrid and Bujewski, Utemaria, *Militärdienst für Frauen*? (Frankfurt am Main: Campus Verlag, 1982). Excellent introduction to women and the military.

—— *Frauen im Militär, Dokumentiert am Beispiel der Vereinigten Staaten von Amerika*, Miltärpolitik-Dokumentation 1981/20 (Frankfurt am Main: Haag und Herchen, 1981).

Bajohr, Stefan, *Die Hälfte der Fabrik: Geschichte der Frauenarbeit in Deutschland 1914 bis 1945* (Marburg: Schriftenreihe der Studiengesellschaft für Sozialgeschichte und Arbeiterbewegung, Nr. 17, 1984). History of women's work in Germany 1914–45.

Brändle-Zeile, Elisabeth (ed.), *Frauen für Frieden* (Stuttgart: Die Grünen Baden-Württemberg, 1984). Biographies of pacifist women.

Brinker-Gabler, Gisela (ed.), *Frauen gegen den Krieg* (Frankfurt am Main: Fischer, 1980). Historical anthology.

Daniel, Ute, 'Fiktionen, Friktionen und Fakten: Frauenlohnarbeit im Ersten Weltkrieg', in *Arbeiterschaft in Deutschland 1914–1918*, Düsseldorf, 1985, pp. 277–323. Women workers in the First World War.

Frauen unterm Hakenkreuz (Berlin: Elephanten Press, 1983). Amply illustrated overview on women in the militarized Nazi society.

Frauenwiderstand in Hunsrück: Frauengeschichten 1983–1985 (Frankfurt am Main: Selbstverlag Frauenwiderstand, 1985). Anthology on women's resistance camp in Hunsrück.

Gegen welchen Krieg—für welchen Frieden? special issue of *Beiträge zur feministischen Theorie und Praxis* 8 (1983).

Geiger, Ruth-Esther and Johannesson, Anna (eds.), *Nicht friedlich und nicht still: Streitschriften von Frauen zu Krieg und Gewalt* (Munich: Frauenbuchverlag, 1982). Challenging ideological essays by German feminists on war and violence.

Gersdorff, Ursula von, *Frauen im Kriegsdienst 1914–1945* (Stuttgart: DVA, 1969). Standard reference work on women in world wars, with 400 pages of documents.

Hecht, I., Henry, R. and Meves, Christa, *Frauen im Wehrdienst: Erinnerungen; und ein aktueller Diskussionsbeitrag von Cordula Koepke* (Freiburg: Herderbücherei, 1982). Recollections from three women from the Second World War, with an overview on the topic.

Janssen, Renate, *Frauen ans Gewehr*? (Cologne: Pahl-Rugenstein, 1980). German debate on alternative forms of women's suggested service against a historical background.

Krieg und Unfrieden, special issue of *Feministische Studien* 2 (1984), Weinheim, Beltz-Verlag.

Lippert, Ekkehard and Rössler, Tjarck, *Mädchen unter waffen? Gesellschafts- und sozialpolitische Aspekte weiblicher Soldaten* (Baden-Baden: Nomos Verlag, 1980). Material on women in the militaries of several countries with ample statistical data.

Not am Mann—Frau muss ran? Bremen, Fachgruppe 'Frauen und Kriegsdienstverweigerung' in der Evangelischen Arbeitsgemeinschaft der Kriegsdienstverweigerer (EAK), 1985.

Quistorp, Eva (ed.), *Frauen für den Frieden. Analysen, Dokumente und Aktionen aus der Friedensbewegung* (Bensheim: päd.-extra-Buchverlag, 1982). Contemporary anthology on women and peace from a wide perspective.

Randzio-Plath, Christa (ed.), *Was geht uns Frauen der Krieg an*? (Hamburg: Rowohlt, 1982). Analyses about women and war by a number of contemporary writers.

Schenk, Herrad, *Frauen kommen ohne Waffen: Feminismus und Pazifismus* (Munich: C.H. Beck, 1983). Feminist overview on women's roles in a male-dominated society from a pacifist point of view.

Schwarzer, Alice, 'Von Flintenweibern und Flintenkerlen', *Emma* 6 (1984). Leading German feminist advocates military service for women, who can only become true pacifists once they become conscientious objectors.

Seidler, Franz W., *Frauen zu den Waffen? Marketenderinnen, Helferinnen, Soldatinnen* (Koblenz and Bonn: Wehr und Wissen, 1978). Essential source book on women and the military. Authoritative history on German women's participation in the Second World War. Very thorough and detailed sections on several countries, especially Soviet Union and several Eastern European countries. Concentrates on the Second World War and on the present situation.

—— *Blitzmädchen: Die Geschichte der Helferinnen der Deutschen*

Wehrmacht im Zweiten Weltkrieg (Koblenz and Bonn: Wehr und Wissen, 1979). German women's service in the Second World War II, amply illustrated.

Szepansky, Gerda (ed.), *'Blitzmädel', 'Heldenmutter', 'Kriegerwitwe': Frauenleben im Zweiten Weltkrieg* (Frankfurt am Main: Fischer, 1986). Accounts of German women of their experiences in the Second World War.

Publications in Other Languages

Femmes, Guerre et Revolution. Dossier. *Cahiers du féminisme* 27 (Winter 1984).

Fleron, K., *Kvinder i modstandskampen* (Odense: Sirius Risskov, 1964). Women in the Danish resistance during the Second World War.

La Femme grécque au combat (Athens, 1975). Greek women in combat.

Larson, Margareta, *De arbetade för fred. Kvinnoföreningar i Sverige med fred på sitt program 1898–1940* (Stockholm: Författares bokmaskin, 1985). Study about Swedish women's organizations with peace on their agenda 1898–1940.

Lottorna i samhällets tjänst (Stockholm: Militärhistoriska förlaget, 1984). Official publication on past and present of the Swedish women's voluntary Lotta corps.

Lukkarinen, Vilho, *Suomen Lotat: Lotta Svärd-järjestön historia* (Porvoo/Helsinki/Juva: WSOY, 1981). Authoritative history of the Finnish women's Lotta Corps, 1921–1944.

Murmantseva, V., *Sovetskie zhenschiny v velikoi oteschestvennoi voine* (Moscow: Mysl, 1974). Slanted yet extremely detailed and informative on all branches in which women participated during the Second World War, with ample documentation.

Thebaud, Françoise, *La femme au temps de la guerre de 14* (Paris: Stock, 1986).

Index